*The Invention of
Terrorism in France, 1904–1939*

The
INVENTION
of
TERRORISM
in
FRANCE
1904–1939

CHRIS MILLINGTON

STANFORD UNIVERSITY PRESS
Stanford, California

Stanford University Press
Stanford, California

© 2023 by Christopher Daniel Millington. All rights reserved.

No part of this book may be reproduced or transmitted in any form or by any means, electronic or mechanical, including photocopying and recording, or in any information storage or retrieval system, without the prior written permission of Stanford University Press.

Printed in the United States of America on acid-free, archival-quality paper

Cataloging-in-Publication Data available upon request.
Library of Congress Control Number: 2022055294
ISBN: 9781503636521 (cloth), 9781503636750 (paper) 9781503636767 (ebook)

Cover design and art: Jason Anscomb

For Alexandra, Madeleine, and Matthew

CONTENTS

Figures and Tables   ix
Acknowledgments   xi

Introduction   1
Cultures of Terrorism

ONE
Made in Russia   25
Emerging Perceptions of Terrorism Before the Great War

TWO
The Anarchist and the Tiger   54
Emile Cottin and the Shooting of Prime Minister Georges Clemenceau, February 1919

THREE
The Giant Assassin   80
Paul Gorguloff and the Killing of President Paul Doumer, May 1932

FOUR
Killing a King   108
The Assassination of King Alexander I of Yugoslavia, October 1934

FIVE
Bombings, Piracy, and Kidnapping 141
Terrorism in France During 1937

Conclusion 175
Terror in the Dark Years, 1940–1944

Glossary of the French Press 195
Notes 201
Select Bibliography 273
Index 285

FIGURES AND TABLES

Figure 1	*La Lanterne. Le Supplément*, 1 June 1907	45
Figure 2	Front page of *Excelsior*, 20 February 1919, reporting Cottin's attack on Clemenceau	60
Figure 3	The assassination of President Paul Doumer, as depicted in *Le Petit Journal illustré*, 15 May 1932	85
Figure 4	The assassin of President Doumer, Paul Gorguloff, pictured soon after his arrest on 6 May 1932	97
Figure 5	Paul Gorguloff on trial at the assizes court of the Seine	101
Figure 6	The moment of the attack in Marseille, 9 October 1934	117
Figure 7	Ustashe fighters at a training camp, likely in Italy	121
Figure 8	The building at the rue de Presbourg following the bomb attack of 11 September 1937, published in the socialist *Le Populaire*	155
Figure 9	Terrorist cosplay: a party of "Cagoulards" gathered round a box of "Incendiary Bombs"	159
Table 1	Principal French News Publications, 1900–1939	23
Table 2	"Terrorist attacks" committed in France during 1936–1937	146

ACKNOWLEDGMENTS

Most academic work owes a great debt to funders, institutions, archives, libraries, publishers, reviewers, colleagues, and students. I will thank them in due course. Contrary to convention, I would like first to thank my family for their love and support. The completion of this book depended on one person: my wife Alexandra. As important as support from the world of academia may be, no archivists, librarians, or colleagues did the far more important job of looking after our children while I worked at home and abroad throughout this project. My name may appear on the cover but Alexandra did all the hard work. Her role is particularly deserving of recognition given the context in which this book was written. The project began in earnest when my wife, my daughter, and I lived in Cardiff. It was completed at our current home in Liverpool. Along the way, our wonderful daughter transformed from a toddler into a schoolchild, and we welcomed a beautiful son into the world. We endured (like many others) the strangest and saddest of years in 2020, losing three close family members and coming very close to losing a fourth. Yet through the darkness there shone many moments of light: the coloring and drawing at the kitchen table; the crafting of houses, castles, stables, hospitals, and dinosaur worlds out of old cardboard boxes; the frustrations and accomplishments of lockdown home schooling; the trips to the park; the miles walked pushing a pram; the cups of tea made for me; the wistful looks between tired parents that one day—one day!—we might get to spend an hour alone together; the make-believe games ("You be the dog, daddy!"); the playing with Hot Wheels and Duplo bricks; the building of dens; the mornings at soft play; the Disney films; the conversations with Jorgie; the walks to and from school; the nursery dropoffs and (even better) the nursery pickups. I often paused the writing of this book when I looked up to see my daughter jump down from the back door, closely pursued by my son, both either running, jumping, or skipping toward me in our garden office (aka The Shed). All of this meant that, despite our losses, the writing of this book during the pandemic was not at all an unhappy time and for that I must thank Alexandra, Madeleine, and Matthew. It is because of them (not to mention all the brothers, sisters, mums, dads, aunties, uncles, nieces, and nephews), that I can write without the shadow of a doubt, and perhaps a little professional authority, that I am the luckiest man in history.

I would like to offer my heartfelt thanks to the Gerda Henkel Stiftung. Their generous funding made this project possible. They understand the importance of academic work, and they are truly a model funder. I thank Swansea University for granting me a sabbatical at the beginning of the project. I had many brilliant colleagues and friends in south Wales, and I will always look back on my time there with great affection. I thank my colleagues at Manchester Metropolitan University for welcoming me there in 2018.

I am indebted to the readers who provided insightful comments on previous versions of this work. I have enjoyed many conversations over FaceTime with Caroline Campbell, about French history and life. Kevin Passmore and Garthine Walker continue to provide support for my work, and friendship too; it is a shame that we no longer live in the same city. Gayle K. Brunelle and Annette Finley-Croswhite made useful comments and suggestions on the manuscript and gave kind encouragement throughout the publication process. David Uhrig and Marguerite Momesso met me with their usual warm hospitality during my research trips to Paris. Martin Alexander gave some useful advice via email.

Several people provided important assistance with this project. Daniel Baker and Vanda Wilcox took photographs for me in French archives when I could not travel myself. Jean-Yves Le Naour told me where to find the archives of the Emile Cottin case online. I also thank the staff at the Archives Nationales (Pierrefitte-sur-Seine), the Archives de la Préfecture de Police (Le Pré-Saint-Gervais), and the Bibliothèque Nationale François Mitterand, as well as the staff closer to home at the university libraries of Cardiff, Manchester Metropolitan, and Swansea.

*The Invention of
Terrorism in France, 1904–1939*

INTRODUCTION

Cultures of Terrorism

"Terrorism." When you saw this word, what came to mind? Was it planes flying into buildings or massacres in nightclubs? Maybe it was government offices or hotels gutted by bombings. Or wedding parties obliterated in a drone strike. When you read the word "terrorist," whom do you imagine? A balaclava-clad paramilitary fighter? A bearded "martyr" in a suicide vest? A white supremacist? Or maybe a suit-wearing statesman? Few other words have the power to evoke such immediate mental images and to trigger prejudices and preconceptions about what we "know" of a phenomenon. Yet save for students and scholars, we rarely stop to consider the origins or accuracy of this "knowledge." From where and from whom do we "learn" about terrorism? The answer is, from an array of sources, from the news media and the political establishment to cinema, literature, and video games. We rarely question the content of, or motives behind, these sources yet we are nevertheless sure that we "know what terrorism is."

People in the past also "knew" what terrorism was. This book is the first work to reconstruct this "knowledge" through an examination of representations and perceptions of terrorism in French political and cultural discourse during the period of the late Third Republic. It analyzes the interpretations of terrorism by antagonists and observers to understand how these actors perceived, experienced, and reacted to terrorist violence. The investigation uses the narratives produced about terrorist attacks and their perpetrators, as well as the responses of the police, army, and ministers of the democratic Third Republic, to uncover "cultures of terrorism," defined as the frameworks of values and qualities that informed common beliefs about the nature, operation, and goals of terrorism and its perpetrators. "Terrorism" is therefore understood here not only as a "brute fact,"[1] but also as a political and cultural construction of violence composed from a variety of discourses and deployed in particular circumstances by commentators, witnesses, and perpetrators. The political and cultural battles inherent to perceptions of terrorism spoke to numerous concerns, not least anxieties over immigration, antiparliamentarianism, representations of gender, and the future of European peace. The book thus recognizes terrorism as a stake in early twentieth-century political conflict. It sheds light on the previously understudied historical antecedents of French notions of terrorism in the twenty-first century, the roots of which scholars often locate in the post–Second World War era of decolonization. In doing so, it offers an original and highly significant contribution to the field of terrorism studies and European twentieth-century history.

The years under examination here broadly coincide with a period of sharp political conflict in France that some scholars (though by no means all) have characterized as the "French civil war."[2] The global ideological conflict of the time marked the French profoundly, as competing visions of a future France—primarily the democratic Republican, the fascist, and the communist—vied for supremacy. Persistent economic depression, governmental instability, and factional rivalries in parliament undermined confidence in the Republic. French groups from the extreme right-wing extra-parliamentary leagues to the extreme left-wing Communist Party drew inspiration from foreign models to offer alternatives to democracy. Theirs were not voices crying in the wilderness. Hundreds of thousands of French joined associations committed to a radical shakeup of the nation. Regular street violence between political opponents and the police heightened the sense of crisis.[3]

French involvement in episodes of fighting abroad—notably official intervention in the Russian Civil War of the early post-war years and unofficial intervention in the Spanish Civil War after 1936—as well as the suspected presence in France of hostile foreign spies, agents, and terrorists further implicated the country in wider European political struggles. The Franco-French conflict reached a bloody climax during the years of Nazi Occupation. Marshal Philippe Pétain's Etat Français at Vichy persecuted minorities and repressed dissenters with legal sanction and violence. Resistance groups initially reacted with caution, uncertain of the loyalties of the population and in fear of reprisals from the German Occupier. Following the invasion of the Soviet Union in summer 1941, communist operatives committed the first violent attacks against German soldiers and French collaborators. Vichy responded with ferocious repression and exceptional judicial measures that stripped "terrorists" of their basic legal rights. In the final year of the war, numerous resistance groups took the fight to their enemies as best they could, with limited supplies of weapons and in the face of bloody violence from the regime's Milice Française.

Historians have mined this period of internecine strife extensively, yet terrorism as a subject of analysis has received relatively short shrift. It is treated as either tangential to, or the backcloth of, other subjects, namely the paramilitary politics of the years after 1934. The relegation of terrorism as a subject of secondary importance in the scholarly literature may reflect historians' belief that people living during the 1930s and 1940s likewise dismissed the phenomenon. Heinz-Gerhard Haupt and Klaus Weinhauer claim that after 1918 civil war and revolution "absorbed public attention leaving only little room for the pre-1914 discourses on individual acts of terrorism."[4] Newer paramilitary cultures subsumed terrorism.[5]

It is to some extent true that the 1930s ideological conflict in Europe informed interpretations and representations of terrorist acts, organizations, and perpetrators. Yet in France, aspects of a pre-1914 culture of terrorism persisted and adapted to the new political climate. French perceptions of terrorism were not "reset" in the wake of the Great War. Rather, they evolved, retaining aspects of understandings from the pre-war period while acquiring new meanings derived from the context of the interwar years. As the home-grown anarchist threat of the 1890s subsided (but did not disappear), terrorism as a political strategy came to be associated with the struggles of Russian revolutionaries. The press and popular cultural productions framed the Russian population of Paris as a nihilist enclave that exported terrorism back home.

Ideas about terrorism had changed subtly by 1919. Emile Cottin's attempted assassination of Prime Minister George Clemenceau in February 1919 demonstrated that older ideas of anarchist and nihilist violence, while persistent, were gradually giving way to a fear of Soviet terrorism in France as continental politics reconfigured after the war. In the wake of several attacks, especially the October 1934 assassination of King Alexander I of Yugoslavia in Marseille, the French came to perceive their own country as a battleground for foreign terrorist fighters, loyal to either communism or fascism, who imported their conflict from abroad. Significantly, by the mid-1930s France was not considered the target of terrorism. This belief persisted into the latter half of the decade. By 1937, the fear that terrorists (still largely understood as foreigners) were now targeting French interests gained traction thanks to a series of bombings in Paris and the south of the country. If in the early 1930s terrorists had struck in France, as war approached at the close of the decade terrorists struck at France. This conception strengthened throughout the war years as both Vichy and the resistance accused each other of harming French interests. At the Liberation, the triumph of a democratic, Republican, and "French" vision of France ("French" because Vichy's opponents long depicted the regime as a foreign puppet) reinforced perceptions of terrorism as an "unFrench" and anti-Republican phenomenon, perceptions that persist today.

There were two threads of continuity throughout the evolution of the French culture of terrorism in the first half of the twentieth century. First, terrorism was an "unFrench" entity, that is, a thing that was not simply "foreign" or non-French but contrary to certain ideas of "Frenchness."[6] Certainly, the figure of the foreigner loomed large in representations of the terrorist, from the Russian nihilist of the early 1900s to the Spanish Francoist agent of the late 1930s. He (and, more rarely, she) was generally an immigrant, resident in France as a refugee, an asylum seeker or illegal alien, or a spy. The terrorist abused French hospitality by committing illegal acts of political violence in the country. Terrorist violence became a factor in discussions over immigration control and the refugee crisis of the 1930s, and it exacerbated xenophobic feeling during the decade. In this sense, the French of the 1930s confronted challenges already encountered earlier in the twentieth century in Great Britain and the United States where violence perpetrated by migrant anarchists had prompted a tightening of immigration and citizenship legislation.[7] Conversely, the French governments of the 1890s had responded to the threat of anarchism with the so-called "Villainous Laws" (*lois scélérates*) that targeted anarchist movements and publications rather than foreigners.

Beyond the framing of terrorist violence as simply foreign, the casting of terrorism as "unFrench" amounted to an appreciation of the phenomenon as different from a French "mentality." This mentality, and the behaviors associated with it, rested on a subjective perception of national values. The right generally perceived terrorism to be a communist tactic, directed from Moscow with the intent of spreading global revolution. During the Second World War, right-wingers also blamed London for directing terrorism in France. In both cases, terrorism was depicted as harmful to the national interest: it was the unpatriotic and treacherous activity of foreign and French-born citizens in the service of a foreign government. When terrorist violence was perpetrated in the name of reactionary or fascist ideologies, right-wingers trivialized such terrorism or passed over its motives in silence. Political considerations likewise informed left-wing perceptions of "Frenchness" and terrorism. The left saw the hand of international fascism behind acts of terrorism. It considered perpetrators to be either the agents of fascist secret services or the French puppets of Germany, Italy, Francoist Spain, or a "fascist international." In this context, terrorists sought to undermine Republican France with the intention of installing a fascist dictatorship. Consequently, when looking to discover attitudes to terrorism, we must recognize that such attitudes had political origins and aims. Yet despite the ideological differences that right and left perceived behind terrorism, and their subjective notions of "true" Frenchness, a point of agreement emerged: any French worthy of the name simply did not—could not—perpetrate terrorism.

Second, throughout the period under investigation here, gendered understandings of terrorism came to the fore when police or press investigations revealed the participation of women in terrorist plots. Some of these women played significant roles in the execution of terrorist operations. However, the female terrorist proved an object of fascination simply because of the apparent unlikeliness that women should be involved in such things. This assumption persists into the twenty-first century.

On the one hand, the perception that terrorism is a largely, if not uniquely, male act rests, first, on the marginalization of women in terrorist groups themselves. Let's be clear: this marginalization tends to pertain solely to the public face of the organization. Women feature less frequently in propaganda, and their concerns may be presented as relating solely to assumed "women's issues" such as family life.[8] In private, the situation is more complex. It is generally the case that few women occupy leadership positions in terrorist organizations. However, the roles they do fulfill—as organizers, propagandists, recruiters, and logistical operators—are vital to the survival and success of the group.[9] This is as true for the Russian terrorists of the late nineteenth century as for the Islamic-inspired fighters or white supremacists of today.

On the other hand, deeply rooted notions of women as less likely to commit violence than men have obscured women's participation in terrorism.[10] Yet it is precisely this belief that garners the female terrorist a disproportionate amount of attention when she "emerges" into the public consciousness through an act of violence. The assumed unusualness of the female terrorist prompts a question rarely posed about male attackers; namely how could someone of that gender do such a thing?[11] In the early part of the twentieth century, responses to this question involved speculation about the terrorist's past, her mental state, and, frequently, her sexuality. Despite the bewilderment with which some French received the news of women terrorists, there was also something familiar about the phenomenon. Quite aside from the fact that, as readers will discover, women were featured in reports of terrorism time and again (as both perpetrators, accomplices, and acquaintances of terrorists), the figure of the *femme fatale* appeared in popular cinema and fiction: for example, George Fitzmaurice's 1931 *Mata Hari*, starring Greta Garbo as the wartime spy, played in French movie theaters throughout the 1930s.[12] Accordingly, if female terrorists attracted interest from the media, they were in fact "not-so-unusual suspects."

Terrorism: Definitions and Constructions

The study of terrorism is fraught with problems of definition. Indeed, within several years of the emergence of the phenomenon, the meaning of terrorism had changed. Originally, "terror" described the system and policy of the revolutionary government in France between spring 1793 and summer 1794. On 5 February 1794, Maximilien Robespierre set out the dual necessity of "virtue" and "terror" in his "On the Principles of Political Morality." "Terror" for Robespierre was "nothing but prompt, severe, inflexible justice" served to the counterrevolutionary enemies of France.[13] In practice, "terror" meant legal and physical abuse, violence, and execution: during the Great Terror of June-July 1794, thirty people on average lost their head each day.[14] Only after the Terror ended did its opponents refer retrospectively to "terrorism," with the "terrorist" described as "an agent or partisan of the Terror that arose through the abuse of revolutionary measures" (according to the dictionary of the Académie Française). Anglo-Irish writer and politician Edmund Burke put it another way: the terrorists were "Hell hounds."[15] The terrorism of 1793–94 resembled most closely the contested contemporary concept of "state terrorism."[16] The notion of terrorism as a means of *opposition* to the state appeared first in 1866 and became popular only during the 1890s.[17] Scholars usually trace the origins of modern antistate terrorism to late-nineteenth-century Russia and the violent campaign of Narodnaia Volya (People's Will) that culminated in the March 1881 killing of Tsar Alexander II (though some historians have located the emergence of terrorism in 1870s Ireland and 1890s France, too).[18]

To account for terrorism's multiple historical forms—Walter Laqueur suggests that it is more accurate to speak of "terrorisms"[19]—researchers have identified a series of transitions in the history of the phenomenon. Alex Schmid identifies six stages in the history of terrorism: the Robespierrist stage (1790s); the anarchist stage (1890s); the Communist/Fascist stage (1920s–1930s); the anticolonialist stage (post-1945); the urban guerrilla stage (post-1960s); and finally the religious fundamentalist stage (1990s–present).[20] David C. Rapoport famously identified four overlapping "waves" of modern terrorism since the nineteenth century, namely the anarchist, anticolonial, Marxist, and religious fundamentalist waves.[21] Attempts to periodize the history of terrorism continue, as do efforts to draw attention to new and emerging forms.[22]

Given the multiple changes that terrorism has undergone since the 1790s, it is reasonable for the reader to ask, "What *is* terrorism?" It is a ritual in terrorism studies for authors to tackle the matter of how best to define this object of study, only to claim that such a feat is devilishly difficult but not *too* difficult to prevent the formulation of a definition that suits the author's purpose.[23] The problem is not that terrorism *cannot* be defined—there are hundreds of definitions in the scholarly literature—but rather that there is a surfeit of sometimes contradictory definitions.[24] Attempts to draw a line under the issue have foundered. Schmid's so-called "Revised Academic Consensus Definition of Terrorism," compiled from a survey of the field, would raise objections from scholars who consider state violence legitimate in all contexts (point eight of Schmid's list claims the contrary).[25]

How is the historian to navigate this definitional quagmire? If the debate over the definition of terrorism once threated to become "the great Bermuda Triangle of terrorism research," other approaches to the study of the subject have emerged.[26] One alternative lies in "rejectionism." Rejectionists refuse to use the term "terrorism" altogether, considering it to be too loaded with moral and political baggage to be useful.²⁷ It is true that terrorism has acquired a "nigh-inescapable value judgement," and its use by governments and media is seldom disinterested.²⁸ Yet if rejectionism offers a quick way out of some definitional and moral quandaries, for a historian seeking to understand the meaning of terrorism in the past (rather than one who seeks solely to categorize) it is problematic. We must engage with the "t" word (as Dominic Bryan, Liam Kelly, and Sara Templer call it) for the simple fact that past societies used it (and our own society continues to do so).²⁹

"Constructivism" offers a more fruitful avenue of research for historians. In this respect, Joseba Zulaika and William A. Douglass's 1996 *Terror and Taboo* is salutary. In this book, Zulaika and Douglass deconstruct the discourse of terrorism that emerged in the West during the 1970s, arguing that it "becomes more relevant to examine the nature of the behavior labelled 'terrorism,' as well as the labelling process itself, rather than to focus upon the ostensible 'face value' of particular terrorist events and episodes."³⁰ This approach has become characteristic of what Richard Jackson has described as a "literary turn" in terrorism studies.³¹ It does not allow that "terrorism" is a timeless and objective phenomenon observable in the past and the present if only we might find the correct definition.³² Rather, it understands terrorism to be a "social and cultural construct, defined within a particular historical-cultural context and shaped by the assumptions embedded within it."³³ If we accept that discourse is constitutive of reality, rather than vice versa,³⁴ terrorism may only be understood according to "the way in which it is discursively constructed through language and social practices," in a given context.³⁵

Despite its value for historical investigation, constructivism can lead to some ostensibly alarming assertions. Ondrej Ditrych rejects all exercises aimed at defining terrorism in favor of constructivism: "There is no terrorism beyond the discourse of terrorism," he argues.³⁶ While the victims of terrorist attacks would doubtless attest to its reality, Ditrych does not seek to question the authenticity of violence described as terrorism but rather the process by which it is labeled as such. As Rainer Hülsse and Alexander Spencer contend, "[Terrorist] events [do] not speak for themselves, but [need] to be interpreted."³⁷ The constructivist focus falls squarely on this process of interpretation.

I sympathize with constructivism when applied to historical terrorism. My academic background in the study of fascism in France has demonstrated the futility of searching for a consensus definition of a contested concept.³⁸ Historians of French fascism are beginning to move beyond the stale debate over how best to define the phenomenon, in belated recognition of Gilbert Allardyce's contention that "[t]here is no such *thing* as fascism. There are only the men and movements that we call by that name."³⁹ I draw, too, on a genealogical approach to terrorism outlined by Martyn Frampton. Frampton underscores the importance of context and contingency in historical understandings of terrorism, as well as their centrality to modern notions of terrorist acts.⁴⁰ When it comes to determining whether there was such a *thing* as terrorism, the historian's objective must be to examine the *thing* as contemporaries understood it.

The work of Gregory Shaya and Dominique Kalifa on "imaginaries" has influenced my research. Shaya deconstructed the figure of the "anarchist terrorist" of late nineteenth-century France as represented in the "socialpolitical imaginary: the storehouse of words, images, and stories that shape social and political action, the what-goes-without-saying upon which social and political identities are forged."⁴¹ In his examination of the "underworld" in Western culture, Kalifa defined the "social imaginary" as a "sort of repertoire of collective figures and identities that every society assembles at given moments in history.…Social imaginaries describe the way in which societies perceive their components—groups, classes, and categories—and hierarchise their divisions and elaborate their evolutions. Thus, they *produce and institute* the social more than they *reflect* it."⁴² In this book, I investigate the political and social imaginaries of "terrorism" in France during the first half of the twentieth century. To label an act of violence, a group, or an individual "terrorist" relied on a framework of layered ideas, values, and meanings associated with the term at a given moment in time—a culture of terrorism.⁴³ This discourse built upon, borrowed from, intersected with, and adapted elements of various other available discourses. Discourses of terrorism were not fixed; they formed through a process of interaction with events and broader political and cultural contexts.⁴⁴ This means that, even if we accept that terrorism is a construction, there *is* a relationship between terrorist reality and terrorist myth.⁴⁵ The real exploits of foreign terrorists on French soil—the "concrete events" of history—informed perceptions of the phenomenon in politics, the press, and cultural productions that drew on and adapted available discursive frameworks.⁴⁶

A problem confronting the constructivism purists is that a cursory examination of the French sources reveals that terrorism was a nebulous term. It was applied to both the assassination of heads of state and the sinking of an ocean liner—and everything in between: armed robbery,[47] state repression,[48] inter-state violence,[49] murder,[50] arbitrary and summary punishment,[51] anticolonial resistance,[52] political demonstrations,[53] unlawful imprisonment,[54] strikes,[55] mutilation, acts of vandalism, and the desecration of Church property.[56] In the tense political climate of the period, the word was frequently deployed as an accusation against ideological enemies. In December 1934, the Socialist Party newspaper *Le Populaire* denounced the fascist Francistes as a "terrorist mafia" in the heart of Paris.[57] On the other hand, speaking in the Chamber of Deputies in March 1937, Jacques Poitou-Duplessy, a deputy for the conservative Fédération Républicaine, condemned the Communist Party's attacks on right-wing groups during the previous decade as "acts of terrorism" to which more than five thousand people had fallen victim.[58]

Given the wide-ranging use of the term during the period under investigation, I used a broad definition of terrorism to inform the choice of case studies in this book. The work of terrorism scholars influenced my definition as did the attitudes of the people under study here. A narrow definition can shut down important avenues of research while it can also jar with historical understandings. Bruce Hoffman's perpetrator-focused notion of terrorism, for example, excludes the state. Hoffman claims that it is to "play into the terrorists' hands" to draw an equivalence between wanton and random destruction wrought by terrorists and the careful and precise annihilation of targets by bomber planes.[59] This position contradicts the common interwar and wartime perception that terrorists were agents of a foreign state.

At the other end of the definitional spectrum stands the concept of terrorism as merely the act of violence itself, a tactic available to all actors, state, or substate, revolutionary or democratic, and so on.[60] This approach considers definitions based on the identity of perpetrators and victims as bogged down in subjective ideas of morality. Anthony Richards instead contends that the practice of defining an act as terrorist should remain separate from moral judgment. "Terrorist" is a neutral term used to describe only a form of violence; all political and social actors are capable of terrorism. Richards has no qualms about labeling the violence of the French resistance "terrorist," on the basis of his own definition of the phenomenon as "the use of violence or the threat of violence with the primary purpose of generating a psychological impact beyond the immediate victims or object of attack for a political motive."[61] He claims that "it makes no analytical sense to seek out alternative and more 'positive' labels than 'terrorism' for the same activity just because we might agree with the cause."[62] Whether we perceive terrorism to be "good" or "bad" does not change the fact that it is still terrorism. Yet tactic- or method-focused definitions such as Richards's come unstuck when confronted with historical perceptions of terrorism because the identity of the perpetrator *did* matter to contemporaries. While perceptions were inherently subjective, whether the terrorist was an anarchist, communist, or fascist helped to shape understandings of the broader phenomenon. Moreover, attitudes to terrorism during the war were overwhelmingly negative and resisters rejected the label out of hand.

Similarly, attempts to define terrorism according to its victims prove unsatisfactory in the context of early twentieth-century France. Richard Jackson's proposition that "terrorism is aimed primarily but not solely at civilians" contrasts with interwar French understandings that terrorists chose only high-value political targets.[63] Few civilians died in the terrorist attacks included in this book. Moreover, the League of Nations' convention on terrorism in 1937 considered only civilian *representatives of the state* as potential victims of terrorism. French plans to broaden the definition to "private persons by reason of their political attitude" were rejected. According to French perceptions of terrorism in the early decades of the twentieth century, terrorists did not kill civilians indiscriminately.

I define terrorism thus:

Terrorism is the premeditated use of violence in pursuit of a political goal, through the injury or elimination of a person, persons, or institution, and the simultaneous terrorization of a broader audience through intimidation or violence in order to communicate a political message or cause a change in behavior or policy. A range of actors perpetrates terrorist violence, regardless of political group, party, relationship to the state, or tradition.[64]

This minimal definition serves as a starting point only, and no definition can ever be final.[65] It is a basis from which to explore historical instances of terrorist violence in early twentieth-century France. It is not intended to constrain research through the categorization of historical violence as either "terrorist" or "not terrorist." Rather, it permits the drawing of broad parameters around the phenomenon under investigation while allowing the freedom to explore the variable and contingent factors that shaped past perceptions of terrorist violence.[66] The reader should remain aware that this definition is one of many in the literature and that this book is *a* history—rather than *the* history—of French perceptions of terrorism.

This book's attempt to reconstruct the culture of terrorism relies to a large extent on media reportage and comment. While the analysis is not explicitly based on the theory of "news frames," defined as the presence in the news of "persistent patterns of selection, emphasis, and exclusion that furnish a coherent interpretation and evaluation of events," the reader may perceive in the book an exploration of historical "framing."[67] Yet this book does not rely solely on the media's depiction of terrorism, taking into account, for example, fictional works that include terrorist characters or incidents. Consequently, the focus falls less on the mediatization of terrorism and more on a broader process of mediation that begins with the act of violence itself. It is important to acknowledge the role of terrorists themselves in this process. If terrorism is a means to communicate a political message, then this communication does not end with the attack ("The [terrorists'] message is not the violence or destruction itself," according to Joseph S. Tuman.[68]) Terrorists can help to mold their own image in the media. Organizations may have sympathizers or allies in the press who are well placed to influence news coverage. Statements from groups, or interviews with their leading figures, offer another means by which to contribute to the terrorists' self-representation. Even so-called "lone actors" can popularize their politics through manifestoes and court appearances that are widely relayed to the public via the press. Given the variety of actors involved in the mediation of terrorism, terrorist acts can take on meanings not intended by their perpetrators. This may be the case when political interests wish to take advantage of a situation to further their own agenda. Terrorists may thus lose control of the "meaning" of their act in the interactional process that helps to construct "terrorism" in the popular imaginary.[69]

History, Historians, and Terrorism: An Overview

It was long a truism of "terrorism studies" that history and terrorism did not mix. In 1984, Rapoport noted that "[t]here is no authoritative history of modern terrorism."[70] Seventeen years later, Laqueur began the introduction to the 2001 edition of *A History of Terrorism* thus: "The history of terrorism goes back a very long time, but the very fact that there is such a history, has frequently been ignored or even altogether suppressed."[71] It was perhaps the case that "serious" scholars held themselves aloof to the field of terrorism studies: military historian Michael Howard once described the majority of publications on the subject as the "incompetent and unnecessary" works of "phoneys and amateurs."[72] Historians were not alone in their skepticism about the study of terrorism: in sociology, the subject was long considered "something dirty" that risked either holding back the careers of students who chose to study it or drawing unwelcome attention from the authorities (this latter fact prompted French terrorism scholar Michel Wieviorka to devote his time to non-French manifestations of the phenomenon).[73]

Even the explosion in literature on the subject after 9/11 left historians unmoved; academic studies of the history of terrorism actually declined in number after September 2001.[74] Between 2002 and 2004, less than 2 percent of articles published in the leading journals in the field dealt with historical terrorism.[75] Rather, the flood of new publications emanated largely from researchers and self-appointed "terrorism experts" focused on Islamic-inspired terror and with a policy-objective in mind.[76] This "presentist" bent was reinforced by a tendency to perceive contemporary terrorism as novel and more destructive than past manifestations. Even the work of great scholars in the field betrayed this bias. Laqueur suggested in 1998 that we abandon altogether the use of the word "terrorism" for it did not encapsulate effectively "the new age of unrestrained violence" emerging at the end of the 1990s. The label was better suited to the past when "[t]errorism...was little more than an irritant."[77] The "presentist" inclination subsequently threw up both the concept of "New Terrorism," an idea in vogue since 9/11 (but which, as Laqueur proves, predated the attacks themselves) and the propensity of all societies to perceive their present as the "age of terrorism"[78] (one can trace this phrase at least as far back as 1874, at which time it referred to the French revolutionary Terror[79]).

Twenty years after Rapoport's observation on the poverty of historical terrorism studies, Isabelle Duyvesteyn noted that genuine historical study of terrorism was still lacking.[80] In 2009, Colin Wight surmised that "terrorism research post-9/11 [has] an almost complete lack of historical awareness," something that acted not only to the detriment of academic study but also to the struggle against contemporary terrorist threats.[81] In 2011, Ann Larabee warned historians not to enter lightly into the field of terrorism studies, for in "developing a historiography of terrorism" without the necessary precision over "definitions, classifications, and origins," they risked serving as the accomplices of domestic counterterrorist forces.[82] As recently as 2016, Randall Law noted in his updated *Terrorism: A History* that historians had made only "limited forays" into the subject, content to leave the field largely to social science researchers.[83]

However, historians began to work on terrorism during the formative years of the "terrorism studies" discipline in the 1970s. Laqueur's *A History of Terrorism*—frequently framed as the first history of the topic—appeared in 1977. Laqueur followed this work in 1978 with a collection of historical primary sources on terrorism (*The Terrorism Reader: A Historical Anthology*). A book of essays published in 1982—the fruits of a conference held in 1979 on "social protest, violence, and terror" during the nineteenth and twentieth centuries—also addressed terrorism in history. Still, editors Wolfgang J. Mommsen and Gerhard Hirschfeld admitted in their preface that contemporary studies on nonlegal violence and terrorism lacked historical awareness: "Contrary to currently fashionable beliefs, recourse to violence in deliberate violation of the law, as well as of governmental authority, is a widespread phenomenon throughout history."[84] It seems that historians' awareness of the "historical amnesia" in the field goes back a long way.[85]

Historical monographs on terrorism have appeared in recent years. Notable among these publications (for the purpose of this book) are Richard Bach Jensen's *The Battle Against Anarchist Terrorism* (2014), the product of a career's research in numerous archives around the world; *The Dynamite Club* (2009) and *Ballad of the Anarchist Bandits* (2017), John Merriman's duo of books on French anarchism; Vivien Bouhey's 2009 *Les Anarchistes contre la République*; and Gayle K. Brunelle and Annette Finley-Croswhite's *Murder in the Metro* (2012) and their 2020 *Assassination in Vichy*, both dealing with terrorism in France during the 1930s and 1940s. Nevertheless, studies of historical terrorism grounded in empirical research remain uncommon. Giovanni Mario Ceci was premature when in 2016 he predicted a "historical turn" in terrorism studies and a coming "age of the history of terrorism."[86] If scholars of terrorism usually preface their work with some historical context, this often constitutes a mere "glance over the shoulder" (to borrow Rory Cox's phrase) rather than a serious engagement with the past.[87] Furthermore, recent publications with a historical focus largely concern theory building rather than drawing on excavations from the coalface of primary research.[88]

Whether historical research monographs interest scholars in the broader field of terrorism studies is an open question. Certainly, the field of terrorism studies is poorer for its lack of engagement with history if only for the fact that an absence of historical awareness can prompt unfounded comments on terrorism. Mikkel Thorup claims that until 1945, terrorism was often denuded of its political character or intentions and tarred with the same brush as anarchism—"as a violent doctrine seeking destruction from the mere pleasure of destroying."[89] Readers of this book may conclude otherwise. History—or rather, certain periods of history—still gets a raw deal from terrorism scholars. In the 2018 *Routledge Handbook of Terrorism and Counterterrorism*, editor Andrew Silke pointed out that Leonard Weinberg's chapter on historical terrorism was "rightly the longest in the volume."[90] In twenty pages of text, Weinberg devoted just over four pages to terrorism before 1945.[91]

"An Omnipresent Phenomenon": Terrorism in French History

What about terrorism in France? A history of modern France published in 2015 considers the post-9/11 "War on Terror" as the most significant development in the country's recent past (the book begins with a reconstruction of the Paris attacks of 13 November 2015).[92] Readers who can recall the killings of 2015 and 2016, notably the January 2015 *Charlie Hebdo*/Hypercacher murders (17 dead), the multiple murders of 13 November 2015 (130 dead), and the Nice lorry attack of July 2016 (84 dead), will need little reminding of France's contemporary experience of terrorism. The construction of a security perimeter around the base of the Eiffel Tower, including half a kilometer of bulletproof glass, is an indication of the country's continued fear of terrorist attack.[93] Yet the country has long been at "the bleeding edge" of terrorism, having experienced multiple forms of terrorist violence in the past two centuries.[94] Jenny Raflik has gone as far as to describe terrorism as omnipresent in France since the Revolution.[95] It is therefore a little surprising that in the six hundred pages of the 2021 *Cambridge History of Terrorism*, France merits neither its own chapter nor an entry in the index.

One encounters in the literature on terrorism in France a tendency to study some periods at the expense of others. Recent outbreaks of violence garner the lion's share of attention. Wieviorka claims that terrorism "began to appear as a major challenge" in France only during the 1960s and 1970s; he labels this period that of "classical terrorism" (a label that apparently consigns terrorism before 1960 to ancient history).[96] Some scholars have attempted to draw lessons from France's experience with (Islamic) terrorism only since the 1980s.⁹⁷ The numerous attacks perpetrated on French soil since the turn of the millennium have attracted much attention if only for the fact that they provide new and fertile case studies for academics, analysts, and policymakers. Researchers have studied French responses to the attacks of the 2010s from a variety of angles, including their implications for Republican democracy, the discursive constructions of terror and counterterror, the effects on political behavior, and changing conceptions of national identity.⁹⁸ Even texts that take account of France's long-term history of terrorism still display certain historical blind spots. The authors of the edition of the popular series *Que sais-je?* on "Le terrorisme" (published in 2006) wrongly locate the first French antiterrorism legislation in the 1980s. The wartime Vichy regime was in fact the first government to legislate against terrorism.⁹⁹

There are several works on late nineteenth-century French anarchism, yet few take terrorism specifically as their focus (even if they cover the subject to a greater or lesser extent). Jean Maitron's classic two-volume history of the French anarchist movement covers the "terrorist era" of 1892–94.¹⁰⁰ Maitron ascribes the attacks of these years to violent individuals out of step with the attitudes of the broader anarchist milieu. It is true that Russian nihilist violence had inspired some French anarchists and their "propaganda by the deed," yet from 1886 the movement began to turn away from murder as a political and social strategy.¹⁰¹ Activists understood that violence was having a detrimental effect on their cause, especially when the French government introduced repressive legislation in 1893 and 1894 (the *lois scélérates*). Maitron concluded that "during [this] tragic period, no anarchist newspaper *ever* made an unreserved apology for terrorism."¹⁰² Vivien Bouhey's 2008 history of French anarchist networks likewise explores the anarchist "guerrilla against capitalist society."¹⁰³ Bouhey distinguishes between attacks that served propaganda purposes and those that amounted to anarchist vendettas (such as the exploits of the infamous Ravachol), perpetrated in an "exclusively terrorist and vengeful" spirit by anarchist commandos.¹⁰⁴ Attacks continued after 1900 yet the broader movement fell into decline.

Both Merriman's *The Dynamite Club* (2009) and *Ballad of the Anarchist Bandits* (2017) offer in-depth accounts of two of anarchism's most infamous terrorists, Emile Henry, bomber of the Café Terminus in February 1894, and Jule Bonnot, the criminal gang leader whose violence garnered much media attention during 1911–12. Merriman credits Henry with "[i]gniting the age of modern terror,"[105] noting that his bombing was a "defining moment in modern history [because it] was the day that ordinary people became the targets of terrorists."[106] He further perceives in the nineteenth century "war on terror" a "gossamer thread connecting [Islamist fundamentalists and Emile Henry]."[107] Merriman—not the only author to compare historical anarchism with modern Jihadism—does not follow up on this point.[108] He instead leaves the reader to assume that social inequalities and state repression lay at the heart of both nineteenth-century French anarchist violence and contemporary Islamic terror. Merriman's study of Bonnot's criminal exploits likewise leaves aside deeper analysis of terrorism, noting simply that the anti-anarchist laws of 1893–94 "identified terrorism with anarchism."[109] France features as an illustration in other works on anarchist terrorism, too.[110]

Few authors have considered perceptions of terrorism and the term's construction and application as a label, beyond its use to tarnish opponents of the state, "[dressing] the terrorist wolf in anarchist clothing."[111] A recent article, in which France features as an aside, is an exception to this rule: Richard Bach Jensen's 2018 publication on the June 1904 assassination of Nikolai Bobrikov, Russian governor general of Finland.[112] Using several online press databases that permit a keyword search, Jensen found that after 1904 (and especially in the French press) the terms "terrorism" and "terrorist" began to replace "anarchist" to identify and categorize "ground-up politically motivated violence," in Russia and, to a lesser extent, elsewhere in Europe. Jensen therefore identifies the beginning of a process that saw "terrorism" trump all other words for the description of substate violence; the process was completed during the 1930s.[113]

In comparison with the "first wave" of anarchist terror, the interwar period has received relatively little attention, as if these years marked a hiatus in terrorism.[114] Writing is generally limited to the state terrorism of the Nazi and communist regimes or the case of Ireland as a precursor to post-war sectarian violence.[115] There are some limited studies of French terrorist acts during the 1930s. Katherine Foshko and Karelle Vincent have investigated the response to the Russian Paul Gorguloff's assassination of French president Paul Doumer in May 1932.[116] Péter Kovács, Virginie Sansico, and Ben Saul have shed light on the legal response to the problem of interwar terrorism from France and the League of Nations, respectively.[117] Mario Jareb and Frédéric Monier have examined aspects of the assassinations of King Alexander I of Yugoslavia and French foreign minister

Louis Barthou by the Croatian revolutionary movement the Ustashe in Marseille on 9 October 1934.[118] Scholars from other disciplines, notably law, English, and international relations, have also brought this incident under investigation.[119] However, if Ditrych's claim (made in 2013) that the 1934 Marseille attack "is yet to be recognized in the history of terrorism" is no longer tenable, few scholars have examined this incident—or, for that matter, others in 1930s France—for what it may tell us about understandings and representations of historical acts of terrorism.[120]

Extreme right-wing French terrorism during the 1930s and 1940s has recently attracted the interest of historians. Gayle K. Brunelle and Annette Finley-Croswhite have worked extensively on the Organisation Secrète d'Action Révolutionnaire Nationale (OSARN), otherwise known as the "Cagoule," and its plan to install a fascist-style regime in France. Few historians had considered the organization seriously until Brunelle and Finley-Croswhite's 2012 *Murder in the Metro* (Joel Blatt and D.L.L. Parry had authored chapter-length studies only).[121] In fact, historians were more likely to dismiss the group altogether than bring it under close analysis. Michel Winock, for example, claimed that the Cagoule "belongs to the history of secret societies more than that of fascism," with its leader, Eugène Deloncle, "particularly at ease in the world of plots, oaths, mysteries." The OSARN warranted not so much as a page in Winock's updated four-hundred-page history of nationalism, antisemitism, and fascism in modern France.[122] The violence of the Cagoule in 1937 sat alongside other incidents of terror, including an attempt to steal a Spanish Republican submarine from Brest, the abduction of White Russian General Miller from Paris, and a series of minor bombings (in which the Cagoule was doubtless involved.)

During 1940–44, both the French Vichy regime and the Nazis denounced resisters as terrorists. Even if we dismiss this label as propaganda, we can examine the values and qualities for which it apparently stood to examine wartime perceptions of terrorism. It was under the Vichy regime that the term "terrorism" first appeared in French law when, on 5 June 1943, Marshal Pétain's regime established "Special Sections" within courts for the trial of crimes that promoted or encouraged "terrorism, communism, anarchy, social or national subversion," or "rebellion against the established social order." Vichy's laws did not define terrorism, and the application of the term remained at the discretion of the authorities. Vichy's propaganda was to some extent successful: long after the Liberation former resisters complained that their neighbors considered them still little better than bandits and terrorists.[123] Resisters countered Vichy's smear campaign with the argument that the regime's security forces, especially the paramilitary Milice Française, were the "real" terrorists. Resistance groups worked to reframe their own violence in a more palatable fashion, as military operations. Contrary to Vichy's portrayal of the resisters as bandits operating in the shadows, the groups attempted to legitimize their actions by framing them as precise and surgical, aimed solely at the Nazis and their French lackeys. Historians of France have likewise classified the resistance's armed struggle according to military or paramilitary categories such as "urban guerrilla," "partisan warfare," "subversive warfare," and "civil war." In line with modern definitions of terrorism, the use of the term "terrorist" to describe resistance violence is broadly rejected out of hand because this violence, committed in the name of national liberation, was neither indiscriminate nor directed at civilians.

Terrorism and "Greater France"

Readers may be surprised that France's overseas possessions—especially those in North Africa, given the violence of the years 1954–62—do not feature in this book. I do not deny the importance of "Greater France" to the French mainland and vice versa. As Gary Wilder writes, "The metropole and its overseas colonies exercised a reciprocal influence upon one another," and this influence was present throughout politics, culture, society, and economy.[124] The interwar years in particular saw the emergence of a "national imperial imaginary," in which citizens and subjects perceived the colonies to be "integral, if legally ambiguous, parts of the French nation."[125] Yet it is wrong to assume that imperial territories and anticolonial movements loomed large in the French culture of terrorism. There is little evidence that the terrorism label was applied in a French colonial context.

One finds only sporadic use of the terms "terrorism" and "terrorist" in press reports of anticolonial unrest. News of the uprising at Yên Bài (Indochina) in February 1930 saw *Le Matin* blame a "minority of terrorists" in the local population; conversely, socialist Marius Moutet condemned French repression of the rebels as "terrorism."[126] These examples are rare. Equally rare is the use of "terrorism" or "terrorist" to describe opposition to imperial rule in the missives of colonial administrators and their counterparts in Paris. For the press and the political establishment, anticolonialists were "agitators,"[127] "separatists,"[128] or "ringleaders," holding an impressionable population in thrall.[129] Blame for acts of violence lay with "rioters,"[130] insurrectionists,[131] "rebels,"[132] "felons," and "zealots."[133] Yet they were not terrorists.[134]

What explains the absence of colonial subjects from the French culture of terrorism? The answer to this question lies in, on the one hand, understandings of terrorism as an inherently political act inspired by European continental politics and, on the other hand, a racist condescension to colonial peoples that considered them incapable of political engagement. Several examples serve to illustrate this point. In 1922, a secretary of the Communist Party in Relizane (Algeria) reported that the "savage" indigenous population lacked the education to understand communism. This secretary warned the party against making appeals to such people, whom he predicted would fall back on their "ancestral barbarism" when they finally evicted the French.[135] In 1923, Governor General of Algeria Théodore Steeg reassured Minister of the Interior Maurice Maunoury that communism had found little favor with Algerians who, save for "some well-read urban Arabs," were "unfit to absorb" communist propaganda.[136] Later that decade, French opinions had hardly changed. A 1928 report claimed that "only some ambitious agitators" considered communism a means to national liberation but the majority of "indigènes" rejected this European doctrine.[137] In 1937, General Charles Noguès (an army commander in North Africa) described Muslim public opinion in Morocco as "unable to give the facts [of political conflict] the real value that they hold."[138] Such opinions do not reveal that colonial peoples really were incapable of political action (and by extension terrorism) but that the racism of the colonizing European elite perceived them thus.

This prejudice was reproduced in mainland France. A highly racialized stereotype of Algerians as criminals, primitive savages, rapists, and transmitters of venereal disease and tuberculosis was widely diffused through the press.[139] The Paris police's North African Brigade maintained a watchful eye on the colonial immigrant community in Paris; North Africans were most likely to be arrested for petty criminality such as theft and drunkenness.[140] The French state kept these immigrants under close surveillance, fearing that they would fall prey to criminal gangs[141] or political groups such as the Communist Party or the nationalist Etoile Nord-Africaine.[142] However, bureaucrats and press largely considered these immigrants as different from the political refugees from central and eastern Europe who allegedly brought with them the quarrels of their homeland.[143]

Overseas territories figured in the culture of terrorism as largely tangential to the ideological conflict in mainland Europe. Anxiety about the interference of hostile European powers in North Africa was great. During the Spanish Civil War, the French suspected subversive radio broadcasts to French Morocco from Spain[144] and the operation of Francoist agents in the protectorate.[145] Concern also surrounded potential conflict within the Spanish community in Algeria.[146] With regard to Germany, the French press denounced alleged incitements to riot by Hitler's agents,[147] while the government monitored supposed infiltration of North Africa by anti-French Muslims sent from Berlin (this fear in fact spanned the interwar years).[148] Concomitantly, Moscow loomed large among the worries of French colonizers. Rumors in May 1925 indicated that the Soviet Union sought to undermine the war effort against the Moroccan Rif rebels through the incitement of public disorder and the dynamiting of French ships.[149] Nationalist press and government sources blamed the Rif uprising on communist meddling, and the authorities closely monitored left-wing activists suspected of encouraging subversion.[150] Similar attitudes were evident in Indochina, where the press blamed Moscow-controlled communists for corralling poor peasants into action.[151]

Ultimately, in line with their attitudes to colonial subjects and growing political conflict in Europe, when the French imagined political subversion in their overseas territories, they largely considered it the work of a minority of nationalists or European agents provocateurs. Racism underpinned this attitude, for despite the centrality of "unFrenchness" to perceptions of terrorism—a notion that one might expect to be applied to France's imperial peoples—colonial subjects occupied a space beyond the French-foreigner axis that denuded them of terrorist potential. These findings indicate that to assume that the French considered anticolonial nationalists "terrorists" prior to 1945 is to read history backwards from the post-1945 conflicts. They suggest that greater historical engagement with interwar perceptions of terrorism is necessary.

A Brief Note on Sources

To examine perceptions and representations of terrorism in France between 1904 and 1939, this book uses archival documents (generally ministerial, bureaucratic, and police records), the historical press, memoirs, film, fiction, and, in the case of the assassination of King Alexander of Yugoslavia, newsreel footage. Official documents of the government and the police reveal private discussions and analyses of terrorism as well as the details of criminal investigations. National and local newspapers and "true crime" magazines such as *Détective* devoted much attention to terrorist activity, often running their own investigations parallel to those of the police. Journalists and editors narrated, interpreted, and framed terrorist acts for public consumption, placing each event in its perceived historical and contemporary context while drawing on prevailing attitudes to, and understandings of, the phenomenon. Then, as now, the media was wont to sensationalize terrorism. With editors and publishers chasing sales amid growing competition from glossy weekly magazines, reports and exposés blurred news and entertainment and were often richer in dramatic detail than the information released through police channels. As Michael B. Miller writes, "The great sensationalist stories that broke with nearly uninterrupted regularity and came to supersede crime stories [gave] news a palpable presence" in the lives of newspapers' mass audiences.[152] Charles Meyer, director of the Police Judiciaire after 1934, admitted that the truth behind crimes was "often, if not always, more dull and less worthy of a novel than one thinks."[153] Yet beyond embellishment, the press was intimately linked to the reality of terrorism not least through its recording, albeit in a digested (and digestible) form, of government statements, political speeches, and police communications on terrorism.

Given the discussion of terrorism and communication above, and the fact that media "is integral to its [terrorism's] social construction as a cultural object," the influence of the press on popular notions of terrorism was potentially huge.[154] The major titles of the French press had a considerable readership. If many historians of early twentieth-century France rely on press sources, few mention the huge circulation figures of national publications as outlined in Table 1. As Maurice Chavardès notes, the publications of the right, from the center to the extreme, dominated the national press (the reader can find more information about each title in the glossary).[155]

Thirty-two daily newspapers appeared in Paris each day, printing a

TABLE 1. Principal French News Publications, 1900–1939

Publication	Estimated Publication Figure	Frequency of Publication	Political Leaning
L'Action Française	40–70,000 (1935–40)	Daily	Extreme Right
L'Ami du peuple	700,000 (early 1930s)	Daily	Extreme Right
L'Aube	10–20,000	Daily	Christian Democratic Right
Détective	250,000 (early 1930s)	Weekly	—
L'Echo de Paris	100,000 (pre-1938)	Daily	Right
Le Figaro	100,000 (mid-1930s)	Daily	Right
Gringoire	500–650,000 (1938)	Weekly	Extreme Right
L'Humanité	200–300,000 (1930s)	Daily	Communist Left
L'Intransigeant	200,000 (1930s)	Daily	Extreme Right
Le Matin	350,000 (1939)	Daily	Right
L'Oeuvre	100–120,000 (1930s)	Daily	Centrist, close to the Radical Party
L'Ouest-Éclair	400,000 (1934)	Daily	Right
Paris-Soir	2,735,000 (1936)	Daily	Right
Le Petit Journal	150,000 (1930s)	Daily	Right
Le Petit Parisien	1,000,000 (1939)	Daily	Right
Le Populaire	100–300,000 (1930s)	Daily	Socialist Left
Le Temps	100,000 (1930s)	Daily	Right

combined 5.5 million copies (right-wing newspapers printed eight times as many daily issues as their left-wing counterparts).[156] Provincial newspapers published 6 million copies per day.[157] They printed original work from their own correspondents as well as copy from the national titles. Newspaper companies used an array of techniques to sell copies, from street hawkers on foot and on bicycles to luminous screens on the façade of each title's publishing headquarters. Crowds gathered in streets and town squares to read placards and posters posted by an array of titles and political groups. Trains carried news across the country.[158]

While newspapers strove to bring events to readers within hours of their happening (through reports telephoned or telegrammed in from local correspondents and technology such as the Belinograph), radio news often reached French ears first.[159] At 7 a.m. on 7 May 1932, for example, the radio delivered the news of the death by assassination of President Paul

Doumer.[160] Likewise, radio reported the assassination of King Alexander I in October 1934 before newspapers could print their evening editions.[161] The transmission of news helped to collapse geographical distance: radio brought details of the Paris bombings of 11 September 1937 to listeners outside the capital within twenty-four hours of the attack.[162] These broadcasts potentially helped to construct immediate understandings and representations of terrorist events. Unfortunately, the transcripts are unavailable. However, one can speculate that the framing of this violence to some extent reflected that found in the press, especially when one considers the connection between newspapers and radio networks. In 1924, *Le Petit Parisien* founded the "Poste du Petit Parisien." This station made use of the newspaper's journalists and correspondents "exactly like a morning daily," according to Maurice Bourdet, one-time journalist and creator of the "Journal parlé" ("Spoken Newspaper") show.[163] Bourdet conceived of a symbiotic relationship between the radio and the daily press: the former brought to listeners "on the spot impressions" and "instantaneous news… the naked event, the raw event," while the latter provided analysis and interpretation.[164] It was not the case, Bourdet continued, that radio would replace the press. In fact, he claimed that when "radio announces [the event] the evening before, the sales of newspapers increase the day after."[165] Newssheets brought the shocking visual nature of an attack to audiences through printed images. Consequently, if the reality of terrorist activity was somewhat different from its presentation in the press—journalist Jacques Bonhomme observed in September 1937 that "reading the newspapers leaves you astounded, [and] with the very disagreeable impression of living surrounded by terrorists"[166]—the print media nevertheless had a considerable influence over cultures of terrorism.[167]

ONE

Made in Russia

*Emerging Perceptions of Terrorism
Before the Great War*

In the early afternoon of 3 May 1906, Russian émigrés Alexandre Sokoloff and his comrade Vladimir Stryga were walking in the Bois de Vincennes when Stryga's trousers exploded.[1] A nail bomb located in his pocket had accidentally detonated. Carnage greeted the people who rushed to the scene. Stryga was horribly injured. *Le Matin* reported that he had "[a] terrible wound, a bloody hole, opened in place of the abdomen, and, at the bottom of this hole, the vertebrae and hip bones appeared; the mass of the intestines hung, horrible, on the thighs, [which were] torn apart, too."[2] The accidental bomber did not have long to live. Sokoloff was shaken and bleeding but his injuries were not fatal; police directed a doctor at the scene to care for him and ignore his mortally wounded companion. Lying prostrate, Sokoloff gestured to Stryga, murmuring, "Him…bomb…not me."[3] Officers tried in vain to question Stryga. They searched his pockets only to find a second explosive device, which a constable moved carefully to the side of the path. The search also turned up a loaded revolver and a photograph of a woman.[4] Stryga moaned in agony for nearly an hour, before dying in front of a crowd of gawking onlookers.[5] Souvenir hunters later combed the area for pieces of the bomb and fragments of bone and flesh.[6]

Following the explosion, speculation mounted in the press about the man who had accidentally blown himself up in a Parisian park. Was his name really "Stryga," as Sokoloff claimed? The victim had registered at a local hotel under the name Benjamin Katz, a twenty-one-year-old student from Minsk.[7] Yet "Katz" was just one of many names attributed in the newspapers to Stryga, along with Guernstein (or Grunstein), Ivanoff, Toldberg, Trida, and Viatzer.[8] Perhaps the dead man was the notorious "Vladimir Lapidus," a Jewish-Polish bomber wanted by the Russian authorities?[9] The identity of the woman in the photograph found on the dying man prompted further questions. Who was this woman with the austere face of a Russian intellectual, "clouded by the sad dream of an impossible humanity?"[10] Was she a fiancée, a lover, or an accomplice? As for the two bombs, investigators strove to determine their target. Sokoloff claimed that he and Stryga had intended only to export the device and others like it to their revolutionary comrades in Russia. The unexploded bomb found on Stryga reportedly resembled the pine-cone shaped explosive used in Paris on 31 May 1905 during an attempt on the lives of King Alphonse XIII of Spain and French president Emile Loubet on the rue de Rohan. It was also reportedly like the explosives used to kill Russian minister of the interior Vyacheslav von Plehve in July 1904 and Grand Duke Sergei Alexandrovich in February 1905.[11]

Stryga was in fact "Lapidus," the veteran of Russian terrorism. He had led a terrorist faction in Russia called the Kommunary, an offshoot of the violent Chernoe Znamia (Black Banner) anarchist group. The Kommunary drew inspiration from the Paris Commune and wanted to stage a similar uprising in Bialystok (from where Stryga originated) and Ekaterinoslav.[12] While Sokoloff denied that the bomb that killed Stryga was intended for use in France, this does not seem to be true. In October 1907, police reported that a group of violent anarchists from Paris's rue des Ecouffes had revealed Stryga's intention to use the device in Paris on 1 May the following year.[13] If there was more to this story than boastful talk, then the terrorist failed to make good on his plan, dying on 3 May. Conversely, Peter Gooderham claims that Stryga was lying in wait for a German banker to pass through the park when his bomb exploded. The Russian had decided to target wealthy French backers of the Russian authorities.[14] In apparent support of Gooderham's hypothesis, Stryga's last letter to his comrades, published posthumously in 1907, excoriated the French bourgeoisie for their repression of the working class. The letter revealed his desire to attack and kill the bourgeoisie in whichever country they lived.[15]

French newspapers had long devoted attention to political violence in Russia, from the nihilists who had assassinated Tsar Alexander II in March 1881 to the terrorists and anarchists of the Party of Socialist Revolutionaries of the early twentieth century. The plots that allegedly emanated from the Russian community in Paris featured regularly in the contemporary press, too. There seems some truth to the apparent revolutionary effervescence of the capital's eastern European expatriates. In 1909, Lieutenant Colonel von Kotten, head of Moscow's political police, described Paris as the refuge of "the most dangerous Russian terrorists."[16] The French police kept a close eye on the activities of Russian anarchist terrorists in the city.[17] Jensen has reason therefore to claim that Paris became a "grand headquarters" for violent revolutionaries fleeing the east, especially after the bloody Tsarist repression of 1905.[18]

Journalists reporting on the explosion at Vincennes in 1906 used the terms "nihilist," "anarchist," "revolutionary," and "terrorist" interchangeably and often simultaneously to describe the victim and his partner. Stryga was a "Russian terrorist" and an "anarchist"; a "nihilist" belonging to a Russian "terrorist" organization; a Russian "nihilist" and an "anarchist."[19] Stryga's Russian nationality—or, rather, his *assumed* Russian nationality—featured prominently in press analyses. It offered an apparent means to explain the affair because Stryga was one of "those Slav nihilists, cranks, gentle and wild at the same time" (according to the conservative *Le Matin*) that committed terrorist acts.[20] Editor of *Gil Blas* Eugène Destez warned that Russian anarchists living in Paris (of which there were "a lot") burned with a "flame of secret revolt" that one could see in their eyes.[21] Destez demanded that such people keep out of French affairs and reserve their barbarism—"which may reign back home"—for their own country.[22] Such comments betrayed an Orientalist attitude to terrorists; they hailed from a far-off land whose traditions were alien to France. Right-wing *L'Intransigeant* summed up the fears of some French when it asked, "[Is] the terrorist action of which the empire of the Tsars has long been the theatre [going] to reach France?"[23] By the time of Stryga's death in May 1906, the link between Russia and terrorism was taking hold in the popular imagination.[24]

This chapter examines French perceptions of terrorism from the mid-nineteenth century to the Great War. During this period, the term "terrorism" began to take on meaning as a form of substate political violence. First, the chapter unravels the semantic muddle that confronts the historian of terrorism in this period. Terms such as "nihilism," "anarchism," and "terrorism," and their attendant practitioners, appear frequently in the sources with little apparent distinction between them. Nevertheless, each term went in and out of fashion, enjoying a high point of usage in three distinct periods: 1879–82 ("nihilisme"); 1892–95 ("anarchisme"); and 1905–10 ("terrorisme"), suggesting that each label was applied to *something* and not just *anything*. What did these words mean to contemporaries and in what contexts were they deployed? Did "terrorism" have a specific meaning or connotation?

Second, the chapter brings the figure of the terrorist after 1905 under investigation. Reports of terrorist violence in Russia, along with the presumed presence of terrorists among the Russian expatriate community in Paris, contributed to the construction of a stereotypical perpetrator. The male terrorist was a fanatical ideologue and a skilled bomb maker who forsook all earthly comforts and pleasures and who inhabited a shadowy and treacherous world. The female terrorist proved a character of particular interest, for she was a zealot whose plain exterior did not blunt her seductive power. Russian nihilist-anarchist-terrorists featured prominently in the French arts, proving a fertile source of inspiration for authors, playwrights, and early filmmakers. These characters and plotlines, along with real-world terrorism, all helped to inform notions of terrorism and the terrorist in early twentieth-century France.

Nihilist = Terrorist = Anarchist? The Revolutionary Equation, 1860–1900
"PROPAGANDA BY THE DEED"

The word "nihilist" entered the French language as a religious term in 1761. It took on political and philosophical meanings during the 1790s.[25] Nihilism came to prominence throughout France and Europe only during the 1860s, thanks to Ivan Turgenev's 1862 novel *Otsy i deti* (translated into French in 1863 as *Pères et Enfants* and into English in 1867 as *Fathers and Sons*). The novel's main character, Bazarov, is described as a "nihilist." According to Turgenev, Bazarov was a "man who does not bow down before any authority, who does not take any principle on faith, whatever reverence that principle may be enshrined in."[26] For Turgenev, nihilism was not a political movement. It constituted a personal philosophy that rejected the ways of the older generation in Russia to embrace the natural sciences, along with tenets of English utilitarianism and French socialism.[27] Nevertheless, the philosophy's rebellious bent garnered most attention, particularly when set against a background of growing unrest in Russia, notably Dmitry Karakozov's failed attempt to kill the Tsar in April 1866. *Fathers and Sons* thus helped to shape understandings of nihilism as a radical and dangerous political idea.[28] By the late 1860s, "nihilism" as a word synonymous with destructive revolutionary violence had entered English and French dictionaries.[29]

Developments in Russian and European politics during the 1870s and early 1880s further ensnared nihilism in the conceptual frameworks of revolutionary politics. European anarchists' understandings—or *misunderstandings*—of the idea prompted a change of tactics at a time when anarchist thinkers had begun to consider a new means to topple the capitalist system. In December 1876, Italian anarchist Carlo Cafiero noted in a letter to his compatriot Errico Malatesta that the "most efficient means of propaganda" was the "insurrectional deed."[30] Caferio and Malatesta acted upon this idea when, during 5–11 April 1877, they led an armed attack in the Benevento province of Italy, burning local archives and redistributing money to the poor. Short-lived, the experiment proved salutary, and the notion of "propaganda by the deed" began to develop.[31] Four months later, in August 1877, French socialist Paul Brousse, in an article titled "Propaganda by the Deed," explored the efficacy of action over words.[32] The anarchist doctrine had the most chance of success, Brousse argued, if its ideas took physical form, in "flesh and bone, living, before the people."[33]

In Russia, nihilism developed nascent links to the concept of terrorism. During 1873, Sergei Nechaiev, revolutionary leader of the Narodnaia Rasprava (People's Vengeance), stood trial in Moscow. A young and charismatic radical, Nechaiev had authored a nihilist manifesto in 1869 titled *Catechism of a Revolutionary* while living at the Swiss home of renowned Russian anarchist Mikhail Bakunin. Nechaiev presented the revolutionary as a single-minded extremist hell-bent on the destruction of the status quo by violent means. According to Martin A. Miller, Nechaiev's manifesto largely "forms the foundation for the theory and practice of modern insurgent terror."[34] During his 1873 trial, the counsel for the prosecution labeled the accused a "terrorist," a moniker that Nechaiev welcomed. Following Nechaiev's imprisonment, the police hunted down and eliminated members of Narodnaia Rasprava during 1874–77.[35]

Between January 1878 and March 1881, the Russian Narodnaia Volya (People's Will) took up Nechaiev's mantle, waging a violent campaign against the state authorities that culminated in the assassination by bomb of Tsar Alexander II on 1 March 1881. The group revived the term "terrorism" in its practical and theoretical work on revolutionary combat. Notably, Nikolai Morozov authored a pamphlet titled "The Terrorist Struggle" and Gerasim G. Romanenko produced a brochure titled "Terrorism and Routine." Each advocated violent struggle as a virtue against autocracy and disconnected terrorism from its Robespierrist roots to define a new form of political struggle.[36] Narodnaia Volya innovated, too, in the realm of revolutionary weaponry. Its chemist, Nikolai Ivanovich Kibalchich, for example, was the first to propose the use of dynamite for political ends.[37] The high publicity value of such attacks saw the group and its sympathizers deepen their commitment to political violence. A cycle of attack and bloody state repression ensued.[38] Some acts of terrorism gained international notoriety, such as Vera Zasulich's attack on Governor Dmitri Feodorovich Trepov of Saint Petersburg on 24 January 1878.[39]

Revolutionaries outside Russia looked to adapt terrorism to their own ends. In September 1880, a small group of anarchists met at Vevey in Switzerland to discuss a new form of violent revolutionary strategy.[40] One of these men, Russian prince-cum-anarchist Peter Kropotkin, advocated in December 1880 an aggressive propaganda, "by the dagger, the rifle, [and] dynamite."[41] In July the following year, the international anarchist congress in London adopted propaganda by the deed as an official policy of the movement. Speakers urged activists to move from legal to illegal action, described as "the only way that leads to revolution," and they enjoined anarchist groups to study the technical and chemical sciences all the better to serve the revolutionary cause.[42] The new course received widespread approbation from France's anarchists.[43] The anarchist press immediately printed advice on the making of bombs and other so-called "anti-bourgeois products."[44] Throughout anarchist publications, an outpouring of violent rhetoric—"Anything goes! But the shadier the means the better. Fire! Blood! Poison! A pact with death!"[45]—accompanied several attacks during the 1880s.[46] The influence of Russian tactics—or at least French understandings of them—on developments in French anarchist action was evident in the manifesto of the "French nihilist women." The document, printed in *Le Drapeau noir* in September 1883, urged French women to poison their bourgeois masters with lead, spoiled meat, or hemlock.[47] An apparent belief in the interchangeability of "anarchism," "nihilism" and "terrorism" in France gave rise to misunderstandings that prompted borrowings and adaptations. Propaganda by the deed as developed in French anarchist circles was a hybrid of anarchist theories of revolutionary propaganda and (mis)conceptions of Russian nihilist tactics.[48]

PERCEPTIONS OF NIHILIST TERRORISM

Beyond the anarchist movement, the image of the nihilist, the anarchist, and the terrorist as kindred perpetrators of gratuitous and destructive violence solidified throughout the final decades of the nineteenth century as European populations endured a wave of bombings and assassinations.[49] The terrorist label still existed in France as a term to describe the country's historical revolutionaries, and it offered a means to link contemporary "revolutionaries" (such as the communards of Paris) to the Robespierrists.[50] Yet by the end of the 1870s, terrorism began to develop a meaning distinct from its French origins. *Le Gaulois* reported in April 1879 that Russian nihilism was "a secret party, audacious and *terrorist*" that desired the complete destruction of society.[51] Political texts, histories, travelogues, plays, novels, and newspapers came to present the nihilist terrorist as an advocate of wanton criminal violence, devoid of ideological goals.[52] The sheer variety of commentaries and productions in which nihilism featured indicated that the movement was in vogue: the French waxwork museum, the Musée Grévin, even featured a display depicting the arrest of Alexander II's "nihilist" assassins.[53] There *were* progressive commentaries on nihilism: Olympe Audouard's 1880 *Les Soupers de la princesse Louba d'Askoff* was a novel that explored the connections between nihilism and women's rights in Russia.[54] Some democratic critics of the Tsar considered the Emperor's assassination understandable, if not excusable: "I reprimand them, but I pity them [too]," wrote "Jean Frollo," pseudonym of the editorial team at *Le Petit Parisien*.[55] "Frollo" dissociated nihilism from the conception that it represented little more than "annihilation." However, the newspaper erroneously attributed the Tsar's death to nihilists.[56]

Sympathetic press coverage of the Russian regime, in the context of increasingly warm relations between Paris and Moscow, generally undermined the anti-Tsarist cause.[57] The dominant representations of the nihilist were those of a raging and revolutionary savage, a bourgeois lout expelled from university, condemned to poverty, riddled with scrofula, and united with his brethren by a singular desire: the "thirst for destruction." The nihilist terrorist carried out his task with automotive efficiency, before committing suicide without hesitation.[58] If ideas of nihilism were crystallizing, one still finds a lack of clarity in some French sources about Russian terrorism. In 1884, *Le Cri du Peuple* attempted to offer a nomenclature of Russian political parties, among which figured the "political terrorist party," the "specific terrorist party," and the "federal terrorist party." Narodnaia Volya figured in this list, yet it was not labeled terrorist.[59]

The 1885 publication of Sergius Stepniak's exploration of the Russian revolutionary milieu, *La Russie souterraine*, further informed French impressions of the terrorists (the book was printed in English in 1882 as *Underground Russia*). Stepniak spoke with some degree of authority on the subject. He was a revolutionary who had murdered the head of the Russian secret police General Nikolai Mezentsov in August 1878. Stepniak's chapters on terrorism did little to contradict French and western European prejudices. He presented the terrorist as a fearful being: "Upon the horizon there appeared a gloomy form, illuminated by a light as of hell, who, with lofty bearing, and a look breathing forth hatred and defiance, made his way through the terrified crowd to enter with a firm step upon the scene of history. It was the Terrorist."[60] According to Stepniak, the terrorist was a new type of revolutionary, one who preferred action and bullets to words and propaganda and who would stop at nothing to achieve his goal.[61] Stepniak's tome had a substantial influence on French and European conceptions of "nihilism."[62] In 1886, Emile Littré's supplement to his dictionary of the French language added a new meaning to "Nihilisme": "Form of Russian socialism, [a] doctrine that prioritizes above all other considerations the destruction of the social organism and which, for the moment at least, seeks to put nothing in its place."[63] Conversely, the meaning of terrorism remained unstable. Littré's definition of "terrorisme" in 1886, for example, was still rooted in its French revolutionary context, as expounded in his dictionary of 1873–74.[64] The label continued to appear in the press as much for the repression of freedoms by the state as the violent deeds of revolutionaries; it could also describe run-of-the-mill crimes, such as the street robberies committed at knifepoint by a Parisian "beggar terrorist" in spring 1890.[65]

In May 1890, nihilist terrorism made front-page news when police arrested a dozen Russians in Paris on suspicion of bomb making. On 12 May 1890, an inhabitant of Le Raincy, northeast of Paris, came across evidence of explosions in the commune, notably damaged trees and craters in the ground. Police investigations led to the Russian community in the Montrouge district of the capital. On 29 May 1890, officers made a dozen arrests and seized several explosive devices. The arrestees faced criminal charges for the illegal possession of dynamite and weapons of war.[66] Reports of the arrests prompted renewed analysis in the press of nihilist terrorism and its origins. Well-established conceptions of nihilism as an extreme and destructive Eastern doctrine reemerged.[67] A connection between nihilism and terrorism persisted: *La Justice* traced nihilist terrorism to 1878, the year that "[t]he terrorist age began."[68] Some newspapers attempted to explain the complexities of Russian revolutionary politics. According to such analyses, "terrorist" denoted one of the two factions in the Russian "nihilist party" (the "propagandists" or "popularists" were the other faction).[69] Each faction comprised anarchists, collectivists, and communists, all united in the "struggle by the pen, the word or dynamite against Tsarism."[70] Terrorism was thus framed as a tactic, a means of political action, rather than an ideology in itself (because the ideology behind terrorism was nihilism).

A good deal of attention fell on the Russian nihilist colony in Paris. Journalists reported that these refugees were generally educated young people of both sexes enrolled at Parisian universities. They came from financially comfortable if not wealthy families. Almost certainly brainwashed by revolutionaries upon their arrival in Paris, these novice political warriors attended bomb-making lessons provided by their revolutionary elders or "professors."[71] Several press outlets cast a perplexed eye toward the nihilists' domestic arrangements. The terrorists led a monkish lifestyle, sharing sparsely furnished and crowded accommodations (men and women shared the same bed!) that doubled as explosives laboratories.[72]

The female nihilist proved an object of fascination. In fact, a special interest in women terrorists as the "unusual suspects" in attacks—despite their continued presence in terrorist organizations—persists into the twenty-first century.[73] During the 1880s, the conservative press depicted the *femme nihiliste* as a radical feminist, destined only for political fanaticism because she was too ugly for both marriage and prostitution.[74] By 1890, aspects of this representation had changed. The right-wing *L'Echo de Paris* described the female nihilist's "terrible and fearful" form and her pretty yet self-consciously masculine look, defined as a preference for wearing short hair, high boots, men's hats, and simple dresses. These manly looks hid a ferocious sexual appetite. The female nihilist was as adept at enticing "beautiful and vigorous males" into carnal relations as she was at seducing "some young girl, still a virgin but already poisoned with the scent of the oleanders of Lesbos."[75] Nonetheless, for these short-haired women and their long-haired male companions, all was subordinated to the bomb; gratuitous destruction remained the goal.[76] These impressions mirrored contemporary fictional portraits of the woman nihilist as a seductress committed wholesale to her cause.[77]

France endured a sustained period of anarchist violence during the 1890s. The country had experienced such incidents before, notably in March 1886 when Charles Gallo attempted unsuccessfully to detonate a bomb in the main hall of the Paris stock exchange.[78] However, contemporaries understood the spiral of attacks between March 1892 and June 1894 as a time of unprecedented violence. It was a period of "terrorist epidemic" and "dynamitomania."[79] The perpetrators of attacks gained huge notoriety in the press. A veritable cult of celebrity developed around "Ravachol" (real name François Claudius Koenigstein), a murderer and bomber whose reign of terror briefly worried the French during March 1892. Then there was Emile Henry, a young bourgeois who bombed a Parisian café in February 1894. His later declaration in court that all members of the bourgeoisie were fair game for anarchists chilled to the bone well-to-do French society. The targeting of the political elite gave Republican authorities great cause for concern. On 9 December 1893, Auguste Vaillant threw a bomb into the Chamber of Deputies when parliament was in session, lightly injuring several parliamentarians. On 24 June 1894, Italian anarchist Santo Geronimo Caserio stabbed to death President of the Republic Sadi Carnot in Lyon.

The French state responded to these outrages with severely repressive legislation aimed at curtailing anarchist associations and their propaganda. These laws, voted on 12 and 18 December 1893, and 28 July 1894, came to be known as the "Villainous Laws" or *lois scélérates*.[80] The Laws denuded anarchism of its political character and instead rendered anarchist crimes punishable by death as common law offences (crimes deemed political were usually subject to a certain indulgence regarding the conditions of one's incarceration). Republican legislators refused to consider the political motivations of attackers. Rather they attributed anarchism to derangement, degeneration, and criminal depravity.[81] The French were not alone in their campaign to repress anarchism: the *lois scélérates* were a single component in a global struggle to stamp out the anarchist terrorist.[82]

To what extent did the French understand the anarchist wave of attacks during the 1890s as terrorism? The labels "terrorism" and "terrorist" were not absent from descriptions of violence during 1892–94, but their deployment was infrequent. They occurred in press reports of anarchist violence to describe the use of violence rather than as a term that had any meaning itself. In 1892, for example, deputy and future prime minister Charles Dupuy condemned the government for responding too slowly to revolutionary violence. Dupuy argued that "using scientific progress, the *terrorists of anarchy* have replaced the guillotine's blade and the communists' rifle bullet with the dynamite bomb."[83] In March 1894, an anonymous author in *L'Echo de Paris* called on the French state to combat anarchism with its own methods and thus "terrorize the terrorists" ("opposer un terreur à ces terroristes") while noting the effectiveness of unrestrained repression against the nihilists in Russia.[84] In August 1894, nationalist author Maurice Barrès speculated that a taste for education among sections of the working class had nurtured "terrorist anarchy" among terrorists such as Ravachol, Henry, and Caserio.[85] One finds further instances of these infamous attackers labeled as terrorists in the contemporary press.[86] In a similar vein, *La Gazette de France* called the anti-anarchist laws the "terrorist laws" (in the sense of their antiterrorism).[87]

Contemporary concepts of terrorism were perhaps still too closely associated with Russian politics for the label to stick to French anarchists. Eugène-Melchior de Vogüé noted that French anarchists were not "forged from the same iron" as their Russian terrorist predecessors despite the similarities between the two groups (not least their educated background, their audacity, fanaticism, and contempt for life).[88] He did allow that the anarchist attacks proved that France was not immune to action once considered "so Slav"[89] (and by extension unFrench). Nevertheless, the violence of this period, which to twenty-first-century eyes might qualify as "terrorist," was mostly labeled "anarchist." "Terrorism" was not, therefore, always synonymous with anarchism.

By 1900, the terrorist label no longer denoted solely the revolutionaries of 1793. Certainly, the term still held such connotations in a historical sense. However, in the closing decades of the century, terrorism came also to signify a means of violent substate revolutionary action. The changing conception of the word owed, first, to interactions, borrowings, and adaptations between European and Russian leftists and attendant attempts to understand the strategy and goals of their comrades, and second, to the often-indiscriminate use of labels. Complexities remained. From the point of view of some 1890s French anarchists, past Russian attacks—particularly those claimed by the "terrorist" Narodnaia Volya—formed part of the history of the anarchist movement. A calendar in the 1894 anarchist *Père Peinard* almanac commemorated the January 1880 dynamiting of the Winter Palace and the March 1881 assassination of the Tsar along with other dates of revolutionary significance. To add to the confusion, the author of the calendar attributed both incidents to "nihilists."[90] On the right, antisemitic nationalist Edouard Drumont drew an equivalence between Henry's infamous statement on the guilt of the bourgeoisie with French revolutionary Lazare Carnot's 1793 declaration that "there are no innocents amongst the aristocrats." For Drumont, both types of terrorists were purely criminals.[91] On the other hand, nationalist Edmond Lepelletier considered the anarchist attacks of the 1890s quite different from the heroic deeds of the eighteenth-century opponents of the French monarchy. Bombs were "Russian products," and anarchist "terrorization" reeked of "Slav barbarism."[92]

CONSTRUCTING TERRORISM AFTER 1904

By the first decade of the twentieth century, propaganda by the deed had passed its high-water mark in France. Unquestionably, agitation still rumbled on, exploding in spasms of sporadic violence such as the bombing at the rue de Rohan in May 1905. Attacks of a mundane character persisted in the form of episodic murders, sabotage, and, later, bank robberies attributed to anarchist criminal gangs. Yet with revolutionary syndicalism and the trade union movement now offering an alternative to individual violence, and with the anarchist movement largely in decline, direct action appealed to fewer and fewer *compagnons*.[93] The apparent lassitude of French anarchist circles frustrated some eastern European revolutionary exiles in Paris. Police reported in December 1907 that a recent arrival in Paris from Warsaw called Leiser Migdal was so frustrated with the inactivity of his French comrades that he planned to take the lead himself and kill Prime Minister Georges Clemenceau in a bomb attack.[94] Similarly, officers learned in September 1908 that a certain Russian named Voronoff was so disgusted with the "inertia" of the French movement that he decided to return to his former revolutionary comrades in Russia.⁹⁵ However, the fear persisted that "true anarchists" had not abandoned violence altogether, and rumors surfaced periodically about planned anarchist attacks and bombings.⁹⁶ Furthermore, bloody attacks on foreign soil received ample attention from the French press and served to remind readers of the deadly potential of anarchism. News outlets continued to use the terms "anarchist" and "terrorist" interchangeably, such as in reports of the attack on the Spanish King's wedding party on 31 May 1906 that killed twenty-four people.⁹⁷ Terminology familiar to anarchism, such as "propaganda by the deed," was sometimes applied to the actions of terrorists in Russia (who were themselves occasionally termed anarchists).⁹⁸ Indicative of this continued association between "anarchism" and "terrorism" was an entry in the index of the 1906 volume of the *Journal du Droit international privé et de la jurisprudence comparée*: "[For] Terrorist—See Anarchist."⁹⁹

The meanings of "terrorist" and "terrorism" were not so straightforward. To begin to understand the sense of these terms, we may look first to their growing usage in the French press between 1900 and 1914. If journalists still relied on "nihilism" and "anarchism" to describe aspects of political violence, "terrorism" now appeared in newspapers at a frequency not witnessed during the past century's high points of nihilist or anarchist activity. Political upheaval in Russia during the first decade of the century—and its association with terrorism—explain this upward trend. Undeniably, the word retained its elasticity, providing a means to cast as illegitimate any action of which one disapproved, including both striking and strike-breaking,¹⁰⁰ the misdeeds of criminal gangs,¹⁰¹ French government policy,¹⁰² police repression,¹⁰³ and resistance to colonial regimes.¹⁰⁴ Moreover, Russia was not the only theater of political violence labeled terrorist. Thanks to the murderous exploits of Spanish anarchists, French socialist André Morizet dubbed Barcelona the "city of bombs" and "the terrifying hideout of the most formidable terrorists."¹⁰⁵ Yet the apparently random nature of Spanish anarchist violence distinguished it from its Russian relation. The Spanish anarchist-terrorist killed "in heaps," when he threw his bomb; this targeting of innocent civilians and bystanders was "incomprehensible."¹⁰⁶ Civilian bystanders died in Russian violence too, but the French understood that Russians generally chose targets of high political value with any civilian casualties being simply collateral damage. Spaniards, however, seemed to plump deliberately for "soft" civilian targets.¹⁰⁷

Even in the case of Russian terrorism, French perceptions underwent some modification. During 1904–6, terrorism was associated with Russian anti-Tsarist revolutionary violence. By 1910, the prevalence of terrorist expropriations in Russia saw the concept of violent criminality and larceny added to long-standing beliefs about terrorism's destructive essence.[108] In March 1912, *Gil Blas* and *La Lanterne* described so-called anarchist Jules Bonnot's holdups as tantamount to "Russian terrorism."[109] Some French anarchists admired greatly the exploits of the Russian expropriators but decided that a similar tactic was not suitable in a French context, believing that the risk in France was greater and that the public was unlikely to tolerate such a tactic.[110] If anything defined understandings of terrorism in France in the early years of the twentieth century, it was the Russianness of the phenomenon.[111]

RUSSIAN "TERRORISM"

Russia experienced a decade of violent political turmoil prior to the outbreak of the Great War. Democratic reformers in the state Duma and revolutionary organizations intent on the violent overthrow of the monarchy confronted an implacable authoritarian regime. The most prominent groups to advocate terrorism were the Party of the Socialist Revolutionaries and its Combat Organization. The former sought to provide a theoretical and political basis for terrorism as a method of attack and defense, as well as a tool to awaken the revolutionary conscience of the masses; the latter was a semi-autonomous group concerned solely with the perpetration of political violence. The Combat Organization's first attack took place on 2 April 1902, when student Stepan Balmashov assassinated Minister of the Interior Dmitry Sipyagin. The Revolutionaries intermittently renounced terror when the government made concessions. The sitting of the Duma between April and July 1906 marked one such hiatus.[112] Terrorist violence quickly resumed each time the Tsar and his ministers reneged on their promises. Even moderates in the Kadet—the Constitutional Democratic Party—supported terrorism in the face of a brutal and repressive autocracy.[113] Socialist revolution motivated some terrorists, but others seem to have cast off the ties of ideology relatively easily. The clandestine life of the terrorist was all-consuming, and assassins committed violence linked tenuously at best to the Revolutionaries and their purported goal.[114] Attacks spread rapidly throughout the empire: between February 1905 and

May 1906 alone, 1,075 state officials and functionaries fell victim to terrorist murder.[115]

In response to the wave of revolutionary action, the apparatus of repression moved at full tilt, supported by private terrorist militia such as the Black Hundreds.[116] These militia staged pogroms, killing hundreds with the connivance of the state.[117] Concomitantly, the government resorted to emergency decree powers and martial law.[118] Arrested Revolutionaries were subject to arbitrary imprisonment and summary execution, whether at the hands of their jailers or at the scaffold.[119] The scale of police and military tyranny drew condemnation from around the world.[120] At the high point of the violence during 1906–7, at least eight thousand died on both sides of the revolutionary struggle, with thirty-eight thousand anti-Tsarist opponents imprisoned by the end of the decade.[121] In total, Anna Geifman estimates that between 1900 and 1916, seventeen thousand people died.[122] Geifman concludes that "nowhere between the turn of the century and the outbreak of World War I were terrorist practices so widespread as in Tsarist Russia."[123]

The French press reported in detail the strife in Russian politics.[124] Newspapers did not bother to translate words such as *knout* (a whip used for punishment) and *ukase* (a decree law), perhaps assuming that their readers were familiar with such terms.[125] Journalists constructed a fearful image of Russian terrorism as a "mysterious and bloody force" operating throughout the eastern empire and beyond.[126] According to these representations, terrorist groups drew on huge financial resources—possibly supplied by Jews, according to French antisemites—to fund their devilish schemes.[127] Their operations reached into all parts of the state, from the police, the army, and the navy to the railways and the telecommunications network.[128] In bomb-making laboratories they produced cutting-edge explosive devices, some as small as a watch, capable of causing terrible destruction.[129] Descriptions of injuries suffered in bombings illustrated their devastating power. In the aftermath of the August 1906 bombing of Russian minister of the interior Pyotr Stolypin's dacha, *La Liberté* reported, "The majority of the dead were blown to pieces [and] the rescuers had to collect [them] from the curtains [and] the drapes....Parts of human bodies were thrown on the road and as far as the river. An officer, who by chance [was sheltered by] a small tree, saw a hand covered in blood and dust fall [to the ground] before him."[130]

Few French commentators beyond the anarchist milieu approved of

Russian terrorist violence.[131] Socialists sympathized to some extent with their revolutionary comrades in Russia, but they ultimately considered individual acts of violence counterproductive. Real political change would come from working-class solidarity and mass action, rather than the sporadic and isolated interventions of terrorists.[132] Centrists likewise disapproved. Radical Joseph Paul-Boncour saw in terrorism a futile tactic that spoke more to a desire for vengeance than any political goal. Boncour pointed out in 1909 that terrorists had not succeeded in preventing a single repressive measure nor had they turned even one civil servant against the Tsarist regime.[133] Right-wing voices were the most vociferous in their criticism. Conservative publications such as *Le Temps* condemned terrorist violence as an offence against civilization.[134] Meanwhile, *Le Matin* saw "the savage brutality of anarchy" in Russian terrorism.[135]

To some extent, historical understandings of anarchism in France provided a lens through which to interpret this new violence. Like anarchism, Russian terrorism sought "to destroy everything" by means of the dagger, the revolver, and the bomb, and the terrorist killed for the sake of killing alone.[136] Typical of this attitude was conservative deputy Georges Berthoulat, who called terrorism a "frenzy for massacre, a sadism for blood… [and] the return to barbarity by scientific methods."[137] If some observers saw an equivalence between anarchism and terrorism, others considered the latter to be more evil in nature than its predecessor. The conservative *La Liberté*'s P. Peyras wrote that "one will not find in the history of revolutions a more hideous mix of bestial ferocity [and] imbecilic savagery" than terrorism.[138] The foreign and unFrench character of terrorism exacerbated its awfulness: a descendant of nihilism—which desired "the destruction of everything that exists"—terrorism was a notion "hardly accessible to the French brain."[139]

However, an attempt to understand terrorism's political goals often appeared in tandem with these condemnations of revolutionary violence. To a degree, these analyses were one-dimensional: terrorists committed their attacks in the name of—or in place of—democratic participation. The anti-Republican *La Croix* even alleged that Russian terrorist violence was the fruit of a democratic education that had poisoned Russian brains (and it detected the same poison in French brains, too).[140] Socialist Lucien Herr argued that Tsarist repression had rendered terrorism "the only possible protest" and the bomb was the unique means of opposition to the autocratic regime.[141] Boncour wrote that the French, from the comfort of their

Republican legality, should not judge the methods of a people under the yoke of an "implacable absolutism" whose victims belonged to the "daily martyrology of freedom."[142] Common was the argument that democracy offered an antidote to revolutionary violence. After all, France had defeated anarchism by parliamentary means. Tsarist support for the Duma would surely end terrorist attacks.[143] Yet French Republicans fretted, too, that terrorist violence would undo the work of parliamentary reformers and ultimately hinder, rather than hasten, progress toward parliamentary democracy.[144]

The impression that terrorists committed their attacks in the name of democracy at times betrayed some sympathy for their methods. This sympathy did not extend so far as to justify revolutionary violence, but it nevertheless presented terrorism as explainable and even understandable. This position rested on the notion that Russia was trapped in a cycle of violence in which unrelenting Tsarist repression (itself framed as a form of terrorism) persistently prompted terrorist retaliation.[145] A similar position was found in Britain: terrorist violence mirrored Tsarist violence.[146] In France, newspapers referred often to a clash between two terrorisms, that from above, directed from the Ministry of the Interior, and that from below, perpetrated by the revolutionaries.[147] An equivalence between *terroristes* and *policiers* was frequently drawn.[148] Following the revelation in 1909 that Russian insurrectionist Yevno Azev (head of the Combat Organization between 1905 and 1908) was in fact a police spy, suspicion of state involvement in the fomentation of revolutionary terrorism—and even the ordering of terrorist assassinations—grew exponentially.[149] The blame for this mutually reinforcing struggle lay with the Tsarist regime. State repression and authoritarian government, combined with the absence of democratic machinery, had prompted the opposition to turn to violence. In the conservative *Le Radical*, for example, Cyrano claimed that "terrorism, has always been, over there, the principal method of government" and if the people now turned to violence it was due to their experience of living under such rule.[150] Once the cycle had begun, arbitrary arrests, imprisonments, and executions achieved little more than the creation of new terrorists.[151] Ultimately, to defeat *revolutionary* terrorism, one first had to put a stop to *state* terrorism.[152]

The French construction of the figure of the terrorist drew on long-established ideas about the followers of nihilism and anarchism. Terrorists were cold-blooded fanatics who displayed an "absolute devotion to their cause," a "contempt for death," and "extraordinary temerity."[153] Their high level of commitment resulted in an absolute servility to their masters and a willingness to die in the name of a greater good.[154] Indeed, the failure to fulfill one's revolutionary destiny through the perpetration of a successful attack was believed to be the cause of many terrorist suicides.[155] Women were particularly prone to this course of action, for they displayed a commitment to the revolution far greater than that of their male partners.[156] So ingrained was the belief in the terrorist's readiness to commit suicide that the press was inclined to attribute unexplained cases of self-inflicted deaths—particularly those of foreigners—to terrorism.[157] As for repentant terrorists who sought to return to a law-abiding existence, there was no way out alive. Anyone who tried to escape was murdered by their former comrades.[158]

The eyes of the press fell episodically on the Russian expatriate community in Paris. Incidents such as the Stryga affair in May 1906 raised fears that terrorism was rife among the capital's Russian exiles. The technical and scientific expertise required to construct bombs led suspicion to fall on university students. The association between Russian students—particularly female students—and terrorism stretched back to the nineteenth century.[159] Universities allegedly provided breeding grounds for terrorists, with Paris's quartier des Ecoles described as a "little world of nihilists."[160] Russian students, many of whom were alleged to be Jews, were thought to lead a Spartan life despite their wealthy backgrounds, shunning material possessions.[161] However, the pitiful garrets of the Russian colony housed a network of chemical laboratories and makeshift explosive workshops.[162]

The bombs made in these "factories" were strictly for export, at least according to the stories of those terrorists apprehended. In the case of Alexandre Sokoloff, tried in July 1906 along with Viktor Sokoloff and Sophie Spéranska, the defense counsel argued that the accused were "anarchists, but in the Russian sense of the word. They wanted [to commit] the greatest number of attacks, but in Russia."[163] Victor Sokoloff told the court, "We are partisans of the bomb in Russia. But here, in France, we are only students [who are] respectful of the hospitality that is offered to us."[164] These arguments offered small comfort to the French in the wake of accidental explosions like those that befell Stryga and Sokoloff in May 1906 and their compatriot Petroff twelve months later. The president of the court at the Sokoloff trial reminded the defendants that, though intended for use in Russia, Stryga's bomb had exploded *in France.*[165]

In September 1907, a group of mothers in Saint-Mandé reported that they had seen a "bad-looking individual, seeming to be of Russian nationality," loitering near a children's play area. They suggested to police that a nearby hotel was home to a "gang of Russian terrorists." Investigators found nothing untoward about the hotel and could find no evidence of Russian terrorism in Saint Mandé. Police noted that the women were "frightened by the newspaper articles on the Stryga affair and the Soleilland affair, as well as by the arrests of lechers reported daily in the press."[166] Russian terrorism was frightening even if the target was not of French nationality. But these untimely detonations did help to expose terrorist operations in the city: retired police leader Marie-Françoise Goron surmised that without the clumsiness of certain Russians, detectives had little chance of uncovering terrorist plots in the City of Light. The Russian terrorist of the early twentieth century was much more difficult to catch than his anarchist forebear.[167]

The world of the Russian terrorist at home and abroad was one of intrigue, betrayal, and disloyalty.[168] This belief rested on the assumption that double-dealing was inherent to Russian politics and even Russian mentalities. According to P. Duchesne of *L'Aurore*, the Azev affair was "incomprehensible anywhere else than in Russia" (though the affair caused some French anarchists to hunt for police moles in their own groups).[169] The case of Marcel Rips in 1910 nurtured such impressions.[170] On 8 May 1910, Rips, a Russian revolutionary-turned-police-agent, attempted to kill his boss, head of the Moscow political police Lieutenant Colonel Michel von Kotten, at Rips's residence in Paris. Von Kotten had bought Rips's loyalty in February 1909 with the promise not to send the terrorist to Siberia for his part in several revolutionary crimes. Rips accepted a role with the secret police and was tasked with the infiltration of terrorist organizations. In secret, he maintained his commitment to the revolution against the Tsar and hoped that his new job would allow him to unmask fellow agents provocateurs.[171] With the case framed as France's own "Azev affair," the court proceedings brought the seemingly treacherous world of Russian terrorism into focus. Vladimir Burtsev (the man who had exposed Azev's treachery) and socialist Jean Longuet (author of the 1909 *Terroristes et policiers* and perhaps France's first terrorism expert) appeared as witnesses at the Rips trial to explain the context of police infiltration of terrorist groups in Russia.[172] After twenty minutes' deliberation, the French jury acquitted the triple agent.[173] The outcome of the trial therefore revealed some amount of French sympathy for the terrorist cause. Burtsev later commented that Rips had succeeded in putting the Russian state police on trial.[174] The case also exposed the extent to which Russian agents operated in France. It not only brought to light Russian intelligence missions directed at the expatriate community in France, but also the prevalence of agents working in the country. Von Kotten himself had been residing in Nice. He claimed that his purpose in the town was to convalesce after receiving a bullet wound to the right shoulder the previous December. However, he remained in contact with Rips throughout his convalescence and was likely in touch with other Russian operatives in France, too.[175]

Physical descriptions of the Russian terrorist constructed a being who was at once unremarkable yet strangely alluring. There were exceptions to this depiction: Eugène Destez of *Gil Blas* described all terrorists, male and female, without exception as "beautiful" with "pale blonde hair" and "porcelain eyes."[176] The delicate features of the male terrorist perhaps hinted at a transgressive effeminacy sometimes attached to these men.[177] Terrorists were not exclusively unmanly, and they could give "a singular impression of energy and will" and a "determined" air, too.[178] The sexuality of the female terrorist featured more prominently in descriptions than that of her male comrade. These women proved an object of special fascination, not least due to the press's appetite for salacious stories to titillate readers. The understanding of anarchism in France as a predominantly male movement underscored further the peculiarity of these women.[179] Female terrorists dressed austerely, creating the impression of honesty, timidity, and a joyless frigidity. This disarmingly colorless exterior was deceptive because *la terroriste* had the iron will of a fanatical and violent revolutionary.[180] Female terrorists were "the most resolute and formidable agents of nihilism and terrorism" and "strong virgins [who] behave like men and surpass them in virility, [and] intrepidity."[181] Older women revolutionaries schooled novices in terrorism: right-wing *L'Intransigeant* alleged that in Paris, a certain Madame Katia of the rue de l'Arbalète, also known as "Mother Bomb," ran such a training "school."[182] The Russian correspondent of the *Journal des débats politiques et littéraires* warned readers not to mistake female commitment to the political struggle for anything other than fanaticism. They did not kill to demonstrate their love for a comrade or to avenge the death of a paramour. On the contrary, "These priestesses of death are of a rare chasteness," ready to "throw themselves headlong into blood and crime."[183]

Concurrently, the female terrorist was sexually appealing. Her demure

Figure 1. *La Lanterne. Le Supplément*, 1 June 1907, 4. See third row from the top, second image from the left. Source: gallica.bnf.fr / Bibliothèque nationale de France

appearance was at odds with a hidden sexual desire: when Stryga's alleged accomplice, Sophie Spéranska, appeared in court in July 1906, a court reporter noted that an impish smile played on her "charming and slightly sensual mouth."[184] *La terroriste*'s dowdy sense of dress concealed a sexually desirable physique. A cartoon published in the supplement to *La Lanterne* on 1 June 1907 showed two Frenchmen looking admiringly at a beautiful young woman (Figure 1). "Beware," one man warns his friend, "she's a Russian terrorist." "What do you see?" replied the second man. "She's carrying two bombs," the first man says, referring to the woman's large bosom.[185]

Certain commentaries implied that sexual promiscuity was common among female terrorists. One male lover was much like the next, and these women asked for neither the life stories nor even the names of their partners.[186] The female revolutionary's sexuality could prove a useful weapon, too, in "the most skillful seduction" of police officers, and she need not fear arrest because her "fragile" appearance dispelled all suspicion.[187] Female terrorist sexuality was thus enthralling, threatening, and titillating. In a smutty song titled "L'Amour nihiliste" (1909), lyricist Paul Verneuil told the story of a young woman and her meeting with a "dangerous" nihilist. Once in his laboratory, she begs the man to show her his "bomb" (described as a "formidable device"). The nihilist agrees, but first the girl must undress and reveal her own "bombs," each adorned with a "pink fuse." Getting out his "bomb," the nihilist reassures the girl that the thing is perfectly safe if one knows how to "handle" it. However, he continues, if it does "go off," she would not come to any harm. The song ends with the young girl enthusiastically pursuing the study of "explosives" on the boulevards of Paris, a "charming profession" in which many bombs continued to explode in her hands.[188]

The proliferation of "terrorist" violence in Russia after 1904 informed French perceptions of the phenomenon and the uses of the label. While one may still find examples of non-Russian terrorism in the French press—for example, in the case of Spanish anarchist terrorism prevalent at this time—the use of the terms "terrorist" and "terrorism" appeared overwhelmingly in relation to Russian revolutionary violence. This violence, while generally considered counterproductive, was not framed as wholly illegitimate. In fact, terrorist violence appeared to be a valid, if misguided, reaction to Tsarist autocracy and indiscriminate repression. Depictions and representations of the Russian expatriate community in Paris further influenced conceptions of terrorism and its perpetrators. Parisian bomb factories were a cause for concern, as were terrorist agents. Male terrorists were determined political activists, with a single-minded focus on the revolutionary crusade. Female terrorists were fearful and cold-blooded killers. Their modest clothing obscured both a steely commitment to their cause and a dangerous and tempting sexuality.

CONSTRUCTING "TERRORISM" IN/AS ENTERTAINMENT

The heyday of Russian terrorism coincided with a period of growing French interest in the country. The Franco-Russian rapprochement during 1891–94 nurtured a Russophilia encouraged by the cultural, financial, and religious elites, all of whom saw profit in the two countries' friendship. More than eight hundred Russian brands went on sale in France as the French embraced their new ally's clothes, shoes, and cosmetics.[189] Slavic cuisine appeared on some menus, along with dishes of more recent creation, such as the "gâteau Franco-Russe" (invented in Angers).[190] The Musée Grévin re-created in wax the coronation of Nicholas II; visitors to the museum could view the ceremony from a mockup of the Kremlin.[191]

Russian terrorism was a rich source of inspiration for the French arts. Authors, playwrights, and early filmmakers readily used terrorist characters and plotlines in their works. The creative industries drew on a stock of stereotypes and clichés from secret meetings in underground hideouts to disguises and codenames. The Russian terrorist provided authors with the perfect villain: in the thirty-two volumes of Pierre Souvestre and Marcel Allain's popular *Fantômas* series, for example, this figure epitomized more than any other a violent and radical challenge to the status quo.[192] Artistic productions reveal contemporary representations of, and attitudes to, terrorism because, according to Philippe Thuin, "The figure of the nihilist expected by the reader had to be conventional in order to be [believable]."[193] In fact, many of the tropes of French terrorist fiction could be gleaned from contemporary press reporting on Russian politics.

Fiction did not just reflect fact; the perception of terrorism drew on an interaction between the two. Journalists would liken real-life stories of terrorist intrigues to "the darkest novels [from] the most imaginative and inventive novelists," or a "page from a novel."[194] Fictional stories drew on real-life events: during 1911, an adventure serial in *Le Grand Echo du Nord et du Pas-de-Calais* brazenly featured an anarchist character named "Stryga," one of three assassins chosen to kill the Emperor of Russia. Stryga operated at the behest of "Number One," a figure who "exerted a sort of dictatorship over the revolutionary world."[195] Fictional terrorist characters were remarkably like portrayals of terrorists in the press. The female terrorist, for example, appeared generally as a martyr and seductress, with strong political opinions and a greater commitment to the revolution than her male comrades.[196]

Several Russian works of literature featuring terrorists were translated into French. Anton Chekov's 1893 *Rasskaz neizvestnovo cheloveka* (*The Story of an Unknown Man*) was translated as *Valet de Chambre* in 1911; Leonid Andreyev's 1908 *Rasskaz o semi povešennyh* (*The Seven Who Were Hanged*) also appeared in 1911 as *Les Sept Pendus*.[197] A translation of Valentine Dmitriev's novel *Le Terroriste*, the story of Nathalie Serguéievna's love affair with the terrorist Stépane Korjov, was published in 1912.[198] Translations of non-Russian terrorist fiction appeared, too: Joseph Conrad's *The Secret Agent* (1907) was serialized in *Le Temps* from 31 May 1910 to 8 July 1910 and published as a novel in French in 1912.[199] French authors also dabbled in the subject: H. J. Magog's 1912 *L'Attentat de la rue Royale* told the story of the relationship between a young French man and a female Russian terrorist in Paris.[200] It seems that terrorist characters were as common in fiction as to prompt some fatigue among readers: a reviewer of Dmitriev's 1912 novel noted that "we are beginning to become bored of this type of hero."[201]

Terrorist characters featured in the newspaper serializations known as *feuilletons*. The first feuilletons appeared during the 1830s as a tool to maintain reader loyalty, and they quickly became popular.[202] Prone to bombast and dramatization, the feuilletons featured stereotypes and prejudices popular at the time, that the reader could easily understand; Russia featured in these quite often during the nineteenth century.[203] The stories relied upon, and helped to construct, contemporary notions of terrorism. Between 1910 and 1912, for example, several newspapers serialized "Le Roman d'une Etoile," billed as "the moving story of a terrorist conspiracy," by award-winning author, poet, and playwright Jeanne Loiseau (published under the pseudonym Daniel Lesueur).[204] Tatiane Fédorowna, the principal female character in Loiseau's tale, had "[an] ugly, poorly tailored, poorly made outfit" with a face typical of a "truly ugly and unusual" race. However, her ill-fitting clothes hid an enticingly "full and pure figure."[205] Such a description was perfectly in line with press reports of Russian terrorist women.

Serialized stories could give voices to terrorist characters as they explained their attitude to violence. In "Le Roman d'une Etoile," the terrorist Ivan Grégorévitch Toulénine—who has committed an attack in which several innocents were killed—justifies his recourse to violence: "The bomb has a moral impact that the revolver or the dagger do not possess. Why do they call us terrorists? Because we willingly spread terror. We direct the thunder like the ancient gods. Does lightning only strike the guilty? Must the redeemers of the world have any more scruples than Nature? She massacres at random. The blood of *our* victims fertilizes the field in which liberty will germinate."[206] Toulénine's male comrades approved of his justification; the female terrorist character Fédorowna did not. Terrorists in Geroges Thierry's "L'île bleue" (published in *La Croix* during 1910–11) expressed similar views. Thierry's story told of a love affair between Russian terrorist Rova Béhring and Jeanina Voroneg, the daughter of the general that Rova is tasked with killing. When Béhring admits to his inability to carry out the assassination because of his love for Jeanina, one of his comrades scoffs, "Goodness gracious! He loves her!...But a terrorist does not love! A terrorist has no heart! He is the arm in the service of an idea!"[207] This image of the terrorist chimed with the right-wing *La Croix*'s excoriation of real-life Russian revolutionaries.

In contrast, a sympathetic view of terrorist violence appeared in Guy-Péron's "Tcherloskoff. Policier et Terroriste," published in *Le Radical* during 1912. In the opening scene, a group of Russian peasants discuss the motives behind terrorism as a group of convicts passes through their village on the long road to Siberia.[208] Police officer Tcherloskof displays little sympathy for the men. In response, local woman Sonia cites police cruelty, and asks, "Whose fault are these attacks, if not our government's?" Likewise, the blacksmith Maximovitch argues that his rough treatment at the hands of the state prompted him to become a socialist. In a later scene from within the Siberian prison camp, the terrorist Lazarowitch, a former member of the Narodnaia Volya (People's Will), also places the blame for revolutionary violence on the Tsarist regime. Intolerable repression and the deprivation of all liberty justified all means of action.[209] This position reflected *Le Radical*'s broadly sympathetic view of the terrorists' democratic aims.

Beyond the printed word, contemporary theater listings and reviews show that terrorism had a presence on the French stage. The content of some productions remains lost to the historian. On 23 May 1909, for example, *Le Journal* advertised a concert at the place des Tourelles during which one could enjoy a Russian *mazurka* or folkdance titled "La Terroriste." Quite what this dance entailed is a mystery.[210] When one can glean some indication as to the content of theatrical productions, one finds that contemporary ideas of terrorism had a significant influence on productions. In 1907, the Grand-Guignol theater in Paris staged André de Lorde and Pierre Chaîne's "La Petite fille," about a "young terrorist" who travels to Paris on a mission to assassinate a Grand Duke.[211] In November 1908, *L'Auto* reviewed a play titled "Les Révoltés," by Henri Cain and Ed. Adenis, showing at the Théâtre Sarah-Bernhardt in Paris. This was a story of love and betrayal among Russian nihilists.[212] Reviewing "Les Révoltés," *Le Figaro* noted that terrorism offered playwrights a rich source of inspiration. The reviewer mentioned, too, that the nihilist had become a regular hero of the theatrical melodrama and one in whom spectators seemed to place great emotional investment.[213] Indeed, in 1912, *Le Figaro*'s Robert de Flers wrote in his review of Barot-Forlière's "La Sentence" (showing at Paris's Odéon theater) that the French public had long had an "extreme interest in nihilism" on the stage. De Flers speculated that within every bourgeois theatergoer there lay a Russian revolutionary.[214] Current affairs likely aroused interest in theatrical productions: in its comment on Léo Marchès and G.-C. Richard's 1910 "L'Attentat," a drama about nihilists and their repression performed at the Grand-Guignol, *La Liberté* acknowledged its "striking timeliness" in the context of the Rips trial.[215] Stage plays thus presented characters typical of French understandings of the Russian terrorist and their experiences. Illustrative of this point is a play called "La Terroriste" that ran at the Grand Théâtre in Angers during 1914, about a revolutionary love triangle that ends in tragedy. The play closed with Nadia, a colonel's daughter-turned-terrorist, throwing a bomb at a group of soldiers, while shouting, "Everything for the cause!"[216]

Acts of terrorism featured in early French cinematic productions. Historical and realist films began to grow in popularity at the turn of the century, thanks to audiences' appetite for newsreels. To capitalize on this interest in current affairs, filmmakers produced reconstructions of newsworthy moments for cinemagoers. Acts of political murder and terrorism featured among these earliest examples of historical reenactments, including Ferdinand Zecca's *L'Assassinat de MacKinley* (1902), Lucien Nonguet's *Assassinat de la famille royale Serbe* (1903) and *L'assassinat du grand duc Serge* (1905), Etienne Thévenon's *L'attentat anarchiste de la rue Montagne Sainte-*

Walburge (1904), and the Société Éclair's *Un attentat anarchiste* (1912). Production teams re-created historical assassinations, such as Charles le Bargy and André Calmettes's *L'assassinat du duc de Guise* (1908) and Albert Capellani's *La mort de Lincoln* (1909). Directors aimed to give spectators a sense of watching these events as they had happened, forging a connection between historical drama and the news in this embryonic form of entertainment.[217]

The news also provided material for fictional cinematic works. Louis Feuillade's 1907 *La Terroriste* (later renamed *Les terroristes en Russie*) was a dramatic portrayal of a nihilist assassination. The *terroriste* of the film's title was Vera (a not-so-subtle reference to Zasulich), a nihilist-terrorist who succeeds in assassinating an unnamed governor. While Vera is in prison for the crime, the governor's widow visits her. The nihilist begs for forgiveness from her victim's wife. The two women then hatch a plan to prevent more killings. The widow swaps clothes with Vera, enabling the nihilist to escape from prison and return to her revolutionary comrades. Reunited with her fellow revolutionaries, Vera attempts to dissuade them from committing further acts of violence. She arrives at the terrorists' hideout just in time: her comrades—described in the film's script as "peasants, students, Jews with coats and glasses, [and] 4 women"—are about to perpetrate a bombing. Unable to convince the nihilists to renounce violence, Vera seizes a bomb and kills herself and everyone around her. According to the script of the film, the final scene focused on the "destroyed hovel [collapsed] on the anarchists' corpses."[218] *La Dépèche* described the film as a "superb drama."[219]

The representation of terrorism in Feuillade's *La Terroriste* encapsulated French representations of the phenomenon as constructed in the press, politics, and the arts in the decade prior to the Great War. The terrorist was a Russian who targeted political representatives of the Tsarist regime. It is significant that Feuillade chose a woman for the lead character. Since the heyday of nihilism, the French had considered the involvement of women as a defining feature of Russian terrorism at home and abroad.[220] The gender, religion, and social background of Vera's comrades constituted the typical panoply of terrorist characters. Antisemites accused Jews of funding terrorism while students in Russia and in France were considered particularly susceptible to revolutionary propaganda. If Vera's repentance is unusual—because *femmes terroristes* supposedly pursued revolution doggedly—her ultimate demise is not: unable to complete her final mission she chooses murder-suicide in the terrorists' seamy lair. This construction—and those evident in other artistic works—drew on terrorist tropes stretching back to the mid-1860s, adapted and modified through the press and cultural works for a twentieth-century audience.

Conclusion

"Terrorism" was a nebulous term. It denoted a form of violence designed to *terrorize* the victim and the public at large. Contemporaries used the word as a catchall term not only for followers of anarchism but also for burglars, armed robbers, murderers, highwaymen, desperadoes, bandits, and anyone of an essentially violent disposition.[221] In a political sense, during the closing decades of the nineteenth century, the "terrorism" label steadily came loose from its moorings in the French Revolution. The emergence of nihilism in Russia—and its misinterpretation as a revolutionary and violent political doctrine outside Russia—gave rise to a new conception of violence as a means of political communication. French and European anarchists appropriated and adapted Russian nihilist and revolutionary tactics—or, at least, their understandings of these—into propaganda by the deed. For the opponents of nihilism (and anarchism), violence had little aim beyond the gratuitous destruction of the status quo and "to make a clean sweep."[222] For both the supporters and the enemies of such substate violence, terrorism as a strategy of violence was the means to do this. Consequently, on the broadest level anarchism, nihilism, and terrorism were understood as kindred forces; all were synonymous with deadly revolutionary violence.

From 1900, perceptions of terrorism began to take a more definite—yet not definitive—shape. Some differentiation between terrorism as a political act and doctrine and terrorism as an anarchist tactic was already under way. The word was not used consistently to describe the anarchist *attentat*: it did not feature, for example, in press articles on the 1905 rue de Rohan attack, committed by a Spanish anarchist. This absence is due to the understanding that terrorism was a political act and a strategy designed to bring about political change. Conversely, the era of anarchist attacks in France during 1892–94 had prompted a criminalization of anarchism. Anarchism and terrorism took on different implications because the anarchist killed with criminal intent whereas the terrorist killed with political intent.

Press reports and artistic outputs brought Russian terrorism to a French audience. The term described extreme anti-Tsarist violence as well as state repression. Certainly, understandings of terrorism had long developed under Russian influence, from the nihilists of the 1860s, through the self-proclaimed terrorists of the early 1880s, to the Socialist Revolutionaries of the early twentieth century. By 1905, with the anarchist threat in France having receded since the mid-1890s, and a growing political and popular interest in France's eastern ally, terrorism as a label to describe a doctrine of political violence took on an even stronger association with Russia. The presence of a Russian exile community in Paris, among whom police sporadically uncovered bomb makers and terrorists, colored notions of terrorism as an import product. Racial ideas about the difference between Slavic peoples, traditions, and psychology further lent Russian terrorism an alien quality. An understanding of terrorism as an "Other" against which the French defined themselves began to emerge. Evident in the pages of novels and newspapers, on the stage and the cinema screen, this othering process was constructed according to, and in interaction with, new political developments and long-established tropes. The Russian terrorist was central to this unmistakably unFrench phenomenon.

TWO

The Anarchist and the Tiger

*Emile Cottin and the Shooting of
Prime Minister Georges Clemenceau, February 1919*

On 19 February 1919, twenty-two-year-old Emile Cottin chased Prime Minister Georges Clemenceau's car along the boulevard Delessert in the sixteenth arrondissement of Paris. Cottin held a revolver at the end of his outstretched arm, and he fired seven shots into the back panel of the vehicle. "Faster!" barked Clemenceau's bodyguard to the driver, as he climbed out of the open side of the vehicle and swiveled to return fire. The brief pursuit ended when Cottin found his gun to be empty of ammunition. He tossed it to one side and raised his arms to surrender. Police constable Théophile Labaigt wrestled Cottin to the ground, and passersby who had witnessed the attack began to beat the young man. Rescuing the would-be assassin from the fury of the crowd, officers bundled him into a taxi. "Don't hurt me! I'll talk!" Cottin shouted. In the prime minister's car, the "Tiger" Clemenceau felt a pain between his shoulder blades. A single bullet had struck him in the back, lodging between the lungs.[1]

The attacker was Emile-Jules-Henri Cottin, a cabinetmaker from Creil (Oise). Discharged from the army in July 1915 due to a long-term heart problem, Cottin spent most of the war as an itinerant worker in factories in Lyon and Paris; between September 1915 and February 1919, he had no fewer than fifteen jobs. Co-workers described him as a quiet, thoughtful, and inoffensive man with a voracious appetite for reading. Cottin was also an anarchist activist. He came to the attention of police in May 1918 when he assaulted several strikebreaking colleagues during a strike at the Hanriot factory in Billancourt. On 5 January 1919, Cottin was among a handful of men questioned by police for attempting to enter a secret meeting of the Fédération Communiste Anarchiste in Paris. He informed the arresting officers that he was a "socialist revolutionary."[2] Police subsequently discovered that Cottin was well known in Parisian anarchist and revolutionary circles, where he went by the name of "Milou."[3]

In the wake of the attempt on Clemenceau's life, Cottin elaborated upon his deep commitment to the anarchist cause. He described himself as "antiauthoritarian, anticlerical, antipatriotic [and] antimilitarist," and he approved of the use of violence in pursuit of what he termed the anarchist "ideal."[4] Cottin's mother, Cathérine, blamed her son's crime on his fellow anarchists: "If he committed this murderous gesture, it was because he was led astray by his readings and the advice of libertarians and anarchists whose meeting places he frequented."[5] The reasons for which this young man turned to anarchism formed the focus of the subsequent investigation.

Cottin's crime was the first of a series of attacks attributed to anarchists that punctuated the early 1920s in France. On 14 July 1922, Gustave Bouvet fired two shots at the car of the prefect of the Paris Police, Armand Naudin, during the celebrations to mark the fête nationale (Bouvet mistook Naudin's car for that of President of the Republic Alexandre Millerand).[6] On 22 January 1923, Germaine Berton murdered Marius Plateau, a leading figure in the Action Française monarchist league, at the headquarters of the organization. On 26 May 1925, Maria Bonnefoy shot dead Action Française treasurer Ernest Berger at the Saint-Lazare metro station. A year later, on 25 May 1926, Sholom Schwartzbard, a Russian-born anarchist, shot to death Ukrainian military officer Simon Petliura in the middle of a Parisian street.[7]

Cottin and Bouvet's attacks reanimated the ghosts of Henry, Caserio, and other notorious anarchist killers of the late nineteenth and early twentieth centuries. The right-wing *La Patrie* dismissed attempts to explain Cottin's crime with reference to suspected mental illness, as left-wingers had done before in the cases of Henry and Ravachol. According to this newspaper, Cottin most resembled Raymond Callemin (also known as Raymond La Science), a member of Jules Bonnot's criminal gang, and was "infatuated with himself, having ingested pell-mell the most abominable readings as well as the most stupid."[8] In what was likely a deliberate attempt to connect Cottin to historical anarchist violence, on 20 February 1919, *Excelsior* printed a photograph of Clemenceau's attacker with the legend, "The Anarchist Emile-Henri Cottin" (the newspaper printed his full name—Emile-Jules-Henri—in the accompanying article).[9] In the wake of Bouvet's attack in 1922, journalist Clément Vautel noted the apparent similarity between anarchist assassins in recent history. All were pensive, quiet, pale young men, voracious readers who were uninterested in women.[10]

If contemporaries sought to present an uninterrupted history of anarchist terrorism from the turn of the century to the interwar years, we must recognize that the Great War had briefly modified the meaning and use of the "terrorist" and "terrorism" labels. The press attached both labels to the German wartime enemy. During the conflict, "terrorism" described the German or Prussian method of warfare and particularly violence perpetrated against civilians. The violent abuse and killing of noncombatants in northern France and Belgium in the first months of the war lay at the basis of this construction. Left-wing journalist Jacques Mesnil labeled the burning of villages in the battle zone "systematic terrorism" that "correspond[ed] perfectly to the ideas of the generals and theoreticians of war."[11] The portrayal of German terrorism as a premeditated and methodical strategy persisted throughout the conflict: it was "a system of war" rooted in Prussian militarism[12] and the "basis of the Teutonic tactic" of warfare that the Germans hoped would be the "principle instrument of [their] victory."[13] Several newspapers reproduced the 1878 contention of Prussian general Julius von Hartmann that terrorism against noncombatants was a "military necessity" when soldiers faced resistance from the civilian population.[14] From the French point of view, German terrorism against unarmed people was akin to a modern Vandal invasion and a "return to a state of savagery" that spoke to the "barbarous instincts" of the enemy.[15] Such language chimed with the broader culture of war in France.[16] It framed terrorism as the calculated perpetration of illegitimate violence against civilians by the armed forces of the state.

The cessation of fighting between Russia and the Central Powers in December 1917 and the political turmoil that followed saw reports of Russian terrorism return to French newspapers. Left- and right-wing publications decried as terrorism the killings of thousands of civilians and the practice of imprisonment without trial. Conservatives attributed this "wave of terrorism" to the Bolsheviks and their alleged German paymasters.[17] As Germany fell into a state of revolution after November 1918, fears emerged that Russian communist terrorism was spreading.[18] In March 1919, US secretary of state Robert Lansing warned his colleagues at the Paris Peace conference that "[l]ike the anarchy which for a year has made an inferno of Russia, the fires of terrorism are ablaze in the states of Germany. Through the ruins of this once great empire the flames are sweeping westward."[19] Indeed, the immediate reaction to Cottin's crime (committed one month before Lansing's statement) betrayed an understanding of his terrorism as an act of Germano-Russian confection. Cottin fed such conspiracy theories with statements on his opposition to France's intervention against the Bolsheviks in Russia and his belief in the fraternity of Germans and French.[20]

The conflation of terrorism with Russian and German communism represented a moment of transition between the pre-war and interwar cultures of terrorism. The long-held assumption that terrorism was a Russian phenomenon emerged in the framing of the assassin as both bearing a physical resemblance to a "typical" Russian and adopting a method of political violence that had first emerged in the east. Right-wingers infused his terrorism with a distinctly new ingredient: (Russian) Soviet communism. Neither Cottin nor his interrogators referred to Bolshevism during the investigation. Nonetheless, the depiction of the crime as a Soviet-inspired, German-backed attack, supported by treacherous French revolutionaries, harbingered the political civil war that would later engulf France.

This chapter begins with a reconstruction of Emile Cottin's attempted assassination of Georges Clemenceau. It examines the immediate response to the attack in the press. The right-wing media depicted the assassination attempt as a plot against France, engineered by Germany and Russia. Cottin was thus an enemy agent deserving of military justice. In part, the authorities agreed: wartime legislation on threats to the security of the state saw Cottin face the third council of war, rather than a civilian court.

The second part of this chapter investigates Cottin's commitment to anarchism. Journalists and military investigators strove to understand how, why, and when the young attacker had committed himself to a cause for which he was prepared to kill. Investigations focused on Lyon and Paris, with the press and officers reaching different conclusions. The reconstruction of Cottin's past revealed the persistence of older prejudices and preconceptions about anarchists and terrorists, as well as understandings about why some activists turned to violence. Readers may draw comparisons between the explanations of contemporaries about Cottin's "conversion" to anarchism and modern debates over radicalization and deradicalization—a process that one journalist in 1919 termed "de-Cottinization."[21]

Shooting the Tiger

Dressed in a yellow Macfarlane coat with a flamboyant blue scarf and a soft felt hat, Emile Cottin cut a strange figure when he arrived at the rue Franklin at 8:30 a.m. on 19 February 1919. He had found the address of the prime minister's apartment building in the Bottin telephone directory.[22] Cottin was not familiar with Clemenceau's morning routine, and so he planned to wait in the street until his target exited the building. In the meantime, he assumed a casual demeanor, perusing the windows of an electrical store, standing near a public urinal, and mixing with commuters and shoppers at a nearby tram stop. The patient assassin was careful not to attract the attention of the five uniformed police officers nearby; he was not likely aware of two plainclothes inspectors from the Renseignements Généraux also circulating on the rue Franklin. Police later reasoned that the security force had forced Cottin to attack the premier's car rather than strike as he left the building.[23]

At 8:45 a.m., Clemenceau left his apartment to take a car to the Ministry of War. He climbed into the rear seat of the vehicle while Decaudin, his bodyguard, took the front seat next to the driver, Conjat. The car drove a hundred meters along the street before slowing to turn onto boulevard Delessert. At this moment, a loud bang sounded. Cottin had fired his first shot at the Tiger. The bullet passed through the thick Triplex glass of the left rear window and exited through the right rear window. It hit constable François Goursat in the face (Goursat was standing on the pavement opposite, at the corner of rue Vineuse and rue Franklin).[24] Reacting to the sound of the detonation, constable Labaigt looked up to see a "young man with long hair, looking like a Russian" take a second shot before setting off to run behind the car. Conjat accelerated but Cottin was fast; one witness, Mlle Nas, recounted that the assassin was so close to the vehicle that she thought "he had clung to it and had just gotten off."[25] Cottin continued to fire as he ran, emptying the seven remaining bullets in his gun into the rear panel of the vehicle. The car sped away, with Decuadin hanging out of the vehicle's side, firing over the head of the pursuer. A bullet, slowed by its trajectory through the bodywork of the car, bruised Decaudin's left arm.[26] Conjat stopped the car when he believed the danger had passed and turned to check on his passenger. "Back home!" barked Clemenceau.[27]

The prime minister was lucky to survive the attack. Four shots found their mark. Two bullets passed straight through Clemenceau's overcoat, exiting harmlessly. Another shot cut through his overcoat and inner jacket but did not enter the body. The single bullet that injured the premier hit near the right shoulder blade and lodged in the thorax between the lungs. Medical examiners did not risk removing the projectile but noted that the seventy-eight-year-old showed little sign of serious illness following the attack.[28] He was able to return to work within two weeks. In the days after the attack, national and local newspapers updated their readers on the prime minister's health, including the rate of his pulse and his temperature, as if monitoring the life of the nation itself (Figure 2).

Officers scrambled to arrest Cottin. The attacker had stopped in the street, tossed his firearm to one side, and raised his hands. A melee ensued as angry onlookers tried to lynch the young man. Constables Labaigt and Ravery were injured as they defended their quarry from popular justice.[29] Two men lent a hand in the arrest of Cottin, at least according to press accounts: they were seventeen-year-old hairdresser Henri Moulin and M. Brugeron, a local bicycle salesperson, and they helped officers to "master" Cottin in the street.[30] Police soon discovered that the tales of everyday heroism related by the press were embellished: Moulin had in fact intervened to help lynch Cottin.[31] Meanwhile, a third man, M. Dreyfus, ran to protect Cottin, from both the crowd and the police. "He has not done anything," Dreyfus shouted before officers arrested him.[32] Labaigt hailed a taxi to transport Cottin and the hapless Dreyfus, now considered an accomplice, to a nearby police station.

During the journey, the would-be assassin pleaded with his captors, "Protect me; I'll tell the truth; don't hit me; I will talk. I absolutely had to do it; I was pushed and forced to do it; I'll tell [you] everything."[33] Thanks to the beating received in the street, Cottin was in a sorry state when he arrived at the police station, "[m]ore dead than alive," according to *L'Eclair*.[34] His violent ordeal was not yet over. Cottin later alleged that officers themselves threw a stool at his head. Bruises marked his abdomen and his eyes were swollen shut. The medical examiner declared Cottin fit for interrogation only on 22 February, three days after the crime.[35]

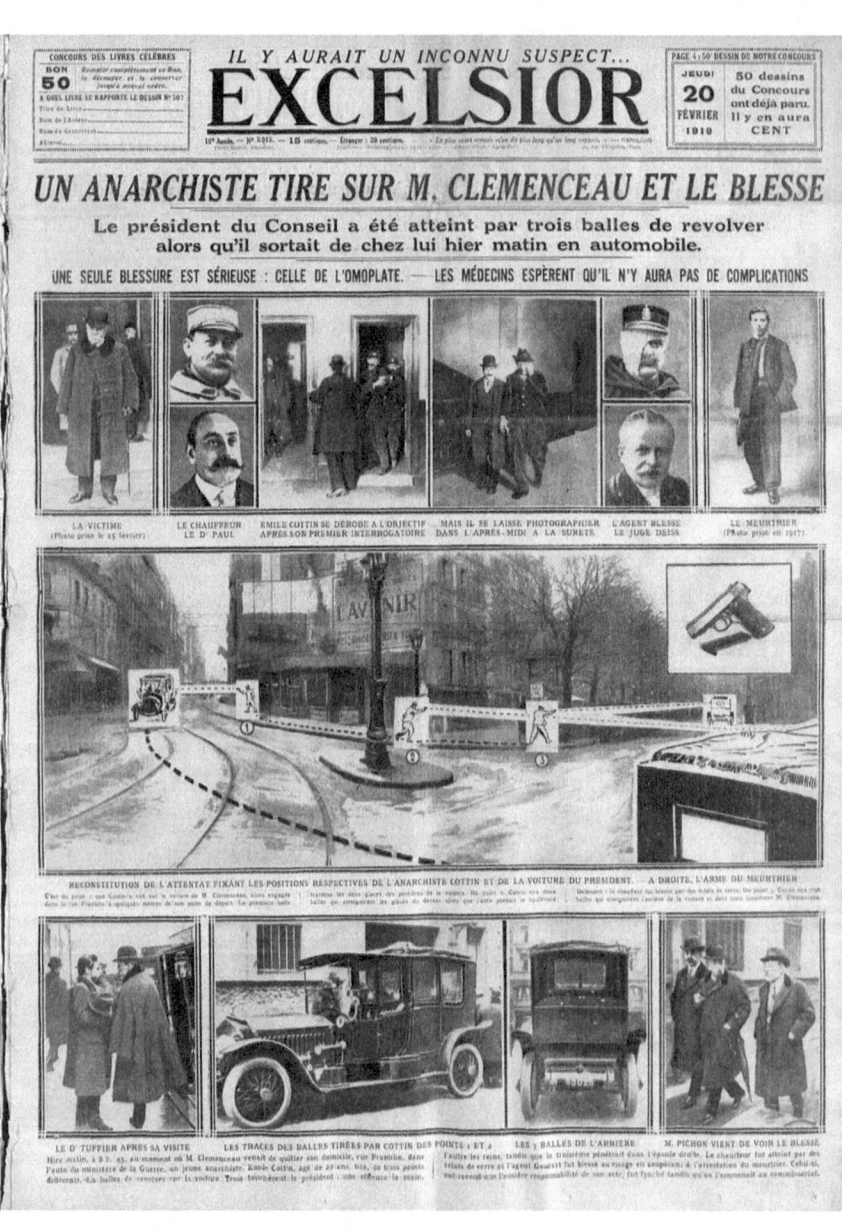

Figure 2. Front page of *Excelsior*, 20 February 1919, reporting Cottin's attack on Clemenceau. Source: gallica.bnf.fr / Bibliothèque nationale de France

At the time of his arrest, Cottin was carrying ammunition, a carving knife, ten francs, and the morning edition of the *Journal du Peuple*, an anarchist newspaper. The weapon used during the attack was an aged 7.65mm caliber revolver of Spanish origin.[36] Cottin claimed to have purchased it from a soldier in a bar on the Faubourg Saint-Antoine in Paris for thirty francs.[37] Suspecting a plot, investigating magistrate Deiss immediately ordered searches of the headquarters of anarchist groups, their affiliates, and the homes of members.[38] The search turned up nothing of interest beyond anarchist propaganda and some banned publications.[39]

Several newspapers carried reports of the attack in their evening editions on 19 February. The apparently uncertain nationality of the attacker featured in these reports. Conjecture rested largely on Cottin's facial features, hair, and style of dress. *Bonsoir* noted that the assailant's long coat and hair gave him "a Russian look." The newspaper speculated that he had committed the attack to avenge the death of his brother on the Archangel front.[40] *L'Heure* reported that Cottin had cried out to the crowd, "I am not Russian!" suggesting that some of his assailants believed him to be so.[41] *L'Intransigeant* was less specific about Cottin's presumed origins, content to relate simply that "[the attacker] has small grey eyes, [and] a flat nose, obviously a physiognomy which, at first glance, does not appear to be from around here."[42]

On 20 February, Cottin's appearance—especially his long blonde hair—drew further comment in the press. His looks seemed to offer clues not only about his origin but also his political motive.[43] According to the conservative *Le Matin*, the twenty-two-year-old was tall and thin with a mop of pale yellow hair and the "general look" of a Russian nihilist.[44] *Excelsior* commented upon the high quality of Cottin's spoken French; was the newspaper suggesting that he was not a native speaker?[45] *L'Avenir* reported falsely that the authorities believed Cottin to be a Russian subject.[46] *Le Journal* noted that his style of dress suggested that he was either a Russian anarchist or a Bolshevik terrorist.[47] A number of newspapers took up this thread. Cottin was a "young communist,"[48] a *libertaire* and a Bolshevist,[49] a self-proclaimed "super-Bolshevist,"[50] a "terrorist,"[51] an "illegalist,"[52] and a "nihilist."[53] The right-wing *La Patrie* was unequivocal in its attribution of Soviet communist motives to Cottin: "only a bandit, in thrall to Bolshevist madness" and with "the dark soul of a disciple of Lenin" could have committed such an outrage.[54] On the other hand, socialist newspapers *L'Humanité* and *Le Populaire* rejected Cottin's individualism, reminding readers that true socialists favored mass action over individual attacks.⁵⁵ Nevertheless, within twenty-four hours of the shooting, accusations of a Bolshevik plot against France were circulating in the French press, based on little more than the fact that Cottin "looked like" a Russian terrorist.

The suspicions of the French press also fell on Germany. In fact, the recent experience of the war informed several responses to Cottin's attempt on Clemenceau's life. First, Clemenceau's status as the architect of the French victory and "the greatest representative of France, the greatest nation" (according to *Le Petit Journal*) saw the crime framed as an attack on the whole nation.⁵⁶ The bullets from the assassin's gun had inflicted a national wound upon France, and the entire population suffered with the injured premier.⁵⁷ The reported reaction of the mob to Cottin's act served to underscore the unified response to the terrorist attack, as men and women from all social classes beat the criminal. In *Le Petit Parisien* Dr. Marbais, an eyewitness to the lynching, described the scene: "Callused hands, big gloved hands, thin hands covered with soft leather gloves and armed either with sticks, or canes, or umbrellas rose and fell incessantly on the murderer. There were butchers, employees, bourgeois who were hitting hard."⁵⁸ Women both stood back from the violence demanding "immediate execution" and became embroiled in the punishment meted out: "A woman was holding him back by his blonde hair, which she squeezed with both hands; another was armed with her hatpin" (as reported in *L'Avenir*).⁵⁹

Second, some sources equated Clemenceau's injury with those suffered during the war. Such depictions in part drew an equivalence between Cottin's weapon and those used at the front. His was described as a military issue automatic pistol akin to those used in battle, especially during trench-cleaning operations.⁶⁰ Emphasis fell on Clemenceau's sangfroid under fire. As the bullets struck the car he was "imperturbable," "showing not the slightest emotion," and describing his wound as "nothing."⁶¹ To illustrate Clemenceau's apparent bravado, a variety of sources attributed sardonic comments to the prime minister, such as, "He's a terrible shot, he missed me!"⁶² He reportedly made further jokes about the anarchists "Tiger hunting" in Paris.⁶³ Several newspapers observed that Clemenceau had braved the bullets of the front to visit the troops only to be struck down on his doorstep.⁶⁴ The premier thus deserved special recognition for his bravery and a wound suffered in the service of France. Georges Leygues, minister of the navy, told his fellow parliamentarians that the homage of the Chamber of Deputies to Clemenceau would equal "the citation on the agenda of the fatherland awarded to the valiant [soldiers] struck down on the battlefield."[65] The Union Nationale des Combattants veterans' association suggested that Clemenceau—the "first poilu of France"—receive the Croix de Guerre for sustaining an injury "on the field of honor."[66]

Third, special legislation on the nation in wartime ensured that the military authorities took over the case against Cottin on 21 February. The French authorities interpreted the attempted assassination as an attack on the domestic security of the state.[67] For this reason, the would-be assassin faced trial at the third council of war rather than a civilian court, and Captain Pierre Bouchardon took over the investigation from magistrate Deiss. Nicknamed the Grand Inquisitor by Clemenceau, Bouchardon had previously prosecuted the spy Mata Hari. The decision to divest the civilian courts of responsibility for Cottin raised opposition from the left-wing press.[68] Ultimately, the military authorities charged Cottin with three separate counts of attempted willful homicide, with premeditation and ambush, each relating to Clemenceau, Goursat, and Decaudin.

Finally, the continued state of war in Europe raised the fear that an unrepentant Germany had ordered the attack. Nationalist author Maurice Barrès declared that Germany had "finally managed to arouse an assassin," and that a "Franco-boche bullet" had struck the prime minister. Germany, after all, "subsidis[ed] anarchy."[69] Other conservative voices connected Germany with Soviet Bolshevism. Editor of *Le Figaro* Alfred Capus denounced the machinations of Germany and Russia that lay behind the attack, while *La Patrie* claimed that Russian Bolsheviks were the "most sure and most faithful auxiliaries" of France's wartime foe.[70]

Cottin denied that he was an instrument in a broader plot. While he had told officers at the scene that he had acted against his will—"I was pushed and forced to do it"[71]—it later transpired that he had made this statement to garner sympathy and avoid further rough treatment. Under interrogation, Cottin stressed that he had acted alone.[72] Within an hour of the attack, he explained his motive: "In a word, I am an anarchist."[73] He went on: "M. Clemenceau was opposed to our anarchist ideas. He obstructed our meetings and stalked us everywhere....After all I heard, I became convinced that he was a man to be eliminated."[74] In a later interview with Captain Bouchardon, Cottin explained that he had acted both to "satisfy his anarchist ideal" and to express his opposition to the premier's repression of anarchism and his policy of intervention in Russia. In a neat reversal of the accusations of complicity with Germany thrown at him, Cottin claimed, "I consider M. Clemenceau like the second Kaiser."[75] The conflict with Germany offered more than one means to frame Cottin's crime.

By the end of February 1919, investigators and journalists had accepted that Cottin was alone responsible for his plot to kill the prime minister. Editors and journalists ended their search for accomplices and co-conspirators. Drawing on established notions about the Russian origins of terrorism, along with continued hostility to Germany, some still believed that the defeated powers to the east of France had the most to gain from the death of Clemenceau. The experience of the war informed representations of the assassin as well as the "brave" behavior of his victim. However, evidence of German or Bolshevik involvement was not forthcoming. Attention turned to the life of the assassin himself. When had Cottin decided to kill the prime minister? Why had he turned to anarchism? What—or who—had transformed Emile Cottin, the young cabinetmaker from Creil, into Milou the anarchist?

From Emile Cottin to Milou the Anarchist

A number of questions preoccupied the press and the police. Who was Emile Cottin? What—or who—had prompted him to turn to anarchism? Why had he decided to kill Clemenceau and had he really acted alone? Parallel investigations into these matters subsequently emerged. Journalists spoke with Cottin's family, colleagues, and acquaintances, old and new. Editors posited hypotheses about matters such as the motive for the crime and the process of Cottin's "radicalization" while warning about the danger that anarchism continued to pose to the nation. They conducted their own analyses of Cottin's statements and compared him to contemporary and historical anarchist terrorists and assassins. There thus emerged a construction of Cottin/Milou in the press. This construction could be quite accurate thanks to the use of official and unofficial statements made to journalists by the police, as well as leaks from people within the investigation. Other aspects of the construction contained a kernel of truth that newspapers subsequently adapted, exaggerated, or distorted. Further features of the press's representation of Cottin were fabricated, while in some cases, newspapers simply did not relate to their readers information that jarred with their own picture of the would-be killer.

The official investigators relied on evidence and testimony as they pieced together their own understanding of Cottin. The focus of the enquiry was not untainted by prejudice. Bouchardon seemed aggrieved by the behavior of a young man whose peers had sacrificed their lives at the front: "At the age when his comrades endured a thousand fatigues and ran the risk of the most terrible of wars, the bibliophile Cottin earned, working as he pleased, up to thirty-seven francs a day. And it is he who complains, finding society unfair and wanting to destroy everything."[76] Cottin had in fact tried to join the army in 1914 but his application was rejected due to cardiac hypertrophy, a condition that had afflicted him since he was seven years old. He was eventually mobilized with the class of 1916 to the ninth engineers' regiment. On 1 July 1915, after barely three months' service, the army declared Cottin unfit for service due to his preexisting heart problem and discharged him without a pension.[77] Nonetheless, Bouchardon considered Cottin a spoiled and arrogant malcontent and represented him as such in his report to the council of war.

One further source informed both the media and the authorities' construction of Cottin: the man himself. Evidence suggests that Cottin self-consciously styled himself as an anarchist and ideological warrior, from his manner of dress to his large collection of anarchist and "sociological" books, about which he boasted to anyone who would listen. Cottin's most recent employer before the attack, Richard Petrelli, told police that he suspected that his young employee was committed to progressive politics because of his "outfit, his flamboyant scarf, [and] his libertarian style."[78] *L'Intransigeant* wondered if Cottin had deliberately fashioned "Milou" after Souvarine, the Russian revolutionary terrorist in Zola's *Germinal*.[79] In interviews with police, Cottin made statements that officers were either able to disprove or unable to corroborate. Cottin's desire to construct his own image (elements of which fed the media's construction of him) seems to lie behind these statements. The construction of Emile Cottin/Milou thus resulted from a process of interaction between police, press, and Cottin himself.

THE ANARCHIST MONK: COTTIN BEFORE THE PRESS

Friends and acquaintances of Cottin and his relatives generally gave positive accounts of Emile's character to the press. People who had known the family in Compiègne and Paris recalled a "good boy" and a loving son and sibling. The concierge at his parent's apartment building described Cottin as "very intelligent, very sweet, never going to the cafe, very hardworking, and so clean, so well turned out!"[80] Impressions of the assassin's parents were likewise favorable, with both his father (a lathe operator) and mother (a laundress) described as respectable and hardworking. Certainly, his father, Lucien, was known for his socialist opinions, yet those who knew him did not consider him an anarchist.[81]

The contrast between the positive testaments to Cottin and his subsequent act of terrorism prompted the question as to how the young *compiégnois* had turned to violence. Lucien Cottin claimed that the change in his son's personality and politics had occurred in Lyon. Cottin had moved to Lyon in September 1915, where he initially lodged with his aunt and uncle. Lucien alleged that anarchists in the city had brainwashed Cottin into joining them.[82] Cottin's mother, Cathérine, recalled that during visits home to Compiègne, her son would discuss anarchist theories over lunch, but he reassured her that anarchism was not synonymous with terrorism.[83] Cathérine claimed, like her husband, that *lyonnais* anarchists had "misled" her son.[84]

The press likewise located Cottin's conversion to anarchism in Lyon soon after he arrived in the city in autumn 1915.[85] *Le Petit Parisien* reported that Cottin had met a Spanish man in the city who had inducted him into anarchism and explained to him "what needed to be done."[86] The newspaper characterized the city as a hotbed of anarchist subversion. It was a meeting place for French, Swiss, and Italian anarchists, where the memory of Caserio's assassination of Carnot was still alive.[87] Géo London, reporting for *Le Journal*, also claimed that Cottin's interest in anarchism had developed in Lyon. However, London cited the influence on the young Frenchman of a mysterious Russian named Michaïl, described as "[a] sort of ascetic with an emaciated face, [with] a blonde, unkempt beard."[88] After meeting Michaïl, Cottin reportedly became more "dark" and "fierce."[89] When investigators raised the subject of Michaïl during questioning, Cottin stated that the man was a fabrication. He knew no one of that name or description in Lyon.[90]

Newspapers referred frequently to another apparent source of Cottin's political conversion: anarchist literature.[91] Cottin possessed a huge library of anarchist and revolutionary books that he spent entire nights "devouring."[92] For media commentators, this hunger for anarchist theory, combined with a primary level of education, was a fatal concoction. Cottin was unable to critique and reflect on the weaknesses in anarchist doctrine, and he therefore followed blindly the incitement to violence contained within. In this way, Cottin was like other young anarchists, poorly educated and provoked to commit violence by their half-understood readings.[93] Conservative journalist Louis Forest bemoaned the fact that, like past anarchists, the young man from Compiègne was one of those "unintelligent intellectuals" who fell under the influence of anarchism.[94] For writer Marie-Louise Néron, Cottin was like both Jacques Clément, assassin of Henri III, and Caserio, assassin of President Carnot, because he "obey[ed] a kind of morbid impulse provoked by perverse doctrines [and] writings, which excite weak and unbalanced brains."[95]

The construction of Cottin's private life following his conversion to anarchy portrayed him leading a monkish existence devoted religiously to anarchism. He enjoyed a Spartan life, living as a vegetarian and a teetotaler, and choosing to remain celibate; his landlady in Montrouge claimed he was so shy he could not look a young girl in the eye.[96] Cottin helped to construct this image, telling his interrogators that he had ended a romantic relationship in Lyon "to devote myself solely to anarchist ideas" (a story widely reported in the press).[97] This decision became a point of interest for some journalists: Vautel suggested that Cottin should have taken out a girlfriend rather than spend his evenings reading anarchist literature.[98] Cottin also took an interest in psychic abilities and hypnotism, attending several meetings of the Société des hypnotiseurs on long-distance hypnotic suggestion (Cottin *was* interested in hypnotism, but soon dismissed it as "humbug").[99] Meanwhile, his attitude to work became overwhelmingly negative.[100] A colleague from Cottin's stint at Haour (in September 1915) claimed that he was "crazy" and "seemed dangerous," though he did not express anarchist views.[101]

Much press attention fell on a visit paid to Cottin on the evening before the attack in February 1919. According to newspapers, Cottin invited a blonde man to his room at the Pizoulet hotel (in Parisian the suburb of Montrouge) for two hours on the evening of the eighteenth. Cottin had met the man twice before, having struck up a conversation with him about anarchism.[102] The press followed the police's fruitless hunt for the "mysterious young blonde man" (later referred to as the "famous young blonde man"), suggesting that the unknown character had conspired with Cottin to kill Clemenceau.[103] According to *Le Matin*, Cottin claimed that the blonde man was interested simply in viewing his library and that he had not conspired with anyone to kill the prime minister.[104] Nonetheless, the conservative *Le Temps* wondered whether the anonymous blonde was in fact the Russian Michaïl.[105] The mystery of the blonde man resurfaced in the media seven weeks after Cottin was jailed in mid-March 1919 when police arrested a blonde anarchist named Cornillon outside Clemenceau's residence. Was this "new Cottin" really the man who had visited the Pizoulet in February?[106]

The press's construction of Cottin presented to readers a poorly educated, naïve young man, underdeveloped both emotionally and physically, converted to anarchism in Lyon under the dark influence of mysterious revolutionaries and intoxicated by the writings of anarchist theoreticians. This process saw Emile transformed into Milou, the joyless and sexless revolutionary ascetic. Vautel summed up: "I am rather suspicious of those young, staunch men who, at the age when it is appropriate to love Margot, are mixed up with loving mankind. We see them wandering, their foreheads heavy with vast concepts, with a singular flame in their eyes....They have read innumerable books which they believe to be very serious and which, in reality, are not serious at all: for them, the Recipe for Happiness is on sale in bookstores, and as they have no critical mind, as they are at that period of existence when one believes in political and philosophical systems, they easily fall into fanaticism. Let a little pride get involved—and here is one more 'martyr'."[107]

SIMPLISTIC AND VAIN: COTTIN BEFORE THE POLICE

Analysis of the police investigation exposes inaccuracies in the press's construction of Cottin. Cottin was not celibate. It is true that his colleagues at Ernest Dryvers aviation parts supplier in Saint-Ouen (where Cottin worked during November-December 1917) said that he showed little interest in women.[108] Yet this apparent aversion to the opposite sex may have been due to the fact that Cottin had spent three days in hospital for the treatment of a venereal disease in October 1917 (and upon his arrest in February 1919, he showed symptoms of gonorrhea, a disease that he claimed to have contracted the previous February).[109] Police collected information, too, on two women with whom Cottin was intimate, including a co-worker in Montrouge in autumn 1918, Marguerite Noël.[110]

The *lyonnais* woman with whom Cottin allegedly ended his relationship in order to devote himself to anarchism was Honorine Giobellina. Cottin lodged with the Giobellina family after June 1916; Honorine's brother, Ricardo Giobellina, was seemingly Cottin's only friend in the city. It is difficult to determine the nature of Cottin's relationship with Honorine. Police described Honorine as Cottin's mistress,¹¹¹ though she was only fourteen when they met, and he was nineteen. Honorine's mother, Valentina, informed police that Cottin intended to marry her daughter.¹¹² This plan did not please Valentina because Cottin's poor state of health concerned her. Consequently, she intervened to put an end to the young man's dreams of marriage.¹¹³ Honorine herself explained that she had rebuffed Cottin's advances because of his sickness. In any case, she was betrothed to another.¹¹⁴ Press reports of Cottin's celibacy conformed more to preconceived ideas about loveless anarchist lifestyles than the truth of the case. However, Cottin himself contributed to the construction of this sexless image through his statement about the reasons for ending his relationship with Honorine Giobellina.

Investigators attempted to determine the point at which Cottin committed himself to anarchism. What they discovered was that Cottin had reconstructed his past as one of a long-held and deep commitment to the anarchist cause. He traced his revolutionary politics to his upbringing, telling colleagues at the Dryvers company that he was "raised in revolutionary principles" by his parents. He further explained to co-workers that his father had named him Emile-Jules-Henri after anarchist bomber Emile Henry, and that his birthdate coincided with Henry's execution.¹¹⁵ This was incorrect: Cottin was born nearly two years after Henry's death on 21 May 1894. This effort to style an anarchist childhood spoke to Cottin's attempts to write a backstory for himself that better suited his later political loyalties.

Cottin explained to Bouchardon that his commitment to anarchism had deepened after an encounter with a Spanish man at the trade union cooperative in Lyon. Cottin ate his meals in the cooperative's restaurant. During dinner one day, the two men struck up a conversation, and the Spaniard advised Cottin to read Sébastien Faure's newspaper *Ce qu'il faut dire*. This was Cottin's first step on the road to anarchist activism. He purchased books advertised for sale in the newspaper, and gradually, he explained, "by dint of reading books, the idea of anarchy won me over. I felt the revolt take hold of me, when I saw that, despite my work, I was earning so little and that I was often unemployed. I said to myself, reading the sociology books, 'Only these people know about misery, [only these people] talk about it and try to do something about it'."¹¹⁶ Police found no trace of the Spanish man with whom Cottin claimed to have met, and investigators cast doubt on the veracity of the story.[117]

Enquiries into the identity of the blonde visitor to Cottin on the evening before the attack were inconclusive. Cottin explained that he had met the man in a local restaurant and invited him to his hotel room; this was the only time that he had seen the unidentified caller. Conversely, M. Pizoulet, in whose hotel Cottin stayed in Montrouge, claimed that the man had visited his hotel on several occasions. However, on one of these occasions, Pizoulet had mistaken Cottin's colleague Maurice Doligé for the stranger. As for the other occasions upon which the man had allegedly visited Montrouge, investigators believed Pizoulet. Still, Cottin provided no more details about the mysterious blonde man, other than the fact that he had *brown* hair.[118]

Investigators exposed Cottin's bald rewriting of his past when they concluded, unlike the press, that his conversion to anarchism had not taken place in Lyon at all. Cottin was in fact unknown in *lyonnais* anarchist circles.[119] The majority of Cottin's acquaintances in Lyon had little reason to suspect Cottin of anarchist sympathies. From his aunt and uncle to Madame Giobellina and her daughter Honorine to his co-workers and employers, interviewees agreed that Cottin had not so much as hinted at an interest in anarchist politics.[120] At best, M. Favier, who employed Cottin between June and August 1916, remembered that the young man had "very progressive socialist ideas" but that he was not an anarchist.[121]

Cottin's former employers in Lyon recalled a committed worker with a good attitude. Between September 1915 and August 1917, he worked in four jobs. His longest term of employment was at the Robert-Esnault-Pelterie (REP) factory, where he worked for twelve months between August 1916 and August 1917. Cottin generally left a favorable impression on his bosses and co-workers. His employer at the REP factory remembered him as a "skillful and consistent worker." Cottin—aged just twenty—was even appointed head of a small team of workers at the factory.[122] Another former employer, Favier, described Cottin as an assiduous worker whose contract he terminated only because the young man was better suited to being a cabinetmaker than a joiner.[123] State investigators subsequently concluded that, while Cottin had joined a trade union in Lyon, he became involved in the anarchist movement only after his return to Compiègne in August 1917.[124]

Once back in northern France, Cottin threw himself into Paris's anarchist movement. He frequented anarchist bookshops and became involved in the publication of the newspapers *La Plèbe* and *Le Libertaire*. Police also noted his connections to several left-wing groups in the capital such as the Comité pour la Reprise des Relations Internationales, the Comité de Défense Syndicaliste, the Jeunesses Syndicalistes, and the Jeunesses Socialistes. He had good relations with several well-known anarchists, including Jules Content and Henri Sirolle. His noisy support for Sirolle at a meeting of the Ligue des Droits de l'Homme on 29 December 1918 drew the attention of police. Cottin was among a small group of anarchists who applauded and cheered when Sirolle spoke in favor of political violence at the meeting. When attendees were asked to approve a motion of sympathy to the fallen of the war, Cottin booed so loudly that the Ligue's president Victor Basch pointed to him and shouted, "Coward! You, the man in the blue shirt, you are a policeman; I'm going to have you thrown out!"[125]

Cottin's involvement in anarchism after August 1917 coincided with a period of instability in his personal and professional life. He lived in the family home in Compiègne until October 1917, when he moved to Paris. He lodged in the city on the boulevard de la Chapelle with Vincent-Antonin Chavrier and Alexis Canet; the three men had worked together at REP in Lyon. Between January and May 1918, he lived with his co-worker Henri Delpy and his family on the rue Duranton. Cottin moved home a further two times before arriving at the Pizoulet hotel in Montrouge in October 1918.[126]

Long-term employment was difficult to come by for the young anarchist. During the eighteen months prior to his attempt on Clemenceau's life, he worked in eleven different jobs, managing to hold down some posts for only a few days. Former colleagues recalled a somber and introverted personality; his last employer, Richard Petrelli, noted that Cottin was so quiet that at first he believed that his new employee lacked the abilities to speak and hear.[127] A number of men who worked with Cottin during this time recalled his anarchist views. At the Caudron factory in Issy-les-Moulineaux (where Cottin worked during December 1917–February 1918), he was known as an "anarchist activist" and was friendly with other socialists and anarchists at the factory such as Delpy.[128] In May 1918, Cottin came to the attention of police when he assaulted blackleg workers during a strike at the Hanriot factory in Billancourt. While his employer expressed surprise that he was involved in industrial action, one might assume that it was hardly likely that an anarchist would make his views known to his boss.[129]

Several former colleagues remembered Cottin's threatening words about Clemenceau, and he was sacked in March 1918 for calling the premier a brigand who had deliberately prolonged the war.[130] The head of the workshop at the Cadoret factory in Montrouge (where Cottin worked during September 1918) recounted to police that Cottin had threatened to "break the face" (*casser la gueule*) of Clemenceau.[131] Cottin told investigators that he had decided to kill Clemenceau in May 1918, during the strike action at the Hanriot factory. When he heard his fellow strikers cry, "Down with Clemenceau!" he thought, "There is more to do. You have to take him down."[132] He explained further: "Everything that Clemenceau did contradicted my ideas and those of my companions. He acted 'like a king' with us. He sent agents to our meetings. He even flew over airplanes to threaten us....Because of him, reaction is in command in France."[133] Interrogation of Cottin also revealed a gendered aspect to his motivation to commit the crime. In his second interview with Bouchardon, the assassin mentioned that he knew fellow anarchists who supported violence in theory, "but they don't feel the courage to go through with it." He, on the other hand, possessed such courage.[134] Moreover, in October 1919, he told co-worker Auguste Jaeger, "I'm not a wimp and soon I'll be able to prove to you that I'm a man."[135] Eight months after deciding to kill Clemenceau, Cottin decided to act on 19 February 1919 as he had lost his job the day before. A lack of work and a desire to avoid homelessness informed his decision to bring his plan to fruition.[136] He expressed no regret about his act; on the contrary, he stated that had he escaped, he would have attempted again to assassinate Clemenceau, if his comrades had approved of his act.[137] Such statements revealed that Cottin had long planned to commit his crime against an enemy of anarchism while his desire to prove himself a man and to avoid the loss of status that his redundancy threatened in February 1919 also informed his decision.

To further determine the origins of the crime and assess Cottin's fitness to face charges, the authorities appointed medical examiner Dr. Roubinovitch to look for evidence of mental or physical abnormalities in the accused. Roubinovitch found none. Rather, he concluded, the roots of the young man's violent act lay in the meeting of anarchist theory with a man of average intelligence. Cottin had given himself over wholly to anarchism yet he was "misguided, insufficiently enlightened, [of] an emotional, impressionable nature that has always been influenced by its milieus."[138] Cottin was "vitiated, made criminal by the theories of the anarchist party.

It was anarchist doctrines that made him into an anti-social being and a murderer."139

Captain Bouchardon's report on Cottin, written after several interviews with the offender and drawing on Roubinovitch's assessment, reached similar conclusions. Bouchardon wrote that Cottin had read widely in anarchist literature yet lacked the intelligence to subject it to rigorous analysis. Simplistic and vain, Cottin's primary level of education, combined with his stubbornness and gullibility, led him to form "a sort of libertarian catechism" according to which he framed himself as a great thinker and ascetic. Bouchardon accepted that Cottin had acted alone. Nevertheless, he laid a portion of the blame on the broader anarchist milieu, in which meetings, pamphlets, and newspapers "overheat brains" and "poison the atmosphere." Bouchardon surmised that it was unsurprising that a Cottin had emerged from such milieus.140 For his part, Cottin bristled at the suggestion that he had fallen prey to "harmful" influences, surmising that "[i]t was only my reading and my reflections that led me to my ideas."141

Bouchardon's enquiry into the crime gave the lie to aspects of the media's construction of Cottin: he was not celibate; he had not converted to anarchism in Lyon; he was generally a good employee (until late 1917); the mysterious blonde visitor was a red herring. The records of the investigation demonstrate that the representation of Cottin in the press was in part founded on assumptions and stereotypes about "typical" anarchists. They reveal, too, that Cottin contributed to the distortion of his character and his past to reinforce his anarchist credentials. Journalists and investigators did agree that the assassin had fallen victim to an ideology that preyed on the naïve and the weak-minded. Ultimately, if Cottin was summoned to answer charges before a council of war, the broader anarchist movement belonged in the dock with him.

The "Poisonous Flower of Anarchy": Cottin on Trial

Cottin appeared before the third council of war in Paris on 14 March 1919, his twenty-third birthday. Captain André Mornet led the prosecution while Oscar Bloch presented the case for the defense. The prosecution called seventeen witnesses to testify. Given his client's confession, Bloch called no witnesses, though he hoped that Clemenceau might appear to speak in favor of clemency.142 Cottin's counsel hoped to convince the justices to grant extenuating circumstances, a move that would win the accused a custodial sentence. If the court decided against clemency, a death sentence awaited Cottin.

Relying on Bouchardon's report, Mornet pursued two lines of attack. First, he drew attention to the brevity of Cottin's war service to illustrate the hypocrisy of a man who claimed to represent the downtrodden yet who had lived an easy life on the home front.[143] Bouchardon had asked Cottin under interrogation why a worker earning a good wage and safe from the risks of fighting should hold a grudge against society. Cottin replied that he had acted not in his own interest but for those less fortunate than himself.[144] Bouchardon concluded bitterly that while his comrades had taken up arms for the nation, the young anarchist had enjoyed a comfortable existence yet "it is he who complains, finding society unfair and wanting to destroy everything. Such is Cottin. [The] [p]oisonous flower growing in anarchist soil."[145] In court, Mornet referred to Bouchardon's damning verdict. He further accused the assassin of undermining the victory and very nearly rendering useless the deaths of millions of young men at the front.[146]

Second, Mornet took up Bouchardon's contention that Cottin was a man of limited intellectual ability who had fallen victim to the influence of dangerous ideas. Cottin did little to respond to this charge beyond the correction of errors in his biography as presented by the prosecution.[147] The prosecutor further accused Cottin and his comrades of being the "apostles of Bolshevism" (Bolshevism had not come up in the investigation into the attempted assassination).[148] Mornet alleged that the attack on the premier was an attempt to import the doctrine to France.[149] At the time of the trial, right-wing commentators likewise framed the crime according to the political upheaval that had engulfed central and eastern Europe. *La Patrie* suggested that Cottin's act was "the first manifestation of Bolshevist evil" in France;[150] *Le Figaro*'s Maxime Girard considered the defendant's antipatriotism to be symptomatic of the "scourge of Bolshevism" that had taken hold in the defeated nations.[151]

Despite the fearful accusations leveled at Cottin in court, newspapers generally expressed surprise and disappointment that "Milou" the anarchist cut a rather pathetic figure in the dock. Cottin appeared "puny, [and] pale" like a "big child, who had grown too quickly," speaking in a slow, high-pitched voice with an accent familiar to Paris's working class, and lacking the eloquence to respond convincingly to Mornet.[152] *Le Petit Parisien*'s Georges de Maizière delivered a harsh verdict on the defendant, describing his "discolored" and "distant" eyes that reflected an "empty brain." He had the unsympathetic and bizarre physiognomy of an imbecile, and the political opinions to match.[153] Other commentators expressed sympathy for a young man seemingly in thrall to anarchism. For Edgar Troimaux in the conservative *L'Echo de Paris*, Cottin's sickly appearance and his child-like voice underscored his status as a victim of anarchism, both its theories and literature.[154] Joseph Mollet of the right-wing *La Croix* agreed: while the punishment of this "poor bland being" was paramount to public safety, the men who had inspired him deserved punishment too.[155] *Le Petit Journal*'s Jean Lecocq was likewise disappointed. Like his fellow anarchist terrorists, Cottin appeared to be intellectually disabled, with a brain "fogged with pride and cluttered with badly digested readings; half-illiterates who constantly have the great words of science and philosophy in their mouths, but who had understood nothing of everything they had read, and whose culture hardly exceeded that of a thirteen-year-old boy who comes out of his village school."[156] Some voices in the press seemed, therefore, to pity the young man just as they later stressed the vulnerability and youth of Germaine Berton, the anarchist killer of Marius Plateau.[157]

The justices of the council of war were not moved to pity Cottin, despite a last-minute plea from Cathérine Cottin to show her son mercy.[158] Following the arguments of the prosecution and the defense, the council withdrew for twenty-five minutes before handing down a guilty verdict for the three charges relating to Clemenceau (but not those relating to Decaudin and Goursat). A capital sentence was delivered. According to the governor of the Santé prison, Cottin accepted his sentence with pragmatism; the verdict had not changed his "usual pallor." Indeed, the sentence seemed to have steeled him in his convictions: "I am condemned to death, but in my association there are some who will avenge me, you will see it, we will shoot others," Cottin told his jailors.[159] The anarchist *Le Libertaire* responded to the news by reprinting articles written by Clemenceau in opposition to the death penalty.[160]

Commutation of Cottin's sentence was swift. A presidential decree on 8 April 1919 reduced Cottin's penalty to ten years' imprisonment. The decision likely had little to do with demands for an immediate revision of the sentence from Cottin's anarchist comrades; a special council of war rejected Cottin's petition for a judicial review on 1 April 1919.[161] Rather, the acquittal of Raoul Villain, the killer of socialist luminary Jean Jaurès, on 29 March 1919 placed the authorities in a difficult position. Public opinion was stupefied that Villain, who had succeeded in murdering his target, could walk free while Cottin awaited execution.[162] The reduction of Cottin's sentence soon followed.

Anarchist newspaper *Le Libertaire* responded with bitterness to the news of Cottin's escape from the guillotine. Imprisonment meant a slow death in the intolerable living conditions of Republican jails.[163] The liberation of Cottin subsequently became a central feature of anarchist propaganda. *La Jeunesse Anarchiste*—the newspaper of the group to which Cottin had belonged—mounted a vigorous campaign for the release of their comrade during 1921 and 1922. The campaign reached as far as French North Africa.[164] Anarchist Louis Loréal even received a prison term of eight months for authoring an article sympathetic to Cottin's crime (he also penned a song titled, "Glory to Cottin!" that celebrated the "act of justice").[165]

Cottin was released from prison on 21 August 1924 for reasons of health. The terms of his release required that he remain in Compiègne until the twentieth anniversary of his crime (19 February 1939). Cottin repeatedly defied this confinement order. Unable to find work locally thanks to his notoriety, he lived and worked in Paris during the 1920s, going by the name of Lucien Barchaulet.[166] The Parisian police kept him under surveillance but were not moved to arrest him. Cottin was not so lucky in Lyon and Toulon.[167] He was arrested in both cities as he searched for a former lover with whom he had fathered a child.[168] The final time that Cottin came to the attention of the authorities occurred in February 1936 when police took him into custody in the Parisian district of Clichy. With several outstanding warrants to his name (for breaking his confinement order and carrying illegal weapons), Cottin received two months' imprisonment.[169] Later that year, and once again free, Emile Cottin traveled to Spain to fight in a unit under the command of Spanish anarcho-syndicalist Buenaventura Durruti. He died in battle during October 1936.[170]

Conclusion

The case of Emile Cottin's shooting of Prime Minister Georges Clemenceau reveals important features of the French culture of terrorism as the country emerged from the Great War. Long-held beliefs about terrorism reemerged in the wake of the attack. Immediate reaction to the crime showed that the notion of terrorism as a Russian political tactic persisted.

This assumption rested not only on the use of the terrorist method itself but also on Cottin's appearance. The slender, pale young man with blonde hair conformed to popular beliefs about "typical" terrorists that originated in the late nineteenth century. Similarly, deeply ingrained assumptions about the anarchist penchant for violence and the dangerously appealing nature of anarchist texts and speeches, especially to men of a certain intellectual ability, were still in evidence in 1919. To some extent, Cottin contributed to this representation. He styled himself deliberately on popular conceptions of the anarchist, from a self-consciously "anarchist" style of dress to the cultivation of a persona as a revolutionary thinker.

Nonetheless, the experience of the war, not least the presumed German use of terrorism, and the post-war explosion of Bolshevism in Europe modified the culture of terrorism. Press and police distorted Cottin's motive. They accepted that he had acted in the name of anarchy yet they set this explanation in the context of France's exit from the war. Cottin had thus acted on the orders of the Kaiser or the newly founded German government, whose aim was to undermine the peace conference and take revenge on Clemenceau, the architect of Prussia's defeat. Simultaneously, Cottin was an agent of communism, a destructive Asian ideology that was slowly spreading westward. Terrorism in 1919 was a Germano-Bolshevik plot against France. The process by which the press, the state, and the terrorist himself invented Cottin/Milou demonstrated a dynamic of interaction that formed representations of terrorism and its perpetrators.

Three years after Cottin's attempted assassination of Clemenceau, young anarchist Gustave Bouvet (or "Juvénis") tried to kill President of the Republic Alexandre Millerand. On 14 July 1922, Bouvet fired two revolver shots at Millerand's motorcade as the president returned from an official event at the Longchamp racecourse. Juvénis missed his mark: he mistook the car of Prefect of Police Armand Naudin for that of the president and opened fire too soon. He was barely able to fire his second bullet before people nearby wrestled him to the ground. According to the press, the crowd moved to warn the president: "Don't approach, [someone] has just fired."[171] Contrary to this depiction, police reported that the president was informed of the attack only upon his arrival at the Elysée palace. So ineffective was Bouvet's act that the presidential car had barely slowed its pace.[172] Constables promptly arrested Bouvet.[173] The case deserves attention here not only because the Cottin family name was implicated in the act, but also because analysis of the 1922 crime reveals similarities between its construction in the press and that of Cottin's case in 1919. It provides further evidence that perceptions of terrorism continued to draw on established representations of the anarchist. However, as in the case of Cottin, certain reorientations were afoot, in the context of the alleged threat from communism in France.

Several right-wing newspapers immediately framed the crime as a "communist attack."[174] In response, communist newspaper *L'Humanité* stressed the individual nature of an attack that did not have the official endorsement of the party.[175] The newspaper later denied that Bouvet was a member of its communist youth wing.[176] Bouvet was in fact a prominent member of the Jeunesses anarchistes group and secretary of its "Ni Dieu ni maître" (Neither God nor Master) affiliate. He managed the *Jeunesse Anarchiste* newspaper during spring 1921. Bouvet's management of the publication ended in June 1921 when he was imprisoned for offences pertaining to anarchist propaganda; he was released in April 1922.[177]

The Cottin family name arose twice in press reports of the crime. First, the center-left *L'Oeuvre* claimed that the *Jeunesse Anarchiste* was the newspaper of the "Cottin group" in the anarchist movement.[178] Indeed, during Bouvet's incarceration, *Jeunesse Anarchiste* mounted a sustained campaign for the liberation of Cottin.[179] Second, several press sources suggested an alternative motive behind Bouvet's crime. During an anarchist meeting in May 1922, Louis Cottin (the brother of Emile) had accused Bouvet of lacking commitment to the revolution. He claimed, too, that Bouvet, released from jail the previous month, was now a police spy. Had he subsequently tried to kill Millerand to prove his revolutionary credentials?[180] At Bouvet's trial, prosecutor Mancel likewise speculated that in killing the president Bouvet had hoped to prove that he was not a traitor.[181]

The description of Bouvet in the press recalled that of Cottin. He was in a poor state of health,[182] of skeletal thinness and suffering from advanced tuberculosis (a fact that exempted him from military service),[183] pale and skinny,[184] "like a plant that had grown too quickly and in the shade."[185] According to *Le Petit Journal*, "[Bouvet] is a tall devil, thin, with a bony face and a pale complexion. His ears stick out from his head, and his face betrays physiological misery and numerous hereditary defects."[186] As for his character, he was reserved, solitary,[187] and quiet.[188] Vautel drew an equivalence between Bouvet and his anarchist terrorist predecessors: these activists were "always the same [type of] pale young man, with feverish expression, and an inspired air." Their families described them as "so sweet, so tidy. He always came home early, he didn't run around after women, he read all the time."[189] Consequently, Vautel continued, it came as a surprise to mothers and fathers when their naïve sons took anarchist theories to their seemingly logical conclusion and committed an attack.[190]

The extent to which Bouvet was responsible for his actions came into question. Concern over Bouvet's sanity was greater than that expressed for Cottin. One of the first reports of the attack, in *La Patrie* on 14 July, suggested that the would-be assassin "did not enjoy the fullness of his mental faculties."[191] The proprietor of the Belleville hotel where Bouvet lived suspected that he was "nuts" yet his regular rent payments dispelled her worries.[192] *L'Ere nouvelle* compared Bouvet to men such as Ravachol, Caserio, and Vaillant, who "are generally isolated and taciturn people whose brain does not assimilate anything normally and in whom the physiological disorder is accompanied by an intellectual imbalance."[193] For the right-wing press, blame for the attack on Millerand lay as much with the anarchist leaders who inspired their followers to violence as with the perpetrators of attacks themselves. Journalist Maurice Prax thus argued that Bouvet was most guilty of being a "big fool," intoxicated with anarchist propaganda and the "drug of hatred."[194] Prax recommended that Juvénis take time to "sober up."[195] French justice agreed. On 8 January 1923, Bouvet received a sentence of five years' forced labor. As he was led away from the court he reportedly shouted, "Down with war! Long live anarchy!"[196]

THREE

The Giant Assassin

*Paul Gorguloff and the Killing of
President Paul Doumer, May 1932*

On 6 May 1932, Russian Paul Gorguloff shot and mortally wounded President of the French Republic Paul Doumer during a book fair at the Hôtel Salomon de Rothschild in Paris.[1] Injured in the head and torso, the president died the following morning. Doumer was the second president of the Third Republic to be assassinated: on 24 June 1894 Italian anarchist Sante Geronimo Caserio fatally stabbed President Marie François Sadi Carnot during a parade in Lyon. Since the end of the Great War, several would-be assassins had made attempts on the lives of French political leaders. As we saw in the previous chapter, in February 1919, anarchist Emile Cottin fired several shots at Georges Clemenceau's car as the French premier left his Parisian home. Struck once in the back, the seventy-eight-year-old man known as the "Tiger" survived the attack. Three years later, during the *fête nationale* celebrations on 14 July 1922, another anarchist, Gustave Bouvet, opened fire on a government car, hoping to kill former president Alexandre Millerand. Millerand was not in the car at the time. In the same month, rumors circulated in the French press that a German monarchist "terrorist organization" planned to assassinate Prime Minister Raymond Poincaré.[2] Still, in 1932 the killing of Doumer came as a terrible shock to the nation. Newspapers heralded the deceased president as the symbol *par excellence* of French democracy and a man whose commitment to France was unquestioned; the measure of the man's patriotism was evident in the loss of four of his five sons at the front during the recent war.[3] On 12 May 1932, thousands of mourners attended the funeral at Notre Dame and a subsequent ceremony at the Panthéon.[4]

Within hours of the attack on Doumer, Minister of the Interior André Tardieu released a statement to the press in which he described the attacker Gorguloff as "a Russian anarchist not seeming to dispose of all his mental faculties."[5] Sections of the press likewise attributed the crime to anarchism: *L'Echo de Paris* claimed that the assassin's act was one that "takes us back to the era of the Ravachols and the Caserios."[6] Socialist Léon Blum, however, echoed Tardieu's concerns about Gorguloff's frame of mind: the Russian was "one of those straitjacketless madmen" the threat from whom hung over all heads of state.[7]

Before long, Tardieu changed his mind. The assassination had occurred just prior to the second round of the French legislative elections, a ballot that Tardieu's left-wing enemies were poised to win. The minister therefore took the opportunity to make political capital out of the killing. In a second press communiqué, Tardieu alleged that the assassin had once belonged to the Communist Party. He continued that Gorguloff had founded a neo-Bolshevik party in Prague and that the Soviet Union frequently used the members of such organizations as agents provocateurs. The implication was plain: Moscow had directed Gorguloff to kill the French president. The right-wing press soon took up this line of argument: "Gorguloff is really a communist," reported *Le Figaro* the day after the assassination.[8] Moscow denied all connections with Gorguloff.[9] French Communist Party newspaper *L'Humanité* instead claimed that a "Tardieu-Chiappe-Gorguloff" conspiracy had planned the assassination as "a new Sarajevo" to unleash a war against the Soviet Union.[10] The threat of an attack by Western bourgeois powers had been a hobbyhorse of the French party since the late 1920s when Moscow decreed 1 August 1929 the first International Day of Struggle Against Imperialist War. In 1932, local communist newssheets toed this line, too.[11] Before the police investigation could begin in earnest, political interests had grafted the ideological conflict of the moment onto the assassination of the French president.

The killing of Doumer marked a moment of transition in representations of the terrorist phenomenon in France. A subtle change in perception occurred, one that saw a departure from interpretations of terrorism grounded in fears inherent to the *post-war* years and a nascent reorientation of notions of terrorism in light of the political and cultural battles of the new decade. Gorguloff was not assumed to be a Russo-German terrorist, as was Cottin in the immediate wake of his 1919 attack on Clemenceau, nor was his attack interpreted as an indication of French weakness next to Germany, like the 1922 "plot" against Poincaré. In addition, while the killing of Doumer was an individual act of assassination, the incident did not revive representations of terrorism as an anarchist crime, despite early attributions of the murder to anarchism. Nineteenth-century-style anarchist violence had receded, and the police—and the right-wing press—now focused their attention instead on communism.[12]

Gorguloff's crime assumed a place on the ideological battlefield of the 1930s, Europe's age of extremes. For the right, the assassination seemed to lay bare France's vulnerability to attacks directed from foreign capitals, namely Moscow (as Tardieu alleged) and their French lackeys. Recent acts of extreme left-wing violence had linked inextricably terrorism and communism in the minds of conservatives and nationalists. In particular, the bombing of the Saint Nadelya church in Sofia, Bulgaria, on 16 April 1925, which resulted in over a hundred deaths, provided apparent proof of the inhumanity of Bolshevik terrorists.[13] Conversely, the French Communist Party perceived in the attack a plot against the Soviet Union by French and White Russian agents (though Gorguloff expressed admiration for Hitler and Mussolini, the French party did not yet see the hand of international fascism behind terrorism in France).[14] For both sides the attack raised fears of a fifth column in the country, an "enemy within," epitomized either in the communist subversive or the nationalist Russian émigré. The foreign terrorist bogeyman would later come to dominate perceptions of the phenomenon in France.

The 1930s ideological conflict was just one (admittedly highly significant) available means for interpreting terrorism in 1932. Understandings of such violence were grounded in a rich political, cultural, and historical terrain. First, the longer history of political killings in France and abroad continued to provide an important reference point. Following the Doumer killing, for example, newspapers ran retrospectives on past regicides, from the 1589 slaying of Henri III to the 1894 death of Carnot.[15] The result saw a mixing of past and present in attempts to determine the motive behind the president's murder. Center-left newspaper *L'Oeuvre* described Gorguloff as both a "Russian fascist" *and* an "anarchist of the extreme right" like

Caserio.[16] Right-wing *Le Figaro* reported that the assassin was at once "a Russian terrorist," "an agent armed by terrorists," "a Russian communist tasked with secret missions by the Soviets," "a disciple of Caserio," and "an imitator of other anarchists."[17] A variety of historical and political precedents informed the French culture of terrorism in 1932.

Second, the Gorguloff case spoke to fears in some quarters that France's border policy was too liberal. In a climate of economic difficulty and rising joblessness, xenophobia flourished as newspapers such as François Coty's extreme right-wing *L'Ami du peuple* stoked anger directed at foreign job stealers. The government responded with steps to protect French workers from foreign competition,[18] but such measures did little to assuage the fear of so-called undesirable immigrants and political agitators. On 8 May 1932, Catholic author and journalist Father Edmond Loutil gave voice to his anxiety when he wrote of Doumer's death, "It's nearly always foreigners who come to commit assassinations in France."[19] Even the expert psychiatrists who examined the Russian assassin suggested that his violent mind-set might be common to *all* refugees in France and to Russians in particular. There developed a connection between "foreignness" (and an unFrench "mentality") and "terrorism" that came to define the phenomenon in the popular imagination.

Finally, we must note that the peculiarities of each terrorist incident could offer additional means of interpretation. The question mark that hung over Gorguloff's sanity, for example, prompted a debate in the press and the courtroom about the criminal responsibility of the mentally ill as well as the role of ethnicity in matters of saneness. *L'Oeuvre* in fact argued that the Doumer assassination demonstrated less that the danger in France lay with immigrant agitators than with "half-crazy people" free to wander.[20] The mental health of so-called "leaderless," "lone actor," or "lone wolf" terrorists remains central to representations of such crimes in the twenty-first century. These representations are not politically neutral: media outlets—particularly those on the right—are twice as likely to attribute far-right (white) "lone actor" attacks to mental illness as those of Muslim attackers. This strategy serves both to depoliticize crimes inspired by reactionary causes and perpetuate the false image of the "insane terrorist."[21] In the case of Doumer's assassin, so keen were conservatives and communists alike to see in Gorguloff an enemy agent that they strove to *prove* his sanity, relying on pseudo-scientific findings on race in the process.

This chapter concerns the assassination of President Doumer, the investigation into the motive behind the crime, and the subsequent trial of the Russian Paul Gorguloff. It explores how contemporary political battles, racial prejudices, fears over uncontrolled immigration, and matters of mental health and criminal responsibility shaped perceptions and representations of this act of terrorism. It further examines how we may perceive in the Gorguloff case the presence of several key tenets of the terrorist phenomenon in the French imagination, namely that terrorism was the enterprise of dark and shadowy groups, directed by foreign powers, operating internationally and knowing no limits to their power. Their agents were immigrant undesirables and operatives bent on destroying France from within. The final section of the chapter focuses on Gorguloff's trial and the attendant debates over his mental health. When much seems at stake in the twenty-first century in proving the madness of the lone actor terrorist, for the political factions in interwar France who sought to use Gorguloff against their enemies, the Russian could not be a terrorist *and* insane.

"It Wasn't a Frenchman, Was It?"
The Crime, the Assassin, and the Motive

At 3 p.m. on 6 May 1932, seventy-five-year-old French president Paul Doumer arrived at the Hôtel Salomon de Rothschild on rue Berryer in Paris. He had an official engagement to attend the eighth Journée du Livre, a book fair hosted by the Great War veterans' literary group the Association des Ecrivains Combattants. The event was of special importance that year: Emir Faysal of Iraq was to attend, along with notables from the French military world, Marshal Franchet d'Esperey, and Generals Gamelin, Gouraud, and Weygand. Upon his arrival, Doumer moved into the crowd of people in the room, speaking with several authors about their work. A tall man in dark glasses then stepped forward. He took out a revolver and fired on the president at close range. Two bullets struck Doumer. The first entered the base of his skull and exited through his right cheek. The second hit the president under his right arm and exited near the shoulder blade, severing the axillary artery.[22] A third bullet injured Claude Farrère, president of the veterans' writers' association. A fourth and final shot did not find a mark (Figure 3).

The president had received several threats to his life in the days preced-

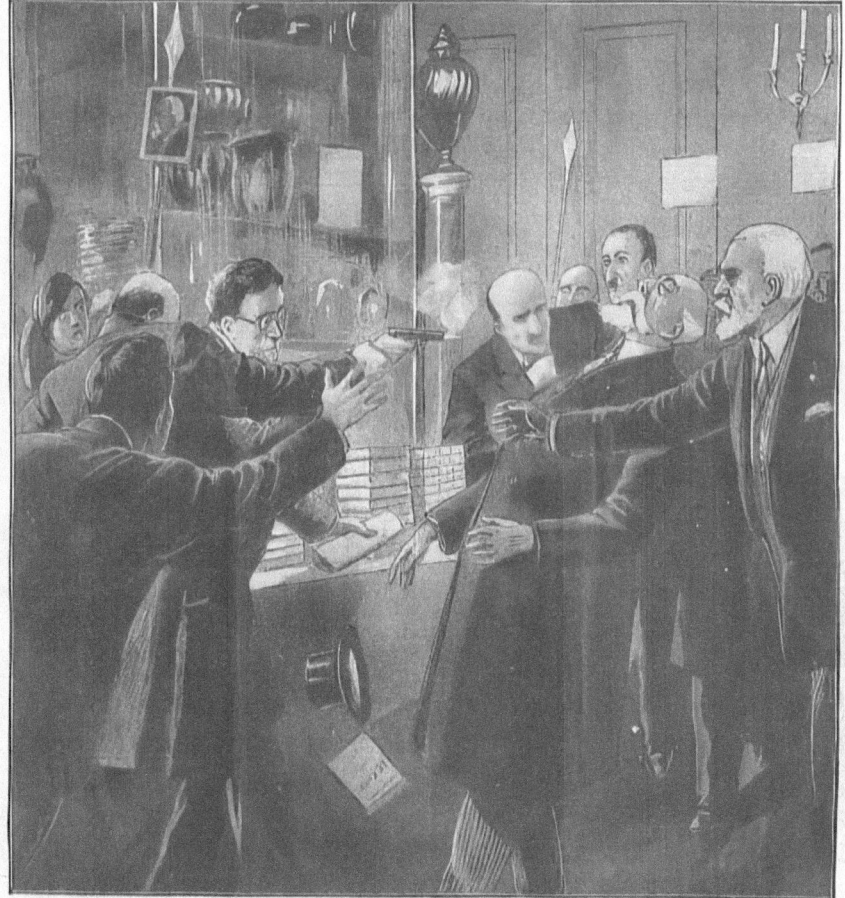

Figure 3. The assassination of President Paul Doumer, as depicted in *Le Petit Journal illustré*, 15 May 1932. Source: commons.wikimedia.org

ing the 6 May attack (though none of these threats came from his eventual killer).[23] Doumer's acquaintances had previously expressed concern about his penchant for mixing closely with the public at official engagements. The president's chief of staff Dr. Edouard Julia noted in his papers that he had broached this subject several times with Doumer before his death. The president simply responded that he desired to remain in contact with the outside world rather than remain closeted in the realm of high politics. In any case, he told Julia, if it was his destiny to die in the service of his country, one could not hope for a better fate.[24] In giving this response, the president was perhaps thinking of his sons, whose deaths came to symbolize for the public the selfless patriotism of Doumer and his wife, Blanche. The president was reputedly a man who "put Duty before everything."[25]

The gunman on 6 May 1932 was Paul Gorguloff, a thirty-six-year-old Russian physician. He had arrived in Paris on 5 May on a one-way ticket from Monte-Carlo. Gorguloff and his wife had resided in the principality of Monaco since autumn 1931. The Russian arrived at the book fair in Paris an hour before the president. He gave his name as "Paul Brède," a veteran author who had suffered an injury to his eyes requiring him to wear dark glasses. "Brède" spoke with Farrère, receiving a copy of the latter's book with a handwritten dedication. Witnesses later remarked upon the strange demeanor of the tall "author": he had moved quickly from stand to stand, appearing nervous. His tinted spectacles and foreign accent further raised the interest of onlookers.[26] Apprehended immediately after the crime—police in fact had to prevent nearby men and women from lynching Gorguloff—the Russian was found to be carrying a small notebook upon which he had written, "Doctor Paul Gorguloff Head-President of the Political Party of Russian Fascists who Killed the President of the French Republic."[27]

Pavel Timoféievitch Gorgoulov came from Labinskaya (Labinsk) in the Kuban region of Russia. He began to train as a doctor prior to the Great War but suspended his studies to serve in the Russian army in a Cossack regiment. Gorguloff took up medicine once again in 1917. During the Russian Civil War, he combined his university training with service in the White army. In 1921, Gorguloff traveled secretly to Poland on false papers to escape persecution by the Bolsheviks (his father had died at the hands of the revolutionaries).[28] Thanks to a friend in Poland, he soon managed to secure a Czechoslovakian visa, and he moved to Prague to continue his medical training. In 1926, Gorguloff graduated and began practicing medicine in Hodonin and Přerov in Moravia. His career there was short-lived. Gorguloff lost his license to practice medicine due to "a deplorable reputation, drunkenness, practicing medicine in suspicious circumstances [and he was] several times implicated in cases of rape and abortion."[29] Medical colleagues in Prague later recalled cases of malpractice. The Russian was said to be a "charlatan who knew little about medical science" and who promised cures to incurable diseases while requesting huge sums of money as advance payment.[30]

On 12 July 1930, Gorguloff arrived in Paris with leave to stay for fifteen days. The authorities later permitted a short extension to this visa on medical grounds. However, Gorguloff remained in the country unlawfully after the expiration of this term, making a living from the illegal practice of medicine among the Russian refugee community in the capital. In February 1931, the French state rejected his request for an identity card, citing his illegal medical practice as grounds for the refusal. Gorguloff received a further refusal of his right to remain in France on 15 November 1931. At that time, police notified the Russian that he had until 30 December 1931 to leave the country. Gorguloff subsequently opened a medical office in Monaco.[31]

Gorguloff's personal life was eventful. His first marriage to fellow medical student Marie Pagorgeloff in Rostov-on-Don failed in July 1921 after only four months thanks to Gorguloff's flight to Poland. A second union with Emilienne Nehafilova in Prague in 1922 ended when Emilienne demanded a divorce. Gorguloff claimed that this demand arose from the fact that he earned too little money. Emilienne insisted, however, that her request for separation came after years of domestic abuse and physical violence.[32] In fact, during divorce proceedings in 1927 Gorguloff threatened to "tear [his wife] to pieces."[33] Gorguloff married his third wife, Kueta Stepkova, in Hodonin in 1928; he later requested a divorce when he discovered that his spouse had previously worked as a prostitute. A fourth and final marriage began on 18 July 1931 to an Anne-Marie Geneg. It was thanks to Geneg's fifty thousand francs dowry that the couple moved to Monaco later that year.[34]

What motivated Gorguloff to kill Doumer? Like Tardieu, sections of the press were quick to judge the assassin as a "madman" and "[mentally] unbalanced." Descriptions of Gorguloff's apparently strange behavior accompanied the use of such labels: it was reported that he had a "mystical expression," and that "[w]hile staring at the ceiling, in a quavering voice, he uttered a stream of prayers of which one could only catch scraps."³⁵ In a long and rambling letter penned in his cell at Paris's Prison de la Santé on 9 May 1932, Gorguloff set out the motive behind his crime. As a supporter of "National Russia," he intended his act as a protest in two senses: first, against the difficulties that faced Russian refugees seeking asylum in Europe and the United States, and second, against the friendship between the Soviet Union and the Western powers. He claimed to have planned to kill President Hindenburg of Germany in 1930 and the Soviet ambassador to France in 1931, later settling on Doumer because of France's good relations with the Soviet Union.³⁶ The Russian therefore had no personal grievance against the president. On 2 June 1932, he told investigating magistrate Louis Fougery that his objective was the political office of the President of the French Republic and that his target, the man, was simply "a victim of the political war, like me."³⁷

Gorguloff's political writings—a "mystic-patriotic hodgepodge," according to historian Amaury Lorin—subsequently came under scrutiny.³⁸ During searches of Gorguloff's home, police found documents relative to the assassin's political party, the "Green Nazis," including a program, party statutes, and organigrams (Gorguloff, the self-styled "Green Dictator," was apparently the only member). Investigators in Czechoslovakia interviewed several people about Gorguloff's past political ambitions. Engineer Vassili Vaziljev had received a letter from the future assassin, who claimed to be head of the "Pan-Cossack Economic Agrarian Federation in Czechoslovakia." Gorguloff wrote that his mission was to destroy Bolshevism and reestablish universal peace." Vaziljev found the claim ridiculous.³⁹ Likewise, Gorguloff's Czech acquaintance Cesar Durchansk told investigators that he considered the Russian to be a megalomaniac.⁴⁰

The assassin's notebooks contained political diatribes against France. "It is France," he wrote, "that contaminated Russia with international Jewish Bolshevism, when it is National Russia that saved France during the war." He believed that France had allowed socialism to take hold in Russia. He therefore planned to take "holy vengeance" on the French. His writings further contained details of his supposed past acts of "clandestine terror," including the derailment of a high-speed train at Břeclav in 1928, several attacks against Czech politician Tomáš Garrigue Masaryk, and the murder of numerous Czechs, especially pregnant women whom he claimed to have "poisoned like rats."⁴¹ It is likely that such claims were little more than violent fantasies.

Partisan interests in France seized upon Gorguloff's self-proclaimed status as a political visionary and avenger as evidence that the assassin was merely a cog in a much larger conspiratorial machine. Conservatives like Tardieu dismissed the Russian's claims that he was an anticommunist reactionary, while former French president Millerand repeated the minister of the interior's accusation that Gorguloff was in fact a communist agent.[42] Right-wing newspapers throughout France reported the Russian's alleged communist affiliation. The allegation drew succor from a report in Belgian newspaper *L'Indépendance belge* that cited supposed sources in the Belgian police who confirmed Gorguloff's loyalty to Moscow.[43] A week later, French true crime publication *Police-Magazine* speculated that Gorguloff was in fact an agent of the fearful Russian State Political Directorate or GPU (often referred to in the French press as the "Guépéou"), the secret police body that succeeded the Bolshevist Cheka.[44] Such theories chimed with past reports of Russian intelligence operations on French soil that appeared sporadically on newsstands.[45] In the minds of conservatives, with the insidious power of the Soviet Union behind the Doumer assassination, the web of conspiracy was potentially huge. *Le Figaro*'s Gaëtan Sanvoisin warned that "never [had] a similar subversion threatened civilization and attack[ed] the universe."[46]

Conversely, the French Communist Party saw a nationalist conspiracy behind Doumer's death, accusing the government of orchestrating the killing to provide a pretext for a war with the Soviet Union. This line of attack fit neatly with communist policy as it stood at the turn of the decade. The specter of international fascism was yet to loom large in the considerations of the French party. Since the mid-1920s the party had instead waged a steadfast campaign against what it perceived to be anti-Soviet imperialism. Tardieu's statements to the press drew a stinging rebuke from communist Henri Barbusse, who in turn alleged the complicity of the minister of the interior in the crime.[47] Communist author Jacques Mortane, a witness to the attack, told *L'Humanité* that the police in attendance had allowed Gorguloff the time to "fire at leisure" at the president.[48] Like the right, the communists warned their members about the intrigues of foreign nationals on French soil, specifically French- and Polish-backed White Russian operatives in General Yevgeny Miller's Paris-based "professional terrorist circles." The party circulated petitions within its factory cells to have White Russian workers fired.[49] The Jeunesses Communistes contacted its sections to alert them to future White outrages, while warning that the

1932 assassination in Paris risked triggering a general European war much as the killing in Sarajevo in June 1914 had sparked the Great War.[50]

Right- and left-wing conspiracy theories spoke to popular perceptions of terrorism as the enterprise of mysterious international interests whose tentacles penetrated everywhere. The secrecy in which terrorists operated, the huge financial and material resources at their disposal, and the efficiency of their operations rendered them at once unknown and unknowable. The sole certainty was the political cause that they served: communism or nationalism (later fascism), depending upon one's view of the world. To read terrorist acts in the light of conspiracy theories gave apparent meaning to ostensibly unconnected events. Conservative author Paul Darlix's *Terrorisme sur le monde* (1932) took three "terrorist" incidents as the focus of his "impartial inquiry" into the subject: the assassination of Doumer, the loss of ocean liner *Georges Philippar* during its maiden voyage in the Gulf of Aden on 15 May 1932, and the killing of Japanese prime minister Inukai Tsuyoshi on the same day.[51] Darlix considered Gorguloff's act the first skirmish in a "gigantic battle" and an "underhand and merciless war" waged against the "civilized Universe" by the Soviet Union.[52] He warned the reader that "[e]verywhere, TERRORISM IS BREAKING OUT IN THE WORLD."[53] Similarly, Philippe Artois, a writer for *Police-Magazine*, perceived behind each of these tragedies "terrorists who work in the shadows and whose existence goes unnoticed most of the time," and he too warned about an approaching global tumult.[54]

Popular publishing houses provided further grist to the mill of conspiracy theorists, churning out memoir after memoir of retired secret agents and former terrorists. Such works often brought to the reader warnings about the threats posed to the contemporary international order. The French translation of Baroness Carla Jenssen's 1930 *I Spy!* (the less snappily titled *J'espionne*, 1931), for example, told of the author's experience with "the enormous machine of post-war espionage."[55] Jenssen went on to signal to the reader that the greatest danger to world peace in the new decade came from both Germany and Russia. Interest in the "original" Russian terrorism rekindled in 1931 with the French translation of Boris Savinkov's 1917 *Vospominanija terrorista* (*Souvenirs d'un terroriste*). Savinkov had been a member of the Party of the Socialist Revolutionaries' Combat Organization.[56] His book described in fine detail several attacks in which he took part as well as the fanatical belief of the terrorists in their ultimate victory over the Tsar. The book appeared in English translation in the same year.[57]

The rate of publication of works such as Jenssen's and Savinkov's attested to a public appetite for literature that exposed the inner workings of spy agencies, the criminal underworld, and the dark machinations of terrorist groups.⁵⁸

Fictional works likewise sought to expose the mysterious intrigues of the terrorist universe. Of note in 1932 was Joseph Lovitch's novel *Tempête sur l'Europe*. This story, about a White Russian who assassinates the French president, bore unnerving similarities to the real-life assassination of Paul Doumer. Worse still for a (conservative) French audience, Lovitch's tale saw the Soviet Union conquer France with the help of a revived and re-armed Germany.⁵⁹ In his preface to the work, French essayist Henri Rollin wondered if Gorguloff had read Lovitch's original Russian text, serialized in the Russian émigré newspaper *Roupor* only weeks before the assassination.⁶⁰ Rollin feared that unnamed foreign powers (though he stated that political assassination was "an old Russian tradition"⁶¹) would look to provoke similar fanatics into action and risk "a conflagration perhaps more serious than that which the attack in Sarajevo triggered."⁶² In his review of Lovitch's work, *Le Quotidien*'s Pierre Le Brun noted the book's apparent blurring of fiction and reality, in an article titled, "When Imagination Anticipates Reality....The Assassination of President Doumer Foreseen and Described by a Russian Novelist."⁶³ In a 1932 pamphlet on the killing, Michel Gorel described Lovitch's story as of a "documentary character" and even suggested that its existence had swayed several members of the jury.⁶⁴ On the other hand, the French communists suggested that Tardieu and his alleged conspirators had used Lovitch's book in their own preparations for the assassination of Doumer.⁶⁵ Neither Rollin, Le Brun, nor the communists dwelled on the evident dissimilarities between Lovitch's story and current affairs: in the novel, the French and British prime ministers are assassinated at the same time as the French president. Still, the book and its apparent prophecy were taken very seriously in 1932; prosecutor Charles Donat-Guigue even mentioned the novel during Gorguloff's trial.⁶⁶

Fact and fiction mixed in one final aspect of the Gorguloff case: the supposed involvement of a blonde female accomplice in the killing.⁶⁷ *Police-Magazine*'s Pierre Bertin reported that witnesses had seen the assassin in the company of a blonde woman on the day before the crime, as well as in the room at the time of the assassination itself (this latest assertion came from a "Mme de Vilmorin," cited in Bertin's article). Bertin suggested that the woman was a prostitute but, having conducted his own investigation among the "professional blondes" of the Latin Quarter, he turned up nothing.[68] The figure of the blonde-haired woman appeared also in Marcel Montarron's report for *Détective* magazine. A local waiter claimed to have served Gorguloff in a café prior to the attack. The Russian, the waiter claimed, had dined with a man, a woman from Martinique, and a blonde-haired woman. Montarron also placed this woman in the room at the time of the attack. After the firing had stopped, this woman allegedly murmured, "At last, he didn't miss."[69] Police reports of the crime did not mention a blonde woman.

Gorguloff had no accomplice. The Russian revealed at his trial that he had met with a prostitute the night before his crime. The two had returned to his hotel room together but she had stayed only for several minutes before leaving and no sexual act had taken place.[70] What is striking about the figure of the blonde woman is the similarity that she bears to characters in fictional portrayals of terrorism during the 1930s. Lovitch's *Tempête sur l'Europe* features the blonde Véra, wife of André Lozine, a journalist, poet, and acolyte of the White Russian activist Ziber. Lovitch explains that Véra's qualities were particularly useful in the underground for she "possessed to a high degree this feminine cunning that blinds men and drives them mad."[71] As we will see, the figure of a woman, sometimes a blonde, reappeared at times of other terrorist attacks during the 1930s. In 1932, as in later instances, she brought the dash of sexual intrigue common to terrorist stories, fictional and otherwise, of that decade.

President Doumer fell victim to Gorguloff's twin desires to save a nationalist Russia that no longer existed and to punish France for its friendship with the Soviet Union. The Russian hoped that a subsequent war might lead to his installation as dictator of a "Green" Russia. His plans were ambitious, given that he was the sole member of his political movement. Yet in the context of the ideological divisions of the early 1930s, French political factions sensed more than a whiff of conspiracy in Gorguloff's manifestoes. Furthermore, the Russian's troubled personal life hinted at a shady side to his character while his dubious medical practices completed the picture of a failed doctor-cum-agent-provocateur. Within days of the assassination, Gorguloff, the delusional quack from Labinsk, was transformed into an international operative of an anti-French terrorist plot whose crime, prophesied in a mysterious novel, threatened to undermine the world order.

The Man from "the Land of Mystery and Blood"

The 1931 census recorded 2.7 million foreigners in France, accounting for roughly 7 percent of the population.[72] France had the highest proportion of foreigners relative to the native population in the world (515 per 100,000 inhabitants).[73] This relatively high number stemmed from immigration policies pursued since the outbreak of the Great War. The shortage of workers during the conflict had prompted the French government for the first time to organize and deploy immigrant labor: by the autumn of 1918, there were 440,000 such workers incorporated into the war economy.[74] Immigration remained high after the war as successive administrations sought to both fill the hole left in the labor market by the war dead and compensate for the country's perceived demographic deficit: 200,000 foreigners entered France annually between 1920 and 1930, and there were 1,150,000 more arrivals than departures.[75] No single body oversaw the immigrant population (Charles Lambert's position as High Commissioner for Immigration and Naturalizations in the 1926 Herriot government lasted only four days).[76] Rather, a division of labor existed between a number of ministries: the Ministry of Labor managed agricultural and industrial workers; the Ministry of the Interior kept suspect foreigners under surveillance and granted identity papers; and, from 1930, the Ministry of Public Health monitored the physical state of migrants entering the country.[77]

In the decade prior to Doumer's assassination, hostility to immigrants was constant. Periodic economic difficulties saw the foreign workforce denounced as job stealers. Spikes in unemployment during 1919, 1921, 1924, and 1927 drew a xenophobic response from French workers and their unions.[78] The presence of large immigrant communities further prompted concerns over the political loyalties of France's foreign population. In September 1926, a police report noted that Italian criminals and political fugitives were arriving in France in large number, prepared to live off only "the fruits of theft, brigandage or other reprehensible acts."[79] The author likewise warned of an Italian Fascist fifth column in France: "One can, definitively, understand as certain that the fascist authorities are carrying out in France underground work toward the organization of terrorism."[80]

The Gorguloff case reinvigorated debates about undesirable foreigners in France. On the one hand, these debates focused on economic migrants. By 1932, the worldwide financial depression had begun to bite in France, with industrial output in decline and unemployment rising. Vociferous demands to protect French workers from immigrant competition multiplied in the press. On the other hand, xenophobia drew on concerns over the activities of foreign political agitators on French soil. Racist newspaper owner and perfume magnate François Coty alerted readers of the right-wing *Le Figaro* to the dangers of the "wog," communists, and the Jewish infiltration of French territory that was evident, he claimed, in the deeds of men such as Gorguloff and Schwartzbard.[81] Coty's extreme right-wing *L'Ami du peuple*—a "veritable anthology of xenophobia and racism" according to historian Ralph Schor—was the newspaper of choice for some three million French by 1930.[82] The Doumer killing itself seemed symptomatic of foreigners' abuse of French hospitality and the danger that "exiled fanatics" represented.[83] On the day of the assassination itself, a police report warned of "the ever starker necessity to rid the country and especially Paris and its suburbs of too numerous foreigners, absolutely undesirable, dangerous for public security, who have become a veritable scourge."[84]

According to the 1931 census, there were 82,900 Russians in France, though other sources placed the true figure as high as 400,000.[85] The first significant Russian migration to France occurred during the final decades of the nineteenth century when Jews and revolutionaries fled to Paris to escape Tsarist persecution.[86] Following the Great War, a number of Russians—including former soldiers of the 1916 Tsarist expeditionary force in the West—remained in France. In the wake of the 1918 Treaty of Brest-Litovsk, they suffered from a reputation as traitors little better than the German enemy. The squalid conditions in which these men lived in French internment camps thus troubled few citizens.[87]

The 1920s witnessed a second significant wave of immigration from the lands of the former Russian Empire, with up to eighty thousand Russians arriving in France as refugees or exiles (prior to the Bolshevik Revolution, thirty-five thousand Russians lived in France).[88] Many of the Russians in France, especially fleeing aristocrats, were legally stateless and able to travel only thanks to the so-called "Nansen" refugee passports.[89] Expatriates generally amassed in Paris thanks to existing social networks and the city's international reputation; the Russian population there more than doubled, turning the City of Light into "the world capital of the Russian diaspora."[90] This wave of immigration brought Russian culture to a French audience. From fashion, perfumes, and cigarettes, to restaurants, cabarets, and publishing (there were 167 Russian newspapers and reviews available) some French sought out products and experiences with "Russian cachet."[91]

The significant number of Russians involved in the Parisian artistic and cultural scene reinforced an idea that these émigrés hailed mainly from the social elites. This was not true: over three-quarters of the active immigrant Russian population worked in the automobile industry.[92]

As the economic crisis worsened during the early 1930s, the image of the Russian community tarnished. A Russian immigrant's average length of unemployment was longer than that of other European communities in France. Vagrancy afflicted many, and the numbers of Russians arrested for this offence grew. Those who could find work were often constrained to accept menial, low-paid posts, condemning them to a miserable existence.[93] Meanwhile, the stigma of organized crime hung over these eastern refugees, and the authorities viewed the Russian immigrant community with suspicion. The export of Russian political conflict to Paris likewise raised French concerns. Incidents such as the kidnapping by Soviet agents of White Russian General Kutepov in broad daylight on a Parisian street in January 1930 caused alarm.[94] Russians were therefore "considerably overrepresented" on the French police's 1932 list of "National Origins of Foreigners Deemed a Threat to Internal Order" in the department of the Seine.[95] They made up 31.6 percent of foreigners on the police's list of October 1932, second only to the proportion of Italians (32.7 percent), and this despite the fact that Russians accounted for only 9.5 percent (or 26,312) of the 275,743 foreigners in the capital.[96]

In May 1932, representatives of the Russian emigrant community were quick to condemn Gorguloff's crime; they were perhaps concerned at the potential damage the crime could do to the already poor reputation of the community in France.[97] There was no public violence against Russians in France (Caserio's assassination of Carnot in 1894 had prompted violence against the French-based Italian community).[98] However, comparisons between Caserio's crime and that of Gorguloff usually focused on the foreignness of the perpetrator.[99] The long history of political violence in Russia in part informed perceptions of the perpetrator's behavior. Gorguloff's alleged admission that he had once belonged to a secret organization founded by Savinkov recalled turn-of-the-century revolutionary terrorism.[100] Darlix attempted to connect Soviet communism with its revolutionary forebear: communism, he argued, was the offspring of "nihilist doctrines hatched in Russia."[101] Meanwhile, the communist *L'Humanité*'s foreign affairs reporter Marius Magnien used a ten-part series to draw attention to the "dens of the white guard terrorists" in France.[102] Yet a certain amount of romance could creep into notions of the Parisian-Russian terrorist underworld. According to *Le Quotidien*, "The living conditions of Russian émigrés [in Paris] are beyond all imagination, where the most extraordinary adventures are forged and [then] vanish, where the bomb, the revolver, the plot, provocations, double, triple, or quadruple agents are not empty ghosts."[103] Popular stereotypes held the Russian to be gripped by alternating states of fervor and depression: "The look of these disconcerting beings, full of an exquisite delicateness, could be riven by flashes of Asiatic savagery."[104] Orientalist notions of Russia, namely that the country was a strange and violent "land of mystery and blood," thus informed attitudes to the Russian immigrant community as depicted in the wake of Doumer's assassination.[105]

Descriptions of Gorguloff's physique likewise betrayed Orientalist attitudes to Russians. While the stigmatization of foreign physical appearances was common to contemporary xenophobic prejudice (Russians were generally appreciated for their imposing physiques),[106] we must further set depictions of Gorguloff within understandings of the physical attributes of terrorists (Figure 4). Witnesses to the shooting described the Russian as a "colossus with tremendously broad shoulders, enormous hands, a low and thick forehead, thin lips, [and] small and narrow eyes."[107] Other sources described a face that was "broad but almost tightened over an overprominent bone structure that bulged at his cheekbones" with a "square and jutting jaw" and protruding ears, "like those of a boxer."[108] As for his body, Gorguloff was "monstrous," "the work of a diabolical sculptor," with "remarkably square shoulders," a "vigorous chest," and unusual strength.[109] Such descriptions were exaggerated, yet the assassin was indeed tall: *Le Figaro* described Gorguloff as "of a colossal size," measuring one meter ninety centimeters.[110] The average Frenchman in 1932 measured one meter sixty-seven centimeters, and it is therefore quite likely that Gorguloff towered over those around him.[111]

Images of Gorguloff in the press contributed to the representation of the assassin as physically monstrous. Photographs showed Gorguloff's tumefied face, with a split cheek, multiple bruises, and a bloody mouth of broken teeth thanks to his rough treatment from the mob at the scene of the crime (and likely from the officers at the police station, too). Such images confirmed Gorguloff as "a rather unsavory alien" and had the potential to shock; as one eyewitness report stated, "One has difficulty in

Figure 4. The assassin of President Doumer, Paul Gorguloff, pictured soon after his arrest on 6 May 1932. Source: commons.wikimedia.org

imagining his normal face."[112] The terrorist Russian was an imposing and monstrous figure.

Popular attitudes to Slavic peoples further emerged in reports of Gorguloff's behavior during and after the crime. The Russian apparently claimed that he had felt himself governed by a supernatural force beyond his control, "an invisible force" that put him "in a sort of hypnotic trance."[113] (Had he acted at the behest of the stars? The review *Croire* noted similarities between Gorguloff's horoscope and that of infamous nineteenth-century triple murderer Henri Pranzini).[114] Pamphleteer Gorel described the assassin as a "dark messenger from another world, a devastated and empty world."[115] Meanwhile, witnesses claimed they saw ecstasy in his eyes during his interrogation as, seemingly not conscious of the act he had committed, he began "murmuring interminable monologues": "Listen to me France, listen to me Europe, I prepared the attack personally myself and killed the President of the French Republic, this is my political terror."[116] His thick Slavic accent and deliberate style of speech created the impression that he was "like a 'seer' in a trance," with bystanders hypnotized by the incessant talking of this "preacher from Hell."[117] Some newspaper sources attempted to re-create this accent for their readers: *L'Echo de Paris* reported Gorguloff as saying, "Moi, je *souis oun* ennemi *dé* la monarchie et *dé* communistes. Je *souis oun* démocrate" ("Me, I *ahm ahn* enemy *ohv* the monarchy and *ohv* communists I *ahm ay* democrat").[118] Such reports contributed to a composite image of Gorguloff as the "mysterious Russian," whose soul, like that of all Slavs, was "indecipherable" and "unfathomable."[119]

The Gorguloff case seemed indicative of France's failed immigration regime. The Russian had lived in the country illegally for over twelve months during 1930–31. He had obeyed an expulsion order, yet this measure had not prevented him from returning to Paris in May 1932 to kill the president. The right-wing *L'Echo de Paris* consequently argued that "our borders are too liberally open to agitators of all nationalities and of all origins who come here to spill French blood."[120] *L'Intransigeant* raised the matter of a foreigner's statute to define and curtail immigrants' rights and reported that ministers were considering legislation. However, such a law required time to formulate and pass, and the newspaper demanded the immediate implementation of stricter controls at the French border.[121] Numerous journalists and political writers made a distinction between "good" and "bad" immigrants. *Comoedia* journalist Jules Véran was prepared to accept "honest" foreigners of the same race as the French ("[an] essential consideration in the question of immigration," Véran noted), yet he railed against the "exotic underworld" of foreign "parasites" in Paris.[122] Ernest Laut's opinion piece in *Le Petit Journal illustré*, while reserving warm words for "good" immigrants, decried the French practice of simply inviting expellees to leave the country, rather than removing them with physical force.[123] In fact, rarely did the police transport expellees to the border, and the result was that "expulsion orders were more often pronounced than implemented."[124]

Gorguloff's crime was refracted through the prism of French prejudice about Slavic people. This prejudice drew on popular ideas of eastern Europeans as mysterious and mystical, as well as on a perceived association between Russian immigrants in France and criminality. Racist descriptions of terrorist perpetrators such as Gorguloff amplified the "Otherness" of this form of political violence. Framed as the evil deed of foreigners, perceptions of terrorism were bound up with anxieties about the apparent insecurity of French borders. The solution seemed to lie in the closing of French borders to all "bad" immigrants (subjectively defined). Until this happened, the threat to France would remain. Coty summed up such thinking shortly after Gorguloff's trial: "The French people, envied on all sides, feel themselves surrounded by all kinds of intrigues, plots, [and] conspiracies, where their fortune, their well-being, their civilization, their very existence is at stake. They feel threatened, besieged by mysterious forces, and undefended."[125] For xenophobes like Coty, the assassination of the president in the heart of Paris had starkly exposed French vulnerability.

The "Emigrant Rasputin" on Trial

The trial of Paul Gorguloff opened on 25 July 1932 at the assizes court of the Seine. The court brought a charge of culpable homicide against the defendant. Neither terrorism nor regicide (or in this case magnicide) were on the French statute book. An archaic imperial law on attacks on the person of the emperor or his family remained in force, yet it went unused until its deletion in 1939. French law considered attacks upon the president as no different to attacks committed against a private individual. The anti-anarchist laws of the mid-1890s further enshrined in common law (*droit commun*) offences that employed terror in the service of a political idea.[126] These crimes were subject to the death penalty. Furthermore, they were exempt from the lenient terms of punishment and incarceration granted to those convicted of a "political" crime.[127] The court scheduled three days to hear the arguments of the prosecution and defense, as well as the testimonies of witnesses and experts. At the end of proceedings, a jury of twelve men selected according to their good moral standing decided Gorguloff's fate.

The trial of the president's assassin was of great public and media interest. Ordinary citizens queued for entry to the public gallery. Extra benches, tables, and chairs allowed a larger than usual audience to watch proceedings. Court attendants also expanded the press box to accommodate the numerous interested journalists (of which there were over two hundred, according to *Le Petit Parisien*).[128] A number of trainee lawyers attended too, eagerly awaiting a lesson in criminal justice from two of the legal world's heavyweights: prosecutor Charles Donat-Guigue and Henri Géraud, the defense attorney who had helped secure the acquittal of Raoul Villain, the assassin of socialist luminary Jean Jaurés.[129] The historical significance of the trial, along with its character as a popular spectacle, raised questions in the press about the possible broadcast of the court's proceedings on the radio (thanks to Tardieu, the radio had broadcast live the president's funeral service and eulogies).[130] In the end, the trial was not heard on the radio.

The theatrical surroundings of the assizes court lent a dramatic air to the event. *Le Petit Journal* described the trial as a "great play," with the entry of the judges like the "raising of the curtain" before the arrival in the dock of Gorguloff, the "star of the show" (another press outlet dubbed the trial "a Dostoyevsky novel").[131] Never had a courtroom awaited the accused with such curiosity and impatience.[132] However, Gorguloff's appearance in court surprised and disappointed some observers (Figure 5). He was certainly tall, but his body, a little stooped, was not that of the colossus described by witnesses.[133] Weeks of incarceration had left the assassin a shadow of his former self. His complexion had yellowed, and his face had wrinkled. Only his square shoulders served as a reminder of his martial past.[134] For the courtroom reporter of *Police-Magazine*, the accused was "an average boy," unremarkable if a little unconventional.[135] Nevertheless, the assassin's behavior in the dock certainly conformed to preconceptions. His darting gaze, his look of a "mystic Slav," his jerky movements, hinted at a "dilapidated" mind.[136] By the end of the trial, Gorguloff had removed his collar, unbuttoned his shirt, and was in a daze; in the final moments before justice was delivered, he had "assumed once again the outline of the madman" that had killed the president.[137]

The most anticipated portion of Gorguloff's trial was the so-called "battle of the psychiatrists."[138] Since the crime of 6 May 1932, investigators had devoted much attention to the matter of the Russian's sanity. Tardieu had raised the issue within hours of the murder, referring to the attacker's claim to be the "Green Dictator" and claiming that his political writings suggested a "mental disorder" (the minister of course quickly recanted).[139] Gorguloff's sanity became a significant political stake in the argument over the motive behind the crime, and it saw a convergence of attitudes between enemies. With the right-wing press and the French Communist Party keen to uncover a conspiracy behind the killing, each presented Gorguloff's "madness" as a ruse intended to obscure his political loyalties either to the Communist Third International or the White Russian cause.[140]

The matter of Gorguloff's mental health had important ramifications for his criminal trial. Article 64 of the 1810 Penal Code stipulated that crimes committed by insane persons were exempt from prosecution.[141] In the aftermath of the assassination, investigating magistrate Louis Fougery tasked three doctors with the physical and psychological examination of Gorguloff in order to determine the accused's mental state, and with it

Figure 5. Paul Gorguloff on trial at the assizes court of the Seine. A bearded Maître Henri Géraud sits directly beneath the defendant. Source: commons.wikimedia.org

"the degree of his criminal responsibility."[142] The medical experts—Truelle, Rogues de Fursac, and Génil-Perrin—were all doctors at the Public Lunatic Asylums of the Seine. They interviewed Gorguloff and subjected him to a physical examination. The doctors also brought under the spotlight his political writings and his professional and personal life, thanks largely to police investigations in France and Czechoslovakia. The result of their work was an eighty-page "Medico-Legal Report" in which the authors concluded that Gorguloff was sane. This diagnosis subsequently formed the basis of the prosecution's case against the Russian.[143]

In conversations with his acquaintances, police investigators *had* uncovered some evidence of Gorguloff's poor mental health. Early enquiries found him to be "obsessive and sly," "an abnormal person," who "destroy[s] all half-used objects (socks, handkerchiefs, braces, etc....) to the sole end that no one [else] may use them."[144] Gorguloff's associates described him to officers as a "fanatic,"[145] while alleged witnesses to his interrogation claimed he was a "crank...bent on some Machiavellian vision."[146] The landlords and hotel owners who had dealt with the Russian during his stays in France and Monaco called him "sly, brutal, proud and unintelligent" and "a bizarre being with a reclusive personality."[147] Dr. Mikhaïloff, an acquaintance in the Monaco medical community, claimed that Gorguloff was "a man who did not enjoy all his mental faculties."[148] His second wife described him as a "devil" who was "not altogether of sound mind."[149] Police discovered that in December 1929, Gorguloff wrote to the director of the state observatory in Prague to request the address of the German inventor Professor Doctor Obrth. Gorguloff had heard about the professor's work on space travel and intended to reserve a seat on the first rocket to the moon.[150]

The state's medical experts took several measures to counter evidence of Gorguloff's "madness." First, a medical examination found that an injury to the head suffered during his service in the Great War had not caused lasting damage. A blood test and lumbar puncture "proved" that the accused's syphilis—contracted in 1916—had neither infected his nervous system nor undermined his intelligence (Gorguloff himself claimed that the disease had prompted the onset of neurasthenia).[151] In any case, the doctors argued, the connection between syphilis and mental ill health was not certain.[152] Second, the experts dismissed Gorguloff's fantastical ideas as simply evidence of his ambitious personality. His grandiose political writings, for example, were those of a "political dreamer" rather than the product of a delusional mind. As for his desire to travel to the moon, serious inventors were examining just such a possibility.[153]

The state's psychiatrists attributed Gorguloff's strangeness to a deficiency in his moral character rather than to mental illness. Their report contained several salacious comments about the Russian's private life, including claims from two of his ex-wives that he was "excitable, abnormal, eating too much, sometimes drunk, [and] eccentric from a sexual point of view."[154] Gorguloff had, after all, boasted in his writings of depriving girls of their virginity, prompting some to commit suicide rather than live with such a dishonor.[155] Thus the "Medico-Legal Report" concluded that the Russian was not mad but rather "an individual of low morality, ceaselessly involved in louche affairs...[and that] he must be considered entirely responsible for his action."[156] The prosecution pursued this line of argument at the trial: Donat-Guigue described Gorguloff as a "runaway doctor, a failure, a rotten bigamist, a sadist, a despoiler of young girls [and] the emigrant Rasputin."[157] Furthermore, the accused's gesticulations in the dock, his frequent interruptions and rambling monologues, during which he demanded to explain his political manifesto, represented nothing more than the sophisticated act of a faker. A qualified doctor like Gorguloff can "play at being mad," alleged the public prosecutor.[158]

The most contentious aspect of the "Medico-Legal Report" (certainly from the point of view of defense attorney Géraud) concerned the psychiatrists' racial explanation for Gorguloff's state of mind. The authors of the report argued that in order to understand the assassin's act, it was necessary to bear in mind that Gorguloff was "an Oriental, a Caucasian peasant...whose mentality has nothing in common with that of our [French] countrymen."[159] If he suffered from delusions, they had ethnic, rather than psychopathic, roots, for he came from a place where "the myth is a form of thought." Indeed, while the doctors noted that behavior like Gorguloff's would mark out as insane a native of Tours or Burgundy, Gorguloff's conduct was quite normal in a man for whom "dream[ing] and cruelty" were inherent to an Oriental disposition.[160] Géraud challenged Truelle on this point at Gorguloff's trial: "You have said...that if [Gorguloff] was from Tours, you would think him mad but as he is Russian, you consider him normal." "Obviously," explained Dr. Truelle. "If I saw a Parisian crossing the Place de la Concorde naked, I would shout, 'Madman!' But if it was a Negro, I would find that more natural." For good measure, Truelle added, "Russians have the habit [of committing] political attacks." Géraud retorted to the court that Gorguloff was not in fact from the Caucasus and that, in any case, how could "madness [be] a simple question of geography[?]."[161] Nonetheless, the "Medico-Legal Report" proceeded to warn that Gorguloff was merely one example of the potential danger inherent in all refugees in France, a country whose "tolerance for wrecks from abroad is rather too great."[162] It could take generations for such exiles and itinerants to adapt to life in their new home, the psychiatrists postulated.[163]

The strategy of Gorguloff's defense team—Géraud, Marcel Roger, and Pierre Xardel—was to prove that their client was insane. Géraud assembled his own panel of medical experts to challenge the findings of the "Medico-Legal Report." Géraud's first expert, Maurice Legrain, was honorary head doctor at the Public Lunatic Asylums of the Seine. The second expert was B. J. Logre, a doctor from the infirmary of the Paris Prefecture of Police. The final expert was Georges Dumas. Dumas came with some hefty academic credentials: he was a professor of experimental psychology at the Sorbonne, a professor of pathological psychology at the University of Paris's Institute for Psychology, and head of the laboratory for pathological psychology at the Clinic for Mental Illnesses at the Paris Faculty of Medicine. In a highly unusual move, the president of the court, Eugène Dreyfus, denied the defense team's doctors the right to examine Gorguloff personally. Dreyfus permitted the defense team's medical panel only to study the official "Medico-Legal Report."[164]

Géraud's team believed that the dossier contained ample evidence of Gorguloff's insanity. Legrain noted that the accused was a paranoiac whose writings marked him out as a danger to society. The Russian required immediate sequestration in an asylum (Legrain later told the court, "I have already locked up hundreds of similar madmen").[165] Logre admitted that it was difficult to arrive at a conclusion without examining the man himself, but he saw in the accused evidence of an "[a]bnormal mind, [and a] dangerous and abnormal psychology."[166] Dumas's assessment of Gorguloff suggested a "morbid mentality" comprising a "messianic spirit, excessive pride, tendencies for ideas of grandeur and persecution, alleged altruism, bombast, ambitious conceptions, initially obsessive and then finally triumphant impulses for murder, [and] warping of his whole personality." His "puerile" political writings were not those of a dreamer but of someone with "mental retardation." In Dumas's opinion, Gorguloff required medical treatment rather than judicial punishment.[167]

In the evening of 27 July 1932, the jury of the assizes court took just twenty-five minutes to deliver a verdict of culpable homicide with premeditation. In a move that all but guaranteed a capital sentence, jurors refused to grant the convict extenuating circumstances.[168] Gorguloff's face remained pale and fixed as he received the jurors' decision. Then he launched once again into a "monotonous lamentation": "Why dishonor me? I am a good Russian soldier. What did I do wrong before the attack? I fought for France. The Germans who, here, had many massacred, you give them identity cards. Me good Russian soldier, no. Why?…You must not kill me like a bandit. You must kill me with a rifle, like a soldier on the fields of honor, like an apostle."[169] Such deranged interjections were merely the "reflection of a literary and Russian soul," *L'Oeuvre* noted acerbically.[170]

In the weeks following the trial, the matter of the condemned man's sanity continued to arouse interest. Victor Basch, president of the civil liberties group the Ligue des Droits de l'Homme, made clear his opposition to the death penalty in the case of a man such as Gorguloff, whose poor state of mental health rendered him free from blame.[171] Basch's protest went unanswered. Doumer's successor, Albert Lebrun, refused Gorguloff a presidential pardon the day before his execution (Lorin speculates that the state wanted to make an example of Gorguloff).[172] At 5:55 a.m. on 14 September 1932, Gorguloff suffered execution by decapitation in front of the Santé prison. A crowd of three thousand people observed from a distance.[173] Interment took place without ceremony in the cemetery at Thiais. Shortly after the execution, the two firearms found upon Gorguloff on 6 May 1932 and the bloodstained book dedicated to "Paul Brède" moments before the attack were donated to the historical museum of the police. Such artifacts from criminal cases were usually destined for auction, yet Donat-Guigue had gotten wind that rich foreign interests were looking to buy the pieces.[174] Interested members of the public could view them at the museum every Thursday afternoon.[175]

Conclusion

The trial at the assizes court of the Seine during July 1932 revealed racial assumptions in French attitudes to terrorism. The report of the state's psychiatrists exposed a belief in the susceptibility of some races (namely the Slavic peoples) to committing acts of political violence. They were the inhabitants of a cruel and enigmatic land where violence was a tradition; the upheavals of the post-war years further predisposed them toward acts of assassination. When one considered such factors, the outrageous act of a Gorguloff was perfectly rational to the exotic mind of the Russian. The medical experts' warning that all refugees from the east were potential Gorguloffs played to contemporary French xenophobic concerns. If all French did not subscribe to such an "unsound, pseudo-scientific method" (as British scientific journal *Nature* described it), the crude racial science of the "Medico-Legal Report" helped to send Gorguloff to the guillotine.[176]

The assassination of President Doumer brought the French culture of terrorism squarely into the political and cultural territory of the new decade. Certainly, the attack drew comparisons with the anarchist outrages of the late nineteenth century. Yet the demise of anarchism and the emergence of new ideological enemies after the Great War meant that Gorguloff was perceived as something more than simply a Caserio for the 1930s. Concomitantly, with the receding of post-war fears of a revived Germany, Berlin no longer seemed to pose a terrorist threat to domestic French politics (though, as we will see, Hitler's accession to power in January 1933 would revive such anxieties). Gorguloff's crime situated terrorism within contemporary debates about France's allegedly liberal immigration regime and the foreign powers who sought to take advantage of it. Doumer's question—"It wasn't a Frenchman, was it?"—spoke for many citizens who feared the activities of foreign political agitators on French soil. In the context of the 1932 assassination, these agitators were agents of the Soviet Union or White Russia. The upshot was that terrorists were foreigners.

The psychiatric evaluation of Gorguloff further pointed to the dangers of those who were allegedly prone to acts of violence, thanks either to the trauma of their experience, their ethnic origin, or both. The government responded with a modification to the terms under which some foreigners could remain in the country. An alien who failed to gain a valid identification card (or who had such a card confiscated) was now subject to immediate expulsion. However, the lack of clarity in the decree left much scope for interpretation: the authorities could henceforth confiscate an identity card (and thus leave the person concerned vulnerable to expulsion) in circumstances when the holder could no longer offer "desirable guarantees" of good residency.[177]

Interpretations of the Doumer assassination did not remain fixed. Political developments at home and abroad provided new lenses through which to view the crime and the motive of its perpetrator. In 1934, reactionary author and journalist Albert Monniot included the president's demise alongside other "mysterious deaths" of public figures in his book on the supposed crimes of a masonic and Republican anti-French mafia.[178] In 1939, Henri Rollin's *L'Apocalypse de notre temps* attributed the 1932 killing to a Nazi plot. Rollin claimed that Doumer's death had in fact been the first of a series of Nazi assassinations in Europe, including the 1933 killing of Romanian prime minister Ion Duca and the 1934 murders of King Alexander I of Yugoslavia, French foreign minister Louis Barthou, and Austrian chancellor Engelbert

Dolfuss.[179] The author warned that Hitler's regime was adept at exploiting a certain "psychological type," of which Gorguloff was a prime example.[180] Rollin's introduction, dated 28 June 1939 (the twenty-fifth anniversary of the Sarajevo assassination) was intended as a warning about the future war that awaited Europe.

FOUR

Killing a King

The Assassination of King Alexander I of Yugoslavia, October 1934

On 9 October 1934, a gunman shot to death Alexander I Karadjordjević, king of Yugoslavia, in Marseille.[1] The monarch had arrived in the port little more than twenty minutes earlier to commence a state visit to France. The attacker struck as the king's official car moved slowly toward the center of town, to the sound of enthusiastic cheers from thousands of onlookers and under the gaze of photographers and newsreel cameras. French foreign minister Louis Barthou, who was at the king's side when the attack occurred, later died from a gunshot wound suffered during the incident. Two civilian bystanders perished in the ensuing mêlée as panicked police officers opened fire on the assassin. Lieutenant Colonel Jules Piollet, part of the king's French escort, slashed the killer on the head with his saber before the enraged crowd pummeled him on the floor. The man later died from his injuries, so disfigured that only his passport and a tattoo of a skull and crossbones offered clues as to his identity: he was Petrus Kelemen, a Croatian with a Czechoslovakian passport and a member of the Internal Macedonian Revolutionary Organization (IMRO).[2]

The assassination revived memories of the Doumer killing of May 1932. Conservative newspaper *Le Temps* lamented the fact that, after Gorguloff, "another foreigner" had come to France to commit murder.[3] In a poster on the streets of Paris the extreme right-wing Jeunesses Patriotes league denounced the "thousands of undesirables" in the country ready to kill a Doumer or an Alexander.[4] Xenophobia in France had sharpened since 1932, when the global economic crisis began to take a toll. By late 1934, the number of unemployed receiving welfare payments had climbed toward half a million yet temporary layoffs brought the true unemployment figure close to one million.[5] The government increasingly looked to safeguard "French" jobs with protectionist measures against economic migrants and, after 1933, refugees fleeing persecution in central and eastern Europe. Antiforeigner prejudice spread beyond the usual confines of the extreme right to take hold in traditionally moderate sectors of society.[6]

Successive governments tried to bring the economy out of the doldrums, but their failures exacerbated antiparliamentarian sentiment. Hostility toward politicians reached a nadir during winter 1933 as the center-left government of the Radical Party became embroiled in the "Stavisky Affair." This scandal centered on the fraudulent dealings of conman Alexandre Stavisky and his seeming protection from prosecution by his well-placed friends in the political establishment, not least the ruling Radicals. Popular discontent climaxed on 6 February 1934 with nationalist demonstrations and rioting in Paris and other French cities. The *six février*— as the night was later known—marked the beginning of a polarization of politics that would last until the German invasion of France in 1940. Furthermore, Stavisky's Ukrainian-Jewish background stoked further the fires of antiforeigner sentiment.[7] Extreme right-wing leagues such as the Croix de Feu experienced huge gains in membership as they blended anti-Republicanism and anticommunism with xenophobia and antisemitism.[8] Yet such hostility was not the preserve of the political extremes. *L'Oeuvre*, the newspaper closest to the Radical Party, asked after the 1934 Marseille assassination that "foreigners not come here [to France] to settle their political scores."[9]

The French left focused less than their political opponents did on the foreignness of the assassin.[10] Rather, the socialist and communist parties— now working together in an antifascist alliance in the wake of the violence of February 1934—drew attention to the *politics* of Kelemen and his accomplices (the right remained largely silent on this issue, save for a few desperate attempts to pin the crime on international communism).[11] Soon after the crime, police had revealed the responsibility of Ante Pavelić's Croatian ultranationalist Ustashe in preparing and committing the crime.[12] Socialist André Leroux declared that the killings were thus "100 per cent" fascist and, in line with the French left's understanding of fascism as an international movement, Socialist Party newspaper *Le Populaire* pointed the finger of blame at Mussolini.[13] Yet French antifascists read the incident according to developments in domestic politics too. According to the communist *L'Humanité*, Kelemen was part of an international fascist movement whose French wing was preparing a "new 6 February" coup.[14]

There were points of convergence between left- and right-wing perceptions of the assassination. First, there seemed something different about terrorism in 1934: it had become a thoroughly political phenomenon. Certainly, Doumer's death in 1932 had raised allegations of Soviet communist and domestic fascist interference in French politics. Yet two years later, references to ethnic mentalities—such as the "Slavic soul" that had so dominated understandings of Gorguloff's crime—were absent from interpretations and representations of the Marseille killings. The 1934 terrorist was a political warrior, moving easily through Europe on false papers, at the behest of a shadowy state or substate group whose tentacles reached everywhere. The assassin and his accomplices—or at least, as we will see, his *male* accomplices—were fanatics, ideologues, and cold-blooded killers, trained in the terrorist profession at the Ustashe's Janka-Puszta camp in Hungary.[15] Such descriptions drew on masculine discourses of the period that foregrounded rational action and sangfroid in understandings of male behavior. These discourses also helped to situate terrorism within the broader interwar European culture of paramilitarism.[16]

Kelemen's female accomplice, Maria Voudracek,[17] raised questions about the role of women in terrorist groups. Voudracek fascinated the press. This fascination did not arise solely from the fact that she escaped arrest. Her physical appearance figured in reports of the attack, as well as in the police investigation, with journalists noting frequently the striking beauty of this "mysterious blonde."[18] Voudracek's presence at the heart of the plot—she had transported the weapons—prompted gendered speculation as to her importance to the Ustashe. Had the conspirators included the beautiful Voudracek merely to maintain the men's morale, possibly with sex? Or was Voudracek a terrorist mastermind, before whose stunning good looks men could but yield?

Second, terrorism was now understood as international. It was a tool to attack the European system of states established in 1919. The Ustashe had struck down the king as part of its campaign for Croatian independence. In this project, it had the backing of Hungary and Italy; the latter had supplied the Ustashe with money, guns, and explosives.[19] Budapest and Rome were engaged in long-running territorial disputes with Belgrade. The collusion between Hungary, Italy, and the Croatian assassination squad seemed to signal a radical departure in terrorism. Henri Donnedieu de Vabres, professor of law and member of the Association Internationale de Droit Pénal (AIDP), a body that worked toward the legal codification of terrorism and other international offences during the 1930s, argued that October 1934 witnessed the emergence of an "original form of 'terrorism'."[20] This "new" terrorism was "a collective blackmail, intended to impose, by intimidation, political or social transformation."[21] The novelty of this international terrorism and its apparent use as an "instrument of state policy" sparked fears of an imminent European war.[22] Commentators in 1934 referred often to the death of Archduke Franz Ferdinand in Sarajevo in 1914, which, like the death of Alexander, also bore the mark of Macedonian terrorism (according to *Le Populaire*).[23] Communist deputy Gabriel Péri did not equivocate in his assessment of the situation: "Europe in 1934 is ready to blow."[24] Such appreciations of the killing, committed by a modern-day Gavrilo Prinċip (according to contemporary Eastern European specialist Robert Seton-Watson) were not confined to France.[25] British author and journalist Rebecca West recalled that upon hearing the news of Alexander's death "[i]t appeared to me inevitable that war must follow."[26] The British Pathé newsreel of the incident asked ominously whether the killings were not "an omen of the future."[27]

War was averted thanks in no small part to the League of Nations. In November 1934, Yugoslavia enjoined the international body to condemn Hungary and, with it, the campaign to revise the borders of southeastern Europe. Budapest alone stood accused of aiding and abetting terrorists as part of a broader plan to redraw the map of eastern Europe.[28] France and Britain succeeded in sheltering Italy from accusations, because both Paris and London desired a closer relationship with Rome at this time.[29] For this reason, too, the French and British managed to divert the energies of the League away from an investigation of the Marseille crime (the matter was formally closed in May 1935) and into a new project for international collaboration against terrorism.[30] The project resulted in the "Convention for the Prevention and Punishment of Terrorism," adopted by twenty-four member states on 16 November 1937.[31] The Convention understood terrorism as a transnational phenomenon directed principally at the apparatus and personnel of the state.[32]

To some extent, the discussions of League members revealed a conception of terrorism like that of anarchism. Terrorism was a "special moral crime" deserving of a singular punishment.[33] In terms reminiscent of those used to describe anarchism, Soviet delegate Maxim Litvinoff described terrorism as "one of the most repugnant and dangerous phenomena in international life."[34] The agreement of the Convention marked the first time that states had discussed the terrorist problem, and the text provided a foundation for future efforts to counter international terrorist violence.[35] Consequently, if Anthony Eden later recalled that, on 9 October 1934, "a nasty corner had been turned" and that the day had witnessed "the first shots of the Second World War," the shots fired in Marseille on 9 October 1934 were in fact the first of the twentieth century's war on terror.[36]

This chapter examines the October 1934 killings in Marseille. It concerns the investigation into the plot behind the crime and its perpetrators, in police records and the press. In addressing French representations of terrorism and the terrorist in the immediate aftermath of the outrage, it explores contemporary perceptions of the phenomenon in the responses to the attack, as well as the ways in which the revelations about the assassin and his accomplices drew upon, and in turn influenced, cultural and political representations of terrorist violence. Much like in 1932, terrorists were understood as foreigners, and the xenophobia of the 1930s provided an available discourse through which to represent Kelemen's act. Yet the political crisis in France and the growing climate of international tension strengthened the perceived link between terrorism, domestic politics, and foreign extremist ideologies. In contrast to 1932, contemporaries rarely posed questions of ethnicity or sanity in their attempts to explain the violence of October 1934. Likewise, the anarchist bomber of the past was no more.[37] The ideological war raging in 1930s France and Europe began to condition the culture of terrorism. Terrorist violence was the work of foreign agents and undesirables, given succor, funding, and arms by hostile states who threatened to overturn the international order.[38]

"The Ride of Death"

King Alexander arrived at the port of Marseille aboard the destroyer *Dubrovnik* during the afternoon of 9 October 1934. A flotilla of French destroyers, battleships, and submarines escorted the royal ship into the port, and a fly-past by seaplanes greeted the monarch as he made landfall.[39] There was much affection for the king in France. Newspapers feted the "king-soldier" as a war hero, and the local *Le Petit Marseillais* printed a greeting to the royal couple in Serbian (Queen Marie was due to meet her husband later that day).[40] The local authorities had ensured that the city itself was "primed and festooned with flags." A large expectant crowd lined La Canebière, Marseille's famed avenue, along which the king's procession would drive.[41] Eighteen mounted police officers preceded the king's car, with two mounted officers of the Mobile Guard bringing up the rear. Over one thousand police constables waited along the route to hold back excited spectators.[42]

The purpose of Alexander's visit spoke to contemporary geopolitical concerns in the Balkans.[43] Paris hoped that the invitation would reassure Belgrade of the continued French commitment to its eastern ally. France's burgeoning relationship with the Soviet Union[44] had concerned the anti-communist Yugoslav monarch, while French overtures to Rome seemed to undermine a long-standing opposition to the revision of the borders set out in the 1920 Treaty of Trianon. Mussolini had recently rebuffed Hitler over the German chancellor's designs on Austria, and an alliance between Italy and France looked possible, at least from the point of view of Paris. Barthou had begun to allay Yugoslav concerns when he addressed the parliament in Belgrade during a visit to Yugoslavia and Romania in June 1934. He spoke of the fraternity between the two nations, telling deputies, "France loves you." The French foreign minister received a standing ovation.[45]

Alexander was less keen than his foreign minister Bogoljub Jevtitch on the prospect of an accord between Belgrade, Paris, and Rome. The king in fact preferred to explore a new relationship with Hitler's Germany.[46] He understood his trip to France largely as a move that would reinforce the commitment of both countries to the "Little Entente."[47] Given the political calculations on both sides, it was not without reason that *Le Matin* hailed the occasion as more than a "banal exchange of international courtesies": "in the tumultuous epoch in which we live," the king's visit signified "a willingness for peace and loyal collaboration" that would have repercussions for "the totality of international questions that currently preoccupy European leaders."[48]

Shortly after 4 p.m., the king met Barthou, General Alphonse-Joseph Georges of the Supreme War Council, and naval minister and deputy for Corsica François Piétri on the dockside. Alexander, Barthou, and Georges climbed into a Delage open-top limousine to take them to the center of town. The itinerary of the king's short stay in Marseille—which local newspapers had printed in street-by-street, minute-by-minute detail—included a wreath-laying ceremony at the city's monument to the Poilus d'Orient and a tea party with Barthou and other high functionaries at the Prefecture. At 6:30 p.m., a train would take the king to Paris, stopping on the way to the capital to collect his wife, the queen.[49]

The car moved away from the dock at a snail's pace—five miles per hour or "little more than [the speed of] a man walking," newspapers later reported.[50] The Delage had traveled barely two hundred meters when a man rushed forward from the crowd, shouting "Vive le roi." He jumped onto the running board of the car and opened fire on Alexander at point-blank range. Several bullets struck the king. Two shots hit Georges as the general tried to protect Alexander. Pandemonium ensued. Constables opened fire on the assassin, spraying bullets into the crowd. Ten bystanders were injured, three of whom suffered serious gunshot wounds.[51] A bullet struck Barthou in the arm, severing his humeral artery. The minister died from blood loss several hours after the attack.[52]

The assassin received several blows from the saber of Colonel Piollet, the mounted officer riding alongside the car. The sword cut down more than two inches into Kelemen's head. Bullets from police hit him in the torso and between the eyes. Grievously injured, he fell to the ground where the crowd beat him half to death, leaving him "a blood-streaked mass that little resembled anything human."[53] Constables fought off the mob and transported the killer to a nearby police station. So disfigured was his face that he did not—or could not—respond to police questions before he died.[54] Officers had already seized the murder weapon on La Canebière: a new model Mauser 7.65 automatic pistol, costing five hundred francs and capable of firing 280 bullets per minute. Upon his body, they found a second Walther pistol and a grenade.[55]

The attack cost the lives of five people, including Kelemen. Alexander died from a bullet that entered his chest and struck the liver. Police were responsible for several deaths, having "fired haphazardly into the crowd."[56] Madame Durbec, a civilian bystander, died from her injuries soon after the incident. Yolande Farris, a waiter in one of the city's brasseries, succumbed on 11 October. She left behind a mother, two younger brothers, and a nine-month-old child.[57] As for Barthou, the injury to the minister's arm, though serious, was treatable. However, in the chaos of the moment, the minister failed to receive immediate medical care. A constable applied a hasty and inefficient tourniquet to the limb before putting the minister into a taxi to take him to the hospital. The taxi driver moved through the crowd with difficulty and without a police escort. By the time the car reached the hospital, Barthou had lost too much blood to survive.[58]

Detailed accounts of the incident appeared in national newspapers barely twelve hours after the king's death. Several Parisian dailies had dispatched journalists to Marseille to report on the king's arrival. These correspondents, some of whom had witnessed the killing, delivered their stories to Paris via telephone for printing. Editors used the immediacy of this method of reporting to reinforce the presumed authenticity of their own publication's accounts and to scoop their rivals: *L'Echo de Paris* printed Jean-Clair Guyot's description under the headline, "The account of the attack made by our special correspondent who witnessed it."[59] Guyot brought home to readers his proximity to the violence: "In front of me, to my right, I saw quite clearly a man come out of the mass of bystanders who, lined up on the pavement, feted the monarch....I saw a colonel, the one escorting the royal car, hit [the man] from up on his horse, with great saber blows....I saw officers fire revolver shots in reply....I saw people on the ground who, wounded, were bleeding."[60] Guyot reported that he ran toward the car and witnessed the last moments of the king's life. He added that so close was he to the ailing monarch that a Yugoslav guard punched him full in the chest to move him away from the scene.[61]

Images of the attack appeared throughout the local and national press. News of terrorist violence has long spread via the medium of images. At the close of the nineteenth century, the nascent picture press helped to construct popular imaginings of terrorism. The illustrated supplement to *Le Petit Journal* had printed vivid and terrifying drawings of the anarchist attacks of the 1890s, notably Auguste Vaillant's nail bomb attack in the Chamber of Deputies on 9 December 1893.[62] The following year, the assassination of French president Sadi Carnot saw the supplement picture the moment of the fatal stabbing, the red of the president's bloodied sash the only flash of color in an otherwise somber scene.⁶³ Among the most striking of the pictures from Marseille in 1934 was a photograph of the moment of the assassination itself, with Kelemen on the running board of the limousine as driver Paul Foissac turned to tackle him (Figure 6). This photograph, taken at 4:20 p.m. on 9 October, appeared in the 5 a.m. morning editions of the Parisian press the following day.⁶⁴ The astonishing speed of its publication lay in the ability to wire a photograph via the telephone line to printers in Paris. The front page of *Paris-Soir*'s 10 October 1934 special edition carried a large image of the dead king, slumped in the rear seat of the limousine. The legend below the image read, "From our special correspondent transmitted from Marseille to Paris-Soir by Belinograph [wire photo] and received by our services forty-six minutes after the attack."⁶⁵ The back page of the newspaper contained further Belinograph images, including one of Kelemen on the car and another of the assassin as he lay stricken on the pavement.⁶⁶ *Paris-Soir* printed one million copies of its 10 October special edition.⁶⁷ In the competitive newspaper market of the 1930s, immediacy was the watchword.

A newsreel film of the attack—the first of a terrorist assassination in history—allowed cinema audiences around the world to experience the horror of the Marseille crowd. Cinema had long re-created acts of terrorism after the fact: French director Ferdinand Zecca's short *L'Assassinat du Président McKinley* appeared in 1902, while Lucien Nonguet produced films of the assassinations of Serbian royals King Aleksandar Obrenović and Queen Draga, Russian minister Plehve, and Grand Duke Serge in 1903, 1904, and 1905, respectively. While these films were artistic reconstructions, cinema listings blurred fact and fiction for they did not distinguish between these "historical" films and the popular "Actualités" (news) showings.⁶⁸

In 1934, audiences could view events as they had happened. Fox-Movietone had dispatched camera operators Georges and Raymond Méjat to Marseille to film the king's visit. The Méjats's film runs from the docking of the Dubrovnik to the scenes of chaos after the killing. Thanks to a hand-operated camera (and relatively lax policing), Georges was able to closely approach the king, capturing the monarch in conversation with Barthou in the rear seat of the Delage. Georges failed to film the moment of the attack itself—he was changing the lens on his handheld camera—yet he captured the lynching of Kelemen and the final agony of the dying Alexander in the rear seat of the Delage. A sound recording of the frenzied

Figure 6. The moment of the attack in Marseille, 9 October 1934. The assassin (center) is on the running board as the driver turns to tackle him. Source: commons.wikimedia.org

screams of the crowd (made thanks to the use of a new sound recording van sent from Paris) amplified the horror of the images. Fox edited the film, added an English-language commentary by broadcaster Lowell Thomas, and distributed it around the world. The footage also featured in an English-language Universal newsreel, with commentary from American radio broadcaster Graham McNamee, and newsreels from Pathé and British Movietone.[69]

Audio narration of the newsreel interpreted the content of the Méjats's images. It served to frame the attack for audiences, acting as another means to construct the meaning of the incident in public minds. Information included in these commentaries was not always reliable. The Fox-Movietone narrator relayed to viewers that the assassin was "a Croat terrorist"; Kelemen was in fact from Bulgarian Macedonia.[70] Commentators used hyperbole and melodrama to dramatize the footage. Universal's McNamee described the images as "the most amazing pictures ever made" as the camera captured the king on his "fateful ride, the ride of death."[71] The commentary for the British Pathé Gazette, though more somber than that of Universal, nevertheless described the attack thus: "Suddenly the Croat murderer sprang from the crowds to the running board and poured a hail of lead into its two occupants."[72] The clamor of the crowds in British Movietone's footage (presented without a musical score, unlike the Universal and Pathé films) provided the drama as cries of "Vive le roi" turned to screams of anguish.[73] For some viewers, no amount of narration could explain the event. Author and journalist Rebecca West dwelt on the newsreel in her celebrated 1941 travelogue *Black Lamb and Grey Falcon*. Despite watching the newsreel repeatedly, West recalled, "I could not understand the event, no matter how often I saw this picture."[74] Other viewers were revolted that the French camera operator had continued to film the king as he drew his final breath.[75]

Beyond its function to inform and entertain, the film served as evidence in the police investigation. In this respect, the newsreel was highly embarrassing for the French authorities. In the days following the killings, French police leaders in Paris and Marseille came under fire for the apparent ease with which the assassin had reached the king.[76] The authorities had stationed constables along the route at intervals of six meters, leaving room for an attacker to break through. Polish consular officer Jan Meysztowicz noted that these officers faced the car rather than watching the crowd for potential troublemakers.[77] Some viewers of the film were "struck cold with horror" at the inadequacy of the security arrangements.[78] *Le Matin* was damning in its assessment of French security pictured in the film: "No etiquette, no organization, scruffy and lacking control, an insufficient or too permissive security force."[79] In the tense political climate, police suspected that some right-wing leagues could take advantage of the general tumult after the killing to attack the police and the minister of the interior for their failure to safeguard Alexander.[80] The government banned the newsreel on 10 October, fearing that the images would expose to audiences the deficiencies in police organization on the day of the attack. The ban on the film was lifted within days, yet this did little to allay suspicions of a conspiracy in government: were the security measures on the day attributable to incompetence or design?[81] Ultimately, propagation of the images and the film of the attack proved a salutary experience for the French authorities. In 1935, the government instructed that, during official visits by foreign dignitaries, all journalists and camera operators were to be held at two hundred and fifty meters from the head of the procession to "better control their location and their activity." Moreover, these steps would help to avoid the "untimely release of 'inappropriate' images" via the media.[82]

Immediate public responses to the attack, as reported in the national and local publications, included shock and great sorrow. In Paris, the "anguished" crowd sought news of the event, women cried, and those who could lay their hands on a newspaper moaned, "It's awful! It's awful!" There was anger against "foreigners who come, weapons in hand, to violate our laws of hospitality."[83] In Marseille, the crowd was stupefied as news of the incident spread. People invaded the street to spread the word while businesses closed early as employees left their posts.[84] Prefectural reports hinted at a diverse response to the tragedy.[85] In departments such as the Aisne and the Calvados news of the attack prompted some nervousness yet there was also calmness in places such as the Basses-Alpes.[86] The assassination left the citizens of Belfort much moved. Memories of a visit to the city by Yugoslavian veterans in 1931 were still fresh, and local ex-servicemen laid a wreath at the town's war memorial in honor of the dead king.[87] Several prefects noted a hardening of public sentiment against foreigners. In the Marne, the prefect reported that people criticized "the ease with which foreigners penetrate France" to take advantage of native hospitality and settle their political scores.[88] In sum, however, prefectural reports that included comment on reaction to the Marseille attack were rare. The continuing financial crisis, the approach of winter, and the death of wartime president Raymond Poincaré on 15 October 1934 preoccupied the French.[89]

The deaths of Alexander and Barthou stunned France and the world. The attack threatened to undermine the European system of states and threw into question the continued viability of France's eastern alliances as well as its nascent relationship with Mussolini. The immediacy with which pictures of the killing appeared in newspapers and movie theaters signaled that terrorism had entered a new media age. Shocking photographs and eyewitness testimony brought terrorism into homes, into cafes, and onto street corners in locations far from Marseille. Newsreels and their accompanying commentaries mediatized terrorism in novel ways: sound and moving pictures combined to amplify the horror of the event while narration helped to condition understandings of terrorism and the apparent inability of the police to prevent it. Some quarters expressed concern about the international response to the newsreels. *Paris-Soir* reported that Londoners had responded with "stupor" to the images and that the failure of the French police had "deeply shocked" English public opinion. The newspaper feared that at a time when the peace of the world depended on Franco-British friendship, the images of French "carelessness...will be etched for a long time in the [British] memory."[90]

The Hunt for the Regicides

Who was the assassin? Press reports immediately after the incident attributed a variety of motives and identities to Kelemen. He was a "Macedonian terrorist,"[91] a persecuted Croat,[92] a *comitadji*,[93] a Soviet agent,[94] an anarchist,[95] and a "Yugoslav fanatic."[96] Petrus Kelemen was not the killer's real name. Investigators soon discovered that his passport was a fake, and Prague confirmed that it had not issued papers in the name of Kelemen. In any case, the document contained several spelling errors.[97] The supply of forged passports was a lucrative business in interwar Europe, not least in France where documents sold for at least three hundred francs. Danish, Swiss, and Austrian passports were most in demand and could earn a forger five thousand francs.[98] To determine the origin of the assailant, French police sent Kelemen's passport photograph to police forces abroad and they used radio transmitters to share information with their foreign counterparts.[99] International collaboration took place on French soil: Yugoslav police official Vladeta Milicević assisted chief inspector Antoine Mondanel of the Police Judiciaire, notably in the interrogation of suspects.[100] The French authorities also combed the foreign press for clues as to the identity of the killer and the motive behind the act.[101]

On 15 October 1934, Bulgarian Legation counsellor Kiroff notified French police of the results of Sofia's investigation into the assassin. The Croatian "Petrus Kelemen" was in fact thirty-seven-year-old Serbian-Macedonian fugitive Vlado Chernozemski. (Further police work later revealed that "Chernozemski" was in fact Veličko Kerin, born in Kamenitsa, Bulgaria, yet he was better known in France by his assumed name).[102] Chernozemski went by the soubriquet "the Chauffeur," so-called for he was the driver of IMRO chief Ivan Mihailov.[103] A member of the IMRO since 1922, he established himself as one of the group's most reliable killers, assassinating Bulgarian deputy Dimo Hadji Dimoff, in 1924, and nationalist dissident Naoum Tomalevsky, in 1931. Imprisoned for the death of Dimoff, Chernozemski walked free on 14 January 1932 thanks to a judicial amnesty. He subsequently left Bulgaria in July that year, sent by the IMRO to act as an "instructor of terrorist gangs" in Pavelić's Croatian Ustashe (Figure 7).[104]

The Ustashe emerged in 1931 within the context of Croatian opposition to the Yugoslav dictatorship.[105] In 1929, Alexander embarked on a project to mold the Serbian, Croatian, and Slovenian peoples into a unified Yugo-

Figure 7. Ustashe fighters at a training camp, likely in Italy. Vlado Chernozemski is in the center. Source: commons.wikimedia.org

slav nation. The plan entailed the end of democracy in the kingdom. The king suspended the Belgrade parliament, banned political parties, and expanded hugely the repressive apparatus of the state. A raft of security laws targeted antistate agitation, terrorism, and ethnic "tribal" dissenters.[106] Alexander had hoped that his visit to France in October 1934 would help to legitimize further his regime in the court of international public opinion. The French left had long criticized the "Belgrade fascist government."[107] Indeed, before the identity of the assassin emerged, communist newspaper *L'Humanité* displayed sympathy for the regicide who had simply killed another bloody dictator.[108]

Pavelić's doctrine—Ustástvo—sought to establish an independent Croatian state, informed by hardline Catholic and anticommunist nationalism. By the early 1930s, the Ustashe had recruited up to two thousand members; a number of these operatives inhabited training camps in Hungary and Italy. During 1932, Pavelić launched a terrorist campaign of "open revolution" against Yugoslavia with an attack on a police outpost in Brusani. The Ustashe made no bones about its desire to kill Alexander. A series of bloodthirsty articles, penned by Pavelić, threatened the king's life.[109]

In mid-September 1934, Chernozemski traveled to Zurich, where he met Pavelić's right-hand man, Eugen Kramer (also known as Eugen Dido Kvaternick). Kramer and Chernozemski (the latter now going by the name of Suk) arranged to meet three Ustashe agents at the city train station. These men were Mijo Kralj, Ivan Rajić, and Zvonimir Pospišil. They had journeyed to Switzerland from a Ustashe training camp called Janka-Puszta in the Zala borderland of Hungary.[110] On 28 September 1934, the five men took a train to Lausanne, where Kramer distributed Czech passports in preparation for the group's journey to France. Kralj received papers in the name of "Malny" and "Willinger"; Rajić in the names of "Beneš" and "Sever"; and Pospišil in the names of "Novak" and "Ungar."[111] Kramer did not reveal the purpose of their mission. To avoid identity checks—and to cover their tracks—the gang of conspirators took a boat across Lake Geneva. Three of the party disembarked at Evian while two entered France at Thonon-les-Bains. The men subsequently traveled to Paris via train and bus.[112]

On 5 October 1934, the men reunited in a café near Paris's Saint-Lazare station. It was here that Kramer revealed the plan to assassinate the king. He instructed Chernozemski and Kralj to travel to Marseille, where the former would kill Alexander; the latter was to remain in the crowd to make a second attempt if Chernozemski failed. Pospišil and Rajić were to remain in Paris. If the king survived his visit to Marseille, these two men would try to kill him once he arrived in the French capital. On 6 October, Kramer, Chernozemski, and Kralj took a train to Avignon, sixty miles northwest of Marseille. Police in the port had begun to round up suspect individuals in preparation for the royal event. A stay in Avignon thus allowed the men to avoid identity checks at the railway station in Marseille. The following day, the trio went to Aix-en-Provence, where they met Maria Voudracek. Voudracek delivered to the men two suitcases packed with weapons. Voudracek and Kramer subsequently left France for Switzerland; Chernozemski and Kralj went to Marseille to plan the attack.[113]

Following the assassination, the hunt for the regicides was short. Pospišil and Rajić fell into police hands at Thonon-les-Bains on 11 October 1934. The two men had returned to the town by train to cross the border. Their inability to speak French raised the suspicions of locals who soon notified the police.[114] Kralj traveled to Fontainebleau via Aix, Avignon, and Paris. When gendarmes questioned him at the town's railway station—because of his "very strong foreign accent"—Kralj panicked and fled into the nearby woods. On 15 October, the fugitive Kralj reappeared at a café in Melun, doubtless desperate for sustenance having gone several days without food and water. His disheveled look and an unusually large tip he left on the bar roused the suspicion of customers, and the police were called.[115] On 19 October 1934, Italian police took Pavelić and Kramer into custody in Turin following a personal request from Mondanel to fascist police chief Arturo Bochini.[116] French inspector Royère traveled to the Italian city to interview the pair, yet fascist officials prevented him from conducting an interrogation. Mussolini would later prohibit the Croatians' extradition.[117] Police located a third conspirator, Ivan Perčević, in Austria. Like Rome, Vienna refused an extradition request.[118] Nevertheless, ten days after the attack, most of the terrorist gang that had operated in France was behind bars. Only Voudracek and Kramer at large.

In preparing the case against Kralj, Rajić, and Pospišil, French prosecutors faced a legal quandary. According to Third Republican law, terrorism was not a crime nor was it an offence to belong to a terrorist organization.[119] Such a situation owed something to the fact that the French anti-anarchist laws of the 1890s did not specifically target terrorism (though the two phenomena were often conflated). This lacuna existed in international law, too. In 1930, the AIDP named terrorism a "universal danger," defined as "crimes and offences [against] the rights of people" that required a "joint struggle on behalf of the civilized community against criminality."[120] This decision marked the first time that the term had appeared in an international legal text. At Copenhagen in 1935, in direct response to the Marseille murders, the AIDP decided that terrorism encompassed "acts having caused a common danger or a state of terror." The body subsequently compiled a list of apparently disparate terrorist offences without reference to the social and political motives behind these crimes. The list testified to the continued debate within the international legal community over the meaning of terrorism.[121]

The trial of Kralj, Rajić, and Pospišil opened on 19 November 1935 at the assizes court of Aix-en-Provence. Media attention was intense. Police reported that ninety-seven journalists attended, with the majority from foreign media outlets.[122] The French telecommunications service, the PTT, installed telephone booths at the courthouse in order that foreign reporters could relay the news home.[123] The court charged the three conspirators with criminal association (*association de malfaiteurs*). Pavelić, Kramer, and Perčević stood trial in absentia for planning the crime and inciting others to commit it.[124] Lawyer Georges Desbons took charge of the six men's defense.[125] Desbons hoped to shed light on the abuses of the Yugoslav regime and expose the royal dictatorship and its French ally to international public opinion; the French government considered him the mouthpiece of the Ustashe.[126]

Controversy struck on the second day of the trial. Following a series of violent rows with public prosecutor Paul Rol and court president Jean de La Broise, the court expelled and disbarred Desbons. The defense lawyer was removed forcibly from the room in the only incident of its kind in interwar France. It is likely that Rol and La Broise wanted to avoid a politicization of proceedings and the embarrassment for France that this would entail. Desbons in turn accused the court of conspiring with the French and Yugoslav governments to have him expelled. The defendants immediately declared a hunger strike and the trial was abandoned.[127]

A second trial opened on 5 February 1936. Emile de Saint-Auban now led a team of lawyers for the defense. François Loison replaced court president La Broise, in a move that perhaps responded to condemnations from across the political spectrum of La Broise's decision to evict Desbons from the earlier proceedings.[128] This second hearing witnessed neither the public trial of the Yugoslav regime nor that of international fascism. The defense refrained from defending the Ustashe's cause while the prosecution mentioned no foreign powers in its arguments.[129] Kralj, Rajić, and Pospišil received sentences of life imprisonment. The court sentenced Pavelić, Kramer, and Perčević to death, yet the three remained beyond the reach of French justice.

Terrorism Imagined

Analysis of the extensive media coverage in the wake of the Marseille assassinations permits the reconstruction of popular perceptions of terrorism. National and local newspapers scrutinized closely the attack, its perpetrator and his accomplices, and the Ustashe. Doubtless thanks to sources within the police force, much information appeared in print about the itinerary of the terrorists prior to their arrival in France, their criminal pasts, and the content of their confessions. Publications supplemented this information with historical accounts of Balkan terrorism, retrospectives on past regicides and incidents of political violence, and no small amount of speculation. Images and artistic depictions of terrorists in the press and popular true crime magazines such as *Détective* and *Police-Magazine* further helped to construct and reveal a culture of terrorism.

FANATICS AND *Femmes Fatales*

The violence of the attack was framed as outrageous and unprecedented. Chernozemski had committed a crime "of which the savagery surpasse[d] the limits of human things."[130] The assassinations represented nothing less than a "disaster" for France, while for the city of Marseille, 9 October 1934 marked the "blackest page in the annals" of the city.[131] As for La Canebière, Marseille's most famous highway was "bloodied for all time."[132] Beyond the French context, the potential consequences of the incident were catastrophic. The murders presented a "grave threat to our whole civilization."[133]

If the police had received much criticism for their failure in Marseille, the terrorists had nevertheless planned the attack in frightening detail, demonstrating a level of sophistication that had undone all preventive measures. The assassination was the result of a "carefully organized plot,"[134] a "vast plot long in the planning and meticulously organized,"[135] and "the outcome of a meticulously prepared project"[136] implemented after "a study that rested on the tiniest of details"[137] by men who "knew well… the weak points of the security network."[138] The planners and perpetrators of the crime were "disciplined and resolute agitators,"[139] "resolute and cold fanatics,"[140] blindly obedient and ready to die for their cause,[141] and "conspirators of death."[142] Rumored sightings of terrorists filled the press throughout October. The conservative *Le Petit Journal* noted, "During the war, we saw spies everywhere. Now, it's terrorists…that witnesses of good faith imagine having seen at the time of the attack in the most diverse of places."[143] Anxiety about the ability of such men to escape justice was high.

The power of the IMRO and the Ustashe, and the strength of their ideological commitment, knew no bounds. The Ustashe was "a veritable terrorist association, that would stop at nothing to reach its abominable goal,"[144] and "a vast international terrorist group."[145] Terrorist agents operated in the shadows, dealing death like "a kind of holy vehme or Croatian or Macedonian camorra,"[146] "an army of crime"[147] planning new terrorist outrages.[148] At its head was a "supreme organizer" and a "mastermind,"[149] and behind him, a "mysterious power designating victims."[150] This shadowy master would not rest until the entire international system lay in ruins. Author Krsta S. Chantitch Chandan warned that "a dark power is striving, with a tenacity worthy of the highest cause, to cloud international politics with terror."[151] Chandan located these "dark powers" in the residences of foreign leaders, where dictators "scientifically and methodically" developed terrorism to serve foreign policy goals. Without firm international action, Chandan warned, the world would collapse "into the barbarism of the Middle Ages."[152] In 1934, the novelty of representations did not lie in their depictions of terrorism as an international force for evil. Rather, the use of international terrorism in the service of ideological political strategies seemed new.

Among the terrorist conspirators, the figure (both literally and figuratively) of Maria Voudracek proved an object of special fascination for the press. Journalists depicted her differently from the other Ustashe operatives. While they emphasized the resolute and fanatical commitment of the male conspirators, they most often described Voudracek as "mysterious"[153] and "enigmatic," if not the "most enigmatic" of all the plotters.[154] Her status as a fugitive added to the mystery around her, and numerous sightings of the blonde woman appeared in the press in the weeks after the assassination.[155] While police were soon able to reveal that she had transported the weapons for the group, newspapers speculated about her past with the terrorist group. *Excelsior*, for example, reprinted a story from Yugoslavian newspaper *Vreme* that (wrongly) revealed the "mysterious blonde" to be Dora Frank, a relation of Eugen Kvaternik, who worked as a courier between Croatian and Macedonian extremist groups.[156]

Voudracek's physical appearance featured in many reports: she was "this beautiful Slav woman with golden chestnut hair,"[157] "a great beauty, very elegantly dressed"[158] "with a statuesque look,"[159] "elegant and pretty,"[160] and "remarkably beautiful."[161] Such emphasis rested on her looks that newspapers sometimes simply referred to Voudracek as "the blonde." She wore elegant clothes and carried "luxurious suitcases," in which she concealed an arsenal under her "delicate linen" and "finely made clothes."[162] Commentators devoted little attention to the physique of her male accomplices. Rare comments on the body of Chernozemski revealed that he was "of large build" and "very muscular."[163] Yet in contrast to the case of Gorguloff two years previous, newspapers commented on neither the facial features nor the physical prowess of the Marseille assassin.

Was Voudracek's role in the attack limited to smuggling weapons? Jacques Klein speculated on this subject in *Le Petit Journal*. Klein mused that perhaps her role was to "galvanize the energies" of the men, to get them "fired up" (*gonfler à bloc*) before they sacrificed their lives. Such innuendo implied sexual relations between Voudracek and the men, an insinuation detectable in other newspapers: *Le Populaire* described her "mischievous look";[164] and *Le Petit Provençal* suggested she was both "inspiration" and "comforter" to the men around her.[165] Klein claimed that all secret organizations made use of beautiful women to carry information and oversee male underlings. On this latter point, Klein wondered if Voudracek was not in fact the "true leader of the expedition."[166] Similar speculation appeared elsewhere in the press. *L'Oeuvre* reported that this woman appeared to be the group's commander.[167] The newspaper in fact called Voudracek "the inevitable 'femme fatale'" involved in all such plots.[168] Casting an eye over the history of terrorism, Jean Lecoq's retrospective on terrorism for *Le Petit Journal illustré* noted that a woman often lay behind the nihilist attacks of Tsarist Russia.[169]

Interest in Voudracek continued after police ended their search for her in late 1935.[170] During February 1936, *Paris-Soir* ran a series of articles in which the newspaper claimed to have finally discovered the identity of the blonde. The source of the revelations, the newspaper claimed, was none other than a novel penned by Pavelić himself. In the story, the Ustashe chief describes a woman who went by the name of "sister Tuga," better known to her comrades as "the blonde Madonna." The Madonna was "sensitive, eager and impressively beautiful," and the charm of this "blonde bombshell" deflected all suspicion; she was thus the perfect shield for the king's assassins. Yet behind the beauty of this woman, seemingly armed only with a smile, lay "a commander of executions by revolver and bomb." In the novel, the Madonna accompanies an assassin to the center of Marseille. She escapes the scene of the crime in a car and manages to cross the border to Italy at Vintimille only to be later killed in an exchange of gunfire with a carabineer.[171]

Chief inspector Mondanel's memoir of the attack revealed the blonde to be US-born Croatian Stana Godina, who, with her husband, Antun, had helped Pavelić smuggle the weapons into France.[172] Inspector Conti of the Italian fascist police came to the same conclusion.[173] French interest in Voudracek indicated that as in the twenty-first century, women were the "unusual suspects" of the terrorist underworld.[174]

FASCISTS AND FOREIGNERS

Alongside the representation of the attack through an international lens, French political factions applied domestic agendas to their analysis. The Socialist Party, in an antifascist alliance with the Communist Party since summer 1934, saw the hand of international fascism behind the attack: "The bullets that bloodied Marseille...are of fascist origin."[175] Indeed, in March 1934, the party had reported on the financial links between Pavelić, his "Oestacha," and the government in Rome.[176] The party used the killing of the king to highlight the danger from *French* fascism, too. A cartoon on the front page of *Le Populaire* titled "The vultures" depicted three extreme right-wing leaguers on a hillside overlooking Marseille. One leaguer tells his comrades, "Well! The body of a swindler [Stavisky] gave us the *six février*...So...a king and a minister, that'll bring a higher return!"[177] The *six février* was important in communist interpretations of the assassination, too. Assistant editor of *L'Humanité* Pierre-Laurent Darnar described the twin goals of fascism as the destruction of international peace abroad and the staging of a "new *six février*" at home.[178] He underscored the kinship between the foreign and domestic extreme right when he noted the striking similarity between the skull and crossbones emblem of the Ustashe and the death's head insignia of Lieutenant Colonel François de La Rocque's extreme right-wing Croix de Feu.[179]

Initially the right attempted to link the terrorists to the extreme left.[180] However, once police revealed that the ultranationalist Ustashe lay behind the violence, conservative and far right commentators opted for silence on the political motivations of the attackers. Instead, the killing revivified right-wing demands for a tougher policy on immigration.[181] On 15 October 1934, the right-wing *Le Matin*'s masthead proclaimed, "Land of Decent People, France Must Not Give Asylum to Undesirables."[182] The following day, the newspaper demanded, "The border must be closed to foreign vermin" and "all the unnamable scum that has rained down on France."[183] Marcel Lucain of *Paris-Midi* lamented the fact that police incompetence had made France the "arena of political murder, of abuse and attacks, where the dregs from abroad, sheltered and protected, provided for by benefits and fed with our labor, believe that anything goes."[184] In the extreme right-wing *Je suis partout*, Pierre Gaxotte warned that in France, fanatics such as Chernozemski were legion; they were asylum-seeking so-called "victims of fascism," the "hooligans, the stateless, criminals, specialists in pimping, spies, international swindlers, cocaine dealers, profiteers of revolution [and] looters of shops."[185] In a similar vein, the extreme right-wing Solidarité Française league launched a savage attack on the "unscrupulous wogs, Jews, revolutionaries chased out of Germany, and all the international scum that sullies the soil of France." Its leader, Jean Renaud, warned that the assassination of the king was the signal for a larger wave of terrorism.[186] Such xenophobia was common throughout the press.[187] Even France's sober conservative paper of record, *Le Temps*, lamented the fact that, following the Doumer killing in 1932, "another foreigner" had come to France to commit murder once again.[188]

Did the press campaign about immigration prompt the government to act? On the surface, parliamentary debate about immigration did not stray from economic matters in the wake of October 1934.[189] During November 1934's discussion of the national budget, deputies raised long-held concerns about the impact of foreign labor upon the French job market. When the debate turned to the alleged foreign exploitation of French "hospitality," deputies focused less on the exploits of enemy agents than on restricting the provision of health care, university scholarships, and primary school places for non-French inhabitants.[190] The decree of 6 February 1935 that rendered more stringent the rules on the granting of identification cards was likewise pitched as a means to eliminate foreign labor rather than shore up national security.[191] Mary Dewhurst Lewis therefore generally refrains from attributing changes in the immigration regime to the October 1934 killings.[192]

However, deputies and ministers *frequently* couched xenophobic arguments in terms of "rational" economics. As France accepted refugees from Germany after 1933, protectionist legislation served to assuage working- and middle-class concerns about the impact of foreign labor, foreign professionals, and foreign entrepreneurs on native businesses, as well as to deter, if not root out, the "Trojan Horse of spies and subversives" (as Edouard Daladier termed asylum-seeking immigrants).[193] Furthermore, Vicki Caron argues that Minister of the Interior Paul Marcheandeau "used the Marseille incident primarily as a pretext to crack down further" on immigrant labor.[194] Severe police repression of immigrants followed the October 1934 murders. Officers submitted forty-one thousand reports on suspect foreigners.[195] Constables raided immigrant districts in French cities, manhandling anyone whose papers were not in order. The number of expulsion orders rocketed while the authorities acted with greater assiduity in their application.[196] By 1935, foreign emigration outpaced foreign immigration.[197] If there was no explicit link between the assassination of Alexander and the government's subsequent action on immigration, the killing nevertheless exacerbated existing tensions about the immigrant "invasion" of France.

AN OFFICIAL CONSPIRACY

The climate of anti-Republicanism in France fostered suspicions of police and ministerial involvement in the assassination. During 1934, worries about police corruption had seen fears of conspiracy in government reach fever pitch. Similar concerns emerged when rumors that the police had received warnings of the Ustashe operation began to circulate. Between May and October 1934, the Yugoslav police had in fact warned Paris three times about threats to the king's life during his planned visit.[198] The French press drew particular attention to the case of a certain Nihomir Nalis, a Yugoslav who had arrived in France in early October 1934 with the intention of killing King Alexander. The publication of a police circular, dated 6 October 1934, requesting that officers search "very actively" for Nalis seemed to confirm suspicions that the police "knew" what was about to happen.[199] Press reports insinuating that Nalis was in fact either Rajić or Kralj added to a sense of outrage that Minister of the Interior Albert Sarraut's reassurances ("We knew nothing, we were not forewarned") could not dispel.[200] Newspapers *did not* report that the municipal police in Menton had apprehended Nalis on 6 October 1934 and deported him to Italy immediately.[201]

The allegedly poor security arrangements for the king's visit fueled further distrust. The press quoted a high Yugoslav official's incredulity that the king should have docked in Marseille, a city known as a "wasps' nest" and a den of scoundrels.[202] Editor of the *Sémaphore de Marseille* Paul Barlatier agreed: Marseille was "one of the most dangerous ports in the country," through which 90 percent of France's suspect individuals passed.[203] Barlatier's counterpart at *Le Petit Marseillais*, Léon Bancal, further remarked that the visit had fallen during the city's cantonal elections when police forces were stretched thinly.[204] However, the Marseille press generally pointed the finger of blame at Paris, especially when it came to light that an official at the Sûreté Nationale in the capital had canceled at the last minute an order for a detachment of police cyclists to ride alongside the Delage (this report appeared in the national press, too).[205] Allegations of conspiracy were not long in coming. The Communist Party noted a troubling comparison between the failure to protect Alexander and Barthou in 1934 and President Doumer in 1932. The latter had also died at the hands of a "fascist" who had encountered little difficulty in committing his crime.[206] The extreme right-wing *Je suis partout* likewise perceived an official conspiracy behind the attack. The cartoon on the front page of the newspaper's 3 November edition depicted two French gazing through a shop window at three funeral wreaths bearing the names of Alexander and Barthou. "This must be the florist of the Sûreté Générale," one man remarked to the other.[207]

Within days of the attack, the government fell into crisis. Both Sarraut and Minister of Justice Henry Chéron resigned from office.[208] The resignations came at a time of high popular hostility to the French regime. The government of Gaston Doumergue had assumed power in February 1934 following the violent protests in Paris. The appointment of Doumergue—a conservative—did little to appease critics of the Republic. The membership of extreme right-wing anti-Republican leagues such as the Croix de Feu subsequently rocketed. Politics moved increasingly to the street—violent clashes were frequent during 1934–37—as more French lost faith in the apparently moribund regime. The attack in Marseille provided another stick with which to beat the Republic. The right-wing *Le Matin* noted how the murders had exposed the shabbiness of a democracy that could not protect official guests on its own soil.[209] Charles Maurras, leader of the antisemitic and monarchist Action Française, alleged a conspiracy between the terrorists, the security services, and Republican politicians.[210] The resignations of Sarraut and Chéron did little to appease critics. On the one hand, socialist leader Blum denounced the resignations as a victory for French fascists who had long demanded the heads of each minister.[211] On the other hand, *Police-Magazine* noted acerbically that Sarraut and Chéron would soon take up once again a ministerial portfolio. The magazine asked why, instead, they should not face trial in a High Court to answer charges of dereliction of duty.[212]

Doumergue's cabinet fell on 8 November 1934, barely a month after the attack. Pierre-Etienne Flandin became prime minister. It is an exaggeration to attribute the dissolution of the Doumergue government to the events of 9 October 1934.[213] Support for Doumergue had waned since February as the premier prevaricated over plans to revise the constitution. He resigned when, in early November 1934, leading Radicals rejected his plans for reform.[214] Nevertheless, the assassination was a huge embarrassment for an increasingly unpopular government.

PROFESSIONAL TERRORISTS

There was some familiarity with Balkan terrorism in France prior to 1934. In 1932, famed investigative journalist Albert Londres published *Les comitadjis ou le terrorisme dans les Balkans*. The book took as its focus the *comitadjis* of the IMRO—the "den of terrorists," according to Londres.[215] The author's aim was to expose to the reader the existence of "a revolutionary organization stronger than the State."[216] On 10 October 1934, some newspapers in fact described "Kelemen" and his accomplices as *comitadjis*.[217] The following day, *Paris-Midi* included an image of the *comitadjis* on its front page, under a quotation from Londres's book: "[These are] the hands in which one puts revolvers."[218] These stories suggest that readers at least recognized the word, even if we cannot be certain that they understood its meaning.

Londres painted a frightening picture of life in Bulgarian Macedonia, the "country of 'Liberty or Death'."[219] He depicted a land in the grip of terrorist master Ivan Mihailov, whose "professors of terrorism" schooled "deferent, attentive, [and] studious pupils" in camps, villages, and towns.[220] Mihailov's aim was to turn these men from mountain-dwelling peasants into modern combatants: Londres described Mihailov as "a modern man who does not like to live in the mountains…clothes-conscious, [he] does not want to tear his trousers."[221] Nevertheless, the IMRO chief was a ruthless killer who "kills those who do not share his opinion."[222] "[Mihailov] is neither mad, nor a crank, nor impulsive," the author continued, "he is a logician. Unable to tolerate obstacles, he gets rid of them."[223] Readers learned of the IMRO's sophisticated training methods, its huge financial resources,[224] and its operation as a state-within-a-state. In the center of Sofia, a labyrinth of streets was under terrorist control. Cafes and restaurants served only IMRO members, while print shops produced propaganda for the organization. A cinema that admitted solely *comitadjis* provided "a training screen for terrorists; a school for the perpetrators of attacks." Londres continued, "The films that are played there are intended to develop in the spectator the taste for firearms: scenes of fusillades, exchanges of fire at ten paces, ambushes."[225] On top of these revelations, Londres warned readers that this terrorist state existed hardly "forty-eight hours by train from the bell towers of the gare de Lyon."[226]

The *comitadjis* returned to French attention in October 1934. Geoffrey Frazer's portrayal of the Balkan terrorists in *Vu* magazine chimed somewhat with Londres's descriptions of the *comitadjis*. The *comitadjis* of old—"a bomb in each pocket, an arsenal on the belt, an unkempt look, bushy moustaches, dragging themselves from hovel to hovel when they [were] not lying in ambush in the wild mountains"—were no more.[227] The modern terrorist was a physically fit, refined gentleman who dressed in elegant sport suits, and who drank fresh orange juice in cafes. (Londres, on the other hand, had described the average *comitadji* fighter as wearing "a cap, a leather waistcoat and, around the calves, strips of wool").[228] Frazer recounted his experience of a meeting with terrorists near Mostar. His terrorist guide—"in brown suit and cream-colored silk shirt"—described the commitment of the contemporary fighter in terms reminiscent of Londres: he was

> a man who has reflected, who is deeply committed to his mission, the liberation of his country. A man ready for anything. A man who has faith and hatred to such a degree that his life has only one goal: the sacrifice that will serve liberation....And when one of [them] falls, there is always someone to step into the breach. Do you know [their] motto? *Liberty or death!* It's generally death. But one day it will be liberty!

Frazer considered such men naïve, romantic warriors in the mold of Goethe's Young Werther and Schiller's Karl Moor, and ripe for exploitation by unscrupulous forces.[229]

A second eyewitness account of life among the Balkan terrorists came to light in France after October 1934. In late 1933, Yugoslavian Jelka Pogorelec published a brochure containing revelations about life in the Ustashe's training camp at Janka-Puszta. Pogorelec had been in a relationship with the Ustashe's Gustav Perčec. She was also an undercover Yugoslav agent. Pogorelec fed information to Belgrade during the eighteen months before fleeing Perčec and writing her memoir.[230] Her story first featured in the Zagreb-based *Novosti* newspaper between 5 and 14 October 1933. It subsequently appeared as a brochure and became widely available in Europe. Pogorelec's exposé appeared to little fanfare in France. However, it received decidedly more attention after the regicide in Marseille and French police possessed a translated version of her work.[231]

Pogorelec exposed the underbelly of terrorist life at Janka-Puszta—the "school for terrorists," according to Yugoslav foreign minister Jevtitch.[232]

On the surface, the camp was a "rustic" and "idyllic" location in which men worked the fields and tended to their animals. However, beneath this calm exterior lay "troubled waters" and "violence."[233] Recruits received instruction in using automatic weapons, supplied by Italy, and bomb making, under the supervision of Hungarian officers.[234] These trainees graduated to commit "fearful crimes against innocent and unknown people, against women and children."[235] Life in the camp was difficult: the men complained that Perčec treated them like a commodity. Virtual prisoners, they were "livestock, to be sold for the highest price possible," fed on meager rations and worked until they dropped.[236] Perčec arranged the executions of his most troublesome followers.[237] The terrorists thus "[sank] in the mud and blood of Yanka Pousta [sic]."[238] Pogorelec also made damaging accusations of collaboration between the terrorists of Janka-Puszta and Hungary and Italy.[239] Perčec and his men were mercenaries in the pay of these "[s]tates who engage individuals across the world to serve for money all their goals even the lowest."[240] The Yugoslav government communicated Pogorelec's findings to Budapest, yet the message received no response. After October 1934, the Hungarian government denied knowledge of the camp, yet it had gradually begun to close such refuges since spring that year.[241]

Pogorelec enjoyed brief notoriety in France as "the terrorist girlfriend." In October 1934, *Le Petit Journal* interviewed "the little Yugoslav dancer" who consorted with regicides. Pogorelec revealed little more to the newspaper than the content of her memoir. However, she did comment on Pospišil and Rajić, whom she knew from her time at Janka-Puszta. These two men, along with Perčec, were the "technicians of Janka Puszta," in charge of the construction of time bombs for use in attacks on trains. For these men, "[t]he manual of the perfect terrorists had nothing to teach them."[242] Pogorelec donated a photograph of herself to the front page of *Le Petit Journal*, autographed and dedicated to the newspaper's readers, a memento from a one-time celebrity terrorist.[243]

Publications on Balkan terrorists before and after 9 October 1934 helped to shape French perceptions of the people who killed Alexander and Barthou. Their depictions of the terrorist fighters were ambiguous. On the one hand, the *comitadjis* resembled peasant farmers and unhappy dupes, forced into terrorism for money and unable to escape. On the other hand, the IMRO and the Ustashe were modern movements of urbane and committed ideologues trained using sophisticated methods and the latest weaponry. They operated thanks to the ignorance (or the connivance) of states that sought to employ these operatives on missions in foreign lands. Regarding Marseille, Yugoslavia alleged that the king's assassins had hatched their plot in "special camps for the execution of acts of this nature." At Janka-Puszta, students of terrorism used images of the king for target practice.[244]

Eyewitness accounts of terrorist life reinforced an image of terrorism as the enterprise of shadowy groups locked in the ideological conflict that afflicted Europe during the 1930s. These groups operated in more than one country, armed with ample financial resources, and it was impossible to know the extent to which they exerted their influence. Male terrorists were cold ideologues, ready to die for the cause. Female terrorists were beautiful and sexually available to the men under their command. The terrorists trained in specialist camps where they learned the science and theory of terrorism. Their goal was to destabilize the international system of states established in 1919. Terrorists were able to operate in France with the complicity of sympathetic political leagues and parties, and even the police and government. At the very least, these domestic sympathizers sought to take advantage of the turmoil created in the aftermath of terrorist outrages to further their own political projects.

Commemorating Marseille

Plans to memorialize the deaths of King Alexander and Barthou began to formulate in Marseille and Paris in the days after the incident. National and local newspapers opened readers' subscription campaigns to accept donations to an as-yet-undecided means of commemoration.[245] Barely a month after the attack, the national Armistice Day focused on the person of the recently assassinated king. The Yugoslav royal standard and the monarch's death mask went on display under the Arc de Triomphe on 10 November for Parisians to visit.[246] The French mint commissioned a souvenir medal, designed by artist André Lavrillier, upon which was engraved an image of Alexander.[247] Exactly two years after the assassination, on 9 October 1936, President Albert Lebrun inaugurated a monument in Paris to King Peter I of Serbia that included a representation of the dead king Alexander.[248] Marseille had not yet erected a monument, and the fact that the capital had stolen a march on the southern port rankled some local politicians.[249]

In Marseille, municipal officials and citizens advanced ideas for commemorative projects. The town council proposed several: renaming the place de la Bourse after the king; naming a street in a new housing development after Barthou; placing effigies of the two men at the Quai des Belges where the king's boat had landed; and siting a commemorative plaque on La Canebière. The final project was the only one to come to fruition.[250] A reader of *Le Petit Marseillais* suggested that the paving stones upon which the king bled be removed and placed in the town's museum as "relics" to which tourists could make a pilgrimage. New flagstones, naming the two men who "fell to the bullets of foreign terrorists," could then be placed on the street. The newspaper endorsed this reader's idea.[251]

Two locations in Marseille now mark the events of October 1934. The commemorative discourse, iconography, and architecture of the Great War lent themselves to both commemorative projects. First, a plaque attached to a lamppost on La Canebière, within sight of the scene of the crime, reads, "Here the valiant King Alexander of Yugoslavia, friend of Marseille and of France, and President Louis Barthou, laid down their lives for peace and liberty…9 October 1934."[252] Elevated on a piece of street furniture, the plaque is barely noticeable to people using the city's busy thoroughfare.[253] Second, an imposing monument sits in the city's sixth arrondissement, near to the departmental prefecture.[254] In the style of a war memorial, it features four women holding bas-relief portraits of Alexander and Barthou. Above the statues is a large shield upon which is inscribed "Pax." An inscription on the base of the monument informs passersby that the king and the minister "fell for peace" (*tombés pour la Paix*). Work on the monument finished in December 1938.[255]

The centrality of "peace" in the text of the plaque and the monument in Marseille served to frame Chernozemski's attack as something more than an act simply intended to reconfigure Balkan politics. Alexander and Barthou had died to save European peace, the very same peace that the terrorists had hoped to destroy. In the wake of the assassinations, no one suggested that the other victims of the attack—Farris and Durbec—receive official recognition, a fact that further underscores the primacy of the perceived international character of the incident over its local impact. Conversely, a plaque dedicated to Chernozemski in his hometown of Kamenitsa, Bulgaria, foregrounds the Balkan context of the assassin's act. Erected in 2005 on the seventy-first anniversary of the attack, the stone carries the following dedication: "Free Macedonia was your ideal. Your sacrifice is our inspiration."[256]

Conclusion

The murders in Marseille on 9 October 1934 stunned the French nation. Monier contends that "[a]mongst all the political murders committed in France between the wars, [the Marseille] attack left its mark the most upon contemporaries and collective memory."[257] The killing of the king was an embarrassment to the government and the French security forces. Inadequate policing, laid bare in Méjat's film, along with rumors that police had expected an attack, pointed to gross incompetence at best, and at worst, conspiracy. The incident sparked a ministerial crisis and, if this predicament did not necessarily cause the fall of the Doumergue government, it did little to improve the prospects of the under-fire prime minister. Several historians have read far broader implications into the loss of Barthou and the consequences that helped tip Europe into war five years later.[258] However, while the killing may have put paid to a nascent alliance between France and Italy and led to a "more conciliatory attitude to the fascist regimes"[259] under Laval's foreign ministry, one cannot draw a straight line from Marseille in 1934 to Poland in 1939.

The events of October 1934 and the subsequent international discussion of terrorism were a landmark in the history of terrorism. On 22 November 1934, Yugoslavia invoked paragraph two of article eleven of the Covenant of the League of Nations to bring before the international body an accusation of Hungarian involvement in the killing of the monarch. Romania and Czechoslovakia supported the move. Yugoslav delegate Jevtitch—who had witnessed first-hand the attack in October 1934—warned that the world stood on the brink of international anarchy and barbarity if crimes like that perpetrated in Marseille went unpunished.[260] Jevtitch set out a number of allegations concerning Hungarian aid to the Ustashe, including the involvement of Hungarian officers at Janka-Puszta.[261] The Yugoslav statement concluded that the Marseille attack was dissimilar to past "isolated and individual [acts of] criminal anarchism."[262] Rather it was an act of a "particularly dangerous form of international criminality" against which "the authorities of a single State are impotent to defend themselves."[263] The Hungarian delegate, Tibor Eckhardt, denied all allegations.[264]

The response of the League disappointed Belgrade. Both France and Britain were keen not to sour relations with Italy. Upon Laval's intervention, the Yugoslav allegations failed to mention Rome's material support for the Ustashe.[265] For the same reason, French pressure later led Queen

Marie to put an end to her civil lawsuit against the terrorists.[266] A League of Nations meeting in December 1934 passed a resolution that left it to the Hungarian regime to investigate the crime itself.[267] The same meeting established a committee of eleven nations—the Committee for the International Repression of Terrorism—to draft a convention; France figured among the nations on the committee.[268] The international community now refocused its energies on a proposed convention on terrorism and a related convention on the establishment of an international criminal court. In the delicately balanced politics of interwar Europe, this outcome embarrassed no one. According to Peter Kovacs, "The basic idea was to say as little as possible about what had been done, and as much as possible about what should be done."[269] Hungary brought the results of its investigation to the League in January 1935. Belgrade made a response in March. In May 1935, the League of Nations, under the impetus of Anthony Eden, removed the matter from its agenda.[270]

Despite this diplomatic fudge, the League of Nations' Convention for the Prevention and Punishment of Terrorism (16 November 1937) was the first international agreement on terrorism.[271] In its first article, the Convention defined "acts of terrorism" as "criminal acts directed against a State and intended or calculated to create a state of terror in the minds of particular persons, or a group of persons or the general public." The article enjoined all states "to refrain from any act designed to encourage terrorist activities directed against another State and to prevent the acts in which such activities take shape."[272]

In two respects, the Convention betrayed the influence of the Marseille murders in contemporary concerns about the terrorist phenomena. First, terrorism was a crime committed regardless of national borders, and it was therefore the responsibility of all states to prosecute and punish its perpetrators. Articles eight, nine, and ten thus dealt with the thorny issue of the extradition of guilty parties. The Convention stated that terrorism was not a political crime from the point of view of extradition treaties. This confirmed previous international efforts to situate terrorism squarely within the jurisdiction of common law.[273] However, if the recourse to extradition failed, the Convention required states to try terrorists in their own territory, regardless of the territory in which they had committed their crime.[274] Second, the Convention understood the principal victims of terrorist violence to be public servants and state property. Article two required signatories to enshrine in criminal law any acts "causing death or grievous bodily harm or loss of liberty" directed against the nationals or national property of all co-signatories, notably heads of state, their families, public functionaries, and state-owned property. Violence directed at members of the public figured fifth on this list.[275] Legal expert Antoine Sottile therefore noted that "a bomb thrown at a bus is not a terrorist act if it is not a service operated by the State."[276] Consequently, article two revealed the understanding of terrorism as a tool of state foreign policy directed principally at the apparatus of an enemy state and not its civilian population.

Twenty states signed the Convention, and ten states signed the associated Convention for the Creation of an International Criminal Court.[277] France agreed to sign the Convention on terrorism with the proviso that the agreement did not apply to its colonies or overseas dependencies. Britain did not sign. Disagreements had longed dogged discussion of the Convention, not least on how best to define the phenomenon itself. Several states even questioned the necessity of specialist domestic and international legislation on terror.[278] In fact, India was the only nation to ratify the text in its domestic legislature.[279] Ultimately, according to Saul, the Convention was useful only in that it diffused international political tensions in the aftermath of the Marseille murders.[280] Yet the Convention also represented the outcome of the first forensic international debate and analysis of terrorism. In this sense it marked a milestone in the history of the phenomenon.[281] The United Nations (UN) brought the matter of terrorism under consideration again only in 1972. Yet in 1972—and in subsequent decades—the UN has encountered the same basic problem faced by the international community in the mid-1930s: how to define terrorism.[282]

In the French context, the representation of terrorism in the wake of the Marseille murders suggested that perceptions of the phenomenon and its perpetrators were changing. In 1932, partisan interests had attempted to construct Doumer's assassination as a crime committed under the direction of Gorguloff's political masters, whether Moscow or the "fascists" Tardieu and Chiappe. Evidence of an international or domestic terrorist conspiracy was not forthcoming, and the charges of terrorism against the Russian assassin in the press generally fell away. In 1934, the details of the crime and its perpetrators enabled the construction of terrorism as an international crime, committed by fanatics who would stop at nothing to destroy the international status quo. The foreignness of attackers inflamed sensitivities about the porousness of the country's borders and the infiltration of enemy agents on French soil. The construction of terrorism as a "foreign" phenomenon, alien to French values, became further entrenched. The rapid apprehension of the suspects likely calmed some immediate concern about the operations of terrorists on French soil. Nevertheless, some voices in the press continued to argue that the truth of the crime had not been fully uncovered: in 1937, *Détective* alleged that the French knew only 10 percent of the truth about the Ustashe network in France.[283] Such suspicions were not unusual in 1937, for a succession of attacks, and the inability of the police to apprehend the perpetrators, pushed the country to the point of a terrorist hysteria.

FIVE

Bombings, Piracy, and Kidnapping

Terrorism in France During 1937

On 5 May 1937, a time bomb detonated in a second-class carriage of the Bordeaux-Marseille express train as it passed between Saint-Martin de Crau and Raphèle-les-Arles. The device immolated railway mechanic and father of two Etienne-Marie Aubert. Five other passengers suffered injuries. The explosion occurred above a wheel of the car on a high-speed section of the track. It was fortunate that the explosion did not derail the entire train, as police suspected was the bomber's intention. Investigators had little idea as to the identity of the bomber, as no person of interest was traveling on the train that morning.[1] With the authorities unable to explain the incident, the local press hypothesized a link between the bombing and the war raging in Spain since the previous summer. In *Le Petit Marseillais*, journalist D. Cristofari claimed that the incident was the latest to worry the south since the outbreak of the Spanish conflict, whose "protagonists come to pursue their fratricidal quarrels on our territory." He recommended that French hospitality to immigrants be "severely curtailed."[2]

France experienced a year of severe violence during 1937. Clashes in the street involving political enemies and the police had resulted in more than a dozen deaths. The deadliest outbreak of violence occurred on 16 March 1937 in the Parisian suburb of Clichy, when an antifascist counterdemonstration against a meeting of the extreme right-wing Parti Social Français (PSF) turned into a riot. Six people, including a police constable, died during fighting.³ The following month, the death of eight-year-old Paul Gignoux in Lyon at the hands of his antifascist peers shocked the nation.⁴ A series of brutal killings further raised tension throughout the country: Russian banker Dimitri Navachine, killed in broad daylight in Paris's Bois de Boulogne on 25 January; bar worker and private detective Laetitia Toureaux, murdered in a Parisian metro carriage on 16 May; and the Italian antifascist brothers Carlo and Nello Roselli, stabbed to death at Bagnoles-de-l'Orne (Orne) on 9 June.⁵ In each case, the attackers remained at large. In French North Africa, colonial governments violently repressed disorder: at Meknès (Morocco) in September 1937 colonial troops killed a dozen inhabitants during a riot.⁶

In the meantime, a series of bombings and attempted bombings troubled France. Small-scale explosions punctuated the year until the autumn. The targets of the attacks in the south of the country, as well as the explosives employed, suggested a link to Spain. The incidents exacerbated the febrile atmosphere in the regions bordering the war-torn Iberian Peninsula, raising fears that France had become an "overspill" zone in the civil war. Had the influx of refugees across the Pyrenean frontier imported terrorist violence to France? The inability of the police to apprehend the perpetrators—the authorities brought just one man to justice in the twelve months between the autumns of 1936 and 1937—indicated a worrying powerlessness to prevent terrorism on French soil.

The most spectacular bombing happened on 11 September, when two devices exploded in the Etoile district of Paris, causing significant material damage and killing two police constables. The culprits were two French men, René Locuty and Léon Macon. Both men were members of the secret extreme right-wing group, the Organisation Secrète d'Action Révolutionnaire Nationale (OSARN), also known as the Comité Secret d'Action Révolutionnaire (CSAR) or the "Cagoule." Eugène Deloncle, a veteran of the 1930s extreme right, directed the Cagoule, while wealthy French business interests bankrolled the organization. Cagoulards carried out missions on French soil for Mussolini's regime, in return for money and weapons (they assassinated the Roselli brothers in exhange for rifles). Members of the group also worked with Franco's nationalist rebels in Spain and, as we will see, France. The French police had long kept the Cagoule under surveillance, yet the authorities were motivated to act only when Deloncle launched an abortive coup on 15 November 1937. In January 1938, Minister of the Interior Marx Dormoy exposed to the French public the frightening scale of this terrorist organization's plot against the Republic.[7] Nonetheless, so thoroughly associated with "unFrenchness" was terrorism at this time that the existence of a *French* terrorist group was difficult to believe, a fact that Deloncle's allies in the right-wing press and political establishment played upon.

A week after the Etoile detonations, reports about a Spanish political operation broke onto the front pages of newspapers. On the night of 18 September, a Francoist commando in Brest, led by military commandant of Irun General Julián Troncoso Sagredo, attempted to steal the Spanish Republican C-2 submarine docked in the French port for repairs. Equipped with firearms and restraints for the crew, the hijackers boarded the craft with the complicity of the C-2's captain. Troncoso offered the sailors a share in a large sum of money to join Franco's nationalist rebels. The operation came to a sudden end when a submariner shot and killed one of Troncoso's men; the Francoist team fled. The subsequent arrest of several of the fugitives, including Troncoso himself, revealed not only the secret activities of a foreign terrorist network in France but also the collaboration of French extreme right-wingers with the Spanish agents.[8] *L'Humanité* subsequently railed against Troncoso, the "agent of Franco and Hitler," and demanded the imprisonment of his alleged "accomplices," leader of the PSF Lieutenant Colonel François de La Rocque and Jacques Doriot, former communist and head of the fascist Parti Populaire Français.[9] After a year of violence and intrigue, on 22 September, Georges Bidault—in 1937, an influential editorialist at *L'Aube*—declared in a column on "dark intrigues" in the country, "We have had enough, more than enough."[10]

On the very day that Bidault made clear his exasperation, Soviet agents kidnapped General Yevgeny Karlovich Miller from a Parisian street. Miller was a White Russian émigré and head of the exiles' Union Générale Militaire Russe. His predecessor in the post, General Alexander Pavlovich Kutepov, was also the victim of a kidnapping in January 1930. Neither Miller nor Kutepov were seen alive again. If the affair of the C-2 in Brest provided the left with ammunition in its propaganda war with the right, right-wingers denounced the "terrorist teams" of the Soviet Guépéou (the GPU) who used France as their "training ground" with the connivance of the French left.[11]

The political civil war that reigned over the country during the 1930s thus subsumed acts of terrorism. Factions bent the facts to suit their own ideologies. On the one hand, Wladimir d'Ormesson reminded readers of *Le Figaro* that, while it was intolerable that Spanish nationalists should operate in France, the Popular Front government had allowed the "comings and goings of revolutionary agents and anarchists" to proceed unchecked.[12] On the other hand, the Communist Party blamed Miller's disappearance on the Gestapo.[13] So important were contemporary political divisions that they provided a lens through which to view terrorism even beyond the borders of France and Europe. Unrest in the British and French empires was attributed to the interference of foreign powers. Italy stood accused of channeling funds via Syria (a French mandate) to anti-British Palestinian terrorists; Damascus itself was a "terrorist recruitment center" for the Arab world.[14] Mussolini ultimately hoped to incite rebellions that would benefit his own plan to control the Mediterranean.[15] Perceived Soviet agitation in French imperial possessions likewise sought to undermine the social order, as communist agents fomented violence throughout colonialist peoples.[16] According to the right-wing *Le Jour*, there was even a special section of Moscow's secret service dedicated to undermining French rule in its colonies.[17] Common to both conspiracy theories was a depiction of colonialist peoples as tools manipulated by foreign terrorist agents for the benefit of European revolutionary projects.

If right and left perceived different enemies behind terrorism in France, each side considered the matter with reference to broader long-established anxieties over the "immigrant problem" and the porosity of French borders. This view continued to make inroads into opinion beyond the extremes.[18] In fact, Bidault's column on 24 September, titled, "Enough Is Enough," called on the government to "terrorize the terrorists" because "[t]he rougher the treatment, the happier the French, and the quieter the foreigner."[19]

This chapter commences with an examination of understandings of the terrorist attacks in France during 1937, specifically those with perceived links to the civil war in Spain. Fears over the terrorist infiltration of France abounded as the left denounced Francoist attacks on Spanish Republicans. Conversely, the right warned that communist and anarchist revolutionaries had crossed the border disguised as refugees and with the connivance of France's own Popular Front government. The frequency of attacks and attempted attacks was concerning. *Détective*'s Montarron depicted an "army of outlaws," exiled to France.[20]

The chapter moves on to examine the culmination of the 1937 wave of terrorism during 11–22 September 1937. Over the course of eleven days, reports of terrorism dominated the press as the Etoile bombings rocked Paris, the existence of the Cagoule emerged in the press, and Spanish and Russian agents executed their operations in Brest and Paris, respectively. This paroxysm of terrorism and its representation in the press entrenched further the notion of terror as "unFrench" in the popular imaginary. Anxieties about immigration, citizenship, and national security combined in calls to combat vigorously the perceived foreign threat from within.

An Army of Outlaws

Between 13 October 1936 and 11 September 1937, police recorded nineteen bombings and attempted bombings in locations throughout France (Table 2). The epicenter of these "acts of terrorism" (as a contemporary source described them) was in the southern region that bordered Spain.[21] The frequency and concentration of terrorist incidents in southern regions indicated to police that there was a connection between each crime. State explosive experts in fact noted significant similarities between the bombs employed at Cerbère (7 March 1937), Perpignan (7 March 1937), Marseille (23 May 1937), Toussus-le-Noble (29 August 1937), and Paris (11 September 1937): all contained TNT.[22] This particular chemical makeup suggested foreign provenance for, as Superintendent Delrieu of the Police Mobile remarked, the fabrication and use of TNT was "very rare" in France yet "certain foreign powers such as Germany and Italy use it"; Superintendent Louis Spotti in Montpellier reached the same conclusion.[23] The internal mechanics of the bombs likewise came from abroad. The time bombs discovered on the banks of the River Têt in Perpignan in March 1937 contained a foreign type of battery and a German brand of alarm clock popular in Spain (details that newspapers revealed to readers).[24] Local investigators concluded that the close resemblance of the chemistry, detonator, and trigger systems of each bomb, as well as the apparent skill of the bomb maker, were evidence of a "mass production" in "specialist workshops" and "foreign military arsenals."[25]

In May 1937, Dr. André Kling of the Parisian Municipal Laboratory drew conclusions similar to those of his provincial counterparts. Kling had received from police several devices discovered in locations around the country. All were disguised as everyday objects such as a petrol can or a tin of

Table 2. "Terrorist attacks" committed in France during 1936–1937.

Date	Location	Incident	Casualties	Judicial outcome (as of 30 September 1937)
13 October 1936	Marseille	Attempted bombing of the Spanish cargo ship Cala Pi	—	Case dismissed
30 December 1936	Marseille	Bombing of a van	—	Case dismissed
2–3 February 1937	Bayonne	Attempted fire-bombing of Spanish ship Maria-Amelin	—	—
7 March 1937	Cerbère	Bombing of a carriage of the Paris–Barcelona train service	—	—
7 March 1937	Perpignan	Bomb found in the courtyard of the Spanish Consulate	—	—
7 March 1937 (discovered on 26 February 1937 and given to the police on 7 March 1937)	Perpignan	Two bombs found on the banks of the River Têt	—	—
8 March 1937	Perpignan	Attempted car-bombing of M. Pierre Fabresse, left-wing activist	—	—
15 March 1937	Montpellier	Bombing of the entrance to the city cathedral	—	—
15 March 1937	Nice	Bombing of M. Arbona's greengrocer shop	—	—
1 April 1937	Villeneuve-les-Maguelonne	Bombing of the town church	—	Case dismissed
1 April 1937	Marseille	Attempted bombing of a berth in the harbor used by Spanish ships	—	Case dismissed
5 May 1937	Saint-Martin de Crau	Bombing of the Bordeaux–Marseille express train	One fatality; five wounded	—

Table 2. "Terrorist attacks" committed in France during 1936–1937 (continued).

Date	Location	Incident	Casualties	Judicial outcome (as of 30 September 1937)
23 May 1937	Marseille	Discovery of explosives on the railway platform from which aid for Spain departed	—	—
24 May 1937	Marseille	Fire-bombing of a supply ship destined for Spain	—	Case dismissed
31 May–1 June 1937	Cerbère	Attempted bombing of the international tunnel between France and Spain	—	Conviction
21 June 1937	Marseille	Bombing near the boat sheds of the Chamber of Commerce	—	Case dismissed
25 August 1937	Villeneuve-sur-Lot	Fire in an aircraft hangar	—	—
28–29 August 1937	Toussus-le-Noble	Fire-bombing of an aircraft hangar	—	—
11 September 1937	Paris	Bombing of the Confédération générale du patronat français and the Union des industries métallurgiques	Two fatalities	—

Note: I designed this table from a dossier on "Attentats terroristes" in AN BB18 6476, undated but compiled after 30 September 1937.

food. None of the bombs contained shrapnel, suggesting that the manufacturer had intended the bombs to demolish rather than to kill and maim. The laboratory subjected the explosives to various tests and experiments to determine their origin. Kling noted that the chemistry and mechanics of the bombs recalled German artisanship.[26] The concerns of French scientists reflected those of their nineteenth-century predecessors: Constance Bantman has shown that during the anarchist scare of the late 1890s, fears focused on the bombers' use of chemistry and modern inventions such as dynamite, exposing fin-de-siècle anxieties about technological and scientific developments.[27] In 1937, news of the sophistication of the *machines infernales* hinted at anxiety about modern war-making capabilities. They betrayed nervousness about the threat of foreign attack in the face of the presumed technological preeminence of France's European neighbors and enemies.

The acts of violence perpetrated in the south suggested a connection to the conflict in Spain. The first incident noted in the police dossier on the terrorist campaign concerned the *Cala Pi*, a Spanish yacht docked at Marseille. At 2:30 a.m. on 13 October 1936, customs officials Jean Pipo and Maurice Thibert glimpsed on the quai de Rive Neuve a small plume of smoke moving slowly along the edge of the jetty. A closer inspection revealed a smoldering Bickford fuse leading to the *Cala Pi*. Pipo and Thibert quickly cut the burning end from the fuse and woke the fourteen men aboard the boat. A search of the rear of the *Cala Pi* uncovered a bomb made from picric acid, cheddite, and dynamite.[28] *Le Matin* reported the "Pyrenean" provenance of the explosives; *Le Petit Marseillais* indicated that the components originated from a factory in the Pyrénées-Orientales department, a fact that suggested a Spanish presence in France.[29] The Socialist Party therefore denounced the "fascist attack" at Marseille as the deeds of "agents of Franco, [and] probably French fascists," too.[30] Yet the motive behind the attempted bombing was unclear. The *Cala Pi* had arrived from Spain on 10 October with a cargo of rice for Marseille and melons for North America. Investigators soon realized, however, that the yacht had docked in the berth reserved for the *Margarita Taherner*, a similar boat that had departed Marseille at 11 p.m. on 12 October loaded with foodstuffs for Republican Spain. The captain of the *Cala Pi* suspected that the bombers had made an error.[31]

At 6:03 a.m. on 7 March 1937, a bomb blew the side off a railway carriage in the station at Cerbère. The attack occurred as the train stood in a siding. It did not therefore seem intended to damage the nearby international railway tunnel, through which trains between France and Portbou in Spain passed. Moreover, it was further unlikely that the perpetrators had this goal in mind because the press had reported widely a government ban on the entry of engines into the tunnel due to the danger of bombardment.[32] Still, the proximity of the blast to the tunnel was worrying. The mystery of the bomb deepened when, on the same day, a faulty device failed to explode at the Spanish Consulate in Perpignan. Police discovered that the explosive was timed to detonate at 4:30 a.m., when it would pose little threat to human life.[33]

The extreme right-wing *L'Action Française* did not equivocate in attributing the bomb at Cerbère to the "red Spanish agitators" who were transforming the south of France into a province of the "Frente popular." These "bloody brutes" operated under the paternal gaze of France's own Republican front.[34] Police were unable to establish a connection between the incident and Spain despite a promising lead discovered in the wake of the attack. Travelers at Cerbère had noticed the presence of a man in blue overalls at the station prior to the explosion. He had frequented the station in the days before the attack and asked questions about the train timetable. Officers apprehended the man at Perpignan, to where he had traveled directly from Cerbère on the day of the attack. Jean Salles was a Frenchman from Toulouse and residing in Béziers.[35] He was, according to the right-wing press, an anarchist.[36] Salles denied neither his anarchist sympathies (he was found with anarchist pamphlets on his person) nor the fact that he made regular trips to Spain, yet he claimed to have no knowledge of the explosion. The right-wing *Le Journal* remarked that Salle's hometown of Toulouse was known for its "very important extremist agitation" in favor of Republican Spain and speculated that Salles intended the attack as a protest against the recent closure of the border.[37] The newspaper situated its analysis of the incident squarely within the context of the Spanish war, with the explosion framed as "overspill" from the conflict. Its front-page report of the crime even featured an unrelated photograph of three nationalist bomber planes over Jarama, east of Madrid.[38] Salles had acted in a suspicious manner at Cerbère station. Around the time of the explosion, he had hurriedly boarded the train to Perpignan, leaving behind a bag filled with Spanish-language pamphlets printed in Barcelona. However, investigators were unable to find any evidence of an incriminating nature, and Salles was soon released.[39] In the end, the authorities could not identify the bomber.

Subsequent acts of terrorism reinforced perceptions of a link to Spain. A week after the blast at Cerbère, on 15 March 1937, a bomb damaged the grocery shop of Jean Arbona in Nice. Locals knew of Arbona's sympathies for the Spanish Republican cause, and his shop was the only store in the town authorized to sell Spanish oranges.[40] On 23 May 1937, police discovered explosives at Marseille's railway station on the platform from which aid for Spain usually departed.[41] Superintendent Spotti noted that the public in the southern Roussillon region followed closely developments across the border. While there had been some division between fascists and antifascists in the region, the mood of the population remained calm. The superintendent feared that terrorists aimed to undo this tranquility.[42] Spotti discounted the involvement of Spanish antifascists in the act, reasoning that left wingers would not want to poison relations with France. He further ruled Spanish anarchists above suspicion, believing that their attacks were "more terrible and more carefully prepared." The Superintendent concluded that the culprits were Francoists, though he did not have any suspects in his sights.[43]

The most lethal of the southern attacks occurred on 5 May 1937. At 7:50 a.m., an incendiary device detonated in a second-class carriage of the Bordeaux-Marseille express train as it passed between Saint-Martin de Crau and Raphèle-les-Arles. The bomb—"an infernal machine of considerable strength," according to the authorities—was placed under a bench near the toilet in car 3713.[44] The explosion killed railway mechanic Etienne-Marie Aubert and injured five other travelers. The location of the bomb and the timing of its explosion caused the public prosecutor to believe that this "purely terrorist act" had intended to blow the carriage from the track.[45] The bombing provided something of a spectacle for the local press. *Le Petit Marseillais* published a photograph of Aubert's burnt body in the wreckage of the carriage, alongside an image of the exterior of the devastated train car.[46] The accompanying report described the scene in detail: in the corridor outside the toilet lay "the horrifying vestiges of what had been a human body. The limbs, the pelvis, the head had been burned and were crumbling under the feet. Only the torso remained, strangely shriveled."[47] Descriptions of the damage to the local environment illustrated for readers the destructiveness of the blast. The bomb had peppered with glass the cypress trees along the banks of the track, while for a hundred meters around the car the bodies of nesting birds lay strewn on the ground.[48] Police sealed the damaged carriage and left it at the crime scene to await further examination. Many people from the surrounding area came to gawk at the curious sight.⁴⁹ Acts of terrorism continued to possess value as entertainment.

"Are we on the threshold of a fearful attack?" asked the front cover of the 20 May edition of *Détective*.⁵⁰ The press had recently reported the arrest of Croatian Stefan Marušić in Paris, described as the "extremely dangerous... right-hand man" of the Ustashe's Ante Pavelić.⁵¹ Marušić's presence in the French capital raised fears of renewed Ustashe activity in France. According to *Le Petit Journal*, "It is difficult to believe that this terrorist...came to Paris, just for a walk about. Much is being done at the present time to find the accomplices of this terrorist. There is even a rumor that a second Ustashe was arrested and that nine bombs were found at his residence."⁵² *Le Petit Provençal* claimed that Marušić would reveal at last the "hidden aspects" of the 1934 Marseille attack—and the identity of the mysterious blonde.⁵³ The arrest of the Croatian prompted *Détective*'s Montarron to recall in detail the assassination of King Alexander. Several images illustrated the article, including photographs of Chernozemski on the footplate of the king's car and of the farm at Janka-Puszta.⁵⁴ The article painted a fearful picture of continued French vulnerability to terrorist infiltration:

Thousands of outlaws roam [Europe], thinking of their lost homeland, and hoping to kill the masters who have hunted or oppressed them. This army of outlaws grows every year, and it is to France, a land of asylum, a legendary land of freedom, that they come in crowds to take refuge....Too often, taking advantage of the welcome offered to them, foreigners have, in contempt of the laws of hospitality, exacted their vengeance and spilled the blood of their enemies on our soil.⁵⁵

Montarron closed with a gloomy observation on the incorrigible nature of terrorists. Incarcerated men such as the Marseille regicides Mijo Kralj, Ivan Rajić, and Zvonimir Pospišil "cannot escape from the infernal circle into which their dreams of revolts threw them. Releasing them, they will only leave their hiding places to rush into the bomb-making laboratories, into the camps where they learn to shoot targets painted in the style of dictators, and where, in the smoke of secret committees, they prepare infernal machines, which must one day shake the world."⁵⁶ It was a bleak and terrifying conclusion.

A further attempted bombing at Cerbère on 31 May 1937 heightened tension. Police officers arrested Italian Guglielmo Gardella as he attempted to plant a bomb at the mouth of the international tunnel. Gardella (calling himself "Cantelli") was carrying a time bomb disguised as a Thermos flask. Under interrogation, he claimed to have received the device the previous day from Armando Ruiz and Carlos Altomonto, two Spanish nationalist refugees living in Italy. French explosives expert Prévost offered apparent confirmation of the story when he ruled that the hexogen found in the bombs likely came from abroad.[57] The attempted bombing was not Gardella's first foray into violence. On 27 February 1937, Ruiz and Altomonto asked Gardella to bomb two locations in France: the Spanish Consulate in Toulouse and a former military hospital in Perpignan from which the Spanish Popular Front ran a recruitment operation. Gardella agreed to carry out the attacks—which Ruiz described as a "service to civilization"—in exchange for ten thousand lira.[58] However, according to the Italian, upon arriving at each target he balked at the thought of committing carnage (a fact that led *Le Matin* to mock Gardella as "the humanitarian terrorist").[59] For the left, the Gardella affair proved the existence of a web of fascist terrorism in France: *L'Humanité* argued that Gardella belonged to an organization that resembled the Ustashe.[60] The Socialist Party questioned Gardella's denial of any commitment to fascism. Socialist Jean-Maurice Hermann observed pointedly that "[h]e's an Italian... recruited in Italy by a devoted agent of Franco." Hermann scorned the supposed "terrorist for reasons of hunger" who had "too sensitive a heart" to kill.[61]

Gardella appeared before the criminal court in Céret on 23 September 1937, charged with the illegal possession of explosives on French soil, as set out in article three of the law of 19 June 1871. Ruiz, Altomonto, and a third accomplice, Lippi, were tried in absentia. Magistrates found the accused guilty. Gardella received three years' imprisonment (the court accepted that he had acted out of financial desperation and had cooperated fully with the police). Gardella's accomplices each received five years' imprisonment and a fine of several thousand francs.[62] Public prosecutor Cassou framed Gardella's crime in the broader context of foreign terrorist activity on French soil, demanding an end to "the quarrels that foreigners come here to settle."[63] The court shared Cassou's concerns.

The series of terrorist outrages in the south of France during 1937 drew anxious commentaries from the press. Foreign agents' infiltration of French territory seemed a reality, as attacks bore evident links to the Spanish war. The left perceived the hand of international fascism behind the terrorist bomb: "All fascists have the same master, Hitler, and the same doctrine, terrorism," *L'Humanité* surmised in April 1937.[64] The right accused Spanish Republicans and anarchists of importing their conflict to France. Accusatory fingers all pointed at foreigners. Likewise, the French authorities apparently believed that the terrorist threat hailed largely from abroad. In reaching their decision, the judges at Gardella's trial in September 1937 noted that "the interest of society demands a severe repression of such acts, if one considers that these are foreigners who, abusing our hospitality, come to sow discord and disorder amongst our communities."[65] Whichever faction one blamed, the foreign terrorist threat seemed real and persistent.

Eleven Days of Terror: 11–22 September 1937

11 SEPTEMBER: THE ETOILE BOMBINGS

On 10 September 1937, René Locuty arrived in Paris. Tall, thin, and with a bespectacled and reserved appearance, Locuty was a chemical engineer at the Michelin works in Clermont-Ferrand. He was a member of the Cagoule's "Enfants de l'Auvergne" provincial affiliate. Leading Cagoulard François Méténier had summoned Locuty to the capital for a special meeting. Méténier introduced Locuty to another Cagoulard boss, Jean Moreau de la Meuse, and the three men visited a secret arms cache on the rue Ampère. It was here that Moreau ordered Locuty to help to construct two time bombs. The six-kilogram bombs were subsequently hidden in two boxes and timed to explode at 10 p.m. on 11 September. With the bombs set, Méténier and comrade Léon Macon took Locuty to the seat of the Groupe des Industries Métallurgiques de la Région Parisienne on rue Boissière and the headquarters of the Confédération Générale du Patronat Français on rue de Presbourg. Both organizations represented French business leaders and industrialists. Macon delivered his package to the former address, while Locuty left his bomb at the latter, at approximately 6:15 p.m. His mission complete, Locuty took the train home to Clermont-Ferrand. Macon disappeared without a trace; he likely fled to Spain.[66] The devices exploded at the designated time. The bomb at the rue Boissière destroyed the entrance hall and staircase. Concierge Paul Baes escaped with cuts and cruises. The bomb at the rue de Presbourg scattered rubble over a twenty-five-meter radius and blew a passing taxi across the road (Figure 8). Debris from the building buried constables Legnier and Truchet as they made their nightly round. Each man suffered multiple fractures to their body and skull; the blast severed Legnier's right arm.[67]

Police had been watching the Cagoule since February 1937.[68] Detectives had picked up the trail of the group when a suitcase belonging to Cagoulard gunrunner Maurice Juif fell into police hands at Lille railway station. The documents seized from the case indicated "the existence of a vast organization" intended to smuggle arms into France for extreme right-wing groups.[69] In June 1937, OSARN operative Fernand Jakubiez was arrested at the Swiss border; under questioning, he provided his interrogators with more information on the group. Police began to arrest members from 16 September 1937 (a fact that received much attention in the press), yet suspicion about the Etoile bombings fell too on the left, notably Aldo Fiamberti, an anarchist who had recently returned to France following armed service in Spain with the Republicans.[70] Cagoulard leaders had in fact hoped that, in bombing the headquarters of two employers' groups, accusatory fingers would point to the extreme left. However, the discovery of time bombs like those used in the attack at a Cagoulard arms store on the rue Ribera in mid-November 1937 led to the arrest of Méténier on 10 December 1937.[71] When police took Locuty into custody on 11 January 1938, the rue de Presbourg bomber gave a full confession.[72]

In the aftermath of the Etoile attack, speculation was rife in the press about the identity of the bomber and his motive. Journalists and commentators described the unprecedented destructiveness of the bombs that had exploded in the country's capital.[73] The anarchist attacks of the late nineteenth century seemed to pale in comparison to an outrage that had left ruin and rubble in its wake.[74] Indeed, images of the damage to the buildings prompted the observation that only modern weapons of great power could wreak such devastation. The French authorities did little to dispel such concerns: police scientists concluded that the material used in the bombs "could only have been made by technicians," in "war factories" and "very well-equipped workshops."[75] Those French who read newspapers were accustomed to seeing such things in reports about Spain; in September 1937, it seemed as if war had now come to Paris.[76]

A new more dangerous era of violence had dawned, and voices on the left and right knew just where to lay the blame: "The perpetrators of the Etoile attacks are blatantly foreign agents" (*Ce Soir*); "This attack...could only have been ordered from abroad" (*Le Petit Journal*).[77] Depending on one's political loyalties, the perpetrators hailed either from Moscow or Re-

Figure 8. The building at the rue de Presbourg following the bomb attack of 11 September 1937, published in the socialist *Le Populaire*. Source: commons.wikimedia.org

publican Spain, on the one hand, or Berlin or Rome, on the other hand.[78] In the interwar culture of terrorism, French hands could not have planted the bombs: "Terrorism is not French…these crimes [are] not French" (*Paris-Soir*);[79] "…the bombs are not French" (*L'Oeuvre*);[80] "…there are weapons that the French do not use. These bombs came from abroad" (*Le Matin*);[81] "'Frenchmen did not do that'…the French temperament is disgusted by these brutal, cowardly, and stupid acts of terrorism" (*Le Petit Journal*);[82] "an attack so un-French" (*L'Ere nouvelle*).[83] The government seemed to agree: Prime Minister Camille Chautemps announced a project to draw up a "Foreigners' Statute." The prime minister attributed the blame for terrorism in France to the immigrant population: "Acts of violence have multiplied on our territory. Bombs have been planted whether on trains, in aerodromes, in stations; crimes have been committed against foreigners and remain unpunished. It seems therefore necessary to modify sensitively our policy on the surveillance of foreign undesirables."[84] The new statute would tighten immigration controls and strengthen the surveillance of foreign nationals in the country.[85] The press hailed Chautemps's announcement as the implementation of a long-overdue reform. Of course, right-wing xenophobes were buoyed: in *Le Matin*, Stéphane Lauzanne even proposed the establishment of concentration camps in southern Algeria or on an unnamed Atlantic island to house this "rubbish."[86] Yet the statute spoke to concerns across the political spectrum that France remain reserved for the French.[87]

Within a week of the bombing, French police moved against the Cagoule with a series of arrests and raids in Paris and the provinces. Among the arrestees were Michel Harispe, OSARN armorer and personal secretary to group luminary Gabriel Jeantet.[88] The recent bombings had given the police new impetus to investigate the group, and investigators were confident of a link between the Etoile attack and the Cagoulards.[89] Political loyalties informed reaction to the arrests: the Communist Party declared the Cagoule a "fascist organization of civil war" while the Action Française alleged that the affair was an electoral stunt designed to tarnish the right and benefit Dormoy's leftist allies.[90] Indeed, as Brunelle and Finley-Croswhite argue, the organization's friends in the press and on the right wing of politics sought to downplay the seriousness of the revelations. *L'Intransigeant* ridiculed the poor results of the raids (five arrests from two hundred searches) and the seizure of some "murderous devices, including a halberd."[91] *Le Figaro*'s fashion column noted a growing penchant for hooded capes among the women of the capital. The garments "confer[red] the lure of mystery to the looks of the beautiful Cagoulardes."[92] There were attempts to disassociate the Cagoule entirely from the Paris bombings of 11 September.[93] While some of these attempts were certainly politically motivated, in some sections of the press there seemed genuine confusion about the provenance of the bombers. In fact, from the extreme left to the extreme right, questions were raised about the timing of the police intervention against the OSARN: was the Cagoule affair designed to distract the public from the fruitless search for the Etoile terrorists?[94]

The arrest of Cagoulards during September 1937 worried the OSARN leadership. The police, apparently long satisfied simply to keep the group under surveillance, had begun to turn the screw on the Cagoule. Meanwhile, OSARN activists grew impatient for action. Time was running out for the group to act. Deloncle thus chose 15 November 1937 as the date for an attempted coup. Operatives were placed in a state of alert while the leadership attempted to induce its contacts in the army to join in putting down an illusory communist insurrection. Army officers failed to take the bait and the night of the "coup" ended in a damp squib. The police swung into action and waves of arrests brought prominent Cagoulards into custody, including Deloncle.[95] Investigators discovered hidden arms stores and underground prisons; they seized documents outlining the seizure of public utilities and water supplies, as well as the imprisonment and likely execution of left-wing leaders.[96] The press ran stories about the sudden discovery of "thousands of terrorists" in France.[97] On 23 November 1937, Dormoy unveiled publicly the extent of the conspiracy, which he termed "a true plot against republican institutions."[98] Speaking in the Chamber of Deputies, Minister of Justice Vincent Auriol asked, "Who can deny that these were acts of terrorism, prepared in secret, with a perverse refinement of the imagination and with cruelty until this day unknown in our country, where even the plots against state security had, in times past, an otherwise chivalrous character."[99] Terrorism, once again, appeared to be an unprecedented threat to the nation. By January 1939, police had impounded a frightening amount of weapons belonging to the group, including 16 machine guns, 259 automatic rifles, over 9,000 grenades, 150 kilograms of picric acid, and an anti-tank gun with 69 shells.[100] This large stockpile of armaments led the public prosecutor to consider the group to be of a terrorist nature.[101]

The terrorist character of the group was less certain in the press. On the one hand, terrorism was so thoroughly understood as an "unFrench" phenomenon perpetrated by foreign agents that the existence of a French group seemed fantastical.[102] Indeed, foreign terrorism provided a means by which to comprehend this French oddity: the Cagoule was a sort of "French Ustashe" modeled on Nazi paramilitarism.[103] Terrorism, it seemed, was still a foreign import. Antifascists described the Cagoule as a local variant of international fascism, controlled either by the German or Italian secret services.[104] The threat from the Cagoule was thus not read solely in transnational terms; domestic politics provided touchstones for understanding.[105] L'Oeuvre admitted that the group was of a "terrorist nature," but claimed it was in the style of the Blanquistes and preached "integral Orleanism."[106] The socialists, however, perceived something different in the Cagoule. Le Populaire referred to the group as a terrorist outfit less frequently than its left-wing allies did. In fact, the newspaper suggested that the organization was much better-organized and well-funded than the average terrorist group. Referring to Cagoulard plans for a coup, it claimed the group was simply another of France's extreme right-wing leagues.[107]

The right-wing press worked to discredit the seriousness of the group. An array of publications ridiculed Dormoy's revelations as a mixture of exaggeration and invention.[108] This interpretation of the Cagoule episode gradually took root in the popular imagination, and the Cagoulards became figures of fun and derision (Figure 9).[109] As Philippe Bourdrel writes: "The fashion in the salons was for Cagoulard parties [with people] decked out in masks and robes. The catherinettes donned a hood as their symbol.[110] Cabaret artists and cartoonists took great pleasure in it."[111] Ultimately, thanks to the right-wing campaign and a deeper understanding of who terrorists were, the idea of a French terrorism was just not credible.

During January 1938, the figure of an "enigmatic" blonde woman caught the attention of journalists. Following his arrest on 11 January 1938, Locuty revealed that, on the afternoon prior to the bombings, he had dined with Méténier and "a young blonde woman, [who was] tall, thin, [and] pretty."[112] Locuty reported that Méténier and the woman had spoken on familiar terms with each other (using the informal *tutoiement* form of address), and he speculated that they were intimate friends. Several newspapers reported that police were keen to speak to this woman. On 19 January 1938, eighteen-year-old typist Jacqueline Blondet turned herself in to the police station in the Saint-Philippe-du-Roule district of Paris. After reading in the newspapers that the police were searching for a blonde woman in con-

Figure 9. Terrorist cosplay: a party of "Cagoulards" gathered round a box of "Incendiary Bombs." Source: commons.wikimedia.org

nection with the Etoile attacks, Blondet decided to speak with police and eliminate herself from their enquiries. She also provided detectives with what little information she had on the OSARN.[113]

Blondet was not the only woman to consort with Cagoulards. Women were, in fact, "indispensable to the mission of the Cagoule," according to Brunelle and Finley-Croswhite.[114] The diary of Aristide Corre, a co-founder of the Cagoule, revealed that women fulfilled important roles in the organization, acting as liaison agents and recruitment officers, and tailing potential targets.[115] Cagoulard Annie Mouraille would, in 1941, plant the bomb that killed Dormoy in his bed at a hotel in Montélimar.[116] Female Cagoulards were objects of fascination for the press. Their sexual promiscuity—women in the OSARN had multiple intimate partners, usually among the organization's leadership—titillated journalists and readers, while their participation in terrorism jarred with contemporary expectations of terrorist attackers and feminine behavior. Both through their sexuality and their violence, women in the Cagoule were doubly transgressive.[117] Media attention on these women arose from an attempt to explain behavior that so contradicted "respectable" standards. Of course, the transgressive behavior of women in the OSARN was constructed. Women were by no means estranged to terrorist violence (as this book has demonstrated); women could be committed to political revolution as much as their male comrades; Cagoulard men, even the married ones, were just as promiscuous.

In January 1938, Blondet admitted to police that Méténier was courting her. However, the two were not lovers. Blondet revealed that the relationship had ended in November 1937, during an evening at a Parisian nightclub when Méténier had made clear his desire to "end the night with her," something that she was not prepared to allow.[118] Blondet's involvement with the Cagoule, however minor, furnished reporters with an opportunity to make salacious speculations about the Cagoulards. The "pretty Jacqueline" provided a welcome distraction from the line-up of colorless stooges and small fry exposed up to that point in police searches.[119] This young girl, "very pretty, with hair like ripened wheat," in the style of a cinema star, brought sex appeal to the scandal.[120] The press cast Blondet as far from a terrorist sympathizer. She was actually attracted to Méténier for his wealth—he owned three cars!—and the fact that he spoiled her with evenings out at restaurants and dancing in Parisian clubs.[121] Her refusal to submit to her suitor's charms amused the writers at *L'Oeuvre*: Méténier's bad luck had spared the young girl from having to describe to police her hours of passion with the scantily clad Cagoulard boss.[122] The newspaper's "L'Ouvrier" used this detail of the affair to pour scorn on the OSARN's political ambitions: the Cagoulards may have considered themselves the "hardest of the hard," but the story of "Blondet-the-Blonde" demonstrated their softness. How could men who lacked the virility to "conquer" a young blonde girl ever hope to conquer the Third Republic?[123] The figure of Blondet became the latest woman on the press's list of titillating female terrorists.

THE AFFAIR OF THE SPANISH SUBMARINE

On the night of 18 September 1937, a Francoist commando attempted to steal the Spanish Republican C-2 submarine docked at Brest. The raid failed: resistance from the submariners resulted in the death of one of the pirates, José Maria Gabarin Goni. Police managed to arrest several of the men within twelve hours of the crime. The leader of the attack was none other than commandant Julian Troncoso Sagredo, Franco's head of the

Border Services of the North of Spain. The subsequent police investigation offered tantalizing clues as to the identities of the perpetrators behind the spate of bomb attacks committed across the south during 1937.[124]

At the outset of the conflict in Spain, Francoist agents established a base at villa Nacho Enea in the French border town of Saint-Jean-de-Luz. Nacho Enea belonged to the Marquis of Caviedes, who, in 1936, leased the property to Frenchman Iñigo de Bernoville, a member of the defunct Croix de Feu, France's largest extreme right-wing paramilitary league. Bernoville was, according to *Le Matin*, Franco's representative in southern France.[125] Under the orders of General Emilio Mola, José María Marcet y Vidal, a military officer from Zaragoza, directed the station's activities, which included propaganda work, aid, intelligence, and field operations against France-based Spanish Republicans.[126] Marcet recruited agents among the expatriate community in Perpignan and developed links with French extreme right-wing groups. He was also in touch with Angelo Tamborini, an Italian spy working in both Toulouse and Paris. Police had received several tip-offs about Marcet's plans to bomb targets in France, and Spotti suspected the group of involvement in the bombing at Cerbère on 7 March 1937.[127] Tamborini later fingered Marcet for the bombing campaign in the south of France, describing him as the head of Franco's espionage in France and the organizer of terrorist attacks.[128]

After French police raided Nacho Enea in October 1936, intelligence operations ceased, and the villa operated openly as the unofficial embassy of the Spanish rebel government in France. The Communist Party denounced the presence of the rebel delegation, calling it a "fascist center" frequented by Francoists and German Nazis.[129] Furthermore, party grandee Paul Vaillant-Couturier claimed that Nacho Enea facilitated collaboration between Francoists and French extreme right-wingers.[130]

Two months after the police search of Nacho Enea, Troncoso took over the Francoist secret service in southern France. His mission was to disrupt trade and communications between Europe and Republican Spain, particularly the supply of arms and food to loyalist soldiers.[131] Troncoso's first action demonstrated an audacity later in evidence at Brest. On 21 June 1937, Francoists hijacked an Air Pyrénées flight between Biarritz and Bilbao. The airline had carried people and correspondence between southern France and the Basque government. On 21 June, the plane's pilot, José Yanguas Yáñez, along with mechanic Pablo Martínez, diverted the plane to a beach at Zarautz. Troncoso's agents had likely paid off both men. Among the handful of passengers on board were Alfredo Espinosa, a minister in the Basque government. Espinosa was later murdered.[132] The French press did not widely report the hijacking.[133]

In September 1937, Troncoso's plans concerned two Republican submarines docked in France: the C-2 at Brest and the C-4 at Bordeaux. Given that the rebels lacked submarines, to steal two of the machines from their enemies would be both a propaganda coup and militarily useful.[134] Troncoso hoped to persuade the submariners to join Franco, much like he had persuaded the crew of the Air Pyrénées flight in June to divert the plane. Troncoso traveled to Bordeaux, where he and his comrades, Antonio Martin Montis (the Marquis of Linares) and Rafael Parella (the Marquis of Maravella and Troncoso's driver), delivered a letter to the crew of the C-4, bidding them to join the nationalist cause. The letter presented the men with a choice between "inevitable disaster and death or rehabilitation, freedom and well-being." In their return communication, the submariners refused the offer of "traitor Julian." However, their commandant, Jesus de Las Heras—a much-respected member of the Spanish navy—deserted to the nationalist camp, sabotaging the C-4 in the process. Troncoso and Parella returned to Irun the same day.[135]

Montis journeyed to Brest to address a similar request to the sailors aboard the C-2. Accompanying Montis was Frenchman Robert Chaix. Chaix was a journalist at the *Presse de Bayonne*, and a well-known activist of the PSF (the successor party to the Croix de Feu) in Saint-Jean-de-Luz.[136] He later claimed that his participation in the plot came from his desire to win a scoop for his newspaper.[137] To sweeten the offer to the crew of the C-2, Montis and Chaix offered a sum of two million pesetas to be shared among the crew should they accept Troncoso's invitation. The sailors were unable to decide on how to respond to the invitation. Nevertheless, Montis felt emboldened enough to return to Irun with the news that, if Troncoso made the proposal in person, the submarine would likely pass over to the rebels.[138]

Troncoso arrived in Brest on 14 September 1937, in the company of Chaix, Montis, and Las Heras, former commandant of the C-4. The men met with C-2 commandant José Luis Ferrando Talayero. The nationalists had set up the meeting through Ferrando's lover, Dominique Fusciardi Rosario, nicknamed "Menga," a Franco loyalist and a dancer of Spanish-Italian heritage at the L'Ermitage club in Brest.[139] Ferrando usually ended his soirées in the town with a visit to the nightspot.[140]

Menga later proved an object of fascination for the press. According to André Salmon of *Le Petit Parisien*, she was the heroine that all good detective stories require.[141] Referred to as the "beautiful Menga," the "pretty Menga," the "audacious Menga," and, invariably, the "dancer," she brought a touch of glamour to the story.[142] When Menga denied recognizing Troncoso (with whom she had undeniably met), *Le Petit Parisien* attributed her amnesia to late nights, cocktails, and champagne.[143] Menga's appeal to journalists partly lay in her sexuality and her intimate relationship with Ferrando. *L'Ouest-Éclair* salaciously asked if this girl with Castilian blood had "used her charms for the benefit of the nationalists."[144] Once again, perceptions of terrorism mixed with sex in the figure of a female protagonist. While the media attributed to Menga an important role in the plot—she was in the center of a rogues' gallery in *Détective*'s feature article on terrorism in September 1937—by the time of the Francoists' trial in March 1938, "the beautiful Menga" was no longer a person of interest and the press had forgotten her.[145]

At the meeting on 14 September, Ferrando—a closet Francoist and former classmate of Las Heras—revealed that he was favorable to Troncoso, despite the reservations of some of his crew. Troncoso returned to Irun, ordering his henchmen Manuel Orendain Arana, Severiano Satrustéguy (also known as Salvador Serrats Urquiza), José Maria Gabarin Goni, and Medina to travel north in preparation for the capture of the vessel. On 17 September, Troncoso arrived in Brest, with Las Heras, Parella, and his deputy in the intelligence service, Captain Miguel Ibanez. A further meeting with Ferrando saw the C-2's captain urge Troncoso to proceed with caution, given the Republican loyalties of some of his crew. He suggested that the commandant board the submarine with his followers under the pretense of bringing new orders from the Spanish Republican government. Troncoso and Ferrando would then announce that the boat was to set sail for Republican waters. In fact, the vessel would travel to a nationalist port.[146]

During the evening of 18 September 1937, Troncoso led a squad of eleven men to the harbor, equipped with revolvers, ropes, and chains to subdue any resistance aboard the C-2.[147] The team included three French: Chaix, Léon Pardo (a member of the PSF in Hendaye, where he was a customs agent), and Luc Robet (a former member of the extreme right-wing Action Française).[148] They waited for the majority of the crew to disembark for a night of entertainment in the city before approaching the submarine in a rowing boat. Las Heras identified himself to the sentries and Ferrando permitted the men to board. The crew gathered in the submarine's main chamber to hear Las Heras—who claimed to speak in the name of socialist politician Belarmino Tomas—declare that the boat would rendezvous with a trawler far from the coast. The ruse hit an immediate snag when the head mechanic, Joseph Hernandez Sanchez, asked to see Tomas's order in writing. An agitated Troncoso pulled a revolver from his coat and pushed it into the chest of the mechanic. His comrades proceeded to restrain the sailors. Captain Ferrando drew his own firearm and disarmed one of his subordinates. Las Heras and Luis Dabouza, a mechanic on the C-2, tried and failed to start the submarine's engines.[149]

As their comrades searched the boat, one sailor, Augusto Diego, refused to leave his post in the turret. In the days before the Troncoso raid, Diego had received a warning from his anarchist comrades about a nationalist attempt to take the vessel by force. He had smuggled several handguns aboard as a precautionary measure.[150] When Gabarin attempted to remove Diego by force, the submariner shot his assailant in the head. Sailor Valardino suddenly tackled Troncoso, knocking him to the ground and threatening to kill him. The commandant and his men fled with Ferrando and submarine mechanic Dabouza.[151] Diego raised the alarm and the police soon arrived. The Spanish Republican *ABC* claimed that Gabarin was a "known terrorist" suspected of involvement in another attack at the port of Marseille in June 1937.[152]

Within twelve hours of the raid in Brest, gendarmes in Belin, a commune south of Bordeaux, arrested Orendain, Satrustéguy-Serrats, Chaix, and Las Heras, along with Ferrando and Dabouza.[153] Officers apprehended Parella several days later.[154] Troncoso—who had escaped back over the border in the trunk of the Argentine ambassador's car—turned himself in to French police on 21 September 1937, believing that he would benefit from diplomatic immunity.[155] Prior to the revelation that Troncoso had taken part in the act, prosecutors brought a charge of complicity in attempted theft against the commandant. Troncoso admitted to the infraction, describing the mission as a "humanitarian act."[156] As for the men arrested at Belin, officers made an initial allegation of illegal arrest and arbitrary sequestration, before it transpired that Ferrando and Dabouza had left the C-2 willingly.[157] Lawyers acting for the detainees requested that their clients be held as political prisoners; the prosecutor denied the request.[158]

The C-2 affair dominated the news in the days after the failed hijacking. The audacity of the plot drew comment. *Le Petit Parisien* described the story as more fantastical than a spy or gangster film and more incredible than the tales of the most popular adventure writers.[159] *L'Ouest-Éclair* agreed: the raid was the stuff of movies.[160] Reports speculated about connections between the Troncoso expedition and previous acts of terrorism in the south.[161] It transpired that the Sûreté Nationale was aware of Orendain and Gabarin's terrorist pasts; the former even had a conviction from November 1936 for smuggling arms and dynamite into France (PSF member Pardo had paid Orendain's bail).[162] The suspected involvement of Spaniards in the year's earlier bombings, combined with the fact that the raid in Brest happened so soon after the Etoile bombings (September 11), nurtured suspicions of a link.[163] Troncoso soon stood accused in several newspapers of being a criminal mastermind and the commander of a "vast terrorist enterprise" in the regions of France that bordered Spain. Had his men committed the Paris bombings, not to mention the attacks at Cerbère, Marseille, Toulouse, Bordeaux, and Toussus-le-Noble?[164] Were these incidents all part of a "single plot"?[165] Communist Lucien Sampaix alleged that Troncoso had directed "terrorist operations" on French soil under the orders of Hitler and the Gestapo. Sampaix thus incorporated these terrorists and pirates into the perceived threat from international fascism.[166]

The investigation into the C-2 raid seemingly offered police the prospect of capturing the perpetrators of several attacks committed that year. A search of Gabarin's rented accommodation uncovered materials like those used in several bombings, including detonators, gunpowder, and two metal cans disguised as sardine tins.[167] In fact, Gabarin's lover, a Mlle Palacin, indicated that the Troncoso squad had undertaken a number of earlier missions. Notably, Palacin alleged that the men were behind the explosions at Cerbère in March 1937 and the attempted bombing of the Spanish Consulate in Bayonne.[168] A further tip-off to the police linked the men to an attack on a Spanish boat, the *Maria-Amelin*, in February.[169] However, there were insufficient grounds to charge the men on these counts. The criminal case against the accused provoked much discussion. The judicial authorities debated at length whether the action at Brest even fell under the jurisdiction of French law; after all, the crime had taken place on a foreign ship.[170] Ultimately, the decision to bring the men to trial in France rested on the fact that the attack had commenced on French "territory": the rowing boat used to reach the C-2 belonged to a Frenchman.[171]

Proceedings commenced on 15 March 1938. The courtroom in Brest was packed with journalists, including famous reporter Géo London, French political activists, and a significant security force.[172] On 22 March 1938, the court convicted Troncoso, Orendain, and Satrustéguy-Serrats for the possession of weapons of war and the carrying of banned weapons. Each man received six months and five days' imprisonment. Chaix was acquitted on all counts.[173] In the case of the Spaniards, the court deducted time already served from the sentence. Consequently, four days after their conviction, Troncoso and Satrustéguy-Serrats were freed. Orendain was transported to Bayonne, where he faced charges relating to another crime. French antifascists deemed the sentences tantamount to an acquittal.[174] As for Ferrando and Dabouza, the French authorities expelled them back to Spain on 27 November 1937.[175]

The C-2 affair again prompted calls for severe measures against foreign undesirables in France. For the socialist *Le Populaire*, the crime threw into relief the threat to French security from enemy agents: "This new scandal underlines the need to rid French territory of the spies and terrorists with which it is infested."[176] Concern over the broader "immigrant problem" conditioned responses. The right-wing *Le Petit Journal* noted that, in all the cases currently under investigation (including Gardella's attempted bombing of the Cerbère tunnel), "the majority of criminals arrested are foreigners!"[177] Terrorism was not simply foreign in character; it was unFrench: "Never would French brains have dreamed of organizing with so much Machiavellian intrigue such a murderous plot."[178] Jacques Lemoine, editor of *La Petite Gironde*, lamented a number of recent and historical terrorist attacks, including the assassinations of King Alexander and Doumer. In a message to foreign troublemakers, he summed up a sense of exasperation felt across the political spectrum: "Clear off!"[179]

"THIS IS PERHAPS A TRAP": THE ABDUCTION OF GENERAL MILLER, 22 SEPTEMBER 1937

On 22 September 1937, General Yevgeny Miller, a White Russian émigré, left his office at rue du Colisée in Paris just after midday. He was not seen alive again. Kidnapped by agents of Stalin's NKVD (Naródnyy Komissariát Vnútrennikh Del, or the People's Commissariat for Internal Affairs), Miller spent the rest of his life as prisoner "Petr Vasil'evich Ivanov" in cell 110 of the Soviet secret police's notorious Lubianka prison. He was executed on 11 May 1939.[180]

As head of the Union Générale Militaire Russe (Rossijskij Obŝevoinskij Soûz, or ROVS), Miller was a well-known figure in Paris's Russian émigré community. Founded in 1924, the ROVS sought to build a network of émigré and exiled officers and soldiers, in preparation for an eventual return to Russia. During the 1930s, the association established friendly relations with Germany and Italy, and several of its members fought alongside Nationalists in Spain.[181] By 1937, the movement claimed 30,000 members.[182] When one considers that the Russian population of France in 1936 was approximately 77,800 (64,000 Russian nationals and 13,800 naturalized citizens), the ROVS apparently accounted for a sizeable proportion of France's emigrant population.[183]

The size of the exiles' association concerned the Soviet leadership in Moscow. NKVD agents infiltrated the group, ultimately hoping to take control of all such organizations in the White Russian community.[184] In 1930, Miller's predecessor as president, General Alexander Kutepov, was betrayed by his chief of staff, General Boris Shteifon, a secret Guépéou operative. On 26 January 1930, Kutepov was bundled into a car in broad daylight on the rue Oudinot in Paris by three Soviet agents, one disguised as a French constable, as he made his way to church.[185] The authorities suspected that the general was killed and taken to a Soviet ship off the Normandy coast. It is also possible that Kutepov suffered a heart attack during his abduction and was buried in an unmarked grave outside Paris. A lack of evidence left the case unsolved.[186] In the wake of the kidnapping, Léon Daudet of the extreme right-wing *L'Action Française* declared Paris the "capital of political crime."[187]

At 12:15 p.m. on 22 September 1937, General Miller left the headquarters of the ROVS to attend a meeting. As he exited the building, he passed an envelope to his comrade General Pavel Kussonski, saying nervously, "Don't think me mad, but this time I'm leaving you a note in a sealed envelope; please open it only if I do not return."[188] Kussonski later opened the envelope when concerns about Miller's safety began to grow. The note read,

Today at 12:30 p.m. I have an appointment with General Skoblin at the intersection of the Rue Jasmin and Rue Raffet. He is supposed to take me to a meeting with a German officer by the name of Strohmann, the military attaché in one of the Baltic countries, and Werner of the German embassy here. Both speak Russian well. The meeting has been arranged on Skoblin's initiative. This is perhaps a trap and that is why I am leaving this note.[189]

Major-General Nikolai Skoblin was head of the ROVS intelligence branch. This body was responsible for monitoring Russian immigrants to France and weeding out Soviet agents in the organization.[190] Ironically, Skoblin was an NKVD agent, and the planned meeting with Miller on 22 September 1937 was indeed a ruse. The two "Germans" with whom Miller was to meet were in fact Kislov, NKVD spy chief in Paris, and Shipel'glas (deputy chief of the NKVD's foreign section). The Russian spy agency hoped to replace Miller with Skoblin as leader of the ROVS.[191] Skoblin and his accomplices likely chloroformed Miller before locking him in a box and loading it into a van belonging to the Soviet embassy. The vehicle traveled to Le Havre, where the box was put onto the Soviet freighter *Maria Oulianoff*. The ship left in a hurry, failing to unload the entirety of its cargo, with the captain claiming that he had received an urgent message to return home. Moscow denied French requests to return the ship to Le Havre.[192]

Miller's comrades reported his disappearance to the police only at 3:15 a.m. on 23 September. Kussonski had opened the General's envelope at 11 p.m. and immediately contacted Admiral Mikhail Kedrow. Kussonski and Kedrow awoke Skoblin at 1 a.m. and asked him to accompany them to make a report to the police. Unusually calm for a man awoken unexpectedly in the early hours of the morning, Skoblin agreed, unaware of the existence of Miller's note. However, the undercover NKVD agent did not want to speak with police. He easily gave the two men the slip and was never seen in France again.[193]

Skoblin's wife, Nadezhda Plevitskaya, was not so lucky. Police apprehended Plevitskaya on 24 September 1937 as she entered the headquarters of the Gallipoli veterans' association on rue de la Faisanderie. Discrepancies between her account of her movements on the day of the abduction and those of witnesses raised suspicions, and detectives soon discovered her own connection to Moscow.[194] Originally a Red Army entertainer, she had joined the White Russian cause when she fell in love with Skoblin. Soviet intelligence recruited the couple during the early 1930s.[195] In 1937, Plevitskaya was charged with complicity in Miller's disappearance.

The abduction of Miller prompted speculation about links between the general's disappearance and other unsolved crimes. On the one hand, memories of Kutepov's kidnapping revived and the Miller case appeared to be a "new" or "second" Kutepov affair. Some comparisons with the vanishing of Kutepov were contrived: *Le Petit Journal* noted that Kutepov had a friend who was a dancer while the wife of Miller's deputy Skoblin was a singer.[196] On the other hand, some commentators proposed a link between the Miller affair and the other unsolved crimes of that year, notably the murders of Navachine and the Roselli brothers.[197] All press outlets agreed that the Miller abduction was the latest in a series of "enigmas" to confront the French police. *Paris-Soir* presented readers with a chronology of "foreign terrorist activity" in France during 1937, beginning with the 7 March explosion at Cerbère and ending with Miller's disappearance.[198] *Le Journal* lamented the "streak of terrorism" that France was enduring.[199]

Appreciations of the origin of this terrorism depended on political loyalties. The conservative press looked to Moscow. Miller had fallen victim to the "terrorist teams" of the Guépéou, who used France as their "training ground."[200] Conversely, the French Communist Party accused international fascism.[201] *L'Humanité* suggested that Hitler and Mussolini had sent a "guardian angel" to Paris to spirit away Miller—a present-day Gorguloff—before his indictment alongside Troncoso's terrorist gang.[202] Communist Pierre-Laurent Darnar even alleged that Berlin and Rome had manufactured the scandal to distract French attention from the C-2 affair. "This spectacular turn of events will only underline the terrorists' relentless hammering of France," he concluded.[203] Suspicion once again fell upon foreigners. Well-worn arguments resurfaced about the desirability of France's "liberal" immigration policy in the face of the "den of bandits" that the country was rapidly becoming.[204] An advertisement for a communist meeting at Paris's Vélodrome d'Hiver on 28 September (featuring party grandees Lucien Sampaix, Paul Vaillant-Couturier, and Maurice Thorez) focused on the exploits of "fascist dynamiters," spies, and terrorists in France, as well as the "measures to take FOR THE LIBERTY AND SECURITY OF OUR PEOPLE. FOR FRANCE FOR THE FRENCH."[205]

The involvement of Plevitskaya proved a boon for the press. Plevitskaya was none other than the famed Russian singer popularly known as "La Plevitskaya," the "Nightingale of Kursk."[206] Journalists delighted in recounting the checkered past of the sixty-two-year-old who had, as a young girl, escaped from a convent, joined a traveling singing troupe, and once charmed the Tsar with a personal performance.[207] Press photographs of "La Plevitskaya" showed her in stage costume and largely dated from her younger days.[208] On 30 September 1937, she featured on the front cover of *Détective*'s "Special Issue on Terrorist Intrigues in France." The magazine noted that the name of "La Plevitskaya," "evokes with pomp the former Russia, the very mysterious soul of the people of icons. The life of this woman is an astonishing golden and bloody adventure story."[209] The framing of Madame Skoblin once again aroused a connection between terrorism and sex: journalists Henry Malric and Luc Dornain wrote that despite her age, "La Plevitskaya" was "still so beautiful, so seductive, [and] she has so much charm."[210] Such descriptions abounded during her trial in December 1938.

The story of "La Plevitskaya" perhaps inspired Jean de la Hire's popular novel *La Loubianskaïa*, completed in October 1937 and published the following year. La Hire was in fact Count Adolphe d'Espie, a prolific novelist who specialized in authoring low-priced adventure stories (*La Loubianskaïa* itself cost just five francs). La Hire presented *La Loubianskaïa* as a semifictional account of an international terrorist plot to develop a new explosive of devastating power. The Loubianskaïa of the title is Véronique Servant, a French secret agent. In the novel, Servant and French spy François Le Brieul attempt to smuggle the plans for the new weapon back to France (Le Brieul has in fact stolen them from central European terrorist Alexandre Lokgachine). Unfortunately, Servant and Le Brieul fall into the hands of female Soviet agent Machka Raïev. While in captivity, Raïev reveals to Le Briec that his companion is in fact the famous Guépéou agent named the "nurse," nicknamed by her friends "La Loubianskaïa" and the "siren of the Guépéou."[211] Le Breuil, who had fallen in love with Servant during their adventure, is dumbfounded. The novel ends in tragedy when Le Breuil shoots dead Servant before he himself is gunned down.[212] Press reviews of the work noted its realism. The book was "based on tragic truths that the entire world suspects, but whose certainty has not yet been accepted by everyone."[213] The character of Servant was "a woman like, without doubt, a lot of them who run at the present time, from country to country."[214]

The trial of the Skoblins (Nikolai was tried in absentia) opened on 5 December 1938. Michael B. Miller calls the proceedings "one of the great spectacles of the decade."[215] Madame Skoblin stood accused of complicity in willful violence and forcible confinement.[216] She continued to deny knowledge of General Miller's whereabouts. Her appearance in court presented lawyer Maurice Ribet, acting in a civil case on behalf of Miller's wife, with an excellent opportunity to theatricalize. During his statement to the court, Ribet described the defendant as a wily actress behind whose hypnotic gaze one glimpsed the "terrible power of her duplicity."[217] He suggested that she was responsible for her husband's conversion to communism and, in fact, had directed the operation to kidnap Miller. Ribet warned the court against falling prey to the seductive powers of "this woman, with her eyes sometimes wet with tears in the face of her terrible guilt, who puts on an act of frightened naivety, [and] who simply responds mournfully to pressing questions, 'I do not know anything'."[218] To underscore this alleged pretense, Ribet referred to Madame Skoblin throughout his speech using her celebrity moniker, "La Plevitskaya."

For the press, the fate of the White Russian general appeared less interesting than the figure in the dock, with reports framing her as a new Mata Hari.[219] Both her character and her appearance drew extensive comment. For celebrated reporter Géo London, Madame Skoblin possessed a "sort of fatalism, which sometimes leaves Slav women insensitive to the hardest ordeals."[220] *Le Jour* described the "enigmatic smile" of this "black sphinx" who remained an "actress in her soul."[221] The court reporter for *Ce Soir* noted the resemblance between the Russian and "the mysterious face of Leonardo da Vinci's women." One perceived still the beauty that had exerted such a power over her husband. Indeed, Nikolai Skoblin's comrades had supposedly suspected that *she* was the real general of their relationship.[222]

The jury of twelve men did not succumb to Skoblin's apparent charms. After fifty minutes' deliberation, jurors convicted the Russian but allowed for the application of extenuating circumstances. The court sentenced "La Plevitskaya" to twenty years' forced labor and ten years' exile from France, a punishment whose severity would, according to *Le Figaro*'s Henri Vonoven, assure her a front-row place among the "beautiful heroines" of the assizes court.[223] La Plevitskaya, crushed, accepted the verdict with resignation.[224]

Conclusion

In 1938, Belgian Nick Gillain published *Le Mercenaire*, a memoir of the author's service in the International Brigades in Spain. Gillain explained the ease with which many fighters traveled via France. From his home in Ostend, Gillain journeyed to Perpignan via Ypres, Lille, and Paris. Arriving in Perpignan with about five hundred others, "unemployed and foreigners," he received false papers from the local trade union headquarters and was advised, "If they ask why you don't speak Spanish, say that you left the country as a baby."[225] Gillain and his new "Spanish" comrades boarded a coach and passed without difficulty into Spain. Gillain's stories would likely have sounded remarkably familiar to any French who read a newspaper in 1937. According to the press, "terrorists" traversed France every day.

In contrast to the rapid apprehension of the regicides in 1934, the inability of the police to catch the perpetrators of the 1937 bombings, attempted bombings, and kidnapping gave cause for nervousness. In some cases, the only clue to the identity of the attackers was their choice of target. The destruction of Spanish property and the interruption of communications between expatriate communities in France and their comrades in Spain seemed to be the aim. The similarity of methods and equipment in each case, as well as the Spanish provenance of components, suggested that an organized and well-supplied Spanish terrorist network was operating in France. As for the abduction of Miller, the fate of General Kutepov in 1930 and the revelations regarding Skoblin and Plevitskaya apparently proved Soviet involvement. Representations and interpretations of these acts throughout 1937 were consonant with existing perceptions of terrorism as the settling of scores by foreigners on French territory. The flow of refugees into the southwest of the country further raised concerns over the "import" of terror by an army of outlaws.

Francoist operations in France during 1937 also revealed the complicity of members of the French extreme right, even if the Caudillo's agents were not directly commanding these men. Chaix—the former Croix de Feu who had taken part in the raid in Brest—admitted to police that, aside from Troncoso, he had other contacts in the Spanish nationalist camp whom he had presumably cultivated during visits to Irun, Saint-Sebastian, Burgos, Pamplona, and Salamanca. He provided intelligence about shipping between France and Spain to nationalists across the border.[226] The left had long accused domestic fascists of involvement in international terrorism.

In the space of eleven days during September 1937, four sensational affairs shook France. The responses to these affairs drew upon, and helped to reinforce, the culture of terrorism in late 1930s France. The dominant theme of this discourse framed terrorism as the "Other"—a crime that could not be committed by "true" French men and women in the name of French values (such values, however, were subjectively defined). Recent French experiences of terrorist violence informed this representation, as did fears over the deterioration of European peace, exemplified most violently in the Spanish conflict. It is unsurprising that French anxiety over terrorism manifested in the announcement of a Foreigner's Statute, inspired by, and directed at, terrorism. The term "undesirable," long employed by the xenophobic right to describe the archetypal foreign wrongdoer, now became commonplace in the language of all political factions and parties.[227]

The "problem" of foreigners in France who had "abused" their hosts' hospitality and "imported" terrorism seemed particularly severe during the wave of terrorist attacks in 1937. That France was near-fatally afflicted with terrorist violence seemed obvious. Albert-Petit surmised the French predicament in a January 1938 article in the *Journal des Débats*: "It's self-evident, and it is not flattering. We are the country of choice for all the apostles of terrorism and propaganda by the deed. It's here that all those people not wanted anywhere else pile up."[228] Yet the plan for a Foreigners' Statute was not realized before Chautemps lost his position in spring 1938, and the project subsequently foundered.[229] It is telling that no government considered a special law on *homegrown* terrorism, despite the exposure of the OSARN. Were the Cagoule "terrorists or jokers"?[230] The answer was not clear.

Edouard Daladier's administration (10 April 1938–21 March 1940) introduced tough new immigration laws on 2 May 1938, in what Mary Dewhurst Lewis calls "an unprecedented crackdown on migrants' civil liberties" and "the largest crackdown on immigrants the republic had ever known."[231] Daladier's decrees included new repressive measures aimed at those people deemed "unworthy" of French hospitality.[232] Further measures followed the May decrees. The Ministry of the Interior, for example, later established a special fund within its budget to ensure that foreigners expelled according to the decree law of 2 May 1938 returned home.[233]

Lewis attributes Daladier's decrees to both the continued arrival of refugees from Germany and "a *vague* fear" that these asylum-seekers posed a security risk to France.[234] On the contrary, throughout 1937 this fear of foreign undesirables in France assumed a well-defined form: the fear of terrorism. Daladier's decrees, after all, drew much inspiration from Chautemps's failed proposal for a Foreigner's Statute.[235] Continuity of personnel in government also ensured that the concerns of late 1937 were addressed in spring 1938: Albert Sarraut was minister of the interior in both the Chautemps and the Daladier governments. In May 1938, his government's decrees cracked down on immigrants and, by extension, terrorists.

While conceptions of terrorism in 1937 drew largely on those familiar to recent years in France, the attacks of 1937 prompted a subtle change. France was now the *target* of a terrorism directed by hostile powers—and in some cases their French lackeys—whose aim was to divide and demoralize the people, incite civil conflict, and undermine the nation prior to invasion. In April 1939, the minister of the interior issued a warning to all prefects and the governor of Algeria that foreign state-sponsored terrorists were active in France.[236] The minister listed a number of objects that could house bombs: lactometers, fountain pens, pencils (each of which could contain an ampule of incendiary liquid), children's puzzles and building blocks, and suitcase time bombs.[237] With war approaching, the terrorist had now become an agent of the fifth column. In the febrile atmosphere of the late 1930s, terrorism was warfare by other means.

CONCLUSION

Terror in the Dark Years, 1940–1944

On 27 August 1941, twenty-one-year-old Paul Collette shot and wounded Pierre Laval during a military ceremony at the Borgnis-Desbords barracks in Versailles. Laval had acted as deputy prime minister of the French state, headquartered at Vichy, between July and December 1940. During this time French leader Marshal Philippe Pétain had announced his willingness to collaborate with Germany. Two bullets from Collette's automatic pistol passed through Laval's arm; one projectile entered his chest and lodged above the heart. "They got me," Laval allegedly murmured as he held onto those around him for support. Marcel Déat, head of the collaborationist Rassemblement National Populaire (RNP), was also injured in the stomach during the attack. Both Laval and Déat were at Versailles to review the first contingent of troops of the Légion des Volontaires Français, a collaborationist militia. Collette, a metalworker living in Caen, had attended the ceremony as a legionnaire. He later informed police that he did not regret his crime. "I joined the Légion to commit an attack," he allegedly stated. His motive: a sense of patriotic duty and an opposition to collaboration with Berlin.[1] Collette reportedly said that he had targeted the French rather than the Occupier because the Germans in France were simply doing their duty.[2] Fernand de Brinon, Vichy's liaison with the Nazis, claimed that the young man was the tool of a "terrorist organization" against which there was no solution but the use of force.[3]

For collaborators like de Brinon, one did not have to look far for the

175

origins of Collette's terrorism: Moscow and London had directed their followers in France to prepare and commit the attack.[4] *Le Cri du Peuple*, newspaper of the collaborationist Parti Populaire Français (PPF), blamed the communists, who had turned "to the terrorist methods of their origins," and the incitements to violence from the "Jewish-Bolshevik" radio in London.[5] The Catholic newspaper *La Croix* later described the murder of a Jewish man in Paris in August 1941 as a reprisal for Collette's attack on Laval and Déat: "Terrorism leads automatically to counter-terrorism," the newspaper remarked coldly.[6]

A matter of days before the shooting, the French government at Vichy had introduced stringent new repressive measures against resisters (especially communists) and dissidents. The law of 14 August 1941 (published in the *Journal Officiel* on 23 August 1941) established "Special Sections" within the French court system to try the "perpetrators of all criminal offences, whatever they are, committed with a communist or anarchist motive" ("dans une intention d'activité communiste ou anarchiste").[7] The legislation stripped defendants of rights long protected in French law (such as the right to appeal) and granted justices the power to deliver capital sentences. Swiftness and severity were the order of the day. The regime intended the Special Sections to deliver "a highly desirable local repression from the point of view of exemplarity."[8] Jurist Henri Donnedieu de Vabres described in his 1943 *Traité élémentaire de droit criminel et la législation pénale comparée* the practically limitless power and absence of accountability in the Special Sections. Judges were authorized to deliver sentences as they saw fit, regardless of previous laws on similar offences.[9] The law of 14 August 1941 thus founded a stark and arbitrary jurisdiction in which the Etat Français would later try "terrorists" for the first time.

In the Occupied north of France, the first session of the Special Section in Paris looked to make an example of the accused. Eleven men faced charges. Three—Emile Bastard, André Bréchet, and Abraham Trzebrucky—received capital sentences. Six received sentences of forced labor, including leading communist Lucien Sampaix, and two were imprisoned.[10] Police had arrested forty-five-year-old driver Bastard on 10 January 1941 on suspicion of fabrication and distribution of communist propaganda. A search of his home uncovered various types of propaganda and a copying machine. Bastard had previous convictions for theft, the violation of multiple confinement orders, and pimping. Twenty-year-old Bréchet was a communist activist who had previously worked as a secretary to deputy

Prosper Môquet. Upon his arrest, Bréchet was acting as a liaison between party leaders. He was found in possession of false identity papers and large amounts of propaganda. Trzebrucky was a fifty-four-year-old traveling salesclerk. Previously expelled from France, he had returned to the country with a false passport. Investigators alleged that he was a Jewish communist who spread propaganda among his Jewish friends.[11] The three men were executed at 7 a.m. on 28 August 1941, the day after their conviction. The court did not pass a capital sentence after its first session in August 1941.

The Etat Français continued to strengthen its repressive legislation as resistance activity intensified. Notably, the law of 5 June 1943 extended the remit of the Special Sections to include "all criminal offences, whatever they are, if they are committed to promote *terrorism*, communism, anarchy or social and national subversion or to stir up a state of rebellion against the legally established social order."[12] In a circular to provincial justices, dated 2 July 1943, Minister of Justice Maurice Gabolde further explained the particulars of the new legislation. The minister sought to impose an "uncompromising repression" against wrongdoers of all political loyalties. Such repression had become necessary due to the recent increase in armed attacks as well as a growing number of escapes from prison. Gabolde recognized that the term "terrorism" required some explanation: "By the expression 'terrorism' we must understand any activity—whatever the ideological, doctrinal or political motive which animates it ([communism], Trotskyism, Gaullism, etc....)—which provokes either recourse to crimes or misdemeanors endangering human life or undermining the respect due to property, such as assassinations, attacks of any kind by destructive or murderous devices, fires, looting of foodstuffs, clothing, theft, etc."[13] Consequently, in a time of war, the theft of resources qualified as terrorism.

Vichy was therefore the first French regime to write the crime of terrorism into the French statute book (though the lawmakers of Vichy left the phenomenon of terrorism undefined). With respect to the legal sanctioning of terrorism, the French government acted before the German Occupier. According to Roger Pannequin, the Occupation authorities officially designated resisters as terrorists only after the Allied invasion of 6 June 1944. The use of the word "terrorism" to legally categorize and punish resisters as terrorists thus originated in the French legal establishment.[14]

The enshrining of terrorism in French law is a significant landmark in the history of the phenomenon in France. Yet as the case of Collette demonstrates, Vichy and its sympathizers had denounced terrorism in the country long before June 1943. In September 1941, *L'Oeuvre*—now a collaborationist newspaper close to Déat—reported that the Tribunal d'Etat (a high court established according to the law of 7 September 1941) would "repress terrorism." The legislation that established this body referred to the trial of anyone who should "disturb order, internal peace, public tranquility, international relations or, in general, to harm the French people"— but it did not mention terrorism.[15] In March 1942, the French police leadership announced that, during the previous twelve months, officers had conducted a large operation against "antinational intrigues," namely communist propaganda and "acts of terrorism."[16] One finds in the sources the label used alongside other terms, such as "criminal," "communist," or "Gaullist."[17] Officials could refer to criminal cases as "communist and terrorist intrigues (*menées*)."[18] Prior to its entry into French law in June 1943, terrorism existed—much as it had under the Third Republic—as a social phenomenon without a juridical definition. Yet Vichy's failure to define terrorism in June 1943, along with the deeply rooted constructions of terrorism in the popular imaginary, ensured that the legal and social nature of terrorism remained fluid.

"Terrorism" continued to serve as shorthand for a variety of violent crimes. In this sense, the term was ostensibly used interchangeably with other descriptors of so-called criminality and criminals, such as "bandits" and "banditry," "wrongdoers," and "resistance." Certain parties appear to have preferred these latter terms when singling out specific enemies for opprobrium. The PPF's *Le Cri du Peuple*, while not shying from use of the terrorism label,[19] preferred labels such as "bandits," "banditry," and "Stalin's bandits" when attacking communists. On the other hand, by 1943, Déat used the term "terrorist" to describe both communist resisters *and* de Gaulle's loyalists.[20] Yet "terrorist" and "terrorism" had connotations beyond that of delinquency, and its power to delegitimize rested on the images that it conjured in the minds of the audience. Resistance groups recognized this later in the war. The issue so concerned the Conseil National de la Résistance that in late 1943 the body issued a statement that denounced Vichy's attempts, "under the pretext of 'terrorism'," to depict "the acts of legitimate self-defense" perpetrated by resisters as the "villainous crimes" of bandits.[21]

To some extent, wartime perceptions of terrorism drew on those of the interwar years.[22] For both the Etat Français and its resistance opponents, terrorism originated from foreign lands, whether Moscow, London, or Berlin. In this vein, Vichy's law of 27 July 1940 that introduced the death penalty for actions committed in the pay of a foreign power anticipated later counterterrorist measures.[23] Nevertheless, in the context of the Franco-French civil war of the early 1940s, if neither side could deny the French origins of many perpetrators, each cast doubt on the authenticity of the terrorists' "Frenchness," defined according to one's assumed political commitment.

Beyond representations of terrorism, the reality was often more complicated. Historical actors may have used neatly delineated criteria to define themselves and their enemies, but these boundaries often blurred "on the ground." One-time Cagoulard terrorist Gabriel Jeantet, for example, ended the war in a German prison camp for acts of resistance.[24] Jeantet was one among many "eleventh hour" resisters who had a violent collaborationist past. Distinctions within the resistance were not so clear-cut by 1944 and beyond. Former maquisard Edouard Montcouquiol recounted in 1982, "The regular army officers still treat us as outlaws. Because we were once against the law we'll always be seen as 'terrorists.'...Once a terrorist, always a terrorist in their eyes."[25] Such complexity may have informed the decision of the Ministry of Justice at the Liberation to review convictions for offences with "terrorist or subversive intent" on a case-by-case basis.[26] While wartime antagonists presented quite clearly defined representations of terrorism and terrorists (as explored further on), by the end of the war it was not so clear who the terrorists were.

"Professional Murderers": The Collaborationist Perception of Terrorism

Mercenaries, gangsters, bandits, madmen, and terrorists: the Vichy regime and its collaborationist allies employed a range of epithets to denounce fighters of the resistance and Charles de Gaulle's Free French operating in France and its overseas territories. Given the right-wing bent of the regime and its lackeys in the media, the revolutionary terrorist bogeymen of the interwar nationalist imaginary reappeared. Collaborationists consequently denounced the interference of the "henchmen of the defunct Cheka [the forerunner to the GPU]" and the Guépéou in France.[27] Communist operatives were "robot assassins" trained in Leningrad in the arts of sabotage, spying, and the handling of explosives.[28] They were at once ideological fanatics, feeling neither "the least sensitivity, the least remorse...driven

[only] by an ideology of evil," and mercenaries and professional criminals working for money alone.[29] Enemies of more recent date assumed a place in the rogues' gallery of terrorism, too: agents of the British intelligence service and the Free French allegedly trained terrorists and raised funds for operations across the English Channel.[30] The Jew came to the fore of collaborationist conceptions of terrorism. This development is unsurprising given the antisemitic nature of the Vichy regime. The German Occupier also blamed resistance terrorism in 1941 and 1942 on Jewish Bolsheviks, as Hitler's war in eastern Europe intensified.[31] Collaborationists thus railed against the "Judeo-Bolshevik mafia" and the "age-old hand of the Jew" behind terrorism.[32] Ultimately, terrorist gangs operated "in the pay of foreigners," who directed their agents to "pillage, steal, sabotage and kill."[33] An image thus emerged of France and Europe in the grip of a terrorist epidemic. In June 1942, *La Croix* lamented the frequency of recent outrages: "The number of attacks committed by terrorists can no longer be counted. In all countries, at all latitudes, individuals acting in isolation or belonging to organized gangs are showing overwhelming activity in this area."[34] At the close of 1942, Déat depicted France as a country overrun: "The attack comes from all quarters, in all three spatial dimensions, and in all humanly visible directions."[35] Terrorists were everywhere.

One perceives in collaborationist propaganda the well-worn claim that terrorism was "unFrench." This concept depended on an understanding of the mentality of resisters as different to that of "patriotic" and peace-loving French supporters of Vichy and collaboration. If, according to Déat (writing in September 1941), the terrorists' aim was to sow disorder in France, they would be sorely disappointed, for "recourse to the methods of terrorism is not in the French temperament."[36] In April 1942, de Brinon remarked upon the courage and determination with which two men had apprehended a terrorist; they had acted according to their "good French reflex."[37] As 1944 began, historian René Martel wrote in *Paris-Soir*, in an article titled "Foreigners and Terrorism," that he found it "regrettable" that foreigners participated in attacks against "the person and property of *authentic* French."[38] He continued that France had for too long been the dumping ground of Europe and that in the "interests of decent foreigners," it was time to sort the wheat from the chaff.[39] Such sentiments would not have been out of place in the final decade of the Third Republic.

Further elements of the collaborationist terrorist imaginary echoed those of the interwar years. First, collaborationists depicted terrorism as a motiveless crime inspired by a desire for wanton destruction. *L'Oeuvre* reported in March 1942 that a group of terrorists had admitted to killing a German at the Bastille metro station because, having failed to eliminate their previous target, "[they] did not want to return empty-handed."[40] Propaganda feature films and newsreels relayed images of apparently senseless murders, crop burnings, and train derailments to cinema audiences.[41]

Second, the scale of terrorist planning and expertise was terrifying. Terrorist attacks bore the mark of "specialists long trained in raids."[42] Speaking to the American press in August 1941, de Brinon claimed that recent acts of sabotage in France were perpetrated by "people knowledgeable of...special [techniques]."[43] Déat wrote in September 1941 that the terrorists' method betrayed "[the] presence of an organized group, disciplined, probably small in number, and composed of specialists."[44] Arrests in April 1943 uncovered "a terrorist organization exceptionally well organized and directed by leaders already responsible for numerous attacks of every kind."[45] Terrorists had frightening arsenals of weapons at their disposal. In November 1943, *Le Matin* recounted that between 11 September and 31 October that year, police had confiscated 92 automatic weapons, 786 rifles and muskets, 528 pistols and revolvers, and large quantities of explosives.[46] Added to the size of such stockpiles was the perception that the terrorists' weapons were more powerful than those of their predecessors.[47]

Finally, terrorism was overwhelmingly male. Women featured rarely in press pieces on terrorism. The French public was of course familiar with the figure of the female terrorist. Under the Occupation, the sexuality of the female terrorist receded as her place as a vital cog in the terrorist machine came to the fore. She provided logistical support for comrades on the front line and brought specialist skills to the fight (*Le Matin* described terrorist women as "seasoned specialists in forgery").[48] Still, female terrorists were prepared to use "the means peculiar to their sex to hide the documents given to them" and act as shuttles between male resisters.[49] While heavily indebted to the interwar imaginary, the collaborationist construction of terrorism did innovate in its gendered reading of the phenomenon. Collaborators (and, as will be seen, resisters) invested terrorist and counterterrorist behavior with values and qualities that drew on broadly held ideas of manly and unmanly conduct. This fact is unsurprising because notions of gender informed interwar cultures of violence in France. However, these notions were less visible in representations of terrorism between the wars than in those depictions of other forms of violence such as street fighting.[50]

Their prominence in wartime readings of terrorism may owe something to the fact that, as Luc Capdevila has revealed, "The appeal to virility, in every shape and through every medium, was part of everyday reality for the French from 1940 to 1944."[51] Both Vichy and its opponents based their attempts to mobilize support "on the appeal to a virile identity based on patriotic values, military virtues and voluntary action."[52]

Gendered descriptions of terrorism rested on a dichotomy between the resister-terrorist coward and the collaborationist counterterrorist warrior. Press and propaganda condemned the resister-terrorist's cowardly attacks, launched from the shadows, against defenseless victims, and striking always in the back.[53] In 1941, for example, *L'Oeuvre* referred to "the terrorists who bloody our soil, then go to ground, hiding in the shadows watching the consequences of their cowardice."[54] Leading collaborator and propagandist Philippe Henriot wrote in November 1943, "The [terrorist] attack is almost always carried out with abominable cowardice; they are four or five or ten to one; they are masked; they choose the night which makes pursuit almost impossible; they strike in the back; a sort of infernal sadism presides over these killings."[55] Unlike real soldiers—and, by implication, real men,—terrorists fought without honor. They epitomized "the underworld of vandals and muggers."[56] Such descriptions appeared throughout the collaborationist press.[57]

The other side of the collaborationists' gendered construction of terrorism was the masculine counterterrorist warrior, epitomized in the figure of the *milicien* or militiaman. The Milice Française was a paramilitary force founded in January 1943 to combat growing resistance throughout France. Milice propaganda framed the fight against resistance "terrorism" according to the masculine values of courage, togetherness, discipline, energy, devotion, and will; it was a struggle of real men—"strong men" of "willpower" and "revolutionary ardor"—against cowards.[58] Déat described these men as neither thugs nor fanatics but disciplined war veterans, skilled with weapons yet masters of their nerves, who sought to avoid the fight rather than agitate for it.[59] Nevertheless, these men were ready to sacrifice their lives for France: they were a cohesive and resolute group whose muscles provided armor to protect the public against the terrorist scoundrel.[60] Milice chief Joseph Darnand was depicted as a paragon of courage and the "prototype action man."[61] The extreme right-wing newspaper *Je suis partout* described this veteran of fascist politics as "[n]either a brilliant conversationalist, nor a subtle intellectual…[m]uch better than that: a male."[62]

There was more: "There radiates from him an impression of certainty and serene strength which would restore hope to the most discouraged. This stocky man, with grey temples, square chin, clear and cold eyes, it is understandable that he always inspired total confidence in his subordinates, that he never lacked volunteers for the most perilous missions."[63] Successful counterterrorism depended on the discipline, spirit of organization, and strength of such men.[64]

Alongside the operations of specialist formations such as the Milice, the Vichy regime sought to co-opt the French public into its counterterrorist struggle. As communist resistance hardened during autumn 1941, senior Vichy functionary Paul Marion called for a public response to the fight against terror similar to that witnessed at the signing of the Armistice in June 1940; that is to say, a patriotic and national "rallying" of all good French was necessary.[65] Marion repeated this call in December 1941, at which time he described counterterrorist efforts as a "prolongation of the war" in the name of national unity.[66] At the same time, the collaborationist RNP called on all "honest French" to provide information on the identities and whereabouts of attackers, while the party enjoined "resolute men" to take "energetic decisions" in the struggle.[67] The Vichy government even set aside funds to reward anyone who provided information on terrorists.[68] In October 1942, prefect of the Doubs René Linarès offered a prize of a hundred thousand francs for the capture of four fugitives accused of killing a German captain on the road between Besançon and Le Valdahon.[69] In April 1944, a poster in the Yonne offered a sum of up to twenty thousand francs for the arrest of anyone accused of committing terrorist offences.[70] The following month, in May 1944, a "Madame Madeleine" received a prize of five thousand francs for providing information that led to the arrest of a "dangerous terrorist" responsible for the deaths of three gendarmes and a civilian.[71] Such appeals and rewards perhaps stemmed from a concern that public complicity frequently allowed attackers to escape justice; this was in fact a recurring charge in the collaborationist press.

Much of the collaborationist construction of terrorism drew on long-established tenets of France's culture of terrorism. Terrorists were evil fanatics bent on pointless destruction and operating at the behest of foreign powers. The French who became embroiled in their schemes were not worthy of their nation. If not entirely novel to the French culture of violence, the use of gendered imagery to describe attacks in collaborationist propaganda on terrorism was new. The appeal to the public for help in rooting out terrorists was also a new development; French governments had not had to combat "homegrown" fighters for decades. There were sporadic calls to treat terrorists sympathetically, derived from an understanding of terrorists as lost sheep, brainwashed, or "rebellious [and] brainless youths."[72] The PPF's Simon Sabiani wrote in December 1943 that the conversion of communists from terrorism to the PPF was preferable to their murder. He claimed that the communist resistance recruited terrorist soldiers among workers and these same workers could provide "the best soldiers of the antiterrorist army," once they had been shown the error of their ways and exposed to the true National Revolution (Vichy's project for a root-and-branch renovation of France).[73] *Le Matin*'s Robert de Beauplan wrote as late as February 1944 that the maquis rural partisans were "young boys who let themselves be carried away by leaders or who yielded to the perfidious exhortations of Gaullist radio, but who are not therefore terrorists or communists."[74] However, such opinions jarred with widespread demands to snuff out terrorism with violence.

Not Terrorists but Soldiers: The Resistance and Terrorism

The response of resistance groups to Vichy's propaganda on "terrorism" betrayed a sensitivity to the importance of language in influencing public perceptions of their violence. Resisters, for example, generally refrained from using the word "attentat" for it conjured images of historical killings at the hands of anarchist bombers and fanatics.[75] While resisters were long aware of the power of the "terrorist" label to tarnish their reputation, only in late 1943 did the groups mount a coordinated response to Vichy's propaganda. This response was facilitated by the recent unification of several major associations under the aegis of the Conseil National de Résistance (CNR). The emergence of the maquis partisans and the focus of Vichy's propaganda on resistance "terrorism" perhaps also prompted the reaction. In November 1943, the CNR issued a statement on the subject and the importance of fighting Vichy's campaign of misinformation: "Public opinion, which knows what to expect about the truthfulness of a treacherous press, a slave radio station and infamous propagandists, must understand that the information delivered, concerning alleged terrorism, comes from those who have an essential interest in deceiving about the reality of things, by slandering the defenders of the Nation for the sole benefit of those who exploit, plunder and debase it."[76] Resisters were not terrorists but "courageous patriots who harass the Occupier's troops, destroy its munitions dumps, obstruct its war production and punish its accomplices."[77]

Resisters certainly understood the power of the word to smear its target. Vichy and German propaganda on "terrorism" was "an evil all the more contagious for it plays above all *with words*," and all the more dangerous because these words exploited the unconscious of the audience.[78] With details of attacks published daily in the press, "terrorism" was a frightening specter about which everyone was speaking, whether they had witnessed an incident of violence or not, and resisters expressed concern that Vichy's campaign was gaining traction with members of the public.[79] One gains a sense that the resisters felt themselves to be at a disadvantage in this propaganda war. A group in Marseille advised members to "clarify [*faire la mise au point*] each time it is necessary in conversations, on the trains, in queues, at the cinema, etc.…We must never miss an opportunity to correct and denounce in the eyes and ears of public opinion by graffiti, stickers, and speech."[80] It urged readers of its newssheet to challenge Vichy's terrorism discourse wherever they encountered it, "in conversations, on the train, in queues, at the cinema, etc."[81]

In this war of words, resistance propaganda adopted two tactics. First, resisters threw the accusation of terrorism back at their accusers.[82] The men of the Milice were "authentic terrorists," criminals, thugs, and the "scum" of society.[83] Milice terrorists mutilated the bodies of their victims in the worst example of the "abominable ferocity of fascists."[84] Second, resistance groups worked to reframe their own violence in a more palatable fashion. Contrary to Vichy's portrayal of the resisters as bandits operating in the shadows, the groups attempted to legitimize their violence by framing it as precise and surgical, as "authentic acts of war" and "veritable military operations" aimed solely at the Nazis and their French lackeys.[85] They depicted their members as soldiers in all but name: thus the Communist Party described the "uniformless soldiers" of the FTP (Francs Tireurs et Partisans) as the vanguard of the Liberation Army.[86] Resistance saboteurs acted "on the reliable indications of expert technicians" when they blew up power hubs to deprive factories working for the Germans of electricity.[87] They were "instructed, directed, [and] commanded, whenever possible, by military men or experts."[88] Acts of sabotage and attacks were steps on the road to Liberation, and they could be a more effective contribution to the war effort than allied bombing raids: "To cut a train line, stop a locomotive, put a factory out of action, sabotage always and everywhere: it's a little step closer to victory, it's to render a bombing raid unnecessary and it's furthermore to save French lives."[89] In December 1943, resister G. Le Mainois used an article in *Défense de la France* to counter the accusation of terrorism against the maquis. Resistance attacks were "veritable military operations"; the assassinations of German officers and soldiers and their French collaborators were "transactions in justice" against spies and traitors.[90] "*We are in a state of legitimate self-defense,*" the author argued.[91] One detects the influence of gendered ideals in this method of framing resistance violence. The *Courrier français du témoignage chrétien* attributed martial and masculine values to the "disciplined" and "rigorous" young men of the maquis.[92] The gendering of resistance violence was more explicit in resistance newspaper *Défense de la France*: resisters undertook their missions with "male resolve"; they were "an elite who, more than any other, deserves to be called an army. Those who make it up are not anarchists, rogues, or terrorists, they are soldiers."[93] Like Vichy, the resistance gendered the terrorist struggle.

The resistance's rejection of the terrorist label was not total. Several groups were unafraid to publicize the violence of their action. *Libération* was willing to claim responsibility for "terrorist" attacks: "[Vichy's] publicity does not displease us. In 'terrorism,' there is terror: [the terror] that we inspire." Nevertheless, the newspaper was careful to frame the violence as "legal" and part of an "underground war" for liberation.[94] The newspaper claimed responsibility for so-called terrorism in these terms: "To disobey is a duty, to strike remains an honor: our 'terrorism' is revolutionary legality."[95] According to the founder of *Défense de la France*, Philippe Viannay, in 1943 the desperation of the hour presented a choice for all French: to fight or to desert one's duty as a Frenchman. "Against those who refuse to fight," he continued, "we will use, if necessary, TERROR." This terror involved the assassination of collaborators and police officers ("those who have tortured will be tortured"), collaborator mayors and their underlings. As for the *mouchards* (informers), "A FRENCHMAN WHO SELLS OUT ANOTHER FRENCHMAN DESERVES TO BE TORTURED."[96] *Combat* followed a similar line. The so-called "terrorists" were nothing of the sort; in fact, legality rested with them as the "upholders of the law." Those who were executed in "terrorist" attacks were simply paying for their crimes against France.[97] Justice was an important theme in the resistance's justification of its violence for it distanced resisters from Vichy's accusations of wild and rageful acts read as feminine.[98]

Following the Liberation, the newly installed Republican authorities and their supporters deployed the "terrorist" label against recalcitrant former Nazis and Vichyites. On 1 September 1945, *Combat* published a communication from the Comité Parisien de la Libération. The Comité asked citizens to "redouble [their] vigilance and action" against snipers on the capital's rooftops. The end of the communiqué was striking. The Comité specified that "all those [men] or all those [women] who will bring aid and assistance to terrorists, by accommodating them, feeding them or [assisting] in some other way, will be considered as their accomplices and punished as such. The Prefect of Police fully associates himself with this call."[99] Former resister-terrorists now became operatives of counterterrorism, "ready to respond on the spot to all terrorist attacks by the Hitlerian enemy of its agents of the [fifth] column" looking to subvert the institutions of the newly restored Republic.[100] The Communist Party likewise called on patriots to defend "French order" and the French Republic against Nazi terrorism and the "traitors of the fifth column."[101]

The fluid meaning of terrorism presented a legal quandary for the newly installed French authorities: following Vichy's implementation of France's first counterterrorist law, what would be the attitude of Republican justice to imprisoned "terrorists"? Shortly before the liberation of Paris, de Gaulle's order of 9 August 1944 rendered the Vichy regime and most of its legislative program null and void. Article Three of the order deleted "[a]ll acts that instituted exceptional jurisdictions."[102] On 4 October 1944, Minister of Justice François de Menthon informed his subordinates that the order of 9 August 1944 also "amnest[ied] offences committed to terrorist or anarchist ends" (thus making good on a provision set out in the Free French order of 1 July 1943).[103] However, the order of 1 July 1943 did not mention "terrorism." Rather, it promised to repeal the anticommunist decree law of 26 September 1939 and the law of 14 August 1941 that established the Special Sections.[104] De Menthon recognized that the order of 1 July 1943 failed to consider subsequent modifications made to this repressive legislation. Notably, the 1 July 1943 order did not concern the provisions of the law of 18 November 1942 that repressed attacks on the external security of the state and acts committed in the name of social or national subversion. This omission was deliberate: Republican lawmakers feared that collaborators would claim amnesty on these grounds after the Liberation.[105] De Menthon further recommended the amnesty of all convictions made under the decree of 26 September 1939 and the law of 14 August

1941 prior to 1 July 1943, if they related solely to communist or anarchist motives. All other offences with "terrorist or subversive intent" required revision on an individual basis.[106] At the root of this stipulation lay the contemporary application of the terrorist label to *opponents* of the Liberation government. The minister of justice was perhaps concerned that a wholesale amnesty of "terrorists" would inadvertently benefit collaborators whose wartime violence was now considered "terrorism."

The Invention of Terrorism in France: Assessments

This book has traced the development of a French culture of terrorism during the first half of the twentieth century, elucidating the frameworks of values, qualities, perceptions, and meanings used to represent and understand violence labeled "terrorist" and its perpetrators.

It has explored the discursive constructions through which contemporaries perceived terrorism thanks to the mediation of a variety of actors in the wake of terrorist acts. In doing so, the book has shed light on the historical antecedents of French notions of terrorism in the twenty-first century, the roots of which are often located in the post-war era of decolonization.

Perceptions of terrorism in France during the late Third Republic were highly contextualized. Largely absent were the understandings and explanations of terrorism as a symptom of hereditary degeneracy or the duping of the "weak-minded" so popular during the 1890s. These concerns spoke to the anxieties of French society as it approached the end of the nineteenth century. Nonetheless, there was a period of transition between such ideas and the understandings of terrorism as a political phenomenon, as the case of Emile Cottin in 1919 demonstrated. Press and police considered Cottin a dupe and a political agent. The terrorism of the 1930s was understood in terms of the European ideological confrontation of the period and an attendant fear of foreign intervention in domestic politics. The rise of fascism at home and abroad, the revolutionary threat posed by the Communist International, and the influx into France of political refugees from Spain and central and eastern Europe nurtured a "common sense" representation of the terrorist "Other" as an immigrant whose "undesirable" and "unFrench" nature rested on partisan attitudes to their nationality, ethnicity, and political ideology. Terrorism became a stake in discussions over immigration control, national identity, and the political future of France.

From the 1860s, the term "terrorism" became detached from its original meaning as a system of government during the French Revolution. The emergence of nihilism in Russia—and its misinterpretation as a revolutionary political doctrine outside Russia—gave rise to a new conception of violent action that developed throughout the 1870s and 1880s, latterly under the influence of Russian "terrorists." French and European anarchists appropriated and adapted these Russian revolutionary tactics into violent "propaganda by the deed." By the 1890s, the French had come to understand nihilism, anarchism, and terrorism as kindred doctrines. The labels were employed interchangeably to describe acts of political violence.

From 1904, conceptions of terrorism began to shift. Renewed violence in Russia against the Tsarist regime was reported in the French press as terrorism. Now, with the anarchist threat in France receding, terrorism acquired a foreign character. This marked a significant step in the nascent "othering" process of terrorism: it was a tactic employed abroad, largely (but perhaps not solely) by Russians, and certainly not by anyone French. The presence of a significant Russian exile community in Paris, among whom police sporadically uncovered terrorists and bomb makers, further colored such notions of the phenomenon, as did the figure of the Russian female radical, a dowdy yet seductive character. At this time, France was the laboratory for exported terrorist violence; it was not yet a target. By 1914, if the term still lacked a settled meaning, its perceived alien essence was unmistakable.

The attempted assassination of Prime Minister Clemenceau in February 1919 demonstrated the continued influence of established ideas about terrorism. The assumption that Cottin was Russian informed early accounts of the crime. In this context, understandings of the assassin as a traditional nihilist terrorist mixed with newer fears of Bolshevik intervention in France. The recent war with Germany and the political upheaval that beset France's wartime enemy raised suspicions that the young Frenchman had acted on behalf of a Germano-Russian conspiracy. When such accusations proved unfounded, attention turned to Cottin's "conversion" to anarchism, and the well-worn argument that such a dangerous ideology held an inordinate attraction for the poorly educated and socially maladjusted.

The assassination of President Doumer in May 1932 likewise raised the prospect of a return to the nineteenth-century era of assassinations. However, though Paul Gorguloff's act drew comparisons with the deeds of past anarchists, reaction to the crime spoke to contemporary concerns over immigration and the threat that both communism and anticommunism (embodied in the figures of the White Russian and the conservative Republic) posed to domestic French affairs. Indeed, the notion of terrorism as a foreign phenomenon directed from abroad and perpetrated by foreigners in contradiction to French values began to take shape. The nature of these values depended on one's politics, for if the Doumer killing had detached terrorism from a fleeting wartime association with Germany (giving it once again a Russian aspect), interpretations drew largely on one's appreciation of communism. Anticommunists claimed that Moscow had ordered the killing of the French president to spread the cause of revolution. The left blamed reactionary White exiles for the outrage. Both sides accused each other of treachery to France. Alongside political conceptions of terrorism sat an Orientalist prejudice that ascribed ethnic and racial explanations to the assassination: it was a violent tactic suited especially to the "barbaric" Slavs. Consequently, state-appointed psychiatrists dismissed concerns about Gorguloff's mental health in favor of racist explanations of his supposed preference for violence.

Two years after the death of Paul Doumer, the assassination of another head of state in Marseille drew international attention to terrorism as never before. The murder of King Alexander I of Yugoslavia revealed terrorism to be the strategy of substate groups enmeshed in state-sponsored transnational networks intent on undermining international peace. Explanations of terrorism based on ethnic mentalities and "Slav mysticism" were now absent. The terrorist was a committed, highly trained, and well-equipped political warrior. The female terrorist was reconstructed as a sexy blonde bombshell far removed from the drab Russian intellectual of the turn of the century. Whatever Maria Voudracek's role in the conspiracy against Alexander—was she simply an agent of terror or the mastermind behind the plot?—the press exploited her supposed sex appeal. The female terrorist became a mainstay of the French culture of terrorism. These women—Voudracek, Dominique Fusciardi Rosario ("Menga"), Nadezhda Plevitskaya, Jacqueline Blondet—allowed the press to titillate readers with salacious allegations and innuendo about the role of women in terrorist groups. Looking beyond the exploitation of female figures, we may perceive that while women were framed repeatedly as the "unusual suspects" in terrorist conspiracies, they were also closely involved with them.

Significantly, in 1934, the perception of terrorism as an organized, cross-border phenomenon raised questions about the permeability of French frontiers. Calls to close the borders to "undesirables" intensified. The left fretted that foreign fascists were operating in France with the support of the growing indigenous extreme right. The right, unable to deny the political affiliation of the Marseille assassins, opted for xenophobia and racism in its demands for a tougher immigration policy. Once again, left and right united in their condemnation of the "unFrench" behavior of the terrorists—yet their notions of this "unFrench" character differed.

France remained in the grip of terrorism (according to contemporaries) as the 1930s ended. During 1937, there were multiple incidents of terrorist violence in the south of the country. The proximity of these attacks to Spain prompted anxiety that Francoist and Republican agents were operating on French territory. Established ideas about the foreign ideologies behind terrorism were deployed once again. Added to these concerns was a new fear that France was now the target of terrorism (thanks to the French Republican government's support for its beleaguered Spanish counterpart). If in the past terrorists had used France as a staging ground to play out quarrels imported from their homeland, it now seemed that some terrorists had decided to strike against France. A succession of terrorist incidents in September 1937 exacerbated these fears. The bombing of two buildings in Paris, the attempted theft of a Spanish submarine from Brest, and the abduction of a White Russian general gave the impression that terrorists operated freely in the country. The attribution of these incidents to foreign groups and agents saw renewed calls in the press, from the extreme left to the extreme right, to tighten up immigration controls. Former minister of the interior Marcel Régnier summed up the political mood when he told *Le Petit Journal* that since 1936, the "dregs of the shady elements" had arrived in France and that the time was now right, in the wake of the attacks, to halt this "invasion."[107] The government established a special panel to examine this perceived problem in the wake of the September events. "Terrorism" had assumed a place—underappreciated by historians—in the Republic's exclusionary attitude to immigrants. The discovery of the Cagoule plot little altered such perceptions. Right-wingers dismissed the group as pranksters or dupes while the left denounced the "hooded men" as the mercenaries of foreign fascism. The rootedness of understandings of terrorism in ideas of "unFrenchness" informed both reactions.

The French culture of terrorism that had developed under the Republic since the early twentieth century persisted under the authoritarian Vichy regime after 1940. Long-standing tenets of this culture lent themselves well to the collaborationist state's depiction of the resistance as a foreign-backed, violently destructive, and criminal organization intent on fatally undermining France. The regime's antisemitism chimed with that of the Occupier, and so when the Nazis blamed early communist resistance terrorism on "Judeo-Bolsheviks," collaborationists took up this attack too. Still, in 1941, to place the blame for terrorism explicitly on Jews was a novelty in France. Equally novel was the collaborationists' use of gendered language to underscore the enemy's underhand and unmanly terrorist behavior. Terrorists had long operated in the shadows, but only during the war was this framed as cowardly. Vichy's opponents in the resistance responded in turn with a gendered construction of their "terrorism" as a (masculine) military operation undertaken in the name of Liberation. The government's smear campaign worried resisters, and they waged a public relations war with Vichy over who were the "real" terrorists—and the true French. Following the Liberation of France, the provisional government urged citizens to remain vigilant to the threat from Nazi and French fascist terrorism (though the crime of terrorism would reenter French law only on 9 September 1986). By the late 1940s, thanks to the experience of the war terrorism had come to imply a violent opposition to the universalist values of the Republic. In this context, "unFrench" behavior could be attributed to both French and foreign-born anti-Republicans.

Scholars of terrorism tend to agree that the form of terrorism in a particular period owes little to historical precedent because terrorism "emerges in response to other events."[108] The specificities of historical cultural context give rise to novel forms of terrorism rendering the production of a history of the phenomenon difficult. However, the originality and significance of this book lie in its demonstration that, while in the French context terrorism during 1904–39 differed in terms of its goals and its perpetrators, from the Russian nihilist bomber to the French extreme right-wing Cagoulard, perceptions of terrorism across periods drew on similar themes. The ultimate victory of the resistance helped to solidify a culture of terrorism in which Republicans associated terrorist violence with opposition to France, defined as the embodiment of universal democratic values. The longevity of the Republican project since 1944 and its encounters with successive manifestations of terrorism have ensured that this broad understanding of terrorism as a phenomenon residing at the intersection of matters of national security and national identity, immigration, citizenship, and "Frenchness" remains. To appreciate fully post-war representations of terrorism—including those of the twenty-first century—we must look to the age of fascism.

GLOSSARY OF THE FRENCH PRESS[1]

L'Action Française

Founded in 1899. The newspaper of the extreme right-wing monarchist league of the same name, *L'Action Française* was an antisemitic and pro-fascist publication. Its circulation declined from a high point of a 100,000 in 1936 to approximately 45,000 in 1939.

L'Ami du peuple

Founded in 1938. Cheaply priced at two francs, this daily newspaper was owned by extreme right-wing antisemite and businessperson François Coty. Sympathetic to Italian fascism, it sought to attract a middle-class readership of shopkeepers, small business owners, and salaried workers. Maurice Chavardès estimates a circulation of 55,000 copies; Pierre Milza suggests the figure 700,000. *L'Ami du peuple* ceased publication in 1937.

L'Aube

Founded in 1932. A Christian Democratic daily newspaper, hostile to fascism, *L'Aube* had a circulation of up to 20,000 copies.

La Croix

Founded in 1883. A Catholic, conservative, and anticommunist daily, *La Croix* was largely positive about fascism (though its attitude depended on the relationship between Mussolini and the Vatican). The newspaper had an estimated circulation of between 150,000 and 280,000 copies.

Détective

Founded in 1928. Costing little more than a baguette, this cheap weekly magazine was the product of a collaboration between publisher Gaston Gallimard and Joseph and Georges Kessel. Known for its sensationalism and its photojournalism, the magazine claimed to have 500,000 readers just six months after its first publication.[2]

L'Echo de Paris

Founded in 1884. A right-wing newspaper, tending toward Catholicism, with a circulation of approximately 100,000 copies, it pursued a nationalist and anticommunist line. *L'Echo de Paris* merged with Léon Bailby's *Le Jour* in 1938.

Le Figaro

Founded in 1854. *Le Figaro* represented moderate conservatism. Following its sale to Coty in 1934, the newspaper briefly moved closer to the extreme right before returning to the moderate right (Coty subsequently used *L'Ami du peuple* as his racist, rabble-rousing mouthpiece). The newspaper had an estimated circulation of 100,000 copies.

L'Humanité

Founded as a socialist newspaper in 1904, *L'Humanité* became the Communist Party's daily publication in 1921. Stridently antifascist throughout the interwar years, the newspaper came to recognize Hitler as the most serious threat to France after 1935. Chavardés estimates the circulation of the newspaper to be 180,000; Milza suggests the higher figure of between 200,000 and 300,000.

L'Intransigeant

Founded in 1880. A right-wing newspaper—"solidly conservative" according to Milza; "right-wing antiparliamentarian" according to Chavardès—it generally looked favorably on fascism. *L'Intransigeant* had a circulation of about 200,000 copies.

Je suis partout

Founded in 1930. *Je suis partout* was a virulently antisemitic and nationalist weekly newspaper that moved toward a desire to work with German Nazism and Italian Fascism by the end of the 1930s. The circulation of *Je suis partout* reached approximately 100,000 copies in 1936.[3]

Le Journal

Founded in 1892. A conservative newspaper with a generally positive attitude to fascism abroad, its circulation reached 400,000 copies. This was one of the "big five Paris dailies," according to David Wingeate Pike.

Journal des débats politiques et littéraires

Founded in 1789. The *Journal des débats* was a conservative and anticommunist publication with a circulation of about 50,000 copies.

La Liberté

Founded in 1865. This was a moderately conservative newspaper until 1936 when it moved to the extreme right, following its purchase by Jacques Doriot's Parti Populaire Français.

Le Matin

Founded in 1884. This daily newspaper appealed to a conservative audience of small businesspeople and managers. *Le Matin* was very positive about fascism and Italy and came to advocate rapprochement with Germany. The newspaper had a circulation of approximately 300,000 copies by the end of the 1930s, and was one of the "big five Paris dailies," according to Pike.

L'Oeuvre

Founded in 1902. *L'Oeuvre* was close to the Radical Party, and several Radical deputies, such as Edouard Daladier and Edouard Herriot, contributed to its pages. It had an estimated circulation of 120,000 copies.

L'Ouest-Éclair

Founded in 1899. This was a regional Christian Democratic and antifascist newspaper with a large circulation (perhaps as large as 400,000 copies in 1934).

Paris-Soir

Founded in 1923. A very successful national daily newspaper with a circulation that regularly exceeded two million copies, *Paris-Soir*'s conservative outlook largely reflected that of its sister publication, *Paris-Midi*. This was one of the "big five Paris dailies," according to Pike.

Le Petit Journal

Founded in 1863. *Le Petit Journal* was purchased by Lieutenant Colonel François de La Rocque's Parti Social Français in 1936 and became the mouthpiece of this extreme right-wing party. It had a circulation of about 150,000 copies. This was one of the "big five Paris dailies," according to Pike.

Le Petit Parisien

Founded in 1876. *Le Petit Parisien* was a right-wing daily newspaper with an estimated circulation of 1.7 million copies by 1939. This was one of the "big five Paris dailies," according to Pike.

Le Populaire

Founded in 1918. The newspaper of the Socialist Party (Section Française de l'Internationale Ouvrière or SFIO), under the guidance of Léon Blum it pursued a resolutely antifascist agenda. Its circulation was between 100,000 and 300,000 copies.

Le Temps

Founded in 1861. *Le Temps* was a conservative daily aimed at the business and political elites with a circulation of approximately 100,000 copies.

NOTES

INTRODUCTION

1. Terrorism "is fundamentally a social fact rather than a brute fact": Richard Jackson, "In Defence of 'Terrorism': Finding a Way Through a Forest of Misconceptions," *Behavioral Sciences of Terrorism and Political Aggression* 3, no. 2 (2011): 117.

2. Stanley Hoffmann, "The Effects of World War II on French Society and Politics," *French Historical Studies* 2, no. 1 (1961): 36; Robert O. Paxton, *Vichy France: Old Guard and New Order* (New York: Knopf & Random House, 1972), 243; Julian Jackson, *France: The Dark Years 1940–1944* (Oxford, UK: Oxford University Press, 2001), 65.

3. The literature on the "French civil war" is large. Recent publications that concern the political and cultural conflict of the era include Caroline Campbell, *Political Belief in France: Gender, Empire, and Fascism in the Croix de Feu and Parti Social Français* (Baton Rouge: Louisiana State University Press, 2015); Sean Kennedy, *Reconciling France Against Democracy: The Croix de Feu and the Parti Social Français, 1929–1935* (Montreal; London: McGill-Queen's University Press, 2007); Chris Millington, *Fighting for France: Violence in Interwar French Politics* (Oxford, UK: Oxford University Press, 2018); Kevin Passmore, *The Right in France from the Third Republic to Vichy* (Oxford, UK: Oxford University Press, 2013); Joan Tumblety, *Remaking the Male Body: Masculinity and the Uses of Physical Culture in Interwar and Vichy France* (Oxford, UK: Oxford University Press, 2012); Gilles Vergnon, *Un enfant est lynché. L'affaire Gignoux, 1937* (Paris: Presses Universitaires de France, 2018).

4. Heinz-Gerhard Haupt and Klaus Weinhauer, "Terrorism and the State," in *Political Violence in Twentieth-Century Europe*, ed. Donald Bloxham and Robert Gerwarth (Cambridge, UK: Cambridge University Press, 2011), 191.

5. Haupt and Weinhauer, "Terrorism and the State," 192.

6. Contemporaries perceived terrorism as "foreign" in a sense broader than that of its basic legal meaning, that is, to originate from a country other than France. "Foreignness" could also imply difference and incompatibility with a French "mentality." While I use "foreign" throughout this book to describe non-French actors, and, less frequently, as a term to describe behaviors and attitudes perceived as different to those of the French, I prefer the term "unFrench" when describing notions of terrorism for it captures the sense of the culture of terrorism more effectively. On the terms "foreign" and "foreignness" in French, see Mathieu Couderc, "Etre étranger. Pour une histoire sociale de l'extranéité," *Hypothèses* 20, no. 1 (2017): 15–24. On the changing meanings of "foreign" and "foreignness" in France since the nineteenth century, see Clifford Rosenberg, *Policing Paris: The Origins of Modern Immigration Control Between the Wars* (Ithaca, NY: Cornell University Press, 2006), 3; 21; 28.

7. See Constance Bantman, *The French Anarchists in London, 1880–1914: Exile and Transnationalism in the First Globalisation* (Liverpool, UK: Liverpool University Press, 2013); and William Preston, *Aliens and Dissenters: Federal Suppression of Radicals, 1903–1933* (Urbana: University of Illinois Press, 1994).

8. See, for example, Tammy Castle, "*Morrigan Rising*: Exploring Female-Targeted Propaganda on Hate Group Websites," *European Journal of Cultural Studies* 15, no. 6 (2012): 679–94; Maura Conway, "Determining the Role of the Internet in Violent Extremism and Terrorism: Six Suggestions for Progressing Research," *Studies in Conflict & Terrorism* 40, no. 1 (2017): 77–98; Orla Lehane, David Mair, Saffron Lee, and Jodie Parker, "Brides, Black Widows and Baby-Makers; Or Not: An Analysis of the Portrayal of Women in English-Language Jihadi Magazine Image Content," *Critical Studies on Terrorism* 11, no. 3 (2018): 505–20.

9. See, for example, Mia M. Bloom, "In Defense of Honor: Women and Terrorist Recruitment on the Internet," *Journal of Postcolonial Cultures and Societies* 4, no. 1 (2013): 150–95; S. V. Raghavan and V. Balasubramaniyan, "Evolving Role of Women in Terror Groups: Progression or Regression?" *Journal of International Women's Studies* 15, no. 2 (2014): 197–211.

10. See, for example, Karla J. Cunningham, "Countering Female Terrorism," *Studies in Conflict and Terrorism* 30, no. 2 (2007): 113–29; Kathy Laster and Edna Erez, "Sisters in Terrorism? Exploding Stereotypes," *Women & Criminal Justice* 25, no. 1–2 (2015): 83–99; Mia Bloom and Ayse Lokmanoglu, "From Pawn to Knights: The Changing Role of Women's Agency in Terrorism?" *Studies in Conflict & Terrorism* (2020): 1–16, https://doi.org/10.1080/1057610X.2020.1759263 (last accessd 27 October 2022).

11. About women in terrorism, and representations of women in terrorism, I recommend reading the work of Mia Bloom (*Bombshell: Women and Terrorism* [Philadelphia: University of Pennsylvania Press, 2011]) and Caron E. Gentry and Laura Sjoberg (*Mothers, Monsters, Whores: Women's Violence in Global Context* [London: Zed Books, 2007] and *Beyond Mothers, Monsters, Whores: Thinking About Women's Violence in Global Politics* [London: Zed Books, 2015]).

12. Rosie White, *Violent* Femmes: *Women as Spies in Popular Culture* (Abing-

don, UK: Routledge, 2007), 34–43. Fitzmaurice's film is mentioned in newspaper movie listings as late as 1935.

13. David Andress, "The Course of the Terror, 1793–94," in *A Companion to the French Revolution*, ed. Peter McPhee (Chichester, UK: Blackwell, 2013), 303.

14. Mike Rapport, "The French Revolution and Early European Revolutionary Terrorism," in *The Routledge History of Terrorism*, ed. Randall D. Law (Abingdon, UK: Routledge, 2015), 70.

15. Rapport, "The French Revolution," 4.

16. On this debate see, for example, Lee Jarvis and Michael Lister, "State Terrorism Research and Critical Terrorism Studies: An Assessment," *Critical Studies on Terrorism* 7, no. 1 (2014): 43–61.

17. Alex Schmid, "Terrorism: The Definitional Problem," *Case Western Reserve Journal of International Law* 36, no. 2 (2004): 399.

18. See Lindsay Clutterbuck, "The Progenitors of Terrorism: Russian Revolutionaries or Extreme Irish Republicans?" *Terrorism and Political Violence* 16, no. 1 (2004): 154–81; John Merriman, *The Dynamite Club: How a Bombing in Fine-de-Siècle Paris Ignited the Age of Modern Terror* (London: JR Books, 2009).

19. Walter Laqueur, *The Age of Terrorism* (Boston: Little, Brown, 1987), 9.

20. Schmid, "Terrorism," 399.

21. David C. Rapoport, "The Four Waves of Modern Terrorism," in *Terrorism Studies: A Reader*, ed. John Horan and Kurt Braddock (London; New York: Routledge, 2012), 41–61. Rapoport develops this model in his book *Waves of Global Terrorism: From 1879 to the Present* (New York: Columbia University Press, 2022).

22. See, for example, Bruce Hoffman, "A First Draft of the History of America's Ongoing Wars on Terrorism," *Studies in Conflict & Terrorism* 38, no. 1 (2015): 75–83; Or Honig and Ido Yahel, "A Fifth Wave of Terrorism? The Emergence of Terrorist Semi-States," *Terrorism and Political Violence* 31, no. 6 (2019): 1210–28; Jeffrey Kaplan, "Terrorism's Fifth Wave: A Theory, a Conundrum and a Dilemma," *Perspectives on Terrorism* 2, no. 2 (2008): 12–24; Michel Wieviorka, "Une nouvelle ère du terorrisme?" 29 May 2013, https://wieviorka.hypotheses.org/171 (accessed 30 April 2020).

23. Contrarily, Laqueur postulated that to define terrorism is impossible: Walter Laqueur, *A History of Terrorism*, (Abingdon, UK: Routledge, 2017, originally published 1977), 7. For an introduction to the debate over the definition of terrorism, see Randall D. Law, "Introduction," in Law, *The Routledge History of Terrorism*, 1–11; Schmid, "Terrorism," 375–419; Anthony Richards, "Conceptualizing Terrorism," *Studies in Conflict & Terrorism* 37, no. 3 (2014): 217–19; Anthony Richards, "Defining Terrorism," in *Routledge Handbook of Terrorism and Counterterrorism*, ed. Andrew Silke (Abingdon, UK: Routledge, 2018). 13–21; Leonard Weinberg, Ami Pedahzur, and Sivan Hirsch-Hoefler, "The Challenges of Conceptualizing Terrorism," *Terrorism and Political Violence* 16, no. 4 (2004): 777–94; Andrew Silke, *Terrorism* (London: Hodder & Stoughton, 2014), 1–13.

24. Lisa Stampnitzky, "Can Terrorism Be Defined?" in *Constructions of Terrorism: An Interdisciplinary Approach to Research and Policy*, ed. Michael Stohl, Rich-

ard Burchill, and Scott Englund (Oakland: University of California Press, 2017), 12–14.

25. Alex Schmid, "The Revised Academic Consensus Definition of Terrorism," *Perspectives on Terrorism* 6, no. 2 (2012), 158–59.

26. Stampnitzky, "Can Terrorism Be Defined?"12.

27. Dominic Bryan, Liam Kelly, and Sara Templer, "The Failed Paradigm of 'Terrorism'," *Behavioral Sciences of Terrorism and Political Aggression* 3, no. 2 (2011): 80–96.

28. Caoimhe Nic Dháibhéid, *Terrorist Histories: Individuals and Political Violence Since the 19th Century* (Abingdon, UK: Routledge, 2017), 11.

29. Bryan, Kelly, and Templer, "The Failed Paradigm of 'Terrorism'," 80.

30. Joseba Zulaika and William Douglass, *Terror and Taboo: The Follies, Fables, and Faces of Terrorism* (Abingdon, UK: Routledge, 1996), 17.

31. See Richard Jackson, "The Literary Turn in Terrorism Studies," in Law, *The Routledge History of Terrorism*, 487–501.

32. Jackson, "In Defence of 'Terrorism'," 117.

33. Jackson, "The Literary Turn in Terrorism Studies," 487.

34. Rainer Hülsse and Alexander Spencer, "The Metaphor of Terror: Terrorism Studies and the Constructivist Turn," *Security Dialogue* 39, no. 6 (2008): 576.

35. Jackson, "The Literary Turn in Terrorism Studies," 488.

36. Ondrej Ditrych, *Tracing the Discourses of Terrorism: Identity, Genealogy and State* (Basingstoke, UK: Palgrave Macmillan, 2014), 1.

37. Hülsse and Spencer, "The Metaphor of Terror," 584.

38. For an overview of the debate about the definition of fascism in the historiography of France, see Chris Millington, *A History of Fascism in France: From the First World War to the National Front* (London: Bloomsbury, 2020), 149–65.

39. Gilbert Allardyce, "What Fascism Is Not: Thoughts on the Deflation of a Concept," *The American Historical Review* 84, no. 2 (1979): 369.

40. Martyn Frampton, "History and the Definition of Terrorism," in *The Cambridge History of Terrorism*, ed. Richard English (Cambridge, UK: Cambridge University Press, 2021), 31–57.

41. Gregory Shaya, "How to Make an Anarchist Terrorist: An Essay on the Political Imaginary in Fin-de-Siècle France," *Journal of Social History* 44, no. 2 (2010): 522.

42. Dominique Kalifa, *Vice, Crime, and Poverty: How the Western Imagination Invented the Underworld* (New York: Columbia University Press, 2019), 7. In his earlier work on the Belle Epoque, Kalifa wrote, "Indeed, [t]o name is never neutral. The practice always bears intentions or effects—sometimes technical, but sometimes also political, cultural, commercial [etc]": Dominique Kalifa, *La véritable histoire de la "Belle Epoque"* (Paris: Fayard, 2017), 16–17.

43. See Michel Wieviorka, "Espaces, niveaux et temporalités du terrorisme," *The Conversation* (French edition), 31 August 2017, https://theconversation.com/espaces-niveaux-et-temporalites-du-terrorisme-83263 (accessed 30 April 2020): "[T]errorism distils in a matter of seconds, in a specific place questions that con-

cern as much individuals, people in their singular existence, victims as well as the guilty, as [they concern] communities [whether] local…regional…national…supranational…[or] global. Terrorism is a total phenomenon, spatially complex and of a certain historical thickness, but [one] that shows itself in the form of an instantaneous and localised synthesis, while analysis [of it] quickly uncovers multiple dimensions, concerning spaces, temporalities and distinct levels." Relevant to my approach, too, is the concept of the "genealogy" of terrorism: see Michael Livesey, "Historicising 'Terrorism': How, and Why?" *Critical Studies on Terrorism* (2021), DOI: 10.1080/17539153.2021.1982467 (last accessed 27 October 2022).

44. On pages 24–25 of *Disciplining Terror: How Experts Invented "Terrorism"* (Cambridge, UK: Cambridge University Press, 2013), Lisa Stampnitzky writes, "the emergence of terrorism discourse cannot be explained as a simple reflection of concrete events, nor as a mere rhetorical creation.…While the emergence of "terrorism" as a new problem was certainly a rhetorical achievement, this was not *only* a linguistic transformation. To account more fully for the emergence of the problem of "terrorism" as we know it, we must focus on the trifecta of the emergence of new sorts of *events*, new sorts of *experts*, and the means by which these came together: the application of specific forms of expertise to the problem."

45. This statement draws on Eric Hobsbawm's observation about the public perception of bandits: "If there were no relation between bandit reality and bandit myth, any robber chieftain could become a Robin Hood." See Eric Hobsbawm, *Bandits* (London: Abacus, 2003), 168.

46. Benjamin K. Smith, Scott Englund, Andrea Figueroa-Caballero, Elena Salcido, and Michael Stohl, "Framing Terrorism: The Communicative Constitution of the Terrorist Actor," in *Constructions of Terrorism: An Interdisciplinary Approach to Research and Policy*, ed. Michael Stohl, Richard Burchill, and Scott Englund (Oakland: University of California Press, 2017), 92.

47. Maurice Laffitte, "Les bandits en auto ont commis deux nouvelles agressions," *Ce Soir*, 12 April 1939, 3.

48. "Mussolini supprime le droit d'association," *Paris Soir*, 19 May 1936, 1.

49. "Les principaux épisodes du drame autrichien," *Paris-Soir*, 14 March 1938, 4.

50. "Revue de la presse," *Journal des débats*, 28 February 1934, 3.

51. "Contre le terrorisme bolcheviste," *Paris-Soir*, 16 June 1927, 7.

52. "Les sociétés d'anciens coloniaux, bannières en tête défilent devant la statue de Galliéni," *Le Matin*, 1 June 1931, 2.

53. "Les bagarres sanglantes de Toulon," *Le Matin*, 9 August 1935, 3.

54. "Le docker Joseph Le Pape qui, en Septembre dernier, à Saint-Mâlo, porta un coup mortel au 'Grand Georges', est condamné à 5 ans de réclusion," *L'Ouest-Éclair*, 1 December 1934, 6.

55. "Des ouvriers agricoles grévistes pour la plupart étrangers lapident les ouvriers non-grévistes et sabotent le matériel," *Le Matin*, 4 July 1937, 3; "Un acte de terrorisme syndical," *Journal des débats*, 6 May 1937, 2.

56. "Les efforts soviétiques pour déclencher la révolution en Europe," *Le Matin*, 4 April 1937, 3.

57. "Une mafia terroriste à Paris," *Le Populaire*, 3 December 1934, 1.

58. *Journal Officiel du 24 Mars 1937: Débats parlementaires* 33 (23 March 1937), 1187.

59. Bruce Hoffman, *Inside Terrorism* (New York: Columbia University Press, 2006), 25; 40.

60. Giovanni Mario Ceci, "A 'Historical Turn' in Terrorism Studies?" *Journal of Contemporary History* 51, no. 4 (2016): 892.

61. Richards, "Defining Terrorism," 19.

62. Richards, "Defining Terrorism," 18.

63. Richard Jackson, "An Argument for Terrorism," *Perspectives on Terrorism* 2, no. 2 (2008): 30.

64. I broadly agree with Alex Schmid's "Revised Academic Consensus Definition of Terrorism," in particular with regard to point one: "Terrorism refers, on the one hand, to a doctrine about the presumed effectiveness of a special form or tactic of fear-generating, coercive political violence and, on the other hand, to a conspiratorial practice of calculated, demonstrative, direct violent action without legal or moral restraints, targeting mainly civilians and non-combatants, performed for its propagandistic and psychological effects on various audiences and conflict parties."

65. On this point, see Frampton, "History and the Definition of Terrorism," 49.

66. In his 1987 *Age of Terrorism*, Laqueur recommends using a "vague" definition (145).

67. Pippa Norris, Montague Kern, and Marion Just, "Framing Terrorism," in *Framing Terrorism: The News Media, the Government, and the Public*, ed. Pippa Norris, Montague Kern, and Marion Just (New York; London: Routledge, 2003), 4.

68. Joseph S. Tuman, *Communicating Terror: The Rhetorical Dimensions of Terrorism*, 2nd ed. (Los Angeles; London: SAGE, 2010), 32.

69. On this process, see Tuman, *Communicating Terror*, 32–37. See also Piers Robinson, "Editor's Introduction: Communicating Terrorism," *Critical Studies on Terrorism* 2, no. 1 (2009): 1–5; Michael Stohl, "Don't Confuse Me with the Facts: Knowledge Claims and Terrorism," *Critical Studies on Terrorism* 5, no.1 (2012): 31–49.

70. David C. Rapoport, "Fear and Trembling: Terrorism in Three Religious Traditions," *The American Political Science Review* 78, no. 3 (1984): 672.

71. Walter Laqueur, "Introduction to the Transaction Edition," in Laqueur, *A History of Terrorism*, xxv.

72. The quotation from Howard is in M.L.R. Smith, "Review Article: William of Ockham, Where Are You When We Need You? Reviewing Modern Terrorism Studies," *Journal of Contemporary History* 44, no. 2 (2009): 319.

73. Michel Wieviorka, "Terrorism," in *Concise Encyclopedia of Comparative So-*

ciology, ed. Masamichi Sasaki, Jack Goldstone, Ekkart Zimmerman, and Stephen K. Sanderson (Leiden; Boston: Brill, 2014), 418–19; 426n2.

74. Silke, *Terrorism*, 14. On historians and terrorism, see also Richard English, "History and the Study of Terrorism," in *The Cambridge History of Terrorism*, ed. Richard English (Cambridge, UK: Cambridge University Press, 2021), 3–27.

75. Ceci, "A 'Historical Turn' in Terrorism Studies?", 889.

76. Robert Gerwarth and Heinz-Gerhard Haupt, "Internationalising Historical Research on Terrorist Movements in Twentieth-Century Europe," *European Review of History—Revue européenne d'Histoire* 14, no. 3 (2007): 275–81; Beverley Gage, "Terrorism and the American Experience: A State of the Field," *The Journal of American History* 98, no. 1 (2011): 73–94. See also Adam Roberts, "The 'War on Terror' in Historical Perspective," *Survival* 47, no. 2 (2005): 101–30.

77. Walter Laqueur, "The New Face of Terrorism," *Washington Quarterly* 21, no. 4 (1998): 177.

78. See, for example, the special section of *Modern & Contemporary France* 25, no. 1 (2017): 67–89, titled "What Future for French Politics in an Age of Terrorism?"

79. Isabelle Duyvestyn, "How New Is the New Terrorism?" in Horan and Braddock, *Terrorism Studies: A Reader*, 27–41; *The World's Edition of the Great Presbyterian Conflict. Patton vs Swing. Both Sides of the Question* (Chicago: Geo. MacDonald and Co., 1874), 50.

80. Duyvesteyn, "How New Is the New Terrorism?" 439–54.

81. Colin Wight, "Theorising Terrorism: The State, Structure, and History," *International Relations* 23, no. 1 (2009): 103.

82. Ann Larabee, "Why Historians Should Exercise Caution When Using the Term 'Terrorism'," *The Journal of American History* 98, no. 1 (2011): 106–10.

83. Randall D. Law, *Terrorism: A History*, 2nd ed. (Cambridge, UK: Polity Press, 2016), 28–29.

84. Wolfgang J. Mommsen and Gerhard Hirschfeld, eds., *Social Protest, Violence and Terror in Nineteenth- and Twentieth-Century Europe* (London: Macmillan Press, 1982), ix.

85. This term belongs to Isaac Land: "Introduction," in *Enemies of Humanity: The Nineteenth-Century War on Terrorism*, ed. Isaac Land (Basingstoke, UK: Palgrave Macmillan, 2008), 2.

86. Ceci, "A 'Historical Turn' in Terrorism Studies?" 888–96.

87. Rory Cox, "History, Terrorism and the State," in *The Cambridge History of Terrorism*, ed. Richard English (Cambridge, UK: Cambridge University Press, 2021), 575.

88. See, for example, Marc Sageman, *Turning to Political Violence: The Emergence of Terrorism* (Philadelphia: University of Pennsylvania Press, 2017).

89. Mikkel Thorup, *An Intellectual History of Terror: War, Violence and the State* (Abingdon, UK: Routledge, 2010), 123.

90. Andrew Silke, "The Study of Terrorism and Counterterrorism," in Silke, *Routledge Handbook of Terrorism and Counterterrorism*, 6.

91. Leonard Weinberg, "A History of Terrorism," in Silke, *Routledge Handbook of Terrorism and Counterterrorism*, 34–56.

92. Jonathan Fenby, *The History of Modern France: From the Revolution to the War with Terror* (London: Simon & Schuster, 2015).

93. Juliette Duclos, "Paris: voici le mur de verre de la tour Eiffel," http://www.leparisien.fr/paris-75/paris-voici-le-mur-de-verre-de-la-tour-eiffel-14-06-2018-7772067.php, accessed 5 May 2020.

94. Jeremy Shapiro and Bénédicte Suzan, "The French Experience of Counterterrorism," *Survival* 45, no. 1 (2003): 68; Shaun Gregory, "France and the War on Terrorism," *Terrorism and Political Violence* 15, no. 1 (2003): 124.

95. Jenny Raflik, "La France face au terrorisme d'hier à aujourd'hui," *Outre-Terre* 51, no. 2 (2017): 202–14.

96. See Wieviorka, "Terrorism," 418; 423; Michel Wieviorka, "France Faced with Terrorism," *Studies in Conflict & Terrorism* 14, no. 3 (1991): 157–70; Michel Wieviorka, "From Classical Terrorism to 'Global' Terrorism," *International Journal of Conflict and Violence* 1, no. 2 (2007): 92–104; "Terrorisme, radicalisation, Isla : Michel Wieviorka en conversation avec Marc Sageman," *The Conversation* (French edition), 1 November 2017, https://theconversation.com/terrorisme-radicalisation-islam-michel-wieviorka-en-conversation-avec-marc-sageman-86574 (accessed 30 April 2020). See also Gilbert Guillaume, "France and the Fight Against Terrorism," *Terrorism and Political Violence* 4, no. 4 (1992): 131–35.

97. Frank Foley, "France," in Silke, *Routledge Handbook of Terrorism and Counterterrorism*, 528–39; Gregory, "France and the War on Terrorism;" Dorle Hellmuth, "Countering Jihadi Terrorists and Radicals the French Way," *Studies in Conflict & Terrorism* 38, no. 12 (2015): 979–97; Shapiro and Suzan, "The French Experience of Counterterrorism," 88–93.

98. See, for example, Marie Beauchamps, "Perverse Tactics: 'Terrorism' and National Identity in France," *Culture, Theory and Critique* 58, no. 1 (2017): 48–61; Sylvain Brouard, Pavlos Vasilopoulos, and Martial Foucault, "How Terrorism Affects Political Attitudes: France in the Aftermath of the 2015–2016 Attacks," *West European Politics* 41, no. 5 (2018): 1073–99; Myriam Feinberg, "States of Emergency in France and Israel—Terrorism, 'Permanent Emergencies,' and Democracy," *Z Politikwiss* 28 (2018): 495–506; Gino G. Raymond, "After *Charlie*: The Unravelling of the French Republican Response," *Patterns of Prejudice* 52, no. 1 (2018): 24–38; Ariane Bogain, "Terrorism and the Discursive Construction of National Identity in France," *National Identities* 21, no. 3 (2019): 241–65; Julien Fragnon, "'We Are at War': Continuity and Rupture in French Anti-Terrorist Discourse," *Media, War & Conflict* 12, no. 2 (2019): 131–52.

99. Jean-François Gayraud and David Sénat, *Le terrorisme* (Paris: Presses Universitaires de France, 2006), 62.

100. Jean Maitron, *Le Mouvement anarchiste en France. Tome 1. Des Origines à 1914* (Paris: François Maspero, 1975), 206–61.

101. Maitron, *Le Mouvement anarchiste en France. Tome 1*, 260.

102. Maitron, *Le Mouvement anarchiste en France. Tome 1*, 261. The emphasis is in the original text.
103. Vivien Bouhey, *Les Anarchistes contre la République. Contribution à l'histoire des réseaux sous la Troisième République (1880–1914)* (Rennes, FR: Presses Universitaires de Rennes, 2008), 142.
104. Bouhey, *Les Anarchistes contre la République*, 219–20.
105. Adapted from the subtitle of the book: *The Dynamite Club: How a Bombing in Fin-de-Siècle Paris Ignited the Age of Modern Terror*.
106. Merriman, *The Dynamite Club*, 5.
107. Merriman, *The Dynamite Club*, 3.
108. See Ersel Aydinli, "Before Jihadists There Were Anarchists: A Failed Case of Transnational Violence," *Studies in Conflict & Terrorism* 31, no. 10 (2008): 903–23; Richard Bach Jensen, "Nineteenth Century Anarchist Terrorism: How Comparable to the Terrorism of Al-Qaeda?" *Terrorism and Political Violence* 20, no. 4 (2008): 589–96.
109. John Merriman, *Ballad of the Anarchist Bandits: The Crime Spree That Gripped Belle Époque Paris* (New York: Nation Books, 2017), 142.
110. See, for example, Richard Bach Jensen's *The Battle Against Anarchist Terrorism: An International History, 1878–1934* (Cambridge, UK: Cambridge University Press, 2014).
111. Richard Bach Jensen, "The First Global Wave of Terrorism and International Counter-Terrorism, 1905–14," in *An International History of Terrorism: Western and Non-Western Experiences*, ed. Jussi M. Hanhimaki and Bernhard Blumenau (Abingdon, UK: Routledge, 2013), 17.
112. Richard Bach Jensen, "The 1904 Assassination of Governor General Bobrikov: Tyrannicide, Anarchism, and the Expanding Scope of 'Terrorism'," *Terrorism and Political Violence* 30, no. 5 (2018): 828–43.
113. Jensen, "The 1904 Assassination of Governor General Bobrikov," 835–38.
114. Frampton, "History and the Definition of Terrorism," 40.
115. See, for example, Paul M. Hagenloh, "State Terrorism in Early Twentieth-Century Europe," in Law, *The Routledge History of Terrorism*, 159–77.
116. Katherine Foshko, "The Paul Doumer Assassination and the Russian Diaspora in Interwar Paris," *French History* 23, no. 3 (2009): 383–404; Karelle Vincent, "Le régicide en République," *Crime, Histoire & Sociétés/Crime, History & Societies* 3, no. 2 (1999): 73–93.
117. Péter Kovács, "Le grand précédent: la Société des Nations et son action après l'attentat contre Alexandre, roi de Yougoslavie," *Europe Integration Studies* 1, no. 1 (2002): 30–40; Virginie Sansico, "Le terrorisme, vie et mort d'une notion juridique (1930–1945)," *Archives de la Politique Criminelle* 38, no. 1 (2016): 27–45; Ben Saul, "The Legal Response of the League of Nations to Terrorism," *Journal of International Criminal Justice* 4, no. 1 (2006): 78–102.
118. Mario Jareb, "Marseilles 1934: The Death of the King," in *A Transnational History of Right-Wing Terrorism: Political Violence and the Far Right in Eastern and Western Europe Since 1900*, ed. Johannes Dafinger and Moritz Florin (Abingdon,

UK; New York: Routledge, 2022), 115–28; Frédéric Monier, "Défendre des 'terroristes' dans la France de 1935. L'avocat des 'oustachis croates'," *Le Mouvement social* 240 (2012): 105–20; Frédéric Monier, "L'attentat de Marseille 9 octobre 1934: Régicide et terrorisme dans les années trente," *La Révolution française. Cahiers de l'Institut d'histoire de la Révolution française* 1 (2012), posted online at https://lrf.revues.org/461 (accessed 1 March 2017).

119. See, for example, Jonah Corne, "Regicide on Repeat: The Pensive Spectator in Rebecca West's *Black Lamb and Grey Falcon*," *Criticism* 60, no. 1 (2018): 47–73; Matthew Graves, "Memory and Forgetting on the National Periphery: Marseilles and the Regicide of 1934," *PORTAL. Journal of Multidisciplinary International Studies* 7, no. 1 (2010): 1–21, https://www.researchgate.net/publication/272731584_Memory_and_Forgetting_on_the_National_Periphery_Marseilles_and_the_Regicide_of_1934 (accessed 5 October 2022); Saul, "The Legal Response of the League of Nations to Terrorism."

120. Ondrej Ditrych, "'International Terrorism' as Conspiracy: Debating Terrorism in the League of Nations," *Historical Social Research/Historische Sozialforschung* 38, no. 1 (2013): 200.

121. Joel Blatt, "The Cagoule Plot," in *Crisis and Renewal in France, 1918–1962*, ed. Kenneth Mouré and Martin S. Alexander (New York: Berghahn Books, 2002), 84–104; Gayle K. Brunelle and Annette Finley-Croswhite, *Murder in the Metro: Laetitia Toureaux and the Cagoule in 1930s France* (Baton Rouge: Louisiana State University Press, 2012); and Brunelle and Finley-Croswhite, *Assassination in Vichy: Marx Dormoy and the Struggle for the Soul of France* (Toronto: University of Toronto Press, 2020); D.L.L. Parry, "Counter Revolution by Conspiracy, 1935–1937," in *The Right in France: From Revolution to Le Pen*, ed. Nicholas Atkin and Frank Tallett (London: IB Taurus, 2003), 161–81.

122. Michel Winock, *Nationalisme, antisémitisme et fascisme en France* (Paris: Seuil, 2014), 250–51.

123. Former maquisard Edouard Montcouquiol recounted in 1982, "The regular army officers still treat us as outlaws. Because we were once against the law we'll always be seen as 'terrorists.'…Once a terrorist, always a terrorist in their eyes." H. R. Kedward, *In Search of the Maquis: Rural Resistance in Southern France, 1942–1944* (Oxford, UK: Clarendon Press, 1993), 250.

124. Gary Wilder, *The French Imperial Nation-State: Negritude and Colonial Humanism Between the Two World Wars* (Chicago: University of Chicago Press, 2005), 3.

125. Wilder, *The French Imperial Nation-State*, 4.

126. "Le mouvement révolutionnaire en Indochine," *Le Matin*, 25 February 1930, 1; "Marius Moutet dénonce les methodes terroristes de répression," *Le Populaire*, 11 April 1930, 1.

127. See, for example, Archives Nationales, Pierrefitte-sur-Seine (hereafter referred to as AN) F60 754, "Des agitateurs d'inspiration bolchevik préméditèrent l'émeute de Meknès," *Le Matin*, 16 September 1937; "Le Néo-Destour se solidarise avec les agitateurs marocains et algériens," *La Dépêche de Constantine*, 9 Novem-

ber 1937; AN F60 720, "Commission d'études du Haut-Comité Méditerranéen. Séance du 5 juillet 1937"; AN F60 744, "Lettre de Tunis No. 240 du 8 Février 1936 sur la situation en Tunisie."

128. AN F60 727, Armand Henri-Flaasch, "Ce qu'étaient l'Etoile nord-africaine et son chef: Messali Hadj," *Le Journal*, 27 January 1937.

129. AN F60 754, "Les responsabilités du Protectorat," *Le Petit Bleu*, 28 October 1937.

130. AN F60 754, "Violentes bagarres hier à Khémisset," *Le Petit Marocain*, 23 October 1937.

131. AN F7 13412, "Le communisme en Algérie," *L'Action Française*, 26 February 1923.

132. AN F7 13413, "Le Ministre de l'Intérieur (D'on de la S.G) à MM. les Commissaire Spéciaux," 25 May 1925.

133. "Le salut de la France aux victimes de l'attentat de Yen-Bay," *L'Avenir du Tonkin*, 13 February 1930, 1.

134. Conversely, French newspapers presented violence in *non-French* colonial conflicts as terrorism. In particular, the press used "terrorism" to describe strife in the British Empire, as a method either of repression or of nationalist resistance. See, for example, on Ireland: "Les terroristes irlandais inquiètent l'Angletrre," *Le Journal*, 30 November 1920, 1; "Le spectre sinn-feiner épouvante l'Angleterre," *La Lanterne*, 1 December 1920, 3; "L'action terroriste des sinn feiners redouble de violence," *L'Echo de Paris* 21 February 1921, 1; "Ce fut hier à Belfast une journée de représailles," *Le Journal*, 20 May 1922, 3; "Une série d'attentats terroristes marque la visite des souverains anglais en Irlande," *L'Echo de Paris*, 29 July 1937, 3; "Un vaste plan terroristes découvert à Belfast," *Le Matin*, 5 February 1939, 1; "Les attentats terroristes en Angleterre," *Le Populaire*, 28 July 1939, 3; "La répression du terrorisme en Angleterre," *Le Figaro*, 1 August 1939, 3; "Un complot aurait été découvert en vue de faire sauter le Parlement," *Le Figaro*, 10 August 1939, 3; and on Palestine: "Le terrorisme en Palestine," *Le Figaro*, 3 June 1936, 3; "Les Anglais brisent le terrorisme arabe en Palestine," *Le Figaro*, 2 October 1937, 3; "Au nom du Coran le terrorisme est réprouvé...mais la révolte gronde toujours," *L'Echo de Paris*, 3 November 1937, 3; "La répression du terrorisme en Palestine," *Le Matin*, 21 February 1938, 3; "La recrudescence du terrorisme en Palestine," *Le Matin*, 5 July 1938, 3; "L'iman Ali Khasib assassin à Jérusalem par des terroristes arabes," *Le Populaire*, 13 July 1938, 3; "Un village arabe, nid de terroristes, est détruit en Palestine par les troupes anglaises au cours d'une expédition punitive," *Le Matin*, 17 July 1938, 1.

135. AN F7 13412, "Copie du rapport redigé par le Sieur Laskar Sadis, secrétaire du groupement communiste de Relizane pour être depose par lui en reunion générale des sections communistes départementales à Oran Maison du Peuple le 21 Mai 1922 à neuf heures du matin," n.d.

136. AN F7 13412, "Le Gouverneur Général de l'Algérie à Monsieur le Ministre de l'Intérieur," 26 April 1923.

137. AN F7 14978, "Le parti communiste algérien en 1927," 11 February 1928.

138. AN F60 754, "Le Général Noguès, Commissaire Résident Général de France au Maroc, Commandant en Chef, à son Excellence Monsieur Yvon Delbos, Ministre des Affaires Etrangères," 9 October 1937.

139. Neil Macmaster, "Islamophobia in France and the 'Algerian Problem'," in *The New Crusades: Constructing the Muslim Enemy*, ed. Emran Qureshi and Michael Sells (New York: Columbia University Press, 2003), 292.

140. Rosenberg, *Policing Paris*, 153–68.

141. AN F60 720, "Note au sujet de la régularisation provisoire de la situation des Marocains entrés clandestinement en France depuis le 1er Juillet 1936," 22 December 1937.

142. See, for example, AN F60 720, "Note pour Monsieur le Secrétaire Général," n.d.; "Rapport sur la situation de stravailleurs nord-africains et sur leurs revendications," n.d.; "Le Maire de la Ville de Longwy, Chevalier de la Légion d'Honneur, à Monsieur le Ministre de la Guerre," 27 January 1937; "Circulaire à Messieurs les Maires sous le couvert de MM. les Sous-Préfets (Préfecture du Nord) [from R. Gazagne, Secréatire Général du Nord, on behalf of the Prefect of the Nord]," 25 January 1938; AN F60 720, "Commission d'études du Haut-Comité Méditerranéen. Séance du 5 juillet 1937."

143. AN F60 720, "Note au sujet de la régularisation provisoire de la situation des Marocains entrés clandestinement en France depuis le 1er Juillet 1936," 22 December 1937.

144. AN F60 754, "Le Général Noguès, Commissaire Résident Général de France au Maroc, Commandant en Chef, à son Excellence Monsieur Yvon Delbos, Ministre des Affaires Etrangères," 9 October 1937.

145. AN F60 720, "Note sur le service de protection et d'assistance des indigènes nord-africains à Paris et dans le département de la Seine," 5 October 1936.

146. AN F60 733, "Rapport à Monsieur le Gouverneur Général, from L'Inspecteur Général de l'Administration en Algérie," 31 October 1936

147. AN F60 754, Elie Angonin, "Les émeutes de Meknès sont une conséquence de l'action hitlérienne en Afrique du Nord," *Oran Républicain*, 15 September 1937.

148. AN F7 13412, "Renseignement de Suisse, en date du 12 Janvier 1921"; AN F7 14978, "Renseignement. A.s/Préparatifs pour action musulmane en Afrique du Nord. Source: sérieuse. 10 Août 1935"; AN F60 754, "Au sujet de la propaganda faite par Abdellatif Abdelouahab en faveur de l'Allemagne au Congrès interparlementaire au Caire et au Maroc," 2 December 1938.

149. AN F7 13413, "Traduction," Berlin, 6 May 1925 (this document appears to come from the French Legation in Portugal); "D'un correspondant. Le Parti Communiste Français et les événements au Maroc," 16 May 1925.

150. See, for example, AN F7 13412, "Affaire Tchviklinski," 1 April 1921; "Le Ministre de l'Intérieur à Monsieur le Gouverneur Général de l'Algérie," 30 October 1924; AN F7 14978, "Renseignement. A/S. Stepan Bozadjian," 27 February 1931; "Au sujet du fermier Alexandre Belkine d'Ain Tedelas," 26 July 1928. See also, for example, AN F7 13413, "Le Contrôleur Général des Services de Police

Administrative à Monsieur le Commissaire Spécial de Marseille," 6 February 1926 and the press cuttings from *La Liberté* contained within this file.

151. Alfred-Ernest Babut, "Nous n'avon rien à craindre céans, mais, du dehors?" *La Revue franco-annamite. Revue hebdomadaire des questions de politique indigene en Indochine*, 28 December 1930, 1.

152. Michael B. Miller, *Shanghai on the Metro: Spies, Intrigue, and the French Between the Wars* (Berkeley: University of California Press, 1994), 214–15.

153. Pierre Bret, "L'opinion de Charles Meyer, directeur de la Police Judiciaire," *Marianne*, 29 September 1937, 2.

154. Richard Jackson, Lee Jarvis, Jeroen Gunning, and Marie Breen Smyth, *Terrorism: A Critical Introduction* (Basingstoke, UK: Palgrave Macmillan, 2011), 53.

155. Information taken from Amélie Chabrier et Marie-Ève Thérenty, "*Détective*, histoire, imaginaire, médiapoétique d'un hebdomadaire de fait divers (1928–1940)," *Criminocorpus*, 18 December 2018, http://journals.openedition.org/criminocorpus/5537 (accessed May 5, 2020); Maurice Chavardès, *Une campagne de presse. La droite française et le 6 février 1934* (Paris: Flammarion, 1970), 109–13; Pierre Milza, *L'Italie fasciste devant l'opinion française, 1920–1940* (Paris: Armand Colin, 1967), 255–60.

156. Chavardès, *Une campagne de presse*, 113; Albert Pierre, "Remarques sur la stagnation des tirages de la presse française de l'entre-deux-guerres," *Revue d'histoire moderne et contemporaine* 18, no. 4 (1971): 542–43.

157. Pierre, "Remarques," 542–43.

158. Catherine Bertho Lavenir, "Bombes, protes & pistolets. Les âges médiologiques de l'attentat," *Les cahiers de médiologie* 1, no. 13 (2002): 28.

159. By 1939, there were over five million registered radio sets in the country. Rebecca Scales, *Radio and the Politics of Sound in Interwar France, 1921–1939* (Cambridge, UK: Cambridge University Press, 2016), 12–14.

160. "Le Président Doumer est mort des suites d'un attentat," *L'Echo saintongeais*, 8 May 1932, 2; "Dans nos ports," *Le Petit Provençal*, 8 May 1932, 2.

161. "La loterie nationale. Deuxième tranche," *Le Petit Parisien*, 10 October 1934, 5.

162. A. Laudat, "L'enquête se poursuit sur les criminels attentats terroristes de Paris," *Courrier de Saône-et-Loire*, 14 September 1937, 1.

163. Louis-Leon Martin, "Comment on fait un journal parlé," *Le Petit Parisien*, 17 October 1937, 2.

164. Martin, "Comment on fait un journal parlé," 2.

165. Martin, "Comment on fait un journal parlé," 2.

166. Jacques Bonhomme, "Bombes, cagoules, mitraillettes et glaives...," *L'Express de Mulhouse*, 20 September 1937, 2.

167. Hülsse and Spencer, "The Metaphor of Terror," 580.

CHAPTER 1

1. "Stryga" is sometimes spelled "Striga" in the contemporary press.
2. "Fin tragique d'un anarchiste. Eventré par une bombe," *Le Matin*, 4 May 1906, 1.
3. "Nouvelles du jour. La Bombe de Vincennes," *Journal des débats politiques et littéraires*, 5 May 1906, 2–3.
4. "La bombe de Vincennes," *Le Petit Journal*, 17 July 1906, 3; "La bombe de Vincennes," *Le Matin*, 5 May 1906, 1–2.
5. "Une bombe," *L'Aurore*, 4 May 1906, 1; "60,000 ouvriers réclament les huits heures—Une bombe éclate à Vincennes," *L'Intransigeant*, 4 May 1906, 1; "Fin tragique d'un anarchiste," 1.
6. "Un anarchiste tué par sa bombe dans le bois de Vincennes," *Le Petit Journal*, 4 May 1906, 1.
7. "Les bombes de Vincennes," *L'Aurore*, 11 May 1906, 2; "Anarchistes russes," *La Lanterne*, 18 July 1906, 1–2.
8. "Les bombes de Vincennes," 2; "Les bombes de Charenton," *Le Grand Echo du Nord et du Pas-de-Calais*, 8 May 1906, 4; "Les bombes de Vincennes," *Journal des débats politiques et littéraires*, 9 May 1906, 3.
9. "Les bombes de Vincennes," *L'Aurore*, 24 May 1906, 2; "Stryga?" *L'Intransigeant*, 25 May 1906, 4; "Exploits d'anarchistes. Les fabricants de bombes," *Le Matin*, 11 May 1906, 1–2.
10. "La bombe de Vincennes," (*Le Petit Journal*) 3.
11. V. Maron, "L'Affaire Sokoloff," *L'Aurore*, 17 July 1906, 1; "Anarchistes russes," 1–2; M. Grandgousier, "Faiseurs de bombes," *Le Matin*, 17 July 1906.
12. Paul Avrich, *The Russia Anarchists* (Princeton, NJ: Princeton University Press, 1967), 47–48; Peter Gooderham, "The Anarchist Movement in Russia, 1905–1917" (PhD diss., University of Bristol, 1981), 70–71.
13. Archives de la Préfecture de Police, Le Pré-Saint Gervais, (hereafter referred to as APP) BA 1709, untitled report, Paris, 21 October 1907. See also APP BA 1709, "Le Commissaire de Police, Chef de la 3e Brigade, à monsieur le Directeur Général de Recherches," 23 February 1908.
14. Gooderham, "The Anarchist Movement in Russia," 391n71.
15. APP BA 1709, "Lettre de Wladimir Lapidus (Stryga)," Editions du Groupe boundiste, 1907. Anna Geifman gives the letter credence in *Thou Shalt Kill: Revolutionary Terrorism in Russia, 1894–1917* (Princeton, NJ: Princeton University Press, 1993), 36–37.
16. AN BB18 6464, untitled interview between investigating magistrate du Puy and Lieutenant Colonel von Kotten, 10 May 1909. Gooderham and Avrich also claim that Paris was a favored destination for Russian terrorist theorists and activists.
17. See the reports on Russian anarchists in APP BA 1709.
18. Jensen, "The First Global Wave of Terrorism and International Counter-Terrorism, 1905–14," in *An International History of Terrorism: Western and Non-*

Western Experiences, ed. Jussi M. Hanhimaki and Bernhard Blumenau (Abingdon, UK; New York: Routledge, 2013), 16–34.

19. "Un anarchiste tué par sa bombe dans le bois de Vincennes," 1; "Les bombes de Charenton," 4; "Fin tragique d'un anarchiste," 1.

20. "Fin tragique d'un anarchiste," 1.

21. Eugène Destez, "Engin d'exportation," *Gil Blas*, 4 May 1906, 1.

22. Destez, "Engin d'exportation," 1.

23. "Stryga & le terrorisme russe—A Paris: les grève s'étendent," *L'Intransigeant*, 11 May 1906, 1.

24. Stryga was not the last Russian in Paris to fall victim to his own bomb. Two years later, a certain Petroff survived a similar mishap. As with Stryga, the press determined that Petroff was an anarchist, a nihilist, and a terrorist: see "Terroristes. Une explosion fait découvrir à Paris un refuge d'anarchistes russes," *Le Matin*, 21 May 1907, 1.

25. The precise date of this change in meaning is disputed: Charlotte Krauss favors the year 1793 (see *La Russie et les Russes dans la fiction francaise du XIXe siècle (1812–1917). D'une image de l'autre à un univers imaginaire* [Amsterdam; New York: Rudopi, 2007], 11), while Arthur E. Bestor Jr. prefers 1797 (see "The Evolution of the Socialist Vocabulary," *Journal of the History of Ideas* 9, no. 3 [1948]: 259–302).

26. This quotation is taken from Ivan Sergeevich Turgenev, *Fathers and Children*, translated by Constance Clara Garnett, available at http://www.gutenberg.org/files/30723/30723-h/30723-h.htm (accessed 20 May 2020). See the interesting article on Turgenev by Guy de Maupassant, "L'inventeur du mot 'nihilisme'," *Le Gaulois*, 21 November 1880, 1.

27. Claudia Verhoeven, "The Making of Russian Revolutionary Terrorism," in *Enemies of Humanity: The Nineteenth-Century War on Terrorism*, ed. Isaac Land (New York: Palgrave Macmillan, 2008), 99.

28. Michael J. Hughes, "British Opinion and Russian Terrorism in the 1880s," *European History Quarterly* 41, no. 2 (2011): 264.

29. Verhoeven, "The Making of Russian Revolutionary Terrorism," 259–302.

30. Maitron, *Le movement anarchiste en France. Tome 1*, 75. Emphasis added.

31. Maitron, *Le movement anarchiste en France. Tome 1*, 75.

32. Maitron, *Le movement anarchiste en France. Tome 1*, 76–77. Brousse was not the first to use this phrase. In June 1877, an anarchist named Costa had given a conference on "propaganda by the deed" in Geneva, as advertised in the *Bulletin de la Fédération jurassienne*; this seems to be the first time the phrase was used.

33. Maitron, *Le movement anarchiste en France. Tome 1*, 77. On this period in European anarchist politics and violence, see Gavin Murray-Miller, *Revolutionary Europe: Politics, Community and Culture in Transnational Context, 1775–1922* (London: Bloomsbury Academic, 2020), 198–206.

34. Martin A. Miller, *The Foundations of Modern Terrorism: State, Society and the Dynamics of Political Violence* (Cambridge, UK: Cambridge University Press, 2013), 67–69.

35. Gilles Ferragu, *Histoire du terrorisme* (Paris: Perrin, 2019), 82–85; Miller, *The Foundations of Modern Terrorism*, 67–70.

36. Miller, *The Foundations of Modern Terrorism*, 73–74; Verhoeven, "The Making of Russian Revolutionary Terrorism," 100–102.

37. Bouhey, *Les Anarchistes contre la République*, 150.

38. Ferragu, *Histoire du terrorisme*, 86–94; Laqueur, *A History of Terrorism*, 33.

39. Jay Bergman, "Vera Zasulich, the Shooting of Trepov and the Growth of Political Terrorism in Russia, 1878–1881," *Terrorism: An International Journal* 4, no. 1 (1980): 25–51. See also J. Bourdeau, "Femmes russes," *Journal des Débats politiques et littéraires*, 18 March 1906, 1.

40. Bouhey, *Les Anarchistes contre la République*, 140–41.

41. Maitron, *Le movement anarchiste en France. Tome 1*, 78.

42. Maitron, *Le movement anarchiste en France. Tome 1*, 114–15.

43. Maitron, *Le movement anarchiste en France. Tome 1*, 209; Bouhey, *Les Anarchistes contre la République*, 139.

44. Maitron, *Le movement anarchiste en France. Tome 1*, 206. See, for example, "Produits anti-bourgeois," *Le Drapeau noir*, 12 August 1883, 4; "Produits anti-bourgeois," *Le Drapeau noir*, 21 October 1883, 3; "Produits anti-bourgeois," *Le Drapeau noir*, 4 November 1883, 3; and "Produits anti-bourgeois," *Le Drapeau noir*, 11 November 1883, 3.

45. "Vengeons-nous, méfions-nous," *L'Affamé*, 27 July–9 August 1884, 4; quoted in Maitron, *Le movement anarchiste en France. Tome 1*, 208n12.

46. Maitron, *Le movement anarchiste en France. Tome 1*, 206–12; Bouhey, *Les Anarchistes contre la République*, 149–59.

47. "Manifeste des Nihilistes françaises," *Le Drapeau noir*, 2 September 1883, 3. Benedict Anderson mentions this manifesto on page 74 of his *Under Three Flags: Anarchism and the Anti-Colonial Imagination* (New York: Verso, 2007). However, he does not attribute the manifesto specifically to women, calling it the "Manifeste des Nihilistes *Français*." This error was repeated in the 2013 reedition of this book under the title *The Age of Globalization: Anarchism and the Anti-Colonial Imagination* (74). Maitron uses the correct title in his first volume on the anarchist movement. A footnote states that the same group of "nihilistes françaises" had appeared in police records in 1880 for handwritten proclamations calling for "[t]he gradual and successive debilitation of all the representatives of this cursed breed [the bourgeoisie]": Maitron, *Le movement anarchiste en France. Tome 1*, 207n8.

48. Bouhey, *Les Anarchistes contre la République*, 141.

49. A Russian Nihilist, "The Revolution in Russia," *The North American Review* 129, no. 272 (1879): 23–36; Murray-Miller, *Revolutionary Europe*, 204.

50. "Le Nouvelliste de Versailles," *Le Gaulois*, 25 October 1870, 2; E. de la XXXllerie [first part of the author's surname is illegible], "Entreprise générale de balayage parisien," *Le Figaro*, 8 June 1871, 2; "Le Parlement," *La Gazette de France*, 18 March 1880, 1; "Empoisonnement obligatoire," *La Gazette de France*, 19 June 1887, 1; "Echos de Paris," *Le Figaro*, 31 July 1873, 1; Edouard Drumont, "Rothschild à la Chambre," *La Libre Parole*, 2 May 1894, 1.

51. Marc Gérard, "Nouvel attentat contre S.M. L'Empéreur de Russie," *Le Gaulois*, 16 April 1879, 1. Emphasis added.

52. In the secondary literature, see Michel Niqueux, "Les mystères des *Mystères de Saint-Pétersbourg* (1878)," *Revue Russe* 40 (2013): 61–62; Krauss, *La Russie et les Russes dans la fiction française*, 289–90; 295; 319; Mary Carol Matheson, "Reframing Russia in France: 'Popular Diplomacy' and the Franco-Russia Military Alliance, 1871–1901" (PhD diss., University of British Columbia, Vancouver, 2018), 127–128n423; Janine Neboit-Mombet, *L'Image de la Russie dans le roman français (1859–1900)* (Clermont-Ferrand, FR: Presses Universitaires Blaise Pascal, 2005). In the primary literature see Prince Józef Lubomirski, *Le nihilisme en Russie* (Paris: E. Dentu, 1879); J. B. Arnaudo, *Le nihilisme et les nihilistes* (Paris: M. Dreyfous, 1880); M. Pierre Frédé, *La Russie et le nihilisme* (Paris: A. Quantain, 1880); D. K. Schédo-Ferroti, *L'Avenir de la Russie: le nihilisme* (Paris: Auguste Ghio, 1880); L. Gally-Boutteville, *Tzarisme et nihilisme* (Paris: Imp. Wattier, 1881); Anonymous, *Les nihilistes et la Révolution en Russie* (Paris: E. Leroux, 1882); Charles Rabourdin, *Alexandre II et Louis XIV: La vérité aux nihilistes* (Paris: Ch. Delagrave, 1882).

53. Matheson, "Reframing Russia in France," 234–35.

54. Krauss, *La Russie et les Russes dans la fiction française*, 290–91.

55. Jean Frollo, "Les assassins malgrè eux," *Le Petit Parisien*, 16 March 1881, 1.

56. Jean Frollo, "Le nihilisme," *Le Petit Parisien*, 17 March 1881, 1.

57. Faith Hillis, "The 'Franco-Russian Marseillaise': International Exchange and the Making of Antiliberal Politics in Fin de Siècle France," *The Journal of Modern History* 89, no. 1 (2017): 65–66.

58. A. Périvier, "Figaro en Russie. Les Nihilistes," *Le Figaro*, 27 March 1881, 1.

59. "Etranger. Les partis en Russie," *Le Cri du Peuple*, 22 February 1884, 2.

60. Sergei Stepniak, *Underground Russia: Revolutionary Profiles and Sketches from Life* (Westport, CT: Hyperion Press, 1973), 28–29, https://archive.org/details/undergroundrussoolavrgoog/page/n30/mode/2up. This passage appeared in the French edition too: see Sergei Stepniak, *La Russie souterraine* (Paris: J. Lévy, 1885), 51–52, https://archive.org/details/larussiesouterroostepgoog/page/n60/mode/2up.

61. Stepniak, *La Russie souterraine*, 53–58; 68–69.

62. Verhoeven, "The Making of Russian Revolutionary Terrorism," 99.

63. Emile Littré and L.-Marcel Devic, *Dictionnaire de la langue française. Supplément* (Paris: Hachette, 1886), 242.

64. Emile Littré, *Dictionnaire de la langue française. Tome 4* (Paris, Hachette, 1873–74), 2202; Littré and Devic, *Dictionnaire de la langue française*, 375.

65. See, for example, "Vive la dynamite!" *Le Matin*, 3 June 1884, 1; "En Irlande," *Le Matin*, 23 September 1885, 2; "Le terrorisme," *Le Matin*, 24 April 1887, 1; "Socialistes allemands," *Le Matin*, 23 July 1889, 1; "Statistique judiciaire," *Le Matin*, 16 September 1890, 1; "Mendiant terroriste," *Le Petit Parisien*, 3 May 1893, 3.

66. "Arrestation de terroristes russes," *Le Petit Parisien*, 31 May 1890, 2; "Les 'nihilistes'," *Le Matin*, 31 May 1890, 1.

67. Colomba, "Chronique," *L'Echo de Paris*, 3 June 1890, 1–2.

68. L. M. "Les Révolutionnaires russes," *La Justice*, 2 June 1890, 1.

69. "Les terroristes," *Le Matin*, 30 May 1890, 1; "Fait divers," *L'Echo de Paris*, 31 May 1890, 3; Henry Désormeaux, "L'Anarchie internationale," *Le Gaulois*, 29 August 1900, 1–2; "Arrestation de nihilistes," *La Justice*, 31 May 1890, 2–3.

70. "Les 'nihilistes'," 1.

71. Jehan des Ruelles, "Les Russes à Paris," *Gil Blas*, 2 June 1890, 1.

72. Louis Ganderax, "L'hospitalité de la France," *Le Gaulois*, 8 June 1890, 1.

73. Sylvia Schraut writes that these women are depicted as transgressing "natural" gender boundaries and as being "particularly cruel and irrational when using violence." Sylvia Schraut, "Gender Politics and Terrorist Histories," in *The Cambridge History of Terrorism*, ed. Richard English (Cambridge, UK: Cambridge University Press, 2021), 632–33.

74. A. Périvier, "Figaro en Russie. Les Nihilistes," *Le Figaro*, 27 March 1881, 1.

75. "Chronique," 1–2. See also Ganderax, 'L'hospitalité de la France," 1.

76. Ganderax, 'L'hospitalité de la France," 1.

77. Krauss, *La Russie et les Russes dans la fiction française*, 291; 391–92.

78. Maitron, *Le movement anarchiste en France. Tome 1*, 209–12; Ferragu, *Histoire du terrorisme*, 115.

79. Marius Boisson, *Les Attentats Anarchistes sous la Troisième République* (Paris: Editions de France, 1931), 77; Maitron, *Le movement anarchiste en France. Tome 1*, 212.

80. On this period, see Bouhey, *Les Anarchistes contre la République*, 261–97; Ferragu, *Histoire du terrorisme*, 116–33; Maitron, *Le movement anarchiste en France. Tome 1*, 206–50; Merriman, *The Dynamite Club*, 69–99; 137–63.

81. Robert Nye, *Crime, Madness, & Politics in Modern France: The Medical Concept of National Decline* (Princton, NJ: Princeton University Press, 1984), 179; Ruth Harris, *Murders and Madness: Medicine, Law, and Society in the* fin de siècle (Oxford, UK: Clarendon Press, 1989), 78.

82. Murray-Miller, *Revolutionary Europe*, 206. On this subject, see Jensen's peerless *The Battle Against Anarchist Terrorism*.

83. Charles Dupuy, "Le terrorisme," *La Gazette de France*, 30 March 1892, 1 (emphasis added). The phrase "terrorists of anarchy" appears here, too: "Revue des journaux," *Le Figaro*, 22 January 1894, 2.

84. XXX, "Réflexions d'un indépendant. Les anarchistes," *L'Echo de Paris*, 18 March 1894, 1.

85. "Sur l'anarchie," *Le Matin*, 5 August 1894, 1. The tendency to describe such men as anarchists of the terrorist variety appeared elsewhere—see "Bombe pasionnelle?" *Le Matin*, 16 April 1894, 1.

86. "Ravachol en cours d'assises," *Le Figaro*, 27 April 1892, 1; A travers la politique," *Gil Blas*, 14 June 1892, 2; J. Allemane, "Guillotine ou bagne," *Le Parti Ouvrier*, 5 February 1894, 1.

87. "Les lois terroristes," *La Gazette de France*, 20 December 1893, 1.

88. Eugène-Melchior de Vogüé, "Un Regard en arrière.—Les Terroriste russes," *Revue des Deux Mondes* 122, no. 4 (1894): 204.

89. de Vogüé, "Un Regard en arrière," 204.
90. *Almanach du Père Peinard* (Paris, 1894), 6, 10.
91. Edouard Drumont, "Les compagnons d'autrefois," *La Libre Parole*, 7 May 1894, 1. See also Edouard Drumont, "De l'or, de la boue, et du sang," *La Libre Parole*, 22 January 1896, 1.
92. Edmond Lepelletier, "En attendant l'Explosion," *L'Echo de Paris*, 1 May 1892, 1.
93. Bouhey, *Les Anarchistes contre la République*, 363; 419. Police commented on this development: see APP 1499, untitled report, Paris, 30 January 1907.
94. APP 1709, untitled report, Paris, 12 December 1907.
95. APP 1499, untitled report, Paris, 14 September 1908.
96. See, for example, APP 1499, untitled report, Paris, 4 January 1908, and untitled report, Paris, 20 July 1909.
97. Gérault-Richard, "Bêtes féroces," *L'Aurore*, 5 June 1906, 1. The terms were employed simultaneously in reports about Portugal, too: "La Situation au Portugal," *Le Journal*, 2 August 1913, 2.
98. Alcide Ebray, "L'assassinat de M. Plehve," *Journal des Débats politiques et littéraires*, 29 July 1904, 1; "Attentat contre l'amrial Doubassof," *Le Journal*, 7 May 1906, 1.
99. "Anarchistes et terroristes étrangers," *Journal du Droit international privé et de la jurisprudence comparé*, ed. Edouard Clunet [Avocat à la Cour de Paris] (Paris: Marchal and Billard, 1906), vol. 33, 1471.
100. "Les responsabilités à Calais," *L'Aurore*, 11 February 1901, 1; "Mouvement syndical," *L'Humanité*, 11 July 1904, 3; "Une grève en Allemagne," *La Charente*, 7 January 1904, 1; "La Veille du Grand Soir," *La Justice*, 13 March 1907, 1; "M. Briand riposte," *L'Aurore*, 14 May 1907, 1.
101. "L'apache tatoué," *Gil Blas*, 3 July 1908, 1.
102. "Chambre de députés," *La Charente*, 3 July 1912, 2.
103. "Un manifeste de la CGT," *La Lanterne*, 29 May 1913, 2.
104. "Mouvement révolutionnaire en Indo-Chine," *Le Petit Journal*, 29 April 1913, 1; "Le terrorisme annamite," *Le Temps*, 7 August 1913, 3.
105. André Morizet, "Barcelone, cité des bombes," *L'Humanité*, 3 April 1908, 1.
106. Morizet, "Barcelone, cité des bombes," 1; Gérault-Richard, "Bêtes féroces," 1.
107. "Le Voyage d'Alphonse XIII à Barcelone," *Journal des Débats politiques et littéraires*, 4 April 1908, 2.
108. "Lettre de Russie," *Journal des Débats politiques et littéraires*, 14 May 1910, 2; "A l'étranger. Le terrorisme en Russie," *Journal des Débats politiques et littéraires*, 27 August 1911, 1–2. See also "Lettre de Russie," *Journal des Débats politiques et littéraires*, 22 September 1911, 1–2.
109. "Les Bandits en Auto. One les prendra qu'après une bataille rangée," *Gil Blas*, 30 March 1912, 2; "Les Bandits fantômes sèment l'épouvante et font des victimes," *La Lanterne*, 27 March 1912, 1.
110. APP 1499, untitled report, Paris, 12 January 1908.

111. J. L., "Un complot policier," *L'Humanité*, 23 May 1907, 1. See also E. R., "Le drame d'Interlaken," *L'Humanité*, 5 February 1907, 1, which mentions that Russian activists rejected terrorism in "free" countries.

112. Anna Geifmann, "Aspects of Early Twentieth-Century Russian Terrorism: The Socialist Revolutionary Combat Organization," *Terrorism and Political Violence* 4, no. 2 (1992): 37; John Keep, "Terror in 1905," in *Reinterpreting Revolutionary Russia: Essays in Honour of James D. White*, ed. Ian D. Thatcher (Basingstoke, UK: Palgrave Macmillan, 2006), 23.

113. Keep, "Terror in 1905," 21; 25.

114. Geifman, *Thou Shalt Kill*, 249–51; Geifmann, "Aspects of Early Twentieth-Century Russian Terrorism," 33; Amy Knight, "Female Terrorists in the Russian Socialist Revolutionary Party," *The Russian Review* 38, no. 2 (1979): 147; Stephen Smith, *Russian in Revolution: An Empire in Crisis, 1890–1928* (Oxford, UK: Oxford University Press, 2017), 75.

115. Keep, "Terror in 1905," 25.

116. Hugh Phillips, "The War Against Terrorism in Late Imperial and Early Soviet Russia," in Land, *Enemies of Humanity*, 214. See also Ian Lauchlan, "The Accidental Terrorist: Okhrana Connections to the Extreme Right and the Attempt to Assassinate Sergei Witte in 1907," *Revolutionary Russia* 14, no. 2 (2001): 1–32; Keep, "Terror in 1905," 28–30.

117. Keep, "Terror in 1905," 30.

118. Smith, *Russian in Revolution*, 18.

119. Avrich, *The Russian Anarchists*, 64–66.

120. Phillips, "The War Against Terrorism," 215–16.

121. Avrich, *The Russian Anarchists*, 66; Phillips, "The War Against Terrorism," 216.

122. Geifman, *Thou Shalt Kill*, 21.

123. Geifman, *Thou Shalt Kill*, 251.

124. As did the European press: see, for example, Anne-Marie Bouchard and Alexis Desgagnés, "La révolution russe dans la presse illustrée européenne," *Cahiers du Monde russe* 48, no. 2/3 (April-September 2007): 477–83.

125. See, for example, "Corps législatif," *Le Rappel*, 23 March 1870, 2–3; "Tribunaux," *L'Intransigeant*, 19 October 1881, 3.

126. Ernest Forichon, "La constitution inacceptable," *Gil Blas*, 18 August 1905, 1–2.

127. "Lettre de Russie," *Journal des Débats politiques et littéraires*, 10 September 1906, 3; Forichon, "La constitution inacceptable," 1–2; "Les fabricants de bombes," *Le Petit Journal*, 23 May 1907, 1. On the question of Jewish involvement, see Henri Rochefort, "Entre terroristes," *L'Intransigeant*, 1 August 1904, 1; Joseph Mollet, "Choses russes," *La Croix*, 14 February 1909, 3.

128. Robert Villiers, "Curieuses Révélations," *La Presse*, 27 November 1905, 3.

129. "Les fabricants de bombes," 1.

130. "Les attentats des terroristes en Russie," *La Liberté*, 28 August 1906, 2.

131. For a positive view of Russian "terrorist" violence, see Michel Petit, "La

Révolution en Russie," *Les Temps Nouveaux. Ex-Journal 'La Révolte'*, 4–10 February 1905, 1–2.

132. Jean Longuet and Georges Silber, *Terroristes et policiers. Azev, Harting et Cie. Les dessous de la police russe* (Paris: Librairie Félix Juven, 1909 [reprinted by Creative Media Partners LLC, 2019), 246–47.

133. J. Paul Boncour, "Terroristes et policiers," *La Lanterne*, 6 February 1909, 1.

134. "Bulletin de l'étranger," *Le Temps*, 12 September 1906, 1.

135. "Une Bombe pour tuer M. Stolypine," *Le Matin*, 26 August 1906, 1.

136. "Lettre de Russie," *Journal des Débats politiques et littéraires*, 18 July 1905, 1; "Le terrorisme en Russie," *La Croix*, 30 August 1906, 1.

137. Georges Berthoulat, "Ses 'Camarades'," *La Liberté*, 29 August 1906, 1.

138. P. Peyras, "Le Terrorisme," *La Liberté*, 28 August 1906, 1.

139. "Lettre de Russie," *Journal des Débats politiques et littéraires*, 30 September 1906, 2.

140. "Le terrorisme en Russie," 1.

141. Lucien Herr, "La fin du tsarisme," *L'Humanité*, 31 July 1904, 3. See also "Les réformistes russes," *La Lanterne*, 3 January 1905, 2. The French conceived of Russia as a *northern* European autocratic regime, rather than a country of eastern Europe, much like they considered Imperial Germany: see Krauss, *La Russie et les Russes dans la fiction française*, 8.

142. "Terroristes et policiers," 1.

143. "Bulletin de l'étranger," 1. The closing of the Duma was considered a potential cause of "terrorist" violence: E. Fazy, "La suppression de la Douma," *L'Ouest-Éclair*, 24 July 1906, 1.

144. Jean Frontière, "Opinions. Révélation de la Douma," *La Dépêche*, 21 May 1906, 1; Berthoulat, "Ses 'Camarades'," 1.

145. See, for example, "Les deux terreurs," *L'Intransigeant*, 15 September 1906, 4; "Le terrorisme officiel," *L'Intransigeant*, 17 September 1906, 4; Alcide Ebray, "La tragédie de Moscou," *Journal des Débats politiques et littéraires*, 19 February 1905, 1. For sympatheic views, see "La défense de Sazanov," *L'Humanité*, 14 January 1905, 3; "La revolution en Pologne," *L'Humanité*, 27 June 1905, 1; Gabriel Bertrand, "Les clartés," *L'Humanité*, 23 August 1906, 1.

146. Jane McDermid, "Mariya Spiridonova: Russian Martyr and British Heroine? The Portrayal of a Russian Female Terrorist in the British Press," in Thatcher, *Reinterpreting Revolutionary Russia*, 37.

147. "M. De Plehve," *Le Petit Parisien*, 29 July 1904, 2; De la Carrière, "En Perse. La Russie et l'Angleterre," *L'Ouest-Éclair*, 31 December 1907, 1; Henri Rochefort, "Entre terroristes," *L'Intransigeant*, 1 August 1904, 1. See also Français, "Affaires extérieurs," *La Dépêche*, 30 June 1906, 2; Jean Frontière, "Opinions. La réformation russe," *La Dépêche*, 12 October 1904, 1.

148. Ludovic Nadeau, "Les fastes du terrorisme," *Le Journal*, 17 February 1909, 1; Longuet and Silber, *Terroristes et policiers*.

149. Thadée Natanson, "La pitoyable Russie," *Gil Blas*, 4 November 1911, 1; Ge-

ifmann, "Aspects of Early Twentieth-Century Russian Terrorism," 38–39; Keep, "Terror in 1905," 24–25.

150. Cyrano, "Les deux terrorismes," *Le Radical*, 12 September 1906, 1. See also X., "Comment rétablir l'Ordre?" *Le Petit Parisien*, 29 August 1906, 1.

151. "On jette une Bombe dans la Villa du Président du Conseil russe," *Le Petit Parisien*, 26 August 1906, 1; "Bulletin de l'étranger," 1.

152. See, for example, "L'agitation en Russie. Une bombe de liddyte.—Condamnée," *La Justice*, 30 August 1906, 2: "Sur un attentat," *La Lanterne*, 17 September 1911, 1; Jean Lecoq, "Propos d'actualité," *Le Petit Journal*, 9 February 1907, 1; "Bulletin de l'étranger," 1.

153. "La Crise Russe. L'ère du terrorisme," *Le Petit Parisien*, 18 August 1906, 3; "Lettre de Russie," *Journal des Débats politiques et littéraires*, 7 June 1907, 1–2.

154. "Lettre de Russie," *Journal des Débats politiques et littéraires*, 10 September 1906, 3.

155. "Lettre de Russie," (10 September 1906), 3; S., "Le suicide d'une jeune russe," *La Liberté*, 4 January 1908, 3; Lecoq, "Propos d'actualité," 1.

156. Robert Villiers, "Les Organisations Terroristes," *La Presse*, 23 January 1908, 2.

157. See, for example, "Les bombes de Vincennes," *L'Aurore*, 5 May 1906, 1; "Ce n'est pas un terroriste russe," *La Liberté*, 7 March 1907, 2.

158. Robert Villiers, "Curieuses Révélations," *La Presse*, 27 November 1905, 3; "Lettre de Russie," *Journal des Débats politiques et littéraires*, 4 September 1906, 1–2.

159. "Les terroristes," *Le Matin*, 30 May 1890, 1.

160. "Les Universités russes," *Le Grand Echo du Nord et du Pas-de-Calais*, 23 August 1906, 1; Jean Lecocq, "Propos d'actualité," *Le Petit Journal*, 22 May 1907, 1.

161. "Faits divers. Les terroristes russes de Paris," *La Justice*, 24 May 1907, 3. This article appeared also in other national newspapers including *Le Petit Journal*, *L'Aurore*, and *L'Intransigeant*.

162. "Trida?" *Le Petit Parisien*, 6 May 1906, 3; "Les bombes de Vincennes," (*L'Aurore*), 2.

163. V. Maron, "L'Affaire Sokoloff," *L'Aurore*, 17 July 1906, 1.

164. "Anarchistes russes," 1–2.

165. "La bombe de Vincennes," (*Le Petit Journal*), 3.

166. APP BA 1709, "Le Commissaire de Police, Chef de la 3e Brigade, à monsieur le Directeur Général de Recherches," 23 September 1907. In January 1907, Albert Soleilland murdered a young girl.

167. "Une bombe par jour!" *La Presse*, 11 May 1906, 1.

168. See, for example, Nadeau, "Les fastes du terrorisme," 1.

169. APP untitled report, Paris, 17 November 1909; P. Duchesne, "Les drames du terrorisme," *L'Aurore*, 20 August 1909, 1.

170. The dossier on this case is available in AN BB18 6464.

171. "Pourquoi le faux agent policier tenta de tuer son chef," *Le Petit Parisien*, 15 June 1910, 2; "Gazette des Tribunaux," *Le Figaro*, 15 June 1910, 5

172. "Comment Rips, terroriste, devint policier, puis assassin," *Le Matin*, 15

June 1910, 2; "Pourquoi le faux agent policier," 2; "Terroriste et policier," *Gil Blas*, 16 June 1910, 3.

173. "Le terroriste Rips acquitté par le jury," *Le Petit Parisien*, 16 June 1910, 1.

174. "Comment Rips," 2; "Pourquoi le faux agent policier," 2; "Terroriste et policier," 3.

175. In his interview with the juge d'instruction, von Kotten referred to another of his contacts in France, whose name he refused to supply to the French authorities.

176. Destez, "Engin d'exportation," 1.

177. Schraut, "Gender politics and terrorist histories," 634.

178. "Les deux Sokoloff en correctionnelle," *L'Intransigeant*, 17 July 1906, 1.

179. Richard D. Sonn, *Sex, Violence, and the Avant-Garde: Anarchism in Interwar France* (Philadelphia: Pennsylvania State University Press, 2010), 33.

180. "L'etudiant russe à Paris," *Le Petit Journal*, 5 May 1906, 1; "La vérité sur le drame de Vincennes," *L'Intranisgeant*, 5 May 1906, 1; "Les deux Sokoloff en correctionnelle," *L'Intransigeant*, 17 July 1906, 1; "Anarchistes russes," 1–2; Jean Desvosges, "Terrorisme et czarisme," *La Charente*, 18 September 1906, 1.

181. Bourdeau, "Femmes russes," 1; "Lettre de Russie," (10 September 1906), 3.

182. "Stryga & le terrorisme russe," 1.

183. "Lettre de Russie," (30 September 1906) 2; "Lettre de Russie," (4 September 1906), 1–2.

184. "Les deux Sokoloff en correctionnelle," 1; "Anarchistes russes," 1–2.

185. *La Lanterne. Le Supplément*, 1 June 1907, 4.

186. "Les bombes de Vincennes," (*L'Aurore*), 3.

187. Villiers, "Les Organisations Terroristes," 2; "Lettre de Russie," (10 September 1906), 3.

188. "L'Amour nihiliste [a song]; Paroles de Paul Verneuil; Musique de Ch. Thony," 1909.

189. Hillis, "The 'Franco-Russian Marseillaise'," 39–78; Matheson, "Reframing Russia in France," 338–40.

190. Elena L. Berezovich and Galina Kabakova, "Stéréotypes du 'Russe' et du 'Français' regards croisés," *Revue des études slaves* LXXXVI, no. 4 (2015): 389–412.

191. Matheson, "Reframing Russia in France," 234–35.

192. Philippe Thuin, "L'Anarchiste Français au miroir du nihiliste russe dans la série *Fantômas*," *Belphegor: Popular Literature and Media Culture* 6, no. 2 (2007): n.p. (page references here refer to the page number in the downloadable PDF at https://dalspace.library.dal.ca/handle/10222/47739 [accessed 6 December 2019]).

193. See Thuin, "L'Anarchiste Français."

194. Duchesne, "Les drames du terrorisme," 1; "Gazette des Tribunaux," 5; "Un terroriste russe tente de tuer le chef de la police de Moscou," *Le Petit Parisien*, 9 May 1909, 1.

195. Louis Létang, "La Croix de Chair," *Le Grand Echo du Nord et du Pas-de-Calais*, 1 May 1911, 2. "La Croix de Chair" ran from 6 March 1911 to 9 July 1911.

196. Krauss, *La Russie et les Russes dans la fiction française*, 259; 301.

197. "Vient de paraître," *Le Figaro*, 18 February 1911, 2. See also "Petite chronique des lettres," *Le Figaro*, 24 February 1911, 4–5; "Vient de paraître," *Le Figaro*, 3 April 1911, 2.

198. Mme V.[alentine] Dmitriev, *Le Terroriste*. Traduit du Russe par G. Savitch et E. Jaubert (Paris: Plon, 1912).

199. "Feuilleton du *Temps*: L'Agent Secret," *Le Temps*, 31 May 1910, 1. This ran until 8 July 1910.

200. Etienne Charles, "Revue des livres. HJ Magog: L'Attentat de la rue Royale," *La Liberté*, 17 June 1912, 1.

201. "Romans," *Romans-Revues. Guide Général de Lectures. Mensuel. Littéraire. Pratique* 15 (January 1912): 466.

202. Krauss, *La Russie et les Russes dans la fiction française*, 30.

203. Krauss, *La Russie et les Russes dans la fiction française*, 15; Niqueux, "Les mystères des *Mystères de Saint-Pétersbourg* (1878)," 58.

204. "Nos feuilletons," *La Charente*, 20 April 1912, 2. "Le Roman d'une Etoile" ran in *La Charente* from 15 May 1912 to 20 October 1912. It appeared also in *Le Petit Parisien* (1910), *Le Soleil du Dimanche illustré* (1911), *L'Écho d'Alger* (1912), and *L'Ouest-Éclair* (1914). The story was also published as *Du Sang dans les ténèbres—1er vol.: Flaviana princesse* (1910).

205. "La Lutte inégale" ran in *Le Journal* from 2 May 1913 until 24 May 1913.

206. Daniel Lesueur, "Le Roman d'une Etoile," *La Charente*, 26 June 1912, 4.

207. Georges Thierry, "L'île bleue," *La Croix*, 8 November 1910, 1. "L'île bleue" ran from 8 November 1910 to 14 January 1911.

208. "Tcherloskoff. Policier et Terroriste," by Guy-Péron, ran in *Le Radical* from 15 March 1912 to 17 April 1912.

209. Guy-Péron, "Tcherloskof. Policier et Terroriste," *Le Radical*, 4 April 1912, 2.

210. "Concerts du 23 Mai. De 9h à 10h. Place des Tourelles," *Le Journal*, 23 May 1909.

211. "Premières representations," *Le Petit Journal*, 6 December 1907, 3.

212. "Théâtre et concerts," *L'Auto*, 24 November 1908, 2.

213. "Les Théâtres," *Le Figaro*, 21 November 1908, 4.

214. Robert de Flers, "Les Théâtres," *Le Figaro*, 17 March 1912, 5.

215. "Théâtres," *La Liberté*, 19 June 1910, 3.

216. "La Terroriste," *Comoedia*, 8 March 1914, 3.

217. Richard Abel, *The Ciné Goes to Town: French Cinema, 1896–1904* (Berkeley: University of California Press, 1994), 91–92; Isabelle Marinone, "'L'anarchiste' dans le cinéma de fiction français: un motif singulier entre caricature bienveillante et charge malintentionnée," *Belphegor* 6, no. 2 (2007): n.p., available at https://dalspace.library.dal.ca/bitstream/handle/10222/47741/06_02_marino_anacin_fr_cont.pdf?sequence=1&isAllowed=y (accessed 6 December 2019).

218. "La Terroriste: Scénario," Paris, 1907.

219. "Spectacles de Toulouse," *La Dépêche*, 18 July 1909, 6.

220. De Vogüé, "Un Regard en arrière," 204.

221. Ernest Alfred Vizetelly, *The Anarchists: Their Faith and Their Record Including Sidelights on the Royal and Other Personages Who Have Been Assassinated* (London; New York: John Lane/The Bodley Head, 1911), 295; André Girard, *Anarchistes et bandits* (Paris: Les Temps Nouveaux, 1914), 3.

222. Ivan Aleksandrovic Gontcharof, *Marc le nihiliste*. Traduit du Russe et adapté par Eugène Gothi (Paris: Plon, 1886), i–ii.

CHAPTER 2

1. This account draws on documents available online through the website of the Dépôt Central des Archives de la Justice Militaire at Le Blanc (Indre), hereafter referred to as DCAJM. The landing page for the documents is https://www.memoiredeshommes.sga.defense.gouv.fr/fr/arkotheque/navigation_facette/index.php?f=AffaireCottin (accessed 6 October 2022).

2. DCAJM, Cote 113, "Le Chef du Service des Renseignements Généraux à Monsieur le Commissaire du Gouvernement près le 3me Conseil de Guerre," 25 February 1919; DCAJM, Cote 115, "Rapport," 7 February 1919.

3. DCAJM, Cote 117, untitled report, 24 February 1919.

4. DCAJM, Cote 223, "Affaire Cottin (Emile Jules Henri). Tentatives d'assassinats. Rapport médical sur l'état mental de l'inculpé par Monsieur le Médecin Major de 1ère Classes J. Roubinovitch, du Service Central de psychiâtre du Val-de-Grâce, Médecin-Chef à l'Hospice de Bicêtre," 4 March 1919.

5. "La mère de Cottin a été interrogée," *L'Echo de Paris*, 22 February 1919, 3.

6. See, for example, "Au retour de la grandiose revue de Longchamp un anarchiste tire sur la voiture du préfet de police," *Le Petit Journal*, 15 July 1922, 1.

7. Sonn, *Sex, Violence and the Avant-Garde*, 27–54 (on Berton) and 140–49 (on Schwarzbard). Jensen also refers to some anarchist incidents during the 1920s in *The Battle Against Anarchist Terrorism*, 361–62.

8. "La vie politique," *La Patrie*, 20 February 1919, 1.

9. *Excelsior*, 20 February 1919, 2.

10. Clément Vautel, "Mon film," *Le Journal*, 16 July 1922, 1.

11. Jacques Mesnil, "Le Terrorisme comme Moyen tactique," *L'Humanité*, 26 December 1914, 1–2.

12. Général Bonnal, "Les conditions de la guerre moderne. Le terrorisme allemand," *L'Intransigeant*, 25 May 1916, 1.

13. "La faillite du terrorisme," *Le Temps*, 28 April 1916, 1.

14. See, for example, "L'âme de l'Allemagne," *Le Matin*, 30 June 1915, 1; "La Grosse Bertha s'est encore fait entendre cette nuit," *Le Petit Journal*, 16 April 1918, 3. See also Alex J. Bellamy, *Massacres and Morality: Mass Atrocities in the Age of Civilian Immunity* (Oxford, UK: Oxford University Press, 2012), 79.

15. Général Bonnal, "Les conditions de la guerre moderne. Le terrorisme allemand," *L'Intransigeant*, 25 May 1916, 1; Commandant X, "Pourquoi la victoire est certaine," *Le Matin*, 24 August 1916, 1; Dr. Orestes Ferrara, [président de la

Chambre des représentants de Cuba, who has visited the Western Front], "Une neutralité qui est un crime," *Le Matin*, 18 November 1915, 1.

16. For an analysis of the French culture of war during 1914–18, see Stéphane Audoin-Rouzeau and Annetter Becker, *14–18: Understanding the Great War* (New York: Hill and Wang, 2003).

17. See, for example, "Une initiative des Etats-Unis," *L'Humanité*, 23 September 1918, 1; "Après l'assassinat du comte Mirbach," *L'Echo de Paris*, 9 July 1918, 3; "Nouvelle proclamation de Lénine," *Le Matin*, 24 November 1917, 1.

18. See, for example, "Liebknecht et ses partisans ont attaqué dans le centre de la capitale les troupes du gouvernement," *Le Matin*, 8 January 1919, 1; "Le gouvernement de Berlin proclame la victoire," *Le Matin*, 14 January 1919, 3.

19. "Give Germany peace and food at once, says Lansing, if allies would make her pay for crimes committed during war," *The Chicago Tribune*, 12 March 1919, 1; "L'Allemagne mérite ses souffrances," *Le Matin*, 12 March 1919, 3.

20. DCAJM, Cote 356, "Procès verbal d'interrogatoire et de confrontation," 25 February 1919; "Le criminel," *Le Petit Journal*, 20 February 1919, 1; "Emile Cottin comparaîtra aujourd'hui," *L'Oeuvre*, 14 March 1919, 1.

21. Clément Vautel, "Mon film," *Le Journal*, 27 February 1919, 1.

22. "L'attentat," *L'Echo de Paris*, 20 February 1919, 1.

23. DCAJM, Cote 5, report of Paul Abel Lompre, Commissaire du quartier de la Muette, 19 February 1919, 9:30 a.m.; "L'attentat," 1; APP 1 W/1176 59452, untitled note, 19 February 1919; untitled report, by Daumail and Valette, 19 February 1919.

24. DCAJM, "Rapport de Monsieur Ed. Bayle, Sous-Chef du Service. Examen des Traces de Balles," 4 March 1919.

25. DCAJM, Cote 645, Bouchardon, untitled "rapport" summarizing the affair, 8 March 1919; "L'attentat," 1; DCAJM, Cote 6, "Rapport," from gardiens de la paix Labaigt and Ravery [this last name is almost illegible] to Commissaire de Police du quartier, 19 February 1919.

26. DCAJM, Cote 645, Bouchardon, untitled "rapport"; "L'attentat," 1; "Hier soir, l'état du blesse demeurait satisfaisant," *Excelsior*, 20 February 1919, 2.

27. "Le crime," *Le Journal*, 20 February 1919, 1.

28. DCAJM, Cote 227, "Rapport médical du Docteur Charles Paul," 28 February 1919.

29. DCAJM, Cote 6, "Rapport," from gardiens de la paix Labaigt and Ravery.

30. "L'attentat," 1; "Hier soir," *Excelsior*, 2; "Le drame," *Le Matin*, 20 February 1919, 1.

31. APP 1 W/1176 59452, "Télégramme," 20 February 1919, 11:35 a.m.

32. DCAJM, Cote 7, "Rapport," from gardien de la paix Alfred Chapuy, to Commissaire de Police; Cote 203, "Rapport," 5 March 1919.

33. DCAJM, Cote 223, "Affaire Cottin (Emile Jules Henri)."

34. "L'attentat," *L'Eclair*, 20 February 1919, 1.

35. DCAJM, Cote 225, "Rapport médical du Docteur Charles Paul," 22 February 1919; Cote 356, "Procès verbal d'interrogatoire"; "L'attentat," (*L'Éclair*), 1.

36. DCAJM, Cote 249, "Rapport," by Gastone Reventte, 3 March 1919;

DCAJM, Cote 100, "Rapport," 5 March 1919; Cote 223, "Affaire Cottin (Emile Jules Henri)."
37. DCAJM, Cote 111, "Rapport," 24 February 1919.
38. DCAJM, "Commission rogatoire," 19 February 1919.
39. APP 1 W/1176 59452, "Le Directeur de la Police Judiciaire à Monsieur le Préfet de Police," 24 February 1919.
40. "Qui est Cottin?" *Bonsoir*, 19 February 1919, 1.
41. "L'attentat," *L'Heure*, 19 February 1919, 1.
42. "Comment le crime fut tenté," *L'Intransigeant*, 19 February 1919, 1.
43. See, for example, "L'attentat," (*L'Echo de Paris*), 1; "Cottin fait partie de la Fédértaion communiste," *Le Petit Journal*, 20 February 1919, 1; "Le meurtrier," *L'Oeuvre*, 20 February 1919, 1.
44. "L'enquête," *Le Matin*, 20 February 1919, 1.
45. "Hier soir," 2.
46. "Un communiqué officiel," *L'Avenir*, 20 February 1919, 1.
47. "Le crime," 1; "Au commissariat," *Le Journal*, 20 February 1919, 1.
48. "Attentat contre M. Clemenceau," *L'Echo de Paris*, 20 February 1919, 1.
49. C. Garapon, "Les responsables," *L'Echo de Paris*, 20 February 1919, 1; "La vie politique," *La Patrie*, 20 February 1919, 1.
50. "Emile Cottin explique son crime," *L'Eclair*, 20 February 1919, 1.
51. "Le crime," 1; "La vie politique," 1.
52. "La vie politique," 1.
53. "La vie politique," 1.
54. Interim, "La vie politique," *La Patrie*, 19 February 1919, 1.
55. M. C., "L'attentat," *L'Humanité*, 20 February 1919, 1; Jean Longuet, "Après l'attentat," *Le Populaire*, 21 February 1919, 1.
56. "Aux dernières nouvelles état du blessé satisfaisant," *Le Petit Journal*, 20 February 1919, 1.
57. Such views were expressed in *Journal Officiel*, 20 February 1919, 716; René Wertheimer, "Un attentat contre M. Clemenceau," *L'Eclair*, 20 February 1919, 1; Georges Lecomte, "Clemenceau," *Le Matin*, 20 February 1919, 1. See also Jean Guiraud, "Attentat bolcheviste," *La Croix*, 21 February 1919, 1; "M. Clemenceau a été blessé au poumon," *Le Matin*, 21 February 1919, 1.
58. "Le meurtrier," *Le Petit Parisien*, 20 February 1919, 1.
59. "Notre enquête," *L'Avenir*, 20 February 1919, 1; "L'assassin malmené," *Le Matin*, 20 February 1919, 1.
60. "L'arme du crime," *Le Petit Journal*, 20 February 1919, 1; "L'arme de Milou," *Le Matin*, 20 February 1919, 1.
61. "L'attentat," (*Le Petit Journal*), 1; "La blessure," *La Dépêche*, 20 February 1919, 1; "Le crime," 1.
62. "L'attentat," (*L'Echo de Paris*), 1.
63. See, for example, "La chasse au Tigre," *Le Petit Courrier*, 20 February 1919, 2.
64. See, for example, Léon Bailby, "L'attentat," *L'Intransigeant*, 19 Febru-

ary 1919, 1; Charles Chaumet, "Dix coups de revolver contre M. Clemenceau," *L'Avenir*, 20 February 1919, 1.

65. *Journal Officiel*, 20 February 1919, 717.

66. "L'attentat contre M. Clemenceau," *La Dépêche*, 21 February 1919, 1.

67. Cottin was deferred to the military authorities for prosecution, thanks to article 6 of the law of 27 April 1916 that extended the authority of military tribunals during a time of siege. See DCAJM, Cote 647, "Le Commissaire du Gouvernement près le 3ème Conseil de Guerre de Paris à Monsieur le Général de Division, Gouverneur militaire de Paris," 8 March 1919; "L'état de M. Clemenceau est satisfaisant," *Bonsoir*, 21 February 1919, 1.

68. See "Non cedant arma toga," *L'Oeuvre*, 23 February 1919, 1.

69. "Attentat contre M. Clemenceau," 1.

70. Interim, "La vie politique," 1; Alfred Capus, "Attentat contre M. Clemenceau," *Le Figaro*, 20 February 1919, 1. See also Intérim, "De Ravaillac à Cottin," *La France (Paris)*, 22 February 1919, 1.

71. DCAJM, Cote 223, "Affaire Cottin (Emile Jules Henri)."

72. DCAJM, Cote 356, 'Procès verbal d'interrogatoire"; "L'attentat," (*L'Echo de Paris*), 1.

73. DCAJM, Cote 5, report of Paul Abel Lompre, Commissaire du quartier de la Muette, 19 February 1919, 9:30 a. m.

74. DCAJM, Cote 645, Bouchardon, untitled "rapport."

75. DCAJM, Cote 356, "Procès verbal d'interrogatoire."

76. DCAJM, Cote 645, Bouchardon, untitled "rapport."

77. DCAJM, Cote 100, "Rapport,"; Cote 223, "Affaire Cottin (Emile Jules Henri)."

78. APP 1 W/1176 59452, "Rapport," 20 February 1919.

79. "Cottin a été interrogé ce matin," *L'Intransigeant*, 25 February 1919, 1.

80. "L'attentat', (*L'Echo de Paris*), 1; "Chez la concierge du meurtrier," *Excelsior*, 20 February 1919, 2.

81. Géo London, "Nombreuses perquisitions dans les milieu anarchistes," *Le Journal*, 21 February 1919, 3; "L'attentat," (*L'Echo de Paris*), 1; "Chez la concierge," 2.

82. "Cottin à l'instruction," *L'Avenir*, 21 February 1919, 1; "L'attentat," (*L'Echo de Paris*), 20 February 1919, 1.

83. "L'attentat," (*L'Echo de Paris*), 1.

84. "La mère de Cottin a été interrogee," 3.

85. London, "Nombreuse perquisitions," 3.

86. "L'attentat contre M. Clemenceau," *Le Petit Parisien*, 25 February 1919, 3.

87. "L'attentat contre M. Clemenceau," 3.

88. London, "Nombreuse perquisitions," 3.

89. London, "Nombreuse perquisitions," 3.

90. DCAJM, Cote 357, "Procès verbal d'interrogatoire et de confrontation," 26 February 1919. Jean Yves le Naour attributes the invention of Michaïl to *La Presse*; see *L'Assassinat de Clemenceau* (Paris: Perrin, 2019), 32–33.

91. See, for example, "Au domicile de l'assassin," *L'Eclair*, 20 February 1919, 1; 'L'attentat contre M. Clemenceau," *Le Matin*, 3 March 1919, 2.

92. "Cottin est déféré a la justice militaire," *Le Petit Parisien*, 21 February 1919, 1; "Le poumon a été atteint mais l'état du blessé reste satisfaisant," *Le Petit Journal*, 21 February 1919, 1; Vautel, "Mon film," (27 February 1919), 1; "Emile Cottin comparaîtra," 1.

93. "C'est la justice militaire qui est saisie de l'affaire," *L'Ouest-Éclair*, 21 February 1919, 1; "Le poumon," 1.

94. Louis Forest, "L'ombre des idées," *Le Matin*, 21 February 1919, 2.

95. Marie-Louise Néron, "Lettre d'une bourgeoise de Paris," *Le XIXe siècle*, 24 February 1919, 1.

96. 'Cottin est déféré," 21 February 1919, 1; Gustave Kavanagh, "Après l'attentat," *L'Avenir de la Mayenne*, 2 March 1919, 3; "L'attentat," (*L'Echo de Paris*), 1.

97. DCAJM, Cote 357, 'Procès verbal d'interrogatoire."

98. Vautel, "Mon film," (27 February 1919), 1.

99. DCAJM, Cote 223, "Affaire Cottin (Emile Jules Henri)"; "Cottin s'occupait d'hypnotisme," *Le Matin*, 27 February 1919, 1; "Cottin pratiquait les sciences psychiques," *Le Petit Journal*, 27 February 1919, 1.

100. See, for example, "Chez un des patrons de Cottin," *L'Eclair*, 20 February 1919, 1; Kavanagh, "Après l'attentat," 3.

101. "Cottin et ses complices," *Le Petit Journal*, 23 February 1919, 3.

102. "M. Clemenceau a été blesse," 1.

103. "Le mystérieux jeune homme blond," *L'Echo de Paris*, 22 February 1919, 3; "Le mystérieux jeune homme blond," *Le Matin*, 22 February 1919, 1; "Après l'attentat contre M. Clemenceau," *Le Petit bleu de Paris*, 27 February 1919, 2.

104. "Cottin, interrogé hier, n'a exprimé aucun regret de son acte," *Le Matin*, 26 February 1919, 1.

105. "Le jeune homme blond serait-ce Michaïl?" *Le Temps*, 23 February 1919, 1.

106. "L'attentat contre M. Clemenceau," *Le Petit Provençal*, 5 May 1919, 2; : "Le nouveau Cottin," *L'Intransigeant*, 5 May 1919, 3.

107. Vautel, "Mon film," (27 February 1919), 1.

108. APP 1 W/1176 59452, "Rapport," 21 February 1919.

109. DCAJM, Cote 100, "Rapport,"; DCAJM Cote 223, "Affaire Cottin (Emile Jules Henri)."

110. DCAJM, Cote 100, "Rapport,"; APP 1 W/1176 59452, "Chez les anarchistes. L'Attentat contre M. Clemenceau," 19 February 1919.

111. DCAJM, Cote 12, "Le Commissaire de police, Chef du Service de Sûreté à Lyon, à Monsieur le Capitaine Guillaume, Rapporteur près le Ier Conseil de Guerre de Lyon," 26 February 1919.

112. DCAJM Cote 13, statement to Commissaire de police de la Sûreté Raoul Naud, by Valentina Giobellina, 23 February 1919.

113. DCAJM Cote 13, statement to Commissaire de police de la Sûreté (Valentina Giobellina).

114. DCAJM, Cote 17, statement to Commissaire de police de la Sûreté Raoul Naud, by Honorine Giobellina, 23 February 1919.
115. APP 1 W/1176 59452, "Rapport," (21 February 1919).
116. DCAJM, Cote 356, "Procès verbal d'interrogatoire et de confrontation," 25 February 1919.
117. DCAJM, Cote 55, "Rapport," of le sous-brigadier Riboulet, 4 March 1918; DCAJM, Cote 12, 'Le Commissaire de police, Chef du Service de Sûreté à Lyon, à Monsieur le Capitaine Guillaume."
118. DCAJM, Cote 357, "Procès verbal d'interrogatoire,"; Cote 102 bis, "Rapport," 4 March 1919; Cote 100, "Rapport."
119. DCAJM, Cote 12, "Le Commissaire de police, Chef du Service de Sûreté à Lyon, à Monsieur le Capitaine Guillaume."
120. See, for example, DCAJM Cote 13, statement to Commissaire de police de la Sûreté (Valentina Giobellina); DCAJM Cote 14, statement to Commissaire de police de la Sûreté Raoul Naud, by Anastasie Warmé, 23 February 1919; DCAJM Cote 15, statement to Commissaire de police de la Sûreté Raoul Naud, by Albert Warmé, 23 February 1919; DCAJM Cote 17, statement to Commissaire de police de la Sûreté (Honorine Giobellina); DCAJM, Cote 18, statement to Commissaire de police de la Sûreté Raoul Naud, by Jacques Walker, 23 February 1919.
121. DCAJM, Cote 22, statement to Commissaire de police de la Sûreté Raoul Naud, by Jean Baptiste Favier, 25 February 1919.
122. DCAJM, Cote 12, "Le Commissaire de police, Chef du Service de Sûreté à Lyon, à Monsieur le Capitaine Guillaume,"; Le Naour, *L'Assassinat de Clemenceau*, 41.
123. DCAJM, Cote 22, statement to Commissaire de police de la Sûreté (Jean Baptiste Favier).
124. DCAJM, Cote 223, "Affaire Cottin (Emile Jules Henri)." His friend and former co-worker at REP Vincent-Antonin Chavrier recalled that Cottin began to express extreme anarchist views to him only after both men left Lyon to travel north (Chavrier moved to Paris; DCAJM, Cote 55, Rapport of le sous-brigadier Riboulet, 4 March 1918).
125. DCAJM, Cote 117, untitled report.
126. DCAJM, Cote 100, "Rapport."
127. APP 1 W/1176 59452, "Rapport," (20 February 1919).
128. APP 1 W/1176 59452, "Rapport," by Tollenaers, 22 February 1919.
129. DCAJM, Cote 114, "Rapport," 17 March 1918.
130. APP 1 W/1176 59452, "Rapport," by Inspecteur Isaac, 21 February 1919.
131. APP 1 W/1176 59452, "Rapport," 22 February 1919.
132. DCAJM Cote 356, "Procès verbal d'interrogatoire," 25 February 1919.
133. DCAJM, Cote 223, "Affaire Cottin (Emile Jules Henri)."
134. DCAJM, Cote 357, "Procès verbal d'interrogatoire."
135. DCAJM, Cote 645, Bouchardon, untitled "rapport"; mentioned also in 'L'instruction de l'affaire Cottin', *Le Matin*, 5 March 1919, 2; "Dernier interrogatoire de Cottin," *L'Oeuvre*, 7 March 1919, 2.

136. DCAJM, Cote 356, "Procès verbal d'interrogatoire."
137. DCAJM, Cote 356, "Procès verbal d'interrogatoire."
138. DCAJM, Cote 223, "Affaire Cottin (Emile Jules Henri)."
139. DCAJM, Cote 223, "Affaire Cottin (Emile Jules Henri)."
140. DCAJM, Cote 645, Bouchardon, untitled "rapport."
141. DCAJM, Cote 357, "Procès verbal d'interrogatoire"; Cote 366, "Procès verbal d'interrogatoire et de confrontation," 6 March 1919.
142. "Cottin condamné à mort," *Le Journal*, 15 March 1919, 1.
143. References to the war surfaced in other comments on the trial: the editorial in *La Patrie* condemned the anarchist for living an easy life at home while his fellow workers suffered at the front in Intérim, "La vie politique," *La Patrie*, 14 March 1919, 1.
144. DCAJM, Cote 361, "Procès verbal d'interrogatoire et de confrontation," 3 March 1919.
145. DCAJM, Cote 645, Bouchardon, untitled "rapport."
146. "Cottin condamné à mort."
147. Georges de Maizière, "Cottin à l'unanimité, est condamné à mort," *Le Petit Parisien*, 15 March 1919, 1–3.
148. "Cottin condamné à mort," *L'Avenir*, 15 March 1919, 1.
149. "Cottin à l'unanimité, est condamné à mort."
150. Intérim, "La vie politique" (14 March 1919).
151. Maxime Girard, "L'attentat contre M. Clemenceau," *Le Figaro*, 15 March 1919, 1.
152. Girard, "L'attentat contre M. Clemenceau,"; "Cottin condamné à mort," (*L'Avenir*); "Cottin est condamné à mort," *La Lanterne*, 15 March 1919, 1; "Cottin est condamné à mort par le 3e conseil de guerre," *Excelsior*, 15 March 1919, 2–3.
153. De Maizière, "Cottin, à l'unanimité, est condamné à mort," 1.
154. Edgar Troimaux, "Cottin condamné a mort à l'unanimité," *L'Echo de Paris*, 15 March 1919, 1–2.
155. Joseph Mollet, "Cottin est condamné à mort," *La Croix*, 16 March 1919, 1–2.
156. Jean Lecoq, "Enseignez le sens commun," *Le Petit Journal*, 17 March 1919, 2.
157. Sonn, *Sex, Violence and the Avant-Garde*, 45–46.
158. "Cottin est condamné à mort," *Le Matin*, 15 March 1919, 2.
159. APP 1 W/1176 59452, "Le Directeur de la Prison de la Santé à Monsieur le Préfet de Police, 1re Division, 2ème Bureau," 15 March 1919.
160. See *Le Libertaire*, 16 March 1919.
161. "Le pourvoi en révision de Cottin est rejeté," *Le Matin*, 2 April 1919, 2.
162. See La Naour, *L'Assassinat de Clemenceau*, 121–56.
163. "Notre martyr," *Le Libertaire*, 4 May 1919, 1–2.
164. AN F7 13412, "Le Gouverneur Général de l'Algérie à Monsieur le Ministre de l'Intérieur, Direction des Affaires Algériennes—2e Bureau—Paris," 2 March 1922.

165. "Gloire `a Cottin!," *La Jeunesse Anarchiste. Organe de la Fédération des Jeunesses Communistes Anarchistes* 7, 15 November 1921, 2. Between numbers 7 and 11, *La Jeunesse Anarchiste* newspaper focused on Cottin.

166. APP 1 W/1176 59452, "Le Chef du Service des Renseignements Généraux et des Jeux à Monsieur le Préfet de Police," 3 June 1926; "L'anarchiste Cottin, Emile," 22 May 1936.

167. Rumors reached police that Cottin had entered into talks with Italian fascists in Toulon who were planning to kill deputy Pierre Renaudel. See APP 1 W/1176 59452, untitled report, 23 March 1933.

168. APP 1 W/1176 59452, untitled note, 24 March 1930.

169. APP 1 W/1176 59452, "Le Directeur des Renseignements Généraux et des Jeux à Monsieur le Préfet de Police," 22 May 1936.

170. APP 1 W/1176 59452, untitled report, 23 March 1933; untitled note, 16 October 1936.

171. "Un attentat anarchiste," *Le Sémaphore de Marseille*, 14 July 1922, 1. See also Armand Villette, "Un attentat contre le cortège présidentiel," *Le Gaulois*, 15 July 1922, 1.

172. APP 77 W/6742-737631, "Attentat contre M. Millerand, Président de la République," n. d.

173. "Des coups de feu sur la voiture du préfet de police," *La Patrie*, 14 July 1922, 1.

174. "Un Attentat communiste contre le Préfet de Police a marqué le retour de la Revue de Longchamp," *La Patrie*, 14 July 1922, 1; "L'attentat communiste," *L'Echo de Paris*, 15 July 1922, 3; "Au retour de la revue de Longchamp un communiste, croyant atteindre M. Millerand, tire sur la voiture du Préfet de police," *Le Journal*, 15 July 1922, 1.

175. "Un 'attentat' manqué. Des coups de feu près du cortège présidentiel," *L'Humanité*, 15 July 1922, 1; Ch. L., "A propos d'un 'attentat'," *L'Humanité*, 16 July 1922, 1.

176. Ch. L., "A propos d'un 'attentat'."

177. "L'attentat communiste," 3; "Bouvet en correctionnelle," *Le Libertaire*, 8 July 1921, 2–3; "BOUVET, Gustave, Charles, Joseph 'JUVÉNIS'." https://archivesautonomies.org/spip.php?article3066 (accessed May 12, 2021).

178. "Les fêtes du 14 juillet," *L'Oeuvre*, 15 July 1922, 1.

179. See "Sauvons Cottin!" *La Jeunesse Anarchiste*, 7, 15 November 1921, 1; and Louis Lecoin, "Son geste!" *La Jeunesse Anarchiste*, 7, 15 November 1921, 1–2. See also various pieces in *La Jeunesse Anarchiste* 8, 15 December 1921.

180. "Au retour de la grandiose revue," 1; "Bouvet serait un isolé soucieux de prouver qu'il fut un anarchiste 'bon teint'," *Le Matin*, 16 July 1922, 1; "Bouvet voulait prouver qu'il était 'un pur'," *L'Echo de Paris*, 16 July 1922, 1; "On juge Bouvet qui tira sur M. Poincaré," *La Presse*, 8 January 1923, 1.

181. "Gustave Bouvet qui tira sur le cortège du Président de la République est condamné à cinq ans de travaux forcés," *Le Petit Parisien*, 9 January 1923, 1.

182. "L'attentat communiste," 3.

183. "L'attentat manqué d'un anarchiste contre M. Millerand assombrit un instant l'enthousiasme populaire," *Le Matin*, 15 July 1922, 1.
184. "Les fêtes du 14 juillet," 1.
185. "L'attentat anarchiste contre le président de la République et le président du conseil," *L'Echo de Paris*, 9 January 1923, 3.
186. "Au retour de la grandiose revue," 1.
187. "L'attentat manqué," 1.
188. "Bouvet a-t-il voulu tuer le président?" *La Dépêche*, 16 July 1922, 1.
189. Clément Vautel, "Mon film," *Le Journal*, 16 July 1922, 1.
190. Vautel, "Mon film," (16 July 1922).
191. "Des coups de feu," 1.
192. Villette, "Un attentat," 1.
193. "Editorial," *L'Ere nouvelle*, 16 July 1922, 1.
194. Maurice Prax, "L'attentat," *Le Petit Parisien*, 16 July 1922, 1.
195. Prax, "L'attentat," 1.
196. "Gustave Bouvet," 1.

CHAPTER 3

Sections of this chapter draw on the material used in Chris Millington, "Mad or Bad? Paul Gorguloff, the Man Who Killed the French President in 1932," forthcoming 2023, in a collection of essays published by Brill and under the editorship of Graham Wrightson.

1. Instead of "Pavel Gorgulov," I use "Paul Gorguloff," the assassin's name as it generally appeared in French press and government sources.
2. AN F7 12907, Léon Bailby, "Notre faiblesse," *L'Intransigeant*, 29 July 1922.
3. A. Delpeyrou, "La carrière d'un grand citoyen," *Comoedia*, 7 May 1932, 3.
4. Doumer was interred at a family plot in the Vaugirard cemetery, Paris.
5. "M. Paul Doumer assassiné," *L'Echo de Paris*, 7 May 1932, 1.
6. "M. Paul Doumer assassiné," 1.
7. Léon Blum, "Attentat criminel contre M. Paul Doumer," *Le Populaire*, 7 May 1932, 1; "Les tares mentales de Gorgulov," *Le Populaire*, 16 July 1932, 3. See also "Au procès Gorgulov les aliénistes ont parlé mais ils n'ont pas discuté leurs opinions," *Le Populaire*, 26 July 1932, 1, in which it is written, "Gorgulov remained the madman he had been from the first hour."
8. "Gorguloff est bien un communiste," *Le Figaro*, 7 May 1932, 1. See also Sophie Coeuré and Frédéric Monier, "Paul Gorgulov, assassin de Paul Doumer (1932)," *Vingtième Siècle, revue d'histoire* 65 (January-March 2000): 39–40.
9. "The Soviet and the Assassin," *The Manchester Guardian*, 9 May 1932, 9.
10. Jean Chiappe was prefect of the Paris police and a hate-figure of the French left.
11. "Une chaîne infâme de provocations," *L'Humanité*, 8 October 1932, 1. See also André Marty, "Comme en 1914," *L'Humanité*, 8 May 1932, 1; L. Gatignon, "Gorguloff aux assises," *L'Emancipateur*, 30 July 1932, 1.

12. Sonn, *Sex, Violence and the Avant-Garde*, 173.

13. Maurice Prax, "Pour et contre," *Le Petit Parisien*, 20 April 1925, 1; "Pâques rouges à Sofia," *Le Temps*, 9 May 1925, 1.

14. Amaury Lorin, "Un 'régicide républicain': Paul Doumer, le président assassiné 6 mai 1932," *Criminocorpus: histoire de la justice, des crimes et des peines*, varia (posted online 17 November 2011), 50, https://journals.openedition.org/criminocorpus/435?lang=fr (accessed 26 October 2022; *La fin tragique du Président Paul Doumer racontés par deux témoins oculaires* (Paris: Librairie contemporaine, 1932), 21.

15. Jean Lecoq, "Les attentats contres les Chefs d'Etat," *Le Petit Journal illustré*, 15 May 1932, 4–5; Robert Delys, "Les assassinats politiques," *Courrier de Saône-et-Loire*, 11 May 1932, 4.

16. "Un fasciste russe tire sur M. Paul Doumer," *L'Oeuvre*, 7 May 1932, 1

17. See *Le Figaro*, 7 May 1932.

18. The law of 10 August 1932, debated in the Chamber of Deputies the previous December, was the first of its kind since the 'Millerand' decree of 10 August 1899. See Marianne Amar and Pierre Milza, *L'immigration en France au XXe siècle* (Paris: Armand Colin, 1990), 218; Jeanne Singer-Kerel, "'Protection' de la main-d'oeuvre en temps de crise. Le précédent des années trente," *Revue européenne des migrations internationales* 5, no. 2 (1989): 12; Vincent Viet, *La France immigrée. Construction d'une politique, 1914–1997* (Paris: Fayard, 1998), 43n5.

19. Pierre L'Ermite, "L'heure tragique…," *La Croix*, 8 May 1932, 1.

20. "1894–1932," *L'Oeuvre*, 7 May 1932, 2.

21. Stéphane J. Baele, "Are Terrorists 'Insane'? A Critical Analysis of Mental Health Categories in Lone Terrorists' Trials," *Critical Studies on Terrorism* 7, no. 2 (2014): 226; David Parker, Julia M. Pearce, Lasse Lindekilde, and M. Brooke Rogers, "Press Coverage of Lone-Actor Terrorism in the UK and Denmark: Shaping the Reactions of the Public, Affected Communities and Copycat Attackers," *Critical Studies on Terrorism* 12, no. 1 (2019): 121.

22. Amaury Lorin, *Une ascension en République. Paul Doumer (1857–1932), d'Aurillac à l'Elysée* (Paris: Dalloz, 2013), 312–14.

23. Lorin, "Un 'régicide républicain'," paragraph 3.

24. Edouard Julia, *Papiers, 1895–1933* (Paris: Editions du Temps, 1936), 229; Lorin, "Un 'régicide républicain'," paragraph 9.

25. Michel Gorel, *Pourquoi Gorguloff a-t-il tué?* (Paris: Editions Nilsson, 1932), 13.

26. See, for example, "La mort," *La Croix*, 8 May 1932, 2.

27. AN F7 15960/3, "Au sujet de l'attentat contre le Président de la République Française. Gorguloff, Paul," 6 May 1932; AN 603 AP 4, "Rapport Médico-Légal. Etude du Dossier," 30 May 1932.

28. AN 603 AP 4, "Rapport Médico-Légal."

29. AN 603 AP 4, "Rapport Médico-Légal."

30. AN 603 AP 1, "Extrait du dossier du Tribunal Civil provincial à Prague, relative au divorce. Traduit du tchèque."

31. AN 603 AP 4, "Rapport Médico-Légal."
32. AN 603 AP 1, "Procès-verbal dressé à la Présidence de la Direction de la Police à Prague, le 7 mai 1933 ayant pour l'objet l'interrogatoire de Emilie Gorgouloff," n.d., contained within the "Annexes au rapport général. Traduit du tchèque."
33. AN 603 AP 1, 'Extrait du dossier du Tribunal Civil provincial à Prague"; "Tribunal Civil Régional à Prague Arrivée le 17 janvier 1927. Traduit du tchèque," 17 January 1927.
34. AN 603 AP 4, 'Rapport Médico-Légal"; "L'assassinat du président Paul Doumer," *L'Echo d'Alger*, 16 May 1932, 5.
35. AN 603 AP 4, "Le docteur Paul Gorguloff," unknown newspaper, n.d.; "Attentat criminal," 1. See also the collection of clippings in Géraud's file on the case.
36. AN 603 AP 4, "Prisonnier Paul Gorguloff, assassinat de Président de la république française Paul Doumer, 9 mai 1932, Prison de la Santé, Paris."
37. AN 603 AP 3, "Tribunal de première instance du département de la Seine. Procès-verbal d'interrogatoire et de confrontation," 2 June 1932.
38. Lorin, *Une ascension en République*, 325.
39. AN 603 AP 1, "Procès verbal dressé à la Direction de la Police à Prague le 10 mai 1932 ayant pour object l'interrogatoire informative de l'inégnieur Vassili Vaziljev."
40. AN 603 AP 1, "Procès verbal dressé à la Présidence de la Police à Prague le 10 mai 1932, ayant pour object l'interrogatoire de Cesar Durchansk"; "Assassinat du Président de la République," *Le Figaro*, 7 May 1932, 1.
41. AN 603 AP 4, "Rapport Médico-Légal."
42. "Gorguloff Is a Red, Asserts Millerand," *The New York Times*, 8 May 1932, 20.
43. The report from Belgium was mentioned in several press articles in France. See, for example, "L'enquête sur l'assassinat du président de la République," *La Croix*, 10 May 1932, 3; "Notre enquête," *Le Figaro*, 9 May 1932, 2; "Gorguloff, agent des Soviets," *L'Intransigeant*, 9 May 1932, 3; "Gorguloff, l'assassin de M. Doumer, est un agent secret des soviets," *Feuille d'Avis de Neuchâtel et du Vignoble neuchâtelois*, 9 May 1932, 1; "La politique," *La Croix de Saintonge et d'Aunis*, 29 May 1932, 1.
44. Pierre Bertin, "Gorguloff, l'assassin mystérieux," *Police-Magazine*, 15 May 1932, 13 and 15.
45. B. Bajanov and N. Alexeiev, *L'enlèvement du Général Koutepov* (Paris: Editions Spes, 1930), 3; 82. See also Miller, *Shanghai on the Metro*, 134–35.
46. Gaëtan Sanvoisin, "L'énigme de l'attentat," *Le Figaro*, 8 May 1932, 1.
47. Henri Barbusse, *J'accuse!... un réquisitoire implacable* (Paris: Bureau d'Editions, 1932), 1–2; 24–28.
48. "Deux heures avec Jacques Mortane qui a vu comment a été tué Doumer et qui le dit...!" *L'Humanité*, 27 June 1932, 1–2.
49. "Les coups de revolver hier soir écho des explosions de Mandchourie et de l'attentat de Moscou," *L'Humanité*, 7 May 1932, 3; Ralph Schor, *Histoire de l'immigration en France de la fin du XIXe siècle à nos jours* (Paris: Armand Colin,

1996), 157. Communist luminary Paul Vaillant-Couturier described Gorguloff as a "white Cossack" in his preface to Henri Franklin-Marquet, *La vérité sur l'affaire Gorgoulov. Ceux qui ont tué Doumer...* (Paris: Bureau d'Éditions, 1932), v.

50. AN F7 15960/3, untitled, anonymous report, 11 May 1932; "Directive urgente aux bureaux et comités régionaux," 7 May 1932. See also "L'attentat individuel arme de l'impérialisme," *L'Humanité*, 7 May 1932, 1.

51. Some newspapers made the same connections: Gaëtan Sanvoisin, "L'ère des attentats. Coïncidences ou action concertée...," *Le Figaro*, 16 May 1932, 1; "L'incendie du 'Georges-Philippar' est-il dû à un attentat?" *Le Figaro*, 22 May 1932, 1.

52. Paul Darlix, *Terrorisme sur le monde* (Paris: Editions Baudinière, 1932), 144; 220.

53. Darlix, *Terrorisme sur le monde*, 10.

54. Philippe Artois, "Le 'Georges-Philippar' fut-il victim d'un attentat?" *Police-Magazine*, 29 May 1932.

55. Carla Jenssen, *J'espionne...Histoire vraie d'une femme, agent du service secret*. Traduit de l'anglais par Maurice Remon (Paris: Nouvelle Librairie Francaise, 1931), originally published as *I Spy! Sensational Disclosures of a British Secret Service Agent* (London: Jarrolds, 1930).

56. Boris Savinkov, *Souvenirs d'un terroriste*. Traduit du Russe par Bernard Taft (Paris: Payot, 1931).

57. Boris Viktorovich Savinkov, *Memoirs of a Terrorist*. Translated by Joseph Shaplen with a foreword and epilogue (New York : A. & C. Boni, 1931).

58. On this topic, see Miller, *Shanghai on the Metro*.

59. On this novel, see Coeuré and Monier, "Paul Gorgulov," 41.

60. Joseph Lovitch, *Tempête sur l'Europe. Roman. Préfacé de Henry Rollin* (Paris: Editions La Flèche d'Or, 1932), iv.

61. Lovitch, *Tempête sur l'Europe*, xv.

62. Lovitch, *Tempête sur l'Europe*, iv.

63. AN 603 AP1, "Où l'imagination devance l'effroyable réalité...L'Assassinat du Président Doumer prévu et décrit par un romancier russe," *Le Quotidien*, 23 June 1932, 1–3.

64. Gorel, *Pourquoi Gorguloff a-t-il tué?* 78–79.

65. "Une preuve de plus!" *L'Humanité*, 31 July 1932, 2.

66. "Gorguloff Must Die for Killing Doumer," *The New York Times*, 28 July 1932, 6.

67. The blonde is mentioned in, for example, H. Frédéric Pottecher, "Sténographie du premier interrogatoire du meurtrier," *Comoedia*, 7 May 1932, 3.

68. Pierre Bertin, "Gorguloff, l'assassin mystérieux," *Police-Magazine*, 15 May 1932, 13 and 15.

69. Marcel Montarron, "Le secret de l'assassin," *Détective*, 12 May 1932, 8–9.

70. "L'assassin du président Doumer devant de jury de la Seine," *L'Echo d'Alger*, 26 July 1932, 5; Pierre Causse, "Le mystérieux Gorguloff," *L'Intransigeant*, 9 May 1932, 3; "Attentat criminal," 2.

71. Lovitch, *Tempête sur l'Europe*, 18.
72. Vicki Caron, *Uneasy Asylum: France and the Jewish Refugee Crisis, 1933–1942* (Stanford, CA: Stanford University Press, 2002), 4; Patrick Weil, *La France et les étrangers. L'aventure d'une politique de l'immigration, 1938–1991* (Paris: Calman-Lévy, 1991), 373.
73. Gérard Noiriel, *Le Creuset français. Histoire de l'immigration (XIXe–XXe siècle)* (Paris: Editions du Seuil, 1989), 21.
74. Viet, *La France immigrée*, 36.
75. Viet, *La France immigrée*, 44; Weil, *La France et les étrangers*, 24.
76. Schor, *Histoire de l'immigration*, 53–54.
77. Viet, *La France immigrée*, 37.
78. Schor, *Histoire de l'immigration*, 64–65.
79. AN F7 14747, "Le Commissaire de Police Mobile Balmadier à Monsieur le Commissaire Divisionnaire, Chef de la 1ère Brigade Régionale de Police Mobile," 11 September 1926.
80. AN F7 14747, "Le Commissaire de Police Mobile Balmadier."
81. "Gorguloff est condamné à mort," *Le Figaro*, 28 July 1932, 1. See also François Coty, "'Un front unique' contre le communisme," *Le Figaro*, 13 May 1927, 1; François Coty, "'Un front unique' contre le communisme," *Le Figaro*, 19 May 1927, 1 (this latter article contains a riposte to Coty from Schwarzbard himself).
82. Schor, *Histoire de l'immigration*, 116–17.
83. Coeuré and Monier, "Paul Gorgulov," 38–43.
84. Évelyne Cohen, *Paris dans l'imaginaire national de l'entre-deux-guerres* [online] (Paris: Éditions de la Sorbonne, 2000), https://books.openedition.org/psorbonne/1246 (accessed 21 January 2020), "Chapitre III. Le grand Paris," paragraph 97.
85. Hélène Menegaldo, "L'émigration russe (1919–1939)," in *Histoire de l'immigration en France au XXe siècle*, ed. Laurent Gervereau, Pierre Milza, and Emile Temime (1998), 96. See also Table 1 on page 427 of Timothy Maga, "Closing the Door: The French Government and Refugee Policy, 1933–1939," *French Historical Studies* 12, no. 33 (1982): 424–42. Schor gives the number 71,900 regarding the Russian population in France in 1931, in *Histoire de l'immigration*, 60.
86. Amar and Milza, *L'immigration en France*, 274.
87. Schor, *Histoire de l'immigration*, 51–52.
88. Rosenberg, *Policing Paris*, 65. Marianne Amar and Pierre Milza state that a hundred thousand refugees from Russia arrived during the 1920s, in *L'immigration en France*, 275.
89. John Hope Simpson, "The Refugee Problem," *International Affairs* 17, no. 5 (1938): 610–11.
90. Rosenberg, *Policing Paris*, 65.
91. Catherine Goussef, *L'exil russe. La fabrique du réfugié apatride (1920–1939)* (Paris: CNRS Editions, 2008), 10; Menegaldo, "L'émigration russe (1919–1939)," 100; Schor, *Histoire de l'immigration*, 114.
92. Menegaldo, "L'émigration russe (1919–1939)," 94–96.

93. Mary Dewhurst Lewis, *The Boundaries of the Republic: Migrant Rights and the Limits of Universalism in France, 1918–1940* (Stanford, CA: Stanford University Press, 2007), 171–72.

94. Miller, *Shanghai on the Metro*, 134–35.

95. Donald N. Baker, "The Surveillance of Subversion in Interwar France: The Carnet B in the Seine, 1922–1940," *French Historical Studies* 10, no. 3 (1978): 508–9.

96. Baker, "The Surveillance of Subversion," 509. See also the information from the *Annuaire statistique de la Ville de Paris* (1931) in Cohen, *Paris dans l'imaginaire national de l'entre-deux-guerres*.

97. Lorin, *Une ascension en République*, 320.

98. Vincent, "Le régicide en République," 79.

99. See, for example, Memo, "Menus propos," *Mémorial de la Loire et de la Haute-Loire*, 22 May 1932, 2.

100. X. de Hautecloque, "Le spectre de Boris Savinkov," *Le Petit Journal*, 14 May 1932, 1.

101. Darlix, *Terrorisme sur le monde*, 202, 220.

102. The first part was titled, "Dans les repaires des terroristes gardes blancs. 1.—La France impérialiste contre des provocateurs et assassins de l'émigration russe." *L'Humanité*, 18 May 1932, 1.

103. AN 603 AP 1, "Où l'imagination devance l'effroyable réalité," 1–3.

104. Schor, *Histoire de l'immigration*, 114.

105. Georges Claretie, "Gorguloff ne serait-il pas un simulateur?" *Le Figaro*, 27 July 1932, 1–2. See also Montarron, "Le secret de l'assassin," 8–9.

106. See, for example, Weil, *La France et les étrangers*, 360.

107. *La fin tragique du Président Paul Doumer*, 17. See also, for example, "L'abominable attentat d'un nationaliste russe contre le président de la République," *L'Echo d'Alger*, 7 May 1932, 6.

108. Philippe Artois, "L'assassinat du Président Paul Doumer," *Police-Magazine*, 15 May 1932, 12–13; Darlix, *Terrorisme sur le monde*, 28.

109. "L'interrogatoire de Gorguloff au commissariat," *L'Echo de Paris*, 7 May 1932, 1; "Un fasciste russe," 1; *La fin tragique du Président Paul Doumer*, 21.

110. Or six foot two inches.

111. Or five foot five inches; "Assassinat du Président,"; 'M.-C. Chamla, "L'accroissement de la stature en France de 1880 à 1960. Comparaison avec les pays d'Europe occidentale," *Bulletins et Mémoires de la Société d'Anthropologie de Paris* 6, no. 2 (1964): 207.

112. *La fin tragique du Président Paul Doumer*, 17. See also Catherine Bertho Lavenir, "Bombes, protes & pistolets. Les âges médiologiques de l'attentat," *Les cahiers de médiologie* 13, no. 1 (2002): 29.

113. AN F7 15060/3, "Le Crime de Gorguloff," 17 May 1932, supplied by Agence Fournier.

114. As noted in "Nos échos," *Comoedia*, 4 June 1932, 3.

115. Gorel, *Pourquoi Gorguloff a-t-il tué?*, 15.

116. *La fin tragique du Président Paul Doumer*, 11; 21.

117. Artois, "L'assassinat du Président Paul Doumer,"12–13; Darlix, *Terrorisme sur le monde*, 28.

118. Henri Espiau, "Paul Gorguloff répond devant le jury de la Seine de l'assassinat du président Doumer," *L'Echo de Paris*, 26 July 1932, 1.

119. Georges Claretie, "Le procès de Gorguloff commence aujourd'hui," *Le Figaro*, 25 July 1932, 1; Claretie, "Gorguloff ne serait-il pas un simulateur?" 1–2.

120. "M. Paul Doumer assassiné," 1. See also André Pironneau, "L'assassinat du président Paul Doumer," *L'Echo de Paris*, 8 May 1932, 1.

121. A. de Gobart, "Vers un statut définitif des étrangers en France," *L'Intransigeant*, 20 May 1932, 5.

122. Jules Véran, "Les étrangers à Paris," *Comoedia*, 24 May 1932, 1.

123. Ernest Laut, "L'âme de la foule," *Le Petit Journal illustré*, 15 May 1932, 2.

124. Daniel A. Gordon, "The Back Door of the Nation State: Expulsions of Foreigners and Continuity in Twentieth-Century France," *Past & Present* 186 (2005): 227.

125. "La ténébreuse affaire," *Le Figaro*, 29 July 1932, 1.

126. René Rodière, *Le délit politique/ Contribution à l'étude du délit politique en droit français*, thèse pour le doctorat (Paris: Librairie Arthur Rousseau, 1931), 206.

127. For a discussion of this, see Jean Beaudéant, *L'attentat contre les chefs d'état*, thèse pour le doctorat, Université de Toulouse, Faculté de Droit (Toulouse: Ch. Dirion Librairie-Editeur, 1911), 22–35. See also *Des crimes et délits contre la sûreté de l'Etat, contre la constitution et la paix publique: Droit criminal* (Paris: Carus, 1936), 22.

128. "Gorguloff, l'assassin du président Doumer, a comparu, hier, devant la cour d'assises," *Le Petit Parisien*, 26 July 1932, 1.

129. "Paul Gorguloff devant le Jury," *Le Petit Journal*, 26 July 1932, 1 and 3.

130. "Pour ou contre la diffusion des débats d'assises," *Le Populaire*, 26 July 1932, 4; Vincent, "Le régicide en République," 76.

131. Lorin, *Une ascension en République*, 328; "Paul Gorguloff devant le Jury," 1 and 3; Frédéric Chauvaud, *La chaire des prétoires. Histoire sensible de la cour d'assises* (Rennes, FR: Presses Universitaires de Rennes, 2010), 59.

132. "Gorguloff, l'assassin du président Doumer," 1.

133. Pierre Bénard, "Gorguloff, l'assassin du président Doumer, répond de son forfait devant la Cour d'assises de la Seine," *L'Oeuvre*, 26 July 1932, 1 and 4; "Paul Gorguloff, assassin du président Doumer, devant la cour d'assises de la Seine," *Le Matin*, 26 July 1932, 1.

134. See, for example, "L'assassin du président Doumer le Russe Paul Gorguloff devant le jury de la Seine," *L'Echo d'Alger*, 26 July 1932, 1; "Paul Gorguloff devant le Jury," 1 and 3.

135. C. M., "Gorguloff devant ses juges," *Police-Magazine*, 31 July 1932, 8–9.

136. "Gorguloff, l'assassin du président Doumer," 1.

137. "Gorgulov condamné à la peine de mort," *Le Populaire*, 28 July 1932, 1.

138. "La bataille des psychiâtres autour de l'état mental de Gorguloff," *L'Oeuvre*, 27 July 1932, 1. A short chapter on the trial may be found here: Jean-

Gaston Moore, "Gorguloff, ou le procès de la démence," in *Les grands procès*, ed. Daniel Amson, Jean-Gaston Moore, and Charles Amson (Paris: Presses Universitaires de France, 2007), 120–33. I explore this episode elsewhere: Chris Millington, "Mad or Bad? Paul Gorguloff, the Man Who Killed the French President in 1932," forthcoming.

139. "Gorguloff est bien un communiste," 1.

140. See, for example, André Marty, "De Gorguloff à Fantomas," *L'Humanité*, 25 July 1932, 1; "L'assassin du président Doumer devant de jury de la Seine," 5.

141. "There is neither crime nor offense, when the accused was in a state of insanity at the time of the act": https://www.legifrance.gouv.fr/affichCodeArticle.do?idArticle=LEGIARTI000006490631&cidTexte=LEGITEXT000006071029&dateTexte=18100223 (accessed 21 January 2020).

142. AN 603 AP 4, "Rapport Médico-Légal."

143. AN 603 AP 4, "Rapport Médico-Légal."

144. AN F7 15960/3, "Gorguloff, Paul," 7 May 1932.

145. AN F7 15960/3, "Déclaration de Krinskine (Affaire Gorguloff)," 7 May 1932.

146. *La fin tragique du Président Paul Doumer*, 21.

147. AN 603 AP 4, "Rapport Médico-Légal."

148. AN 603 AP 4, "Rapport Médico-Légal."

149. AN 603 AP 1, "Procès-verbal dressé à la Présidence de la Direction de la Police à Prague, le 7 mai 1933 ayant pour l'objet l'interrogatoire de Emilie Gorgouloff."

150. AN 603 AP 1, "Observatoire de l'Etat de la République Tchécoslavaque à Prague," 7 May 1932; "Copie Médecin practicien Docteur Paul Gorgouloff ancien externe de la Clinique de Maladies des Femmes, Interne de la Peau et Vénériennes, à Prague, Soleil artificiзl—Electrothérapie, Examen du Sang, 5.XII.1929."

151. See, for example, 603 AP 1, "Extrait du dossier du Tribunal Civil provincial à Prague, relative au divorce."

152. AN 603 AP 4, "Rapport Médico-Légal."

153. AN 603 AP 4, "Rapport Médico-Légal."

154. AN 603 AP 4, "Rapport Médico-Légal"; Emilie Gorguloff expressed this view in AN 603 AP 1, "Procès-verbal dressé à la Présidence de la Direction de la Police à Prague, le 7 mai 1933 ayant pour l'objet l'interrogatoire de Emilie Gorgouloff."

155. AN 603 AP 4, "Rapport Médico-Légal."

156. AN 603 AP 4, "Rapport Médico-Légal."

157. Emile Zavie, "Gorguloff est condmané à mort," *Comoedia*, 28 July 1932, 1–2.

158. Zavie, "Gorguloff," 1–2.

159. AN 603 AP 4, "Rapport Médico-Légal."

160. AN 603 AP 4, "Rapport Médico-Légal."

161. Espiau, "Gorguloff devant les Jurés," 3; Pierre Bénard, "Gorguloff devant le jury de la Seine," *L'Oeuvre*, 27 July 1932, 4.

162. AN 603 AP 4, "Rapport Médico-Légal."
163. AN 603 AP 4, "Rapport Médico-Légal."
164. Reported in "Gorguloff est-il un fou ou bien un simulateur?" *Comoedia*, 23 July 1932, 1.
165. AN 603 AP 4, "Affaire Gorgulof. Consultation Médicale," 1 July 1932; AN 603 AP 1, Eugène Quincher, "Au procès Gorgouloff on a entendu six psychiatres," *Le Petit Parisien*, 27 July 1932, 1–2.
166. AN 603 AP 1, Quincher, "Au procès Gorgouloff," 1–2; AN 603 AP 4, "Docteur BJ Logre à Maître Henri Géraud," 2 July 1932.
167. AN 603 AP 4, "Georges Dumas à Henri Géraud," 29 August 1932.
168. "La condamnation à mort de Gorguloff," *Le Petit Journal*, 28 July 1932, 2.
169. "Gorguloff est condamné au mort," *L'Oeuvre*, 28 July 1932, 1.
170. "Gorguloff est condamné," 1.
171. AN F7 15960/3, "Une intervention de la Ligue des Droits de l'Homme," n.d., published by Agence Fournier.
172. Lorin, *Une ascension en République*, 327.
173. AN F7 15960/3, untitled note, 14 September 1932; Lorin, *Une ascension en République*, 329.
174. "Nouvelles diverses," *Le Figaro*, 16 September 1932, 2.
175. "Souvenirs sanglants," *L'Echo d'Alger*, 16 September 1932, 2; "Après l'exécution de Gorguloff," *Le Figaro*, 17 September 1932, 2; "Les scellés de l'affaire Gorguloff seront déposés aujourd'hui au musée de la préfecture de police," *Le Matin*, 17 September 1932, 8.
176. Anon., "Racial character and criminal responsibility," *Nature* 130, no. 3276 (13 August 1932): 217–19.
177. AN F7 16030, "Extrait du *Journal Officiel* de la République Française du 22 mai 1932. Carte d'identité d'étranger"; Lewis, *The Boundaries of the Republic*, 65; 274n47.
178. See Albert Monniot, *Les Morts mystérieuses* (Paris: Nouvelles Éditions Nationales), 9.
179. Henri Rollin, *L'Apocalypse de notre temps. Les dessous de la propaganda allemande d'après des documents inédits* (Paris: Gallimard, 1939), 9–10.
180. Rollin, *L'Apocalypse de notre temps*, 11.

CHAPTER 4

1. I refer to the king with the anglicized name "Alexander." The transliteration of his name from Serbian Cyrillic is "Aleksandar." For an excellent account of the assassination, see Pino Adriano and Giorgio Cingolani, *Nationalism and Terror: Ante Pavelić and Ustasha Terrorism from Fascism to the Cold War* (Budapest: Central European University Press, 2018), 89–119.
2. AN F7 15926/1, "Note Pour Monsieur Blanchet, Ministère des Affaires

Etrangères," 11 October 1934. The IMRO was known in France as the ORIM (Organisation révolutionnaire intérieure macédonienne).

3. E. H., "Du mépris de la vie humaine," *Le Temps*, 15 October 1934, 1.

4. "Une affiche des Jeunesses patriotes," *Le Matin*, 10 October 1934, 3.

5. On unemployment in France during the 1930s, see Nicolas Baverez, "La spécificité française du chômage structurel de masse, des années 1930 aux années 1990," *Vingtième Siècle. Revue d'histoire* 52 (October-December 1996): 41–65.

6. Schor, *Histoire de l'immigration*, 132–33; Caron, *Uneasy Asylum*, 268.

7. See Brian Jenkins and Chris Millington, *France and Fascism: February 1934 and the Dynamics of Political Crisis* (Abingdon, UK: Routledge, 2015).

8. Millington, *A History of Fascism in France*, 51–65.

9. "Le roi Alexandre de Yougoslavie et M. Barthou sont assassinés à Marseille par un Croate," *L'Oeuvre*, 10 October 1934, 1.

10. The Communist Party worried that the government would use the attack as a pretext for "a violent offensive against immigrants" (see "Perquisitions, arrestations, expulsions," *L'Humanité*, 11 October 1934, 2). Sure enough, the Ministry of the Interior ordered raids in the immigrant districts of large urban centers during November 1934: see Caron, *Uneasy Asylum*, 45–46.

11. See, for example, "L'assassinat du roi Alexandre a été préparé par l'Internationale communiste," *Je suis partout*, 3 November 1934, 1–2.

12. The movement was called the Ustaša–Croatian Revolutionary Movement (Ustaša–Hrvatski revolucionarni pokret; or, in French, the Oustasha).

13. André Leroux, "Le crime de Marseille est un crime fasciste," *Le Populaire*, 12 October 1934, 1; "L'organisation terroriste des separatists croates, à laquelle appartiendrait le meurtrier de Marseille, est dirigée et subventionnée par l'Italie fasciste," *Le Populaire*, 11 October 1934, 1.

14. See, for example, P. L. D., "L'étrange contre-ordre," *L'Humanité*, 13 October 1934, 2.

15. P. L. D., "L'étrange contre-ordre," 2; "L'attentat de Marseille," *Le Matin*, 14 October 1934, 8.

16. Haupt and Weinhauer, "Terrorism and the State," 191–92.

17. Sometimes reported as Marija Voudraček or Vondraček.

18. See "Quelle était le visiteur de Mme Voudracek," *Le Matin*, 17 October 1934, 6. Newspapers did not recall the phantom blonde "seen" at the assassination of President Doumer.

19. Monier, "L'attentat de Marseille," paragraph 38.

20. De Vabres would in 1943 refer to this watershed incident in his legal text on resistance terrorism and Vichy's special legislation on the matter in *Traité élémentaire de droit criminel et le legislation pénale comparé. Deuxième edition* (Paris: Librairie du Recueil Sirey, 1943), 2–3.

21. Henri Donnedieu de Vabres's preface to Jerzy Waciórski's, *Le terrorisme politique* (Paris: Edition A. Pedone, 1939), 5.

22. Ditrych, "'International Terrorism'," 203.

23. "Un Croate tire plusieurs coups de revolver sur le roi Alexandre de Yougoslavie," *Le Populaire*, 10 October 1934, 1.

24. Gabriel Péri, "Le roi Alexandre de Yougoslavie est assassiné à Marseille," *L'Humanité*, 10 October 1934, 1.

25. R. W. Seton-Watson, "King Alexander's Assassination: Its Background and Effects," *International Affairs* 14, no. 1 (January-February 1935): 28.

26. Rebecca West, *Black Lamb and Grey Falcon: The Record of a Journey Through Yugoslavia in 1937*, Vol. I (London: Macmillan, 1946), 2. See also Corne, "Regicide on Repeat," 47–73.

27. "Assassination of King Alexander," available to view at https://www.youtube.com/watch?v=6R3dVZdFxxo (accessed 12 October 2022).

28. Ditrych, "'International Terrorism'," 204–5.

29. Ditrych, "'International Terrorism'," 205; Peter Kovacs, "Le grand precedent." For a recent account, see Michael D. Callahan, *The League of Nations, International Terrorism, and British Foreign Policy, 1934–1938* (Basingstoke, UK: Palgrave Macmillan, 2018).

30. J. R., "La répression internationale du terrorisme," *Affaires étrangères. Revue mensuelle de documentation internationale et diplomatique* (November 1937): 518–24; Ditrych, "'International Terrorism'," 200.

31. The Convention may be viewed here: https://www.wdl.org/en/item/11579/view/1/1/ (accessed 26 February 2020). A good discussion of the work of the League is in Charles Townshend, "'Methods Which All Civilized Opinion Must Condemn': The League of Nations and International Action Against Terrorism," in *An International History of Terrorism: Western and Non-Western Experiences*, ed. Jussi M. Hanhimäki and Bernhard Blumenau (London: Routledge, 2013), 34–50.

32. Ditrych, "'International Terrorism'," 205.

33. Saul, "The Legal Response of the League of Nations to Terrorism," 82–87.

34. AN F7 15928/2, *Requête du gouvernement yougoslave en vertu de l'article 11, paragraphe 2, du pacte de la Société des Nations relatives aux responsabilités encourues par les autorités hongroises dans l'action terroriste dirigée contre la Yougoslavie. Actes et documents (22 november–10 décembre 1934* (Beograd, 1935), 112.

35. Ditrych, "'International Terrorism'," 200.

36. Eden's quotation is cited in Lewis, *The Boundaries of the Republic*, 119.

37. The Yugoslav report concluded that the Marseilles attack was dissimilar to past "isolated and individual [acts of] criminal anarchism": AN F7 15928/2, *Requête du gouvernement yougoslave en vertu de l'article 11, paragraphe 2*, 32.

38. Ditrych, "'International Terrorism'," 205

39. "Avant le débarquement," *Le Petit Journal*, 9 October 1934, 3.

40. "Bulletin du jour," *Le Temps*, 9 October 1934, 1; "Marseille se prépare à accueillir chaleureusement le roi-soldat Alexandre Ier de Yougolsavie," *Le Petit Marseillais*, 9 October 1934, 3; Vesna Drapac, "A King Is Killed in Marseille: France and Yugoslavia in 1934," *French History and Civilization* 1 (2005): 225–26.

41. "Avant le débarquement," 3.

42. Konrad Sebastian Morawski, "The Assassination of King Alexander I of Yugolsavia in the Light of Archival Press Articles," *Studia z Dziejów Rosji i Europy Środkowo-Wschodniej* 51, no. 1 (2016): 51.

43. For a summary of this subject, see Vojislav Pavlović, "L'Attentat de Marseille 1934. La fin symbolique d'une alliance atypique," in *La Serbie e la France. Une alliance atypique. Relations politiques, économiques et culturelles, 1870–1940*, ed. Dušan T. Bataković (Belgrade: Académie serbe des Sciences et des Arts, 2010): 575–97.

44. Jean-Baptiste Duroselle, "Louis Barthou et le rapprochement franco-soviétique en 1934," *Cahiers du Monde russe* 3–4 (1962): 525–45.

45. "M. Barthou a quitté Belgrade pour Paris," *Le Petit Journal*, 27 June 1934, 3.

46. Morawski, "The Assassination of King Alexander I," 49; Adriano and Cingolani, *Nationalism and Terror*, 89–90; 94–95.

47. Drapac, "A King Is Killed," 224; Pavlović, "L'attentat de Marseille," 587.

48. "Cet après-midi, Alexandre Ier de Yougoslavie sera l'hôte officiel de la France," *Le Matin*, 9 October 1934, 1.

49. "Marseille se prépare," 3.

50. "L'assassinat du roi Alexandre Ier et de M. Louis Barthou," *Le Matin*, 10 October 1934, 2–3; Morawski, "The Assassination of King Alexander I," 51.

51. AN F7 15928/2, "Liste des blessés," n.d.; François Broche, *Assassinat de Alexandre Ier et Louis Barthou. Marseille, le 9 octobre 1934* (Paris: Editions Balland, 1977), 135; Jean-Emile Néaumet, *Les Grandes enquêtes du commissaire Chenevier. De la Cagoule à l'affaire Dominici* (Paris: Albin Michel, 1995), 69–72. See also Jean Belin, *My Work at the Sûrete* (London: George G. Harrap, 1950), 157–59.

52. Monier, "L'attentat de Marseille," paragraph 22; Adriano and Cingolani, *Nationalism and Terror*, 109.

53. Jean-Clair Guyot, "Le récit de l'attentat fait par notre envoyé spécial qui en fut témoin," *L'Echo de Paris*, October 10, 1934, 1.

54. "L'assassinat tragique de S. M. Alexandre et de Louis Barthou," *Le Petit Marseillais*, 10 October 1934, 3; "Le roi Alexandre de Yougoslavie et M. Barthou sont tués à coups de revolver par un sujet croate," *Le Petit Provençal*, 10 October 1934, 2; Morawski, "The Assassination of King Alexander I," 55.

55. AN F7 15926/1, "Copie de message téléphonique par Chef de la Sûreté de Marseille à Contrôle Général des Recherches Judiciaires à Paris, le 11 Octobre 1934, à 11h40."

56. Guyot, "Le récit de l'attentat," 1 and 3.

57. AN F7 15928/2, "Liste des blessés," n.d.; Broche, *Assassinat de Alexandre Ier*, 135; "Mme Yolande Farris est morte à l'Hôtel de Dieu," *Le Petit Marseillais*, 12 October 1934, 4; "L'assassinat du roi Alexandre Ier," 2–3.

58. "L'assassinat du roi Alexandre Ier," 2–3; "L'enquête sur l'attentat de Marseille et les recherches pour retrouver d'autres complices de l'assassin," *Le Matin*, 13 October 1934, 7; "Si la police avait voulu Barthou pouvait être sauvé," *L'Humanité*, 13 October 1934, 2; Belin, *My Work at the Sûrete*, 159.

59. Guyot, "Le récit de l'attentat," 1.

60. Guyot, "Le récit de l'attentat," 1.
61. Guyot, "Le récit de l'attentat," 1.
62. Bernard Oudin, "L'anar et le canard," *Les cahiers de médiologie*, 1 (2002): 105. See *Le Petit Journal. Supplément illustré*, 23 December 1893.
63. *Le Petit Journal. Supplément illustré*, 2 July 1894; Lavenir, "Bombes, protes & pistolets," 24.
64. See, for example, *Le Petit Journal*, 10 October 1934.
65. "Le roi Alexandre et M. Barthou assassinés," *Paris-Soir*, 10 October 1934, 1; Lavenir, "Bombes, protes & pistolets," 27–28.
66. "Le tragique attentat de Marseille," *Paris-Soir*, 10 October 1934, 10.
67. Jean-Pierre Vallé, "L'assassinat politique du roi Alexandre Ier de Yougoslavie. Un tournant dans la censure des actualités cinématographiques sous la IIIe République?" *Hypothèses* 20, no. 1 (2017): 227.
68. Richard Abel, *The Ciné Goes to Town: French Cinema, 1896–1904* (Berkeley: Univerity of Califormia Press, 1994), 91–92.
69. John Faber, *Great News Photos and the Stories Behind Them* (New York: Dover, 1978), 60–61; Raymond Fielding, *The American Newsreel: A Complete History, 1911–1967* (Jefferson, NC; London: McFarland & Company, 2006), 141.
70. Keith Brown, "The King Is Dead, Long Live the Balkans! Watching the Marseilles Murders of 1934," unpublished paper delivered at the Sixth Annual World Convention of the Association for the Study of Nationalities, Columbia University, New York (5–7 April 2001): 4; available at https://watson.brown.edu/files/watson/imce/research/projects/terrorist_transformations/The_King_is_Dead.pdf (accessed 21 February 2020).
71. This film may be viewed at https://en.wikipedia.org/wiki/Ustashe#Assassination_of_King_Alexander_I (accessed 19 February 2020).
72. This film may be viewed https://www.youtube.com/watch?v=6R3dVZdFxxo (accessed 19 February 2020).
73. This film may be viewed at https://www.youtube.com/watch?v=vCJUjMdnqeA (accessed 19 February 2020).
74. West, *Black Lamb and Grey Falcon*, 19.
75. Monier, "L'attentat de Marseille," 20.
76. On criticism of the police, see "L'assassinat du roi Alexandre Ier," 2–3; Paul Barlatier, "La Leçon du Drame," *La Sémaphore de Marseille*, 11 October 1934, 1; "Le film enregistrant l'attentat est interdit," *L'Humanité*, 12 October 1934, 2; Georges Ravon, "L'attentat," *Le Figaro*, 10 October 1934, 1 and 3; Paul Guitard, "La mort du roi et celle de M. Barthou," *Le Petit Journal*, 10 October 1934, 3.
77. Morawski, "The Assassination of King Alexander I," 51.
78. Seton-Watson, "King Alexander's Assassination," 28.
79. Intérim, "Propos d'un Parisien," *Le Matin*, 13 October 1934, 1.
80. Monier, "L'attentat de Marseille," paragraph 16.
81. Vallé, 'L'assassinat politique du roi Alexandre," 227; Monier, "L'attentat de Marseille," paragraph 19.
82. Vallé, 'L'assassinat politique du roi Alexandre," 228.

83. René Rousseau, "L'émotion de Paris," *L'Echo de Paris*, 10 October 1934, 1–2.

84. "L'émotion dans la foule," *Le Petit Marseillais*, 10 October 1934, 1–2.

85. In the wake of the political turmoil of early 1934, the government required prefects to make regular reports on the state of public opinion in their department. The quality of these reports varies. Much depended on the assiduity with which the author recorded opinions in his department. Furthermore, the distillation of the opinions of thousands of French into a few summary sentences renders the reports a blunt instrument.

86. AN F7 13024, "Le Préfet du Département de l'Aisne à Monsieur le Ministre de l'Intérieur," 22 October 1934; "Le Préfet du Calvados à Monsieur le Ministre de l'Intérieur," 16 October 1934; "Le Préfet des Basses-Alpes à Monsieur le Ministre de l'Intérieur," 15 October 1934.

87. AN F7 13024, "Le Préfet de Belfort à Monsieur le Ministre de l'Intérieur," 15 October 1934.

88. AN F7 13027, "Le Préfet de la Marne à Monsieur le Ministre de l'Intérieur," 13 October 1934. See also AN F7 13024, "Le Préfet du Morbihan à Monsieur le Ministre de l'Intérieur," 15 October 1934; "Exécution des prescriptions de la Circulaire de M. le Ministre de l'Intérieur (Direction de la Sûreté Générale) en date du 16 Mars 1934, no. 3093. Période du Lundi 8 Octobre au Dimanche 14 octobre."

89. See, for example, "Le Préfet de la Haute-Marne à Monsieur le Ministre de l'Intérieur," 29 October 1934.

90. "Le film de l'attentat provoque à Londres une grande stupeur," *Paris-Soir*, 13 October 1934, 3.

91. "Le roi Alexandre Ier de Yougoslavie et M. Louis Barthou assassinés à Marseille par un terroriste macédonien," *Le Matin*, 10 October 1934, 1; "L'assassinat tragique de S. M. Alexandre," 3.

92. Péri, "Le roi Alexandre de Yougoslavie," 1.

93. "Le corps du roi assassiné vogue vers son royaume," *Le Petit Journal*, 11 October 1934, 1.

94. "Le crime soviétique," *Je suis partout*, 13 October 1934, 2.

95. "L'abominable attentat terroriste de Marseille," *Le Petit Provençal*, 10 October 1934, 5.

96. "Le roi Alexandre de Yougoslavie et M. Barthou sont tués," 1.

97. Antoine Mondanel, "Notes sur l'attentat de Marseille, 9 octobre 1934," n.p., n.d. Mondanel's recollections are available online at https://www.interieur.gouv.fr/Le-ministere/Organisation/Mission-des-archives-nationales/Exposition-virtuelle/Attentat-du-9-octobre-1934 (accessed 19 February 2020). The original version is located at the AN (Fontainebleau site), 19790846/265.

98. AN F7 14774, "Le Commissaire de Police Mobile Fabre, à Monsieur le Commissaire de Police, Chef de la 3e Section du Contrôle Général des Services de Police Criminelle à Paris," n.d.

99. "L'enquête à Paris," *Le Petit Journal*, 12 October 1934, 3.

100. Antoine Mondanel, "Notes sur l'attentat de Marseille," n.p.

101. AN F7 15926/1, "Courrier Spécial. M. Paul-Emile Naggiar, Ministre de

France à Belgrade à S. E. M. Laval, Ministre des Affaires Etrangères," 31 October 1934; "Monsieur Labouret, Ministre de France, Sofia, à S. E. Monsieur Pierre Laval, Ministre des Affaires Etrangères," 19 October 1934.

102. AN F7 14754, "La véritable identité de l'assassin du roi Alexandre est connue," *Le Petit Parisien*, 21 September 1935.

103. Monier, "L'attentat de Marseille," paragraph 31.

104. AN F7 14754, untitled document, but headed with a stamp: "1re section," 15 October 1934; AN F7 15926/1, "Le Ministre des Affaires Etrangères à Monsieur le Ministre de l'Intérieur," 19 November 1934.

105. For a discussion of the date of the Ustashe's founding, see Sabrina P. Rament, "Vladko Maček and the Croation Peasant Defence in the Kingdom of Yugoslavia," *Contemporary European History* 16, no. 2 (2007): 218–19. For an English-language book on the Ustashe, see Adriano and Cingolani, *Nationalism and Terror*.

106. See Christian Axboe Nielsen, "Policing Yugoslavism: Surveillance, Denunciations, and Ideology During King Aleksandar's Dictatorship, 1929–1934," *East European Politics and Societies* 23, no. 1 (2009): 34–62.

107. "Un Croate tire plusieurs coups de revolver," 1.

108. Péri, "Le roi Alexandre de Yougoslavie," 1.

109. Seton-Watson, "King Alexander's Assassination," 323.

110. Morawski, "The Assassination of King Alexander I," 68; Monier, "L'attentat de Marseille," paragraph 35.

111. Morawski, "The Assassination of King Alexander I," 69n120.

112. Mondanel, "Notes sur l'attentat de Marseille," n.p. See also Belin, *My Work at the Sûrete*, which contains a version of Kralj's confession (Belin calls him "Kraejimo"), 161–63.

113. Mondanel, "Notes sur l'attentat de Marseille," n.p.

114. "On a arrêté hier à Thonon-les-Bains deux accomplices de l'assassin," *L'Echo de Paris*, 12 October 1934, 1.

115. "Egon Kramer, délégué en France d'Ante Pavelitch, qui prépara le crime de Marseille, est indentifié, mais on croit qu'il a réussi à passer la frontière," *Le Figaro*, 15 October 1934, 5.

116. Mondanel, "Notes sur l'attentat de Marseille," n.p.

117. Mondanel, "Notes sur l'attentat de Marseille"; Monier, "L'attentat de Marseille," paragraph 34.

118. Monier, "L'attentat de Marseille," paragraph 27.

119. "En l'état des textes," *Le Matin*, 22 October 1934, 5; "A propos d'une éventuelle extradition des conjurés yougoslaves," *Le Temps*, 23 October 1934, 2.

120. Sansico, "Le terrorisme," 28–29.

121. Sansico, "Le terrorisme," 29–32; Ben Saul, "Attempts to Define 'Terrorism' in International Law," *Netherlands International Law Review* 52, no. 1 (2005): 59.

122. Monier, "Défendre des 'terroristes'," 113.

123. PTT stands for Postes, Télécommunications et Télédiffusion; Roger

Colombani and Jean-René Laplayne, *La mort d'un roi. La vérité sur l'assassinat d'Alexandre de Yougoslavie* (Paris: Albin Michel, 1971), 205.

124. AN F7 14754, "Les assassins du roi Alexandre seraient jugés en novembre," *Le Figaro*, 10 September 1935.

125. Monier, "Défendre des 'terroristes'," 111.

126. Monier, "Défendre des 'terroristes'," 111–12.

127. AN F7 14754, "L'avocat des oustachis expulsé 'manu militari' de la cour d'assises," *Le Petit Parisien*, 20 November 1935; Colombani and Jean-René Laplayne, *La mort d'un roi*, 206–8; Monier, "Défendre des 'terroristes'," 113–14; 117.

128. Monier, "Défendre des 'terroristes'," 115–16.

129. Monier, "Défendre des 'terroristes'," 117–18.

130. "L'assassinat du roi Alexandre Ier," 2–3.

131. Lucien Romier, "Un désastre français," *Le Figaro*, 10 October 1934, 1; "L'assassinat tragique de S. M. Alexandre," 3.

132. "L'assassinat tragique de S. M. Alexandre," 3.

133. "Bulletin du jour: L'Europe et le terrorisme," *Le Temps*, 14 October 1934, 1.

134. "L'enquête à Marseille sur les circonstances de l'attentat," *Le Matin*, 12 October 1934, 6.

135. "L'un des complices arrêtés à Thonon finit par faire des aveux circonstanciés," *Le Matin*, 13 October 1934, 1.

136. Gaëtan Sanvoisin, "La question de la Police et celle des responsabilités," *Le Figaro*, 11 October 1934, 1.

137. Jean Guignebert, "Sur la piste des terroristes," *Le Petit Journal*, 15 October 1934, 3.

138. "Paris, Marseille, Annecy, recherchent les complices de Kalemen," *L'Oeuvre*, 14 October 1934, 1.

139. "L'un des complices arrêtés à Thonon," 1.

140. "L'attentat de Marseille," 8.

141. P.-L. Darnar, "Le crime de Marseille, crime fasciste!," *L'Humanité*, 14 October 1934, 1–2; Jean Lecoq, "Le terrorisme," *Le Petit Journal illustré*, 21 October 1934, 4.

142. Jacques Klein, "La femme blonde, agent de liaison des conjurés de mort," *Le Petit Journal*, 19 October 1934, 3.

143. "C'est Percetz qui a été arrêté à Liège," *Le Petit Journal*, 21 October 1934, 3.

144. "L'un des complices arrêtés à Thonon," 1.

145. "L'attentat contre le roi Alexandre avait été préparé au camp des terroristes croates de Janka Ruszta," *Paris-Soir*, 14 October 1934, 1.

146. Lecoq, "Le terrorisme," 4.

147. "L'un des complices arrêtés à Thonon," 1.

148. Léon Thévenin, "La politique d'intimidation," *Le Temps*, 5 December 1934, 2.

149. Guignebert, "Sur la piste des terroristes," 3.

150. Lecoq, "Le terrorisme," 4.

151. K. S. C. Chandan, *Le Terrorisme devant la Société des Nations. Réquisitoire*

contre la Hongrie apostolique soutenue par le Vatican et Cie... (Paris: Publications Contemporaines "Frances-Les Balkans," 1935), 101.

152. Chandan, *Le Terrorisme devant la Société des Nations*, 103.

153. "Une femme fut en relations avec les terroristes lors de leur séjour à Aix-en-Provence," *Le Matin*, 13 October 1934, 1; "Après l'attentat," *Le Petit Provençal*, 17 October 1934, 2; "L'arrestation à Turin d'Ante Pavelitch et de Kramer-Kvaternik," *L'Oeuvre*, 19 October 1934, 4.

154. "Malny a avoué sa participation à l'abominable attentat de Marseille," *Le Figaro*, 17 October 1934, 3; Klein, "La femme blonde," 3.

155. "Est-ce la belle inconnue?" *Le Petit Journal*, 19 October 1934, 3; "La femme blonde n'a pas été arrêtée," *Le Matin*, 21 October 1934, 3; "On avait cru voir la femme blonde à Bastia," *Le Matin*, 26 October 1934, 1.

156. AN F7 15928/2, "Le Complot terroriste: La 'femme blonde' est-elle la fille de Joseph Frank chef séparatiste croate?" *Excelsior*, 20 October 1934. Several French newspapers carried this story: see *Le Matin*, 30 October 1934; *L'Echo de Paris*, 30 October 1934; *Le Populaire*, 30 October 1934.

157. "Malny a avoué," 3.

158. "Une jolie femme a transporté les armes," *Le Petit Journal*, 13 October 1934, 5.

159. "La belle étrangère," *Le Petit Marseillais*, 14 October 1934, 5.

160. "A la recherche de Marie Voqdrocek alias Soudroch," *Le Petit Provençal*, 19 October 1934, 4.

161. "L'enquête sur l'attentat terroriste-fasciste de Marseille," *Le Populaire*, 14 October 1934, 3.

162. "A la recherche des complices de l'assassin," *L'Oeuvre*, 14 October 1934, 5.

163. Ravon, "L'attentat," 1 and 3; "L'attentat de Marseille," *Le Petit Journal*, 10 October 1934, 3.

164. "L'enquête sur l'attentat terroriste-fasciste," 3.

165. "A la recherche de Marie Voqdrocek," 4.

166. Klein, "La femme blonde," 3.

167. "A la recherche des complices," 5.

168. "Paris, Marseille, Annecy, recherchent les complices de Kalemen," *L'Oeuvre*, 14 October 1934, 1.

169. Lecoq, "Le terrorisme," 4. See also "A la recherche de Marie Voqdrocek," 4.

170. AN F7 14754, "Les trois Croates detenus à Marseille protestent contre l'accusation d'association de malfaiteurs qui vient de leur être signifiée," *Le Petit Parisien*, 28 July 1935.

171. AN F7 15928/2, "Le mystère de la Femme blonde de l'Ustaša dévoilé par Ante Pavelic," *Paris Soir*, 12 February 1936. See also Ante Pavelić, "J'accomplirai, même au prix de ma vie, tout ce qui me sera commandé....De ce moment, vous êtes des nôtres, soeur Tuga!" *Paris Soir*, 14 February 1936; Ante Pavelić, "Un petit hotel parisien...un coin de rue à Marseille, ce sont les dernières étapes de la mission de soeur Tuga," *Paris Soir*, 15 February 1934.

172. Mondanel, "Notes sur l'attentat de Marseille." According to Adriano and Cingolani, Antun—or Ante—was "head of the Ustasha center in Trieste": *Nationalism and Terror*, 103.

173. Adriano and Cingolani, *Nationalism and Terror*, 103.

174. "Hiding behind their soft appearances, and taking advantage of the existing gender stereotypes, women are almost always the unusual suspects, which makes them formidable perpetrators of suicide attacks." Burcu Pinar Alakoc, "Femme Fatale: The Lethality of Female Suicide Bombers," *Studies in Conflict & Terrorism* 43, no. 9 (2020): 797.

175. André Le Roux, "De Marseille à Genève via Belgrade," *Le Populaire*, 22 November 1934, 2; "Après l'attentat de Marseille," *Le Populaire*, 11 October 1934, 3. See also Charles Reber, *Terrorisme et diplomatie* (Paris: La Technique du Livre, 1935).

176. André Le Roux, "Le government de Mussolini a fourni les fonds pour l'action terroriste en Yougoslavie," *Le Populaire*, 29 March 1934, 3.

177. "Les charognards," *Le Populaire*, 14 October 1934, 1.

178. P.-L. Darnar, "C'est une créature de Tardieu qui fit retirer l'escorte cycliste du roi Alexandre," *L'Humanité*, 18 October 1934, 1.

179. P.-L. Darnar, "Le crime de Marseille, crime fasciste!" *L'Humanité*, 14 October 1934, 1–2.

180. See, for example, "Chez les émigrés révolutionnaires" and "Le crime soviétique," *Je suis partout*, 13 October 1934, 2; "L'assassinat du roi Alexandre Ier," 2–3.

181. *L'Intransigeant*'s review of the press summed up the mood: "The press speaks with one voice to demand in every case a stricter surveillance of foreigners": "Le kiosque à journaux: Surveillons les étrangers," *L'Intransigeant*, 11 October 1934, 2.

182. *Le Matin*, 15 October 1934, 1.

183. Untitled article, *Le Matin*, 16 October 1934, 1.

184. Marcel Lucain, "La France au lendemain du crime," *Paris-Midi*, 11 October 1934, 11.

185. Pierre Gaxotte, "La France envahie," *Je suis partout*, 13 October 1934, 1.

186. AN F7 15928/2, "La Solidarité Française—27 rue Drouot Paris (9e)," 9 October 1934.

187. See, for example, A. Fauchère, "Les étrangers et nous," *Le Petit Journal illustré*, 21 October 1934, 3; Etienne Hervier, "Les régicides," *Détective*, 18 October 1934, 2–3.

188. E. H., "Du mépris de la vie humaine," *Le Temps*, 15 October 1934, 1.

189. Rahma Harouni, "Le débat autour du statut des étrangers dans les années 1930," *Le Mouvement social* 188 (July-September 1999): 62–63.

190. Lewis, *The Boundaries of the Republic*, 120–23.

191. Lewis, *The Boundaries of the Republic*, 126.

192. Lewis, *The Boundaries of the Republic*, 119.

193. Lewis, *The Boundaries of the Republic*, 175; 186.

194. Caron, *Uneasy Asylum*, 46; see also Lewis, *The Boundaries of the Republic*, 119.
195. Rosenberg, *Policing Paris*, 100.
196. Caron, *Uneasy Asylum*, 46; Rosenberg, *Policing Paris*, 92n64; 100.
197. Amar and Milza, *L'immigration en France*, 121.
198. Pavlović, "L'Attentat de Marseille," 593; Adriano and Cingolani, *Nationalism and Terror*, 102.
199. "La police savait…," *Aux écoutes*, 13 October 1934, 17; "Le mystérieux Nalis," *Journal des débats politiques et littéraires*, 14 October 1934, 1.
200. "La police savait…," 17. See also "L'arrestation des complices de l'assassin," *L'Echo de Paris*, 13 October 1934, 3; "Trois jour savant le crime Nalis Malny était signal comme dangereux," *Le Petit Marseillais*, 13 October 1934, 7.
201. AN F7 15926/1, "Rapport," 6 October 1934.
202. "…Et les responsables rendront des comptes," *Le Figaro*, 11 October 1934, 5.
203. Barlatier, "La Leçon du Drame," 1.
204. Léon Bancal, "Où sont les véritables responsabilités?" *Le Petit Marseillais*, 12 October 1934, 1.
205. "Promener ainsi un souverain 'c'est exposer la paix du monde' aurait déclaré un haut personnage," *Le Petit Journal*, 13 October 1934, 5; "L'encadrement de la voiture royale par des gardiens cyclistes," *Le Petit Marseillais*, 13 October 1934, 1; "Une injustice," *Le Petit Provençal*, 12 October 1934, 1.
206. "L'attentat," *L'Humanité*, 10 October 1934, 2; P.-L. Darnar, "Notre enquête à Marseille," *L'Humanité* October 11, 1934, 1–2; P. L. D., "L'étrange contreordre," *L'Humanité*, 13 October 1934, 2.
207. "L'assassinat du roi Alexandre a été prepare," 1–2.
208. "M. Sarraut est démissionnaire," *Le Figaro*, 12 October 1934, 1; "Le remaniement ministériel est fait," *Le Figaro*, 14 October 1934, 1.
209. Intérim, "Propos d'un Parisien," 1.
210. Charles Maurras, "La politique," *L'Action française*, 13 October 1934, 1.
211. Léon Blum, "La 'crise' ministérielle," *Le Populaire*, 13 October 1934, 1.
212. Maurice Laporte, "De la Main Noire à l'ORIM," *Police-Magazine*, 21 October 1934, 2–4.
213. As Morawski does in "The Assassination of King Alexander I," 57–58.
214. See Marc Simard, "Doumergue et la réforme de l'Etat en 1934: La dernière chance de la IIIe République?" *French Historical Studies* 16, no. 3 (1990): 590–92.
215. Albert Londres, *Les comitadjis ou le terrorisme dans les Balkans* (Paris: Albin Michel, 1932), 55.
216. Londres, *Les comitadjis*, 34.
217. "Le corps du roi assassiné," 1; "L'assassinat tragique de S. M. Alexandre," 4.
218. Jean-Jacques Brissac, "*Les comitadjis*: Des mains dans lesquelles on met des revolvers," *Paris-Midi*, 11 October 1934, 1.
219. Londres, *Les comitadjis*, 163–64.

220. Londres, *Les comitadjis*, 163–64.
221. Londres, *Les comitadjis*, 64; 84.
222. Londres, *Les comitadjis*, 67.
223. Londres, *Les comitadjis*, 67.
224. Londres, *Les comitadjis*, 104.
225. Londres, *Les comitadjis*, 87–88.
226. Londres, *Les comitadjis*, 34.
227. AN F7 15928/2, Geoffrey Frazer, "Terroristes balkaniques," *Vu*, 24 October 1934.
228. Londres, *Les comitadjis*, 64; 84.
229. AN F7 15928/2, Frazer, "Terroristes balkaniques."
230. "Les agissements antiyougoslaves de certains émigrés," *L'Ere nouvelle*, 27 October 1933, 3; Miller, *Shanghai on the Metro*, 126; James J. Sadkovich, "Terrorism in Croatia, 1929–1934," *East European Quarterly* 22, no. 1 (1988): 75n26.
231. See, for example, "Les révélations de l'amie du terroriste Percek," *Le Petit Journal*, 17 October 1934, 3; "Les révélations de Mlle Pogoreletch," *Le Populaire*, 17 October 1934, 3.
232. See Broche, *Assassinat de Alexandre Ier*, 41–42; Ditrych, "'International Terrorism'," 205.
233. AN F7 15928/2, "La vie secrète des émigrés criminels: Les révélations de Jelka Pogorelec," n.d, 28–29.
234. AN F7 15928/2, "La vie secrète des émigrés criminels," 29.
235. AN F7 15928/2, "La vie secrète des émigrés criminels," 9.
236. AN F7 15928/2, "La vie secrète des émigrés criminels," 47.
237. AN F7 15928/2, "La vie secrète des émigrés criminels," 31–32.
238. AN F7 15928/2, "La vie secrète des émigrés criminels," 41.
239. AN F7 15928/2, "La vie secrète des émigrés criminels," 11–13; 24.
240. AN F7 15928/2, "La vie secrète des émigrés criminels," 14.
241. Kovacs, "Le grand précédent," *Requête du gouvernement yougoslave en vertu de l'article 11, paragraphe 2*, 20.
242. "Au rendez-vous des tueurs de rois," *Le Petit Journal*, 24 October 1934, 1.
243. *Le Petit Journal*, 24 October 1934, 1.
244. See also Broche, *Assassinat de Alexandre Ier*, 41–42.
245. See, for example, "Le *Petit Journal* demande pour Paris une statue du roi martyr," *Le Petit Journal*, 12 October 1934, 1; La Presse Quotidienne Marseillaise, "Un monument au roi Alexandre," *Le Petit Provençal*, 11 October 1934, 5.
246. "Le solonnel et émouvant hommage de Paris au roi Alexandre de Yougoslavie," *Le Petit Parisien*, 11 November 1934, 1–2.
247. An image of the medal featured on page one of *Le Petit Parisien*, 11 November 1934.
248. Graves, "Memory and Forgetting," 8–9.
249. Graves, "Memory and Forgetting," 11–13.
250. Graves, "Memory and Forgetting," 9.

251. Louis Sabarin, "Une dalle sacrée sur la Canebière," *Le Petit Marseillais*, 16 October 1934, 3.
252. Graves, "Memory and Forgetting," 1–2.
253. Graves, "Memory and Forgetting," 1.
254. Monier, "L'attentat de Marseille," paragraph 45; Monier, "Défendre des 'terroristes'," 119.
255. Graves, "Memory and Forgetting," 15.
256. An image of the stone is available at https://en.wikipedia.org/wiki/Vlado_Chernozemski#Gallery (accessed 20 February 2020).
257. Monier, "L'attentat de Marseille," 1.
258. Brown, "The King Is Dead," 4.
259. Graves, "Memory and Forgetting," 4.
260. AN F7 15928/2, B. Jevtitch, "Requête du gouvernement yugoslave, suivie des communications des gouvernments roumain et tchécoslovque, du 22 novembre 1934," in *Requête du gouvernement yougoslave en vertu de l'article 11, paragraphe 2*, 5–6.
261. See also Broche, *Assassinat de Alexandre Ier*, 41–42.
262. AN F7 15928/2, *Requête du gouvernement yougoslave en vertu de l'article 11, paragraphe 2*, 32.
263. AN F7 15928/2, *Requête du gouvernement yougoslave en vertu de l'article 11, paragraphe 2*, 32.
264. AN F7 15928/2, *Requête du gouvernement yougoslave en vertu de l'article 11, paragraphe 2*, 86–87.
265. Monier, "L'attentat de Marseille," paragraph 39.
266. Monier, "Défendre des 'terroristes'," 108–9. See Mondanel, "Notes sur l'attentat de Marseille."
267. AN F7 15928/2, *Requête du gouvernement yougoslave en vertu de l'article 11, paragraphe 2*, 147–48.
268. AN F7 15928/2, *Requête du gouvernement yougoslave en vertu de l'article 11, paragraphe 2*, 147–49.
269. AN F7 15928/2, *Requête du gouvernement yougoslave en vertu de l'article 11, paragraphe 2*, 147–49; Kovacs, "Le grand précédent," n.p.
270. Monier, "Défendre des 'terroristes'," 117; Jozo Tomasevich, *War and Revolution in Yugolsavia, 1941–1945: Occupation and Collabroation* (Stanford, CA: Stanford University Press, 2002), 35.
271. Ben Saul provides an excellent analysis of the Convention on terrorism in Saul, "Attempts to Define 'Terrorism'," 63–66 and Saul, "The Legal Response of the League of Nations," 78–102. The conference also formulated the Convention for the Creation of an International Criminal Court.
272. AN BB 18 6115, "Convention for the Prevention and Punishment of Terrorism," 15 November 1937, 2.
273. Antoine Sottile, "Le terrorisme international," *Recueil des Cours. III. Tome 65 de la Collection. Académie de Droit International* (Paris: Recueil Sirey, 1938), 105.
274. AN BB 18 6115, "Convention," 3–4.

275. AN BB 18 6115, "Convention," 2.

276. Sottile, "Le terrorisme international," 124–25.

277. Geoffrey Marston, "Early Attempts to Suppress Terrorism: The Terrorism and International Criminal Court Conventions of 1937," *British Yearbook of International Law* 73, no. 1 (2002): 293.

278. Saul, "The Legal Response of the League of Nations," 87–89.

279. Stefan Glaser, "Le terrorisme international et ses divers aspects," *Revue internationale de droit compare* 25, no. 4 (1973): 827; Thomas M. Franck and Bert B. Lockwood Jr., "Thoughts Towards an International Convention on Terrorism," *The American Journal of International Law* 68, no .1 (1974): 70.

280. Saul, "Attempts to Define 'Terrorism'," 65.

281. Ditrych, "'International Terrorism'," 200.

282. Charles Townshend, "'Methods Which All Civilized Opinion Must Condemn': The League of Nations and International Action Against Terrorism," in *An International History of Terrorism: Western and Non-Western Experiences*, 46–47.

283. Marcel Montarron, "A l'affût des terroristes," *Détective*, 20 May 1937, 2–4.

CHAPTER 5

Sections of this chapter draw on the material used in Chris Millington, "Immigrants and Undesirables: 'Terrorism' and the 'Terrorist' in 1930s France," *Critical Studies on Terrorism* 12, no. 1 (2019): 40–59. The article may be found at https://www.tandfonline.com/.

1. AN BB18 6476, "Le Procureur de la République près le Tribunal de Première Instance de Tarascon à Monsieur le Procureur Général près la Cour d'appel d'Aix," 8 May 1937; "Le Procureur de la République près le Tribunal de Première Instance de Tarascon à Monsieur le Procureur Général près la Cour d'appel d'Aix," 21 May 1937.

2. D. Cristofari, "L'attentat contre l'express Bordeaux-Marseille," *Le Petit Marseillais*, 6 May 1937, 5.

3. Millington, *Fighting for France*, 143–50.

4. Gilles Vergnon, *Un enfant est lynché. L'Affaire Gignoux, 1937* (Paris: Presses Universitaires de France, 2018).

5. "La série des attentats," *Ce Soir*, 14 September 1937, 3.

6. AN F60 754, "La Tragédie de Meknès," *Le Dépêche de Fès*, 4 September 1937.

7. "Du complot du CSAR aux bombes de l'Etoile," *L'Oeuvre*, 11 January 1938, 5.

8. On this incident, see Patrick Gourlay's excellent book *Nuit franquiste sur Brest. L'attaque du sous-marin républicain C-2, 1937* (Kerangwenn, FR: Editions Coop Breizh, 2013).

9. "Assez!" *L'Humanité*, 22 September 1937, 1.

10. Georges Bidault, "Menées obscures," *L'Aube*, 22 September 1937, 1

11. J. D., "Le général Eugène de Miller, successeur du général Koutiepoff à

la tête de l'Union des Anciens Combattants de l'armée russe a mystérieusement disparu depuis mercredi à midi," *L'Echo de Paris*, 24 September 1937, 1; J. D., "Qu'a fait le général Skobline le mercredi entre 11h. 50 et 13h. 50?" *Le Jour*, 25 September 1937, 1; "Les rapports de Skobline avec les Soviets se précisent," *Le Jour*, 28 September 1937, 1.

12. Wladimir d'Ormesson, "Foire d'empoigne," *Le Figaro*, 26 September 1937, 1.

13. "L'affaire Miller, oeuvre de la Gestapo," *L'Humanité*, 25 September 1937, 1.

14. "Le centre de recrutement de Damas," *Marianne*, 18 November 1937, 2.

15. Pierre Dominique, "L'Italie à la croisée des chemins," *La République*, 10 December 1937, 1.

16. Emile Thomas, "L'empire français s'écroule sous les coups du marxisme," *Le Petit Marseillais*, 10 March 1937, 1–2.

17. Jean Lecoure, "Le 'Gougobez' organise la révolution," *Le Jour*, 14 November 1937, 5.

18. Caron, *Uneasy Asylum*, 268–69; 285–90.

19. Georges Bidault, "Trop est trop," *L'Aube*, 24 September 1937, 1.

20. Montarron, "A l'affût des terroristes," 20 May 1937, 2–4.

21. "Une cinquième bombe est découverte à Perpignan," *Le Petit Provençal*, 9 March 1937, 6.

22. AN BB18 6476, "Le Commissaire de Police Mobile Delrieu à Monsieur l'Inspecteur Général chargé des Services de Police Criminelle à Paris," 4 October 1937.

23. AN BB18 6476, "Le Commissaire de Police Mobile Delrieu,"; "Le Commissaire de Police Mobile Spotti, Louis, à Monsieur le Commissaire Divisionnaire, chef de la 14ème brigade régionale à Montpellier," 15 March 1937.

24. AN BB18 6476, "Le Commissaire de Police Mobile Spotti Louis à Monsieur le Commissaire Divisionnaire Chef de la 14ème Brigade Régionale à Montpellier," 8 March 1937. *L'Echo de Paris*, for example, reported that the bomb found at the Spanish Consulate contained a Spanish brand of battery and alarm clock: "On découvre à Perpignan deux nouvelles bombes," *L'Echo de Paris*, 9 March 1937, 1.

25. AN BB18 6476, "Le Commissaire de Police Mobile Delrieu,"; "Le Commissaire de Police Mobile Spotti," (15 March 1937); "Le Procureur Général à Montpellier à Monsieur le Garde des Sceaux, Ministre de la Justice," 1 June 1937.

26. AN F7 14683, "Rapport à M. le Directeur Général de la Sûreté Nationale," 13 May 1937. The press got wind of Kling's tests: see "Aucune autre arrestation n'a suivi celle de l'oustachi Mazuric," *Le Populaire*, 13 May 1937, 3.

27. Bantman, *The French Anarchists in London*, 113.

28. AN BB18 6476, "Le Procureur de la République près le Tribunal de Marseille, à Moniseur le Procureur Général, Aix," 13 October 1936.

29. "Des inconnus tentent de faire sauter à Marseille un navire espagnol amarré dans le port," *Le Matin*, 14 October 1936, 1; "Un attentat manqué quai de Rive Neuve," *Le Petit Marseillais*, 14 October 1936, 3.

30. "L'attentat fasciste de Marseille," *Le Populaire*, 14 October 1936, 2.
31. AN BB18 6476, "Le Procureur de la République," (13 October 1936).
32. AN BB18 6476, "Le Procureur Général à Montpellier à Monsieur le Garde des Sceaux, Ministre de la Justice," 15 March 1937.
33. AN BB18 6476, "Le Commissaire de Police Mobile Spotti," (15 March 1937).
34. "Attentats terroristes à Perpignan et à Cerbère," *L'Action Française*, 8 March 1937, 1.
35. "Une bombe éclate dans un wagon en gare de Cerbère—On découvre des engins explosifs à Perpignan," *L'Echo de Paris*, 8 March 1937, 1; "Les bombes de Cerbère et Perpignan," *Le Matin*, 8 March 1937, 3.
36. "Une bombe explose dans un wagon du rapide Paris-Cerbère," *L'Ouest-Éclair*, 8 March 1937, 1.
37. "Attentat dans le Paris-Barcelone. Attentats manqués à Perpignan…" *Le Journal*, 8 March 1937, 3. See also "L'attentat de Cerbère," *Le Petit Journal*, 8 March 1937, 4.
38. "Une bombe explose," 1.
39. AN BB18 6476, "Le Commissaire de Police Mobile Spotti," (8 March 1937).
40. AN BB18 6476, "Le Procureur Général près la Cour d'Appel d'Aix, à Monsieur le Garde des Sceaux, Ministre de la Justice," 17 March 1937.
41. AN BB18 6476, "Le Commissaire de Police Mobile Delrieu."
42. AN BB18 6476, AN BB18 6476, "Le Commissaire de Police Mobile Spotti," 15 March 1937.
43. AN BB18 6476, , "Le Commissaire de Police Mobile Spotti," 15 March 1937.
44. AN BB18 6476, "Le Procureur de la République près le Tribunal de Première Instance" (8 May 1937).
45. AN BB18 6476, "Le Procureur de la République près le Tribunal de Première Instance de Tarascon à Monsieur le Procureur Général près la Cour d'appel d'Aix," 21 May 1937.
46. "Entre Raphaèle et Saint-Martin-de-Crau un engine explosive éclate dans un wagon qui prend feu," *Le Petit Marseillais*, 6 May 1937, 1.
47. "Entre Raphaèle et Saint-Martin-de-Crau," 1.
48. Cristofari, "L'attentat," 5.
49. "L'attentat contre l'express Bordeaux-Marseille," *Le Petit Marseillais*, 7 May 1937, 9.
50. *Détective*, 20 May 1937.
51. "Un Oustachi réputé comme très dangereux arrêté à Paris," *Le Populaire*, 11 May 1937, 1; "L'arrestation de l'oustachi Masurick," *Le Figaro*, 12 May 1937, 4.
52. "'Il est faux qu'on ait arrêté un terroriste croate et que l'on ait trouve des bombes,' affirme la Sûreté Nationale," *Le Petit Journal*, 13 May 1937, 6.
53. "L'Oustachi Marusic connaîtrait les dessous de l'attentat de Marseille," *Le Petit Provençal*, 15 May 1937, 2.
54. Montarron, "A l'affût des terroristes," 20 May 1937, 3–4.

55. Montarron, "A l'affût des terroristes," 20 May 1937, 3.
56. Montarron, "A l'affût des terroristes," 20 May 1937, 3.
57. "Le procès de Gardella 'alias' Cantelli," *L'Oeuvre*, 24 September 1937, 6.
58. AN BB18 6476, "Le Procureur Général à Montpellier," (1 June 1937).
59. AN BB18 6476, "Le Procureur Général à Montpellier à Monsieur le Garde des Sceaux, Ministre de la Justice," 9 March 1937; "La condemnation de l'italien Cantelli qui devait faire sauter le tunnel de Cerbère," *Le Matin*, 24 September 1937, 6.
60. "Les complices du terroriste de Cerbère se seraient réfugiés en Italie," *L'Humanité*, 9 June 1937, 2.
61. Jean-Maurice Hermann, "Gardella devant le tribunal," *Le Populaire*, 24 September 1937, 2.
62. AN BB18 6476, "Le Procureur Général à Montpellier à Monsieur le Garde des Sceaux, Ministre de la Justice," 24 September 1937.
63. "Le procès de Gardella 'alias' Cantelli," *L'Oeuvre*, 24 September 1937, 6.
64. "Blessé dimanche par une balle fasciste un Chinois est mort," *L'Humanité*, 13 April 1937, 2.
65. AN BB18 6476, "Extrait des minutes du greffe du tribunal civil de première instance de Céret (Pyr. Or.)," n.d.
66. AN BB18 3061/2, "1ère partie: Etat actuel de l'information au regard des diverses inculpations et des différents inculpés," n.d., 35; Philippe Bourdrel, *La Cagoule. Histoire d'une société secrète du Front Populaire à la Ve République* (Paris: Albin Michel, 1992), 246–48; 297–98; Brunelle and Finley-Croswhite, *Murder on the Metro*, 99–101.
67. AN BB18 3061/2, "1ère partie: Etat actuel de l'information," 28–31.
68. I have explored the terrorism of 1937 elsewhere: Millington, "Immigrants and Undesirables."
69. AN BB18 3061/2, "Le Procureur Général près la Cour d'Appel de Douai à Monsieur le Garde des Sceaux, Ministre de la Justice à Paris," 5 March 1937; "Le Procureur Général près la Cour d'Appel de Douai à Monsieur le Garde des Sceaux, Ministre de la Justice à Paris," 12 May 1937.
70. AN BB18 3061/2, "1ère partie: Etat actuel de l'information," 31.
71. Bourdrel, *La Cagoule*, 266; 297; AN BB18 3061/2, "1ère partie: Etat actuel de l'information," 32.
72. Bourdrel, *La Cagoule*, 296–300.
73. Maurice Garcon, "A propos des derniers attentats," *L'Echo de Paris*, 5 October 1937, 1 and 5.
74. Léon Daudet, "Histoire de bombes," *Action Française*, 14 September 1937, 1; Marcel Montarron, "A l'affût des terroristes," *Détective*, 23 September 1937, 2–4; Emmanuel Car, "Histoire de bombes. Deux cents ans de machines infernales," *Détective*, 23 September 1937, 5–6.
75. See, for example, "Les recherches de la police s'orientent vers les organisations terroristes ayant leur centre à l'étranger," *L'Echo de Paris*, 13 September 1937, 1 and 3; AN BB/18 3061/2, "1ère partie: Etat actuel de l'information."

76. See the images in *Le Matin*, 11–15 September 1937, 1; *Ce Soir*, 13 September 1937, 1; *L'Echo de Paris*, 13 September 1937, 1; *L'Humanité*, 13 September 1937, 1; *L'Intransigeant*, 13 September 1937, 1; *L'Intransigeant*, 13 September 1937, 1; *Le Petit Journal*, 13 September 1937, 1; *Détective*, 23 September 1937.

77. Gilbert Rougerie, "Les auteurs des attentats de l'Etoile sont manifestement des agents de l'étranger," *Ce Soir*, 14 September 1937, 1; "Un témoin aurait fourni des indications sur les auteurs des deux attentats terroristes," *Le Petit Journal*, 14 September 1937, 4.

78. See, for example, O. Rosenfeld, "Les bombes de la rue de Presbourg et de la rue Boissière rappellent celles de Cerbère," *Le Populaire*, 13 September 1937, 1–2; "La série d'attentats," *Ce Soir*, 14 September 1937, 3; Gilbert Rougerie, "Les attentats de cette nuit," *Ce Soir*, 13 September 1937, 3; Paul Estaque, "Chassons les étrangers indésirables," *Le Petit Journal*, 15 September 1937, 4; "L'Anarchiste italien Tamburini a été arrêté hier dans l'Ariège," *L'Echo de Paris*, 16 September 1937, 1; "Tient-t-on enfin un des auteurs des attentats de l'Etoile?" *L'Oeuvre*, 3 October 1937, 1 and 5.

79. "Le terrorisme n'est pas français," *Paris-Soir*, 19 September 1937, 11.

80. André Guérin, "Les bombes de l'Etoile serait de provenance étrangère et parraissent sortir d'une usine de guerre," *L'Oeuvre*, 13 September 1937, 1.

81. "La France aux Français," *Le Matin*, 14 September 1937, 1.

82. G. P., "On entre en France comme dans un moulin," *Le Petit Journal*, 16 September 1937, 1.

83. "Les attentats terroristes," *L'Ere nouvelle*, 14 September 1937, 2.

84. "'Les millions d'étrangers qui vivent en France vont avoir un statut', déclare M. Camille Chautemps," *Le Matin*, 16 September 1937, 1; "Tamburini, anarchiste (*sic*) est arrêté en Ariège," *L'Oeuvre*, 16 September 1937, 1 and 5; "La déclaration de M. Chautemps," *Le Populaire*, 16 September 1937, 2.

85. "'Les millions d'étrangers,'" 1.

86. Stéphane Lauzanne, "Le dépotoir français se remplit d'étrangers indésirables mais ne se vide pas," *Le Matin*, 22 September 1937, 1.

87. See, for example, *L'Humanité*, 29 September 1937; *L'Oeuvre*, 28 September 1937; *Le Petit Journal*, 15 and 16 September 1937; *Le Matin*, 14 September 1937.

88. Bourdrel, *La Cagoule*, 251.

89. Brunelle and Finley-Croswhite, *Murder in the Metro*, 100–101.

90. "La 'Cagoule,' organisation fasciste de guerre civile," *L'Humanité*, 18 September 1937, 2; Maurice Pujo, "La Sûreté générale et sa cagoule," *L'Action Française*, 19 September 1937, 1.

91. "Et les 'cagoulards'?" *L'Intransigeant*, 24 September 1937, 5.

92. Comtesse de S., "Cagoules ou capuchons?" *Le Figaro*, 27 October 1937, 2.

93. "Les quatre 'cagoulards' inculpés sont entendus par M. Barué, juge d'instruction," *L'Intransigeant*, 18 September 1937, 1; Gallus, "L'affaire des Cagoulards," *L'Intransigeant*, 18 September 1937, 1. See also "La rocambolesque affaire des 'Cagoulards'," *L'Echo de Paris*, 18 September 1937, 1 and 3.

94. See, for example, Maurice Pujo, "La Sûreté brûle ses 'cagoulards'," *L'Action*

Française, 17 September 1937, 1; "Le complot contre le pays," *L'Humanité*, 20 September 1937, 2; Hervé Lauwick, "Voulez-vous un déguisement de cagoulard?" *Le Jour*, 22 September 1937, 1–2.

95. Brunelle and Finley-Croswhite, *Murder on the Metro*, 151.

96. AN BB/18 3061/2, "1ère partie: Etat actuel de l'information."

97. "Des milliers de terroristes: Les 'Milices Secrètes Révolutionnaires' préparaient depuis 16 mois un vaste coup de main contre les institutions républicaines," *L'Oeuvre*, 17 November 1937, 1.

98. "'C'est un véritable complot contre les institutions républicaines'...," *L'Oeuvre*, 24 November 1937, 1.

99. *Journal Officiel*, 10 December 1937, 2811–12.

100. AN BB/18 3061/2, "Etat approixmatif des armes, munitions, explosifs découverts dans les dépots de l'OSARN."

101. AN BB/18 3061/2, "Le Procureur Général près la Cour d'Appel de Pars à Monsieur le Garde des Sceaux," 1 December 1937; "Résumé de trois rapports de Monsieur le Procureur Général à Paris des 31 janvier, 30 mai et 23 juin 1938"; "Etat approixmatif des armes."

102. Philippe Roques, "M. Dormoy fait arrêter M. Pozzo de Borgo sur l'injonction des communistes," *L'Echo de Paris*, 27 November 1937, 1; Gabriel Berthau, "Quand cessera la comédie des complots? Posséder un souvenir de guerre, ce n'est tout de même pas être un factieux," *La Voix du combattant*, 20 October 1937.

103. "Le complot des 'oustachis' français prend d'énormes proportions," *L'Oeuvre*, 18 November 1937, 1; "La chasse aux 'oustachis' continue à Paris, en banlieue et en province," *L'Oeuvre*, 21 November 1937, 5; "L'Organisation du CSAR était calquée sur les formations de combat hitlériennes', *L'Oeuvre*, 21 November 1937, 1; "Comme les frères Roselli, Navachine a-t-il été victime des terroristes du CSAR?" *Paris-Soir*, 14 January 1938, 1; "Jakubiez, Fauran, et Puireux partent pour Domfront à la demande du juge d'instruction," *Paris-Soir*, 14 January 1938, 1.

104. Lucien Sampaix, "Double complot contre la France," *L'Humanité*, 18 September 1937, 1; "Complot de la 'Cagoule'! Complot hitlérien!" *L'Humanité*, 23 November 1937, 2; Gabriel Peri, "Les menées de la 'Cagoule' et la politique du Quai d'Orsay," *L'Humnaité*, 14 January 1938, 3.

105. See also Claude Martial, "Les ingénieurs de la terreur au travail sur notre sol," *Regards*, 23 September 1937, 3–4, which accused French extreme right-wing leaders François de La Rocque and Jacques Doriot of complicity in the affair.

106. G. Joly, "Les Cagoulards," *L'Oeuvre*, 17 September 1937, 5.

107. O. Rosenfeld, "Un complot contre la sûreté de l'Etat," *Le Populaire*, 18 November 1937, 1.

108. See, for example, E. G., "La Sûreté nationale relance avec fracas l'affaire des 'Cagoulards'," *L'Echo de Paris*, 18 November 1937, 1.

109. Brunelle and Finley-Croswhite, *Murder on the Metro*, 156.

110. The Catherinettes were single women under the age of twenty-five who remained unmarried on 25 November (St. Catherine's Day) each year. Each year the Catherinettes would confect a headpiece to celebrate the day.

111. Bourdrel, *La Cagoule*, 242.
112. "Locuty parle…", *L'Oeuvre*, 11 January 1937, 5.
113. "CSAR," *Détective*, 27 January 1937, 3.
114. Brunelle and Finley-Croswhite, *Murder in the Metro*, 120.
115. See Brunelle and Finley-Croswhite, *Murder in the Metro*, 118–20. Brunelle and Finley-Croswhite mention the examples of Marie de Massolles, whose social networks promised to provide important information, and Hélène Dalton, who had information on several military officers. Their source is the diary of Aristide Corre, edited by Christian Bernadac and published as *Les Carnets descrets de la Cagoule* (Paris: Editions Terre-Bleue, 2006).
116. Brunelle and Finley-Croswhite, *Assassination in Vichy*.
117. On the transgressing of gender norms and terrorism, see Schraut, "Gender Politics," 623–44.
118. "Sous toutes réserves," *L'Oeuvre*, 23 January 1938, 5; "CSAR," 3.
119. "CSAR," 2.
120. "CSAR," 2–3.
121. "CSAR," 3.
122. "Sous toutes réserves," 5.
123. L'Ouvrier, "Raccourcis," *L'Oeuvre*, 24 January 1938, 1.
124. The most comprehensive work on the C-2 affair in French is Gourlay's *Nuit franquiste sur Brest*. For a short summary of the case with links to newspaper resources on the incident, see Michele Pedinielli, "L'affaire du sous-marin piraté par des franquistes à Brest," https://www.retronews.fr/justice/long-format/2018/06/05/laffaire-du-sous-marin-pirate-par-des-franquistes-brest (accessed 30 March 2020). Pedro Barruso Barés offers a snapshot of Francoist operations in the south of France in "La guerra del commandante Troncoso. Terrorismo y espionaje en Franci durante la Guerra Civil Española," *Diacronie. Studi de Storia Contemporanea* 28, no. 4 (2016): 1–16.
125. Barés, "La guerra del commandante Troncoso," 5; "Des armes sont trouvées au centre nationaliste espagnol de St-Jean-De-Luz," *Le Matin*, 24 February 1937, 3.
126. Barés, "La guerra del commandante Troncoso," 4–5.
127. AN BB18 6476, "Le Commissaire de Police Mobile Spotti," (15 March 1937).
128. AN BB18 6476, statement of Tamborini to Commissaire Louis Lambert, 15 September 1937.
129. Charles Reber, "Les mystères de la villa Nacho Enaea," *Ce Soir*, 31 March 1937, 8.
130. Paul Vaillant-Couturier, "Et les ligues?" *L'Humanité*, 1 April 1937, 1.
131. Barés, "La guerra del commandante Troncoso," 11.
132. Barés, "La guerra del commandante Troncoso," 9–10.
133. The French local press paid the hijacking a little more attention than did national publications. See, for example, "Un avion français ayant atterri sur la plage de Zarrauz les passagers sont faits prisonniers," *Gazette de Bayonne, de Biarritz et du pays basque*, 23 June 1937, 1.

134. With a length of seventy-five meters, the C-2 was capable of diving to a depth of eighty meters and was equipped with six torpedo shoots: Gourlay, *Nuit franquiste sur Brest*, 16.

135. AN BB18 6476, "Le Procureur de la République de Brest à Monsieur le Procureur Général à Rennes," 16 October 1937; "Le Procureur Général près la Cour d'Appel de Rennes à Monsieur le Gardes des Sceaux, Ministre de la Justice," 14 December 1937.

136. AN BB18 6476, "Le Procureur Général près la Cour d'Appel de Pau à Monsieur le Garde des Sceaux," 21 September 1937. Chaix was also a Cagoulard; see Gourlay, *Nuit franquiste sur Brest*, 38.

137. Marcel Montarron, "A l'affût des terroristes," 30 September 1937, 6.

138. AN BB18 6476, "Le Procureur de la République de Brest,"; "Le Procureur Général près la Cour d'Appel de Rennes."

139. André Salmon, "L'affaire Troncoso," *Le Petit Parisien*, 27 September 1937, 2.

140. Gourlay, *Nuit franquiste sur Brest*, 28–29.

141. Salmon, "L'affaire Troncoso," 2.

142. Salmon, "L'affaire Troncoso," 2; "Dans les petits cafés du port de Brest," *Le Petit Parisien*, 28 September 1937, 2; "La jolie Menga entendue cet après-midi par le juge confirmera-t-elle ses premiers aveux?" *Paris-soir*, 28 September 1937, 5; "Pour dégager son maître Franco…," *Ce Soir*, 1 October 1937, 1.

143. "Dans les petits cafés," 2.

144. "On interroge à Brest une jeune danseuse qui fut l'amie du commandant Ferrando," *L'Ouest-Éclair*, 25 September 1937, 1–2. This quotation is referred to in Gourlay, *Nuit franquiste sur Brest*, 77.

145. Montarron, "A l'affût des terroristes," (30 September 1937), 6; Gourlay, *Nuit franquiste sur Brest*, 78; 113.

146. AN BB18 6476, "Le Procureur Général près la Cour d'Appel de Rennes à Monsieur le Garde des Sceaux, Ministre de la Justice," 20 September 1937; "Le Commissaire Divisionnaire, Chef de la 7e Brigade régionale de Police Mobile à Monsieur le Procureur de la République à Bordeaux," 21 September 1937; "Le Procureur de la République de Brest,"; "Le Procureur de la République à Brest à Monsieur le Garde des Sceaux, Ministre de la Justice," 4 October 1937; "Le Procureur de la République de Brest à Monsieur le Procureur Général à Rennes," 14 December 1937.

147. See Gourlay, *Nuit franquiste sur Brest*, 51–59.

148. Gourlay notes that while the police investigation into the Brest affair did not mention the Cagoule, Robet later explained that the group had provided the Francoists with intelligence: *Nuit franquiste sur Brest*, 39–43.

149. AN BB18 6476, "Le Procureur Général près la Cour d'Appel de Pau," 21 September 1937.

150. Gourlay, *Nuit franquiste sur Brest*, 47.

151. AN BB18 6476, "Le Procureur Général près la Cour d'Appel de Rennes,"; "Le Commissaire Divisionnaire, Chef de la 7e Brigade régionale de Police

Mobile,"; "Le Procureur de la République de Brest,"; Le Procureur de la République à Brest."

152. Fabra, "La pirateria facciosa," *ABC. Organo de union republicana*, 21 September 1937, 8.

153. AN BB18 6476, "Le Procureur Général près la Cour d'Appel de Rennes,"; "Le Commissaire Divisionnaire, Chef de la 7e Brigade régionale de Police Mobile,"; "Le Procureur de la République de Brest,"; Le Procureur de la République à Brest."

154. AN BB18 6476, "Le Procureur Général près la Cour d'Appel de Pau."

155. AB BB18 6476, "Le Procureur Général près la Cour d'Appel de Pau, à Monsieur le Garde des Sceaux," 22 September 1937; Gourlay, *Nuit franquiste sur Brest*, 57–58.

156. AB BB18 6476, "Le Procureur Général près la Cour d'Appel de Pau," (22 September 1937).

157. AN BB18 6476, "Le Procureur Général près la Cour d'Appel de Pau," (21 September 1937).

158. AN BB18 6476, "Le Procureur de la République à Brest à Monsieur le Garde des Sceaux, Ministre de la Justice," 1 October 1937.

159. "Deux autres 'assaillants' sont retrouvés à Bordeaux et à Hendaye," *Le Petit Parisien*, 21 September 1937, 1. See also "Y a-t-il une relation entre le coup de main de Brest et le double attentat de l'Etoile?" *L'Aube*, 21 September 1937, 1. *L'Aube* described the "script" of "this fantastic story."

160. Gourlay, *Nuit franquiste sur Brest*, 55.

161. "Le commandant Troncoso appréhendé lundi à Hendaye fut-il 'l'âme d'une série d'attentats en France?" *L'Ouest-Éclair*, 22 September 1937, 1.

162. "Les affaires de terrorisme," *Le Petit Journal*, 21 September 1937, 4; Gourlay, *Nuit franquiste sur Brest*, 36.

163. "Les affaires de terrorisme," 4.

164. "Instigateur et chef du coup de main de Brest le commandant Troncoso est incarcéré à Bayonne," *Le Petit Journal*, 22 September 1937, 1. *Le Petit Journal* reported that a member of Troncoso's squad, Suprella, was wanted for questioning about the Etoile bombings: "Le 18 septembre, 12 hommes attaquaient à Brest le sous-marin espagnol C II," *Le Petit Journal*, 22 September 1937, 4. See also "Le gouverneur militaire d'Irun incarcéré à la 'Villa Chagrin' sera vraisemblablement transféré aujourd'hui à Brest," *Le Petit Journal*, 22 September 1937, 4; Montarron, "A l'affût des terroristes," (30 September 1937), 6.

165. "Un seul complot?" *La Bourgogne républicaine*, 21 September 1937, 1. See also "Parmi les assaillants du C-2 on retrouve des terroristes recherchés pour les attentats de l'Etoile," *Paris-Soir*, 21 September 1937, 3; "Y a-t-il une relation," 1; "Troncoso en accusation," *Ce Soir*, 23 September 1937, 3; "Oui, mais…qui est Troncoso?" *L'Oeuvre*, 23 September 1937, 1.

166. Lucien Sampaix, "Terroristes, pirates et 'Cagoulards'," *L'Humanité*, 21 September 1937, 2.

167. AN BB18 6476, "Le Procureur Général près la Cour d'Appel de Pau à Monsieur le Garde des Sceaux," 25 September 1937.

168. AN BB18 6476, "Le Procureur de la République à Brest à Monsieur le Garde des Sceaux, Ministre de la Justice," 5 October 1937.

169. AN BB18 6476, "Le Procureur de la République à Monsieur le Procureur Général à Rennes," 11 October 1937; Gourlay, *Nuit franquiste sur Brest*, 36.

170. AN BB18 6476, "Le Procureur de la République à Monsieur le Procureur Général,"; "Le Garde des Sceaux, Ministre de la Justice à Monsieur le Procureur Général près la Cour d'Appel de Rennes," 12 October 1937.

171. AN BB18 6476, "Le Procureur de la République de Brest à Monsieur le Procureur Général à Rennes," 16 October 1937.

172. Gourlay, *Nuit franquiste sur Brest*, 113.

173. AN BB186476, "Le Procureur Général près la Cour d'Appel de Rennes à Monsieur le Garde des Sceaux, Ministre de la Justice," 24 March 1938.

174. Gourlay, *Nuit franquiste sur Brest*, 123–24.

175. Gourlay, *Nuit franquiste sur Brest*, 107.

176. "En plein port de Brest des agents de Franco tentent de s'emparer du 'C2,' sous-marin du gouvernement espagnol," *Le Populaire*, 20 September 1937, 1. See also "L'affaire du 'C-2' amène la découverte de terroristes espagnols dangereux," *Le Populaire*, 21 September 1937, 2.

177. "Les quatre 'affaires' en cours," *Le Petit Journal*, 21 September 1937, 1.

178. "Les quatre 'affaires' en cours," 1.

179. Jacques Lemoine, "En voilà assez!" *La Petite Gironde*, 21 September 1937, 1.

180. Gennady Barabtalo, "Life's Sequel," *Nabokov Studies* 8 (2004): 5; Vladislav I. Goldin and John W. Long, "Resistance and Retribution: The Life and Fate of General E. K. Miller," *Revolutionary Russia* 12, no. 2 (1999): 38n45.

181. Goldin and Long, "Resistance and Retribution," 26; Anastasia Pavlova, "Les Russes et les Soviétiques en France durant la Seconde guerre mondiale. Entre collaboration et résistance," unpublished Masters' thesis, Université Paris I Panthéon-Sorbonne, 27–29.

182. Pavlova, "Les Russes et les Soviétiques," 29.

183. Pavlova, "Les Russes et les Soviétiques," 23.

184. See Daniel Kunzi and Peter Huber, "Paris dans les années 30. Sur Serge Efron et quelques agents du NKVD," *Cahiers du monde russe et soviétique* 32, no. 2 (1991): 285–310; Nicolas Ross, *De Koutiépov à Miller. Le combat des russes blancs, 1930–1940* (Geneva: Editions des Syrtes, 2017).

185. Marina Grey, *Le Général meurt à minuit. L'enlèvement de Koutiépov 1930 et de Miller 1937* (Paris: Plon, 1981), 112–15.

186. For contemporary accounts of this abduction, see "L'étrange disparition du général Koutiépoff," *Le Petit Journal*, 28 January 1930, 1; and Bajanov and Alexeiev, *L'enlèvement du Général Koutepov*. See also Grey, *Le Général meurt à minuit*, 118; Goldin and Long, "Resistance and Retribution," 27; 39n49; Nicolas Skopinski, "Koutiepov, histoire d'un Russe blanc enlevé en plein Paris," *RetroNews*, https://www.retronews.fr/conflits-et-relations-internationales/echo-de-presse/2019/06/21/koutiepov-enleve-en-plein-paris (accessed April 9, 2020); Miller, *Shanghai on the Metro*, 134–35;

187. Léon Daudet, "Paris capitale du crime politique," *L'Action Française*, 1 February 1930, 1.

188. AN F7 15976/1, "Affaire Miller. Cour d'Assises de la Seine. Audience du 7 Décembre (3ème Journée). 17h 15," 7 December 1938; Grey, *Le Général meurt à minuit*, 126.

189. AN 334 AP 72, "Plaidoirie de Me Maurice Ribet," n.d.; Goldin and Long, "Resistance and Retribution," 38n43.

190. AN F7 15976/1, "Affaire Miller."

191. Goldin and Long, "Resistance and Retribution," 27; 38n42.

192. AN F7 15976/1, "Affaire Miller. Cour d'Assises de la Seine. Audience du 5 Décembre (3ème Journée). 19 heures," 5 December 1938; "Affaire Miller. Cour d'Assises de la Seine. Audience du 8 Décembre 1938. 17h 30," 8 December 1938; Barabtalo, "Life's Sequel," 4–5; Miller, *Shanghai on the Metro*, 135; 231.

193. AN 334 AP 72, "Plaidoirie de Me Maurice Ribet,"; Barabtalo, "Life's Sequel," 4–5; Ross, *De Koutiépov à Miller*, 214–19.

194. Miller, *Shanghai on the Metro*, 231.

195. F.-H. Pottecher, "La vie aventureuse de Plevidzkaïa," *Paris-Soir*, 26 September 1937, 5; Miller, *Shanghai on the Metro*, 231.

196. "Sept ans après," *Le Petit Journal*, 25 September 1937, 4; Léon Daudet, "La nouvelle affaire Koutiepoff," *L'Action Française*, 25 September 1937, 1.

197. "Le territoire français servira-t-il longtemps encoure de champ d'expérinece aux assassins du Guépéou?" *Le Petit Journal*, 24 September 1937, 4; "Successeur de Koutiepov à la tête des anciens combattants russes le Général de Miller a disparu comme lui," *Excelsior*, 24 September 1937, 1.

198. "Et depuis de nombreuses affaires ont ému l'opinion," *Paris-Soir*, 27 September 1937, 5.

199. "Le Général Miller successeur de Koutiepoff à la tête des Russes blancs, a disparu depuis mercredi," *Le Journal*, 24 September 1937, 1. See also "Mystérieuse dispartion du général Miller," *Le Matin*, 24 September 1937, 1; "Le territoire français," 4.

200. J. D., "Le général Eugène de Miller," 1; J. D., "Qu'a fait le général Skobline," 1; "Les rapports de Skobline," 1.

201. M. Magnien, "L'enlèvement de Miller par la Gestapo," *L'Humanité*, 25 September 1937, 2.

202. P. L. Darnar, "Le Général de Miller, chef des Russes blancs à Paris, est 'enlevé'," *L'Humanité*, 24 September 1937, 1. The communist *Regards* likewise connected Gorguloff and Miller in the history of the White Russian presence in France: "L'activité secrète des Russes blancs," *Regards*, 28 October 1937, 8.

203. P. L. Darnar, "Le complot contre la France," *L'Humanité*, 24 September 1937, 2.

204. "Des étrangers indésirables multiplient sur notre territoire leurs règlements de comptes politiques," *La République*, 24 September 1937, 1.

205. *L'Humanité*, 24 September 1937, 1.

206. Grey, *Le Général meurt à minuit*, 132–38.

207. "La mystérieuse disparition du général russe Miller," *Le Petit Parisien*, 24 September 1937, 5; "Mystérieuse disparition du général Miller," *Le Matin*, 24 September 1937, 1; Pottecher, "La vie aventureuse," *Paris-Soir*, 26 September 1937, 5.

208. Miller, *Shanghai on the Metro*, 231; Nicolas Skopinski, "1938, la 'Mata-Hari de Koursk' face à ses juges : la cantatrice espionnait pour l'URSS," *RetroNews*, https://www.retronews.fr/conflits-et-relations-internationales/echo-de-presse/2019/03/26/la-plevitskaia-espionne-urss (accessed 9 April 2020).

209. Henry Malric and Luc Dornain, "L'enlèvement du général Miller," *Détective*, 30 September 1937, 10. See the editions of 7 October 1937 and 14 October 1937 for parts two and three of Malric and Dornain's investigation.

210. Malric and Dornain, "L'enlèvement du général Miller," 10.

211. Jean de la Hire, *La Loubianskaïa. Sirène du Guépéou* (Paris: Editions des Loisirs, 1938), 240.

212. De la Hire, *La Loubianskaïa*, 250.

213. "Bibliographie," *Le Progrès de la Côte-d'Or*, 14 April 1938, 4; "Les Livres," *La Voix du combattant*, 16 April 1938, 7.

214. Maurice Perisset, "L'Actualité Littéraire," *Journal de Montélimar*, 2 July 1938, 5.

215. Miller, *Shanghai on the Metro*, 231; Skopinski, "1938, la 'Mata-Hari de Koursk'."

216. AN F7 15976/1, "Information. A.S. de l'affaire Miller," 6 September 1938.

217. AN 334 AP 72, "Plaidoirie de Me Maurice Ribet," n.d.

218. AN 334 AP 72, "Plaidoirie de Me Maurice Ribet."

219. Géo London, "Le Procès de la Plevitzkaïa," *Le Journal*, 7 December 1938, 3.

220. London, "Le Procès de la Plevitzkaïa," 3.

221. "Ce sont bien les Soviets qui ont enlevé le général de Miller," *Le Jour*, 7 December 1938, 2.

222. "La deuxième audience du procès Skobline," *Ce Soir*, 7 December 1938, 5.

223. Henri Vonoven, "La condamnation de Mme Skobline," *Le Figaro*, 15 December 1938, 3.

224. AN F7 15976/1, "Affaire Miller. Cour d'Assises de la Seine. Audience du 14 Décembre 1938 (9ème journée)," 14 December 1938.

225. Nick Gillain, *Le Mercenaire. Carnet de route d'un combattant rouge* (Paris: Librarie Arthème Fayard, 1938), 10–11.

226. AN BB18 6476, interview with CHAIX, Charles Robert, n.d.

227. Schor, *Historie de l'immigration*, 158.

228. A. Albert-Petit, "Un pays bien précieux," *Journal des Débats*, 7 January 1938, 1.

229. Caron, *Uneasy Asylum*, 462n107; 162; 168; Schor, *L'opinion française et les étrangers*, 646.

230. "Terroristes, Cagoulards, Ravisseurs, etc..." *Marianne*, 29 September 1937, 1.

231. Lewis, *The Boundaries of the Republic*, 221; 222. See also Schor, *L'opinion*

française et les étrangers, 666–68; Riadh Ben Khalifa, "La fabrique des clandestins en France, 1938–1940," *Migrations Sociétés* 139, no. 1 (2012): 11–26.

232. "Décret sur la police des étrangers," *Journal Officiel de la République Française. Lois et décrets*, 104 (1, 2 and 3 May 1938): 4967–68; Lewis, *The Boundaries of the Republic*, 219–220.

233. AN F7 14711,"Le Ministre de l'Intérieur à Monsieur le Gouverneur Général de l'Algérie, à Monsieur le Préfet de Police, à Messieurs les Préfets," 21 November 1938; Lewis, *The Boundaries of the Republic*, 220.

234. Lewis, *The Boundaries of the Republic*, 219. My emphasis.

235. Caron, *Uneasy Asylum*, 175; Harouni, "Le débat autour du statut des étrangers dans les années 1930," *Le Mouvement social* 188, no. 3 (1999): 71.

236. AN F7 14684, "Le Ministre de l'Intérieur à Monsieur le Gouverneur Général de l'Algérie, à Monsieur le Préfet de Police , à Paris, à Messieurs les Préfets," 20 April 1939.

237. AN F7 14684, "Le Ministre de l'Intérieur"; "Le Ministre de l'Intérieur, Direction Générale de la Sûreté Nationale à Monsieur le Gouverneur Général de l'Algérie, à Monsieur le Préfet de Police à Paris, à Messieurs les Préfets," 8 July 1939.

CONCLUSION

Sections of this chapter draw on the material used in Chris Millington, "Were We Terrorists? History, Terrorism, and the French Resistance," *History Compass* 16, no. 2 (2018): e12440, https://doi.org/10.1111/hic3.12440.

1. AN AJ 40/553, "Le Préfet de Seine-et-Oise à Monsieur le Ministre Secrétaire d'état à l'Intérieur," 28 August 1941; "Le lâche attentat de Versailles," *L'Oeuvre*, 28 August 1941, 1 and 3.

2. Henri Noguères, with M. Degliame-Fouché and J.-L. Vigier, *Histoire de la Résistance en France de 1940 à 1945. II. L'armée de l'ombre. Juillet 1941–Octobre 1942* (Paris: Robert Laffont, 1969), 106–7.

3. "Le lâche attentat," 3; "M. de Brinon fait le récit de l'attentat," *Le Petit Parisien*, 28 August 1941, 3.

4. "L'attentat de Versailles flétri par Vichy," *Le Matin*, 28 August 1941, 3. The would-be assassin had, in fact, acted alone and was a member of the right-wing PSF. On Collette's background, see AN AJ 40/553, "Le Préfet de Seine-et-Oise à Monsieur le Ministre Secrétaire d'état à l'Intérieur," 28 August 1941.

5. Henri Lebré, "Les coupables," *Le Cri du Peuple*, 28 August 1941, 1.

6. "Répression du terrorisme," *La Croix*, 14 September 1941, 1.

7. AN 3W 54, "Genèse de la loi du 14 Août 1941, d'après le dossier de la Direction Criminelle," n.d.

8. AN 19950395/7, "Copie note dactylographiée de M. le Directeur du Cabinet sur un projet de loi réprimant l'activité communiste ou anarchiste," undated but prior to 14 August 1941.

9. Henri Donnedieu de Vabres [professeur à la Faculté de Droit de l'Université de Paris], *Traité élémentaire de droit criminel et la législation pénale comparée. Deuxième édition* (Paris: Librairie du Receuil Sirey, 1943), 596–97.

10. AN BB30 1887, "Audience de la Section Spéciale de la Cour d'Appel, de Paris, de la date du 27 août 1941."

11. AN BB30 1887: on Bastard: "L'Avocat Général de la Section Spéciale de la Cour d'Appel de Paris `a Monsieur le Garde des Sceaux," 27 August 1941; "L'Avocat Général, près la Section Spéciale de la Cour d'Appel de Paris à Monsieur le Garde des Sceaux," n.d. (document stamped 14 November 1941); on Bréchet: "L'Avocat Général à Monsieur le Garde des Sceaux," 17 August 1941; "L'Avocat Général, près la Section Spéciale de la Cour d'Appel de Paris à Monsieur le Garde des Sceaux," n.d. (document stamped 27 November 1941); on Trzebrucky: "L'Avocat Général, près la Section Spéciale de la Cour d'Appel de Paris à Monsieur le Garde des Sceaux," 5 November 1941.

12. My emphasis. AN 3W 178, "Loi No. 318 du 5 Juin 1943 réprimant les activités communistes, anarchistes, terroristes ou subversives." See pages 1714–15 of *Journal Officiel de l'Etat Français: Lois et Décrets*, no. 150, 24 June 1943.

13. AN 19950398/24, "Le Garde des Sceaux, Ministre Secrétaire d'Etat à la Justice, à Monsieur le Procureur Général près la Cour d'Appel," 2 July 1943. According to Sansico (*La justice déshonorée, 1940–1944* [Paris: Tallandier, 2015]), thanks to the law of 5 June 1943 and Vichy's increasingly violent political discourse, "the term 'terrorism', is integrated into official documents without any safeguards or legal framework, as if a law had suffi ced to validate the shift from a term belonging to the register of political propaganda to a legal notion" (465).

14. Roger Pannequin, "Résistance et terrorisme," *Raison présente* 81, no. 1 (1987): 29–32.

15. "Le tribunal d'Etat pour réprimer le terrorisme siégera à Paris et à Lyon," *L'Oeuvre*, 10 September 1941, 3; *Journal Officiel* no. 252 (10 September 1941): 3850–51.

16. "Il est temps que la population sache que la police la protège declare M. Havard," *Paris-Soir*, 4 March 1942, 1 and 8.

17. See, for example, AN 19950395/7, "Le Garde des Sceaux, Ministre, Secrétaire d'Etat à la Justice à Monsieur l'Ambassadeur de France, Délégué du Gouvernement Français dans les Territoires Occupés," 2 January 1942. This document refers to a report of 18 December 1941 from the Procureur général près la Cour d'Appel de Douai, which "rend compte de l'ensemble de l'activité terroriste" in this district. The actual report—"Le Procureur Général près la Cour d'Appel de Douai à Monsieur le Garde des Sceaux, Ministre, Secrétaire d'Etat à la Justice," of 18 December 1941—does not call the acts "terrorism" but rather, "attentats criminels." See also the examples in AN 19950398/24, "Le Garde des Sceaux, Ministre Secrétaire d'Etat à la Justice, à Monsieur le Procureur Général près la Cour d'Appel," 28 May 1943; AN 19970394/1, "Renseignements sur les condamnés pour menées communistes ou gaullistes [Circonscription Pénitentiare de Rennes]," n.d.

18. See, for example, AN BB18 7056, "Le Commissaire Divisionnaire, Chef

du Service Régional de Police Judiciaire à Paris à Monsieur le Procureur Général près la Cour d'Appel à Paris," 24 August 1942.

19. Some examples, among others, include "L'attentat terroriste contre M. de Brinon" and "La terreur rouge dans nos campagnes," *Le Cri du Peuple*, 20 October 1943, 3 ; "La terreur rouge," *Le Cri du Peuple*, 26 November 1943, 2.

20. Marcel Déat, "Questions aux 'patriotes'," *L'Oeuvre*, 5 November 1943, 1–2.

21. "La campagne contre le 'terrorisme'," *Libération. Organe des Français libres (Nord)*, 23 November 1943, 3–4.

22. The German authorities, on the other hand, associated opponents of the Occupation with the historical "franc-tireur" of past wars with France, though in the context of the Nazis' racial ideology this character took on anticommunist and antisemitic qualities: see Gaël Eismann, "Maintenir l'ordre. La MBF et la sécurité locale en France occupée," *Vingtième Siècle. Revue d'histoire* 98, no. 2 (2008): 130–31; and Barbara Lambauer, "D'une 'dûreté douce pour le futur': Le terrorisme selon l'Allemagne nazie et sa répression," in *Terrorismes. Histoire et droit*, ed. Mireille Delmas-Marty and Henry Laurens (Paris: CNRS Editions, 2010), 91.

23. *Journal Officiel*, no. 185 (29 July 1940): 4589–90.

24. I am grateful to Gayle K. Brunelle and Annette Finley-Croswhite for prompting me to add this observation. On Jeantet during the war, see Brunelle and Finley-Croswhite, *Assassination in Vichy*, 186–87.

25. H. R. Kedward, *In Search of the Maquis: Rural Resistance in Southern France, 1942–1944* (Oxford, UK: Clarendon Press, 1993), 250.

26. AN 19950398/25, "Circulaire. Le Garde des Sceaux, Ministre de la Justice, à Monsieur le Premier Président de la Cour d'Appel," 4 October 1944.

27. See, for example, Marcel Déat, "Le jeu des assassins," *L'Oeuvre*, 25 October 1941, 1–2; "Mesures de répression contre le terrorisme," *La Croix*, 11 December 1941, 1.

28. J.-M. Rochard, "Robots assassins. Les secrets du terrorisme," *Actu*, date illegible (though probably 19 July 1942), 3.

29. AN F7 15312, "27 communistes terroristes, auteurs d'actes de sabotage et d'attentats, passent en jugement," *Le Cri du Peuple*, 9 April 1942; Robert de Beauplan, "L'école des gangsters," *Le Matin*, 20 November 1943, 1.

30. See, for example, Déat, "Le jeu des assassins," 1–2; AN F7 15312, "Vichy commencerait-il à comprendre? La lutte contre le terrorisme combat politique et condition première du salut national," *La France Socialiste*, 9 November 1941, also printed in *Le Petit Parisien*, 9 November 1941; "L'emprunt du terrorisme," *Je suis partout*, 29 October 1943, 2; Philippe Henriot, "Le parlement d'Alger," *Je suis partout*, 29 October 1943, 5.

31. Christopher Neumaier, "The Escalation of German Reprisal Policy in Occupied France, 1941–42," *Journal of Contemporary History* 41, no. 1 (2006): 113–31.

32. AN F7 15312, Jean d'Orsay, "Une mesure bien accueillie," *Le Matin*, 16 December 1941; "Les orateurs du PPF ont proclamé: 'Non, la révolution terroriste n'abattra pas la Révolution nationale'," *Le Cri du Peuple*, 9 December 1943, 1; René Martel, "Le terrorisme juif," *Paris-Soir*, 17 December 1941, 2.

33. AN F7 15312, poster: "L'Armée du crime," n.d.; "A Albert, un ouvrier allemande est lâchement assassiné par des terroristes," *Aujourd'hui*, 4 January 1942.
34. P. H., "Attentats et machines infernales," *La Croix*, 22 June 1942, 3.
35. Marcel Déat, "La Révoltuion menacée," *L'Oeuvre*, 8 November 1942, 1–2.
36. Marcel Déat, "Politique des assassins," *L'Oeuvre*, 24 September 1941, 1–2.
37. "M. de Brinon félicite deux ouvriers qui ont aide à l'arrestation d'un terroriste," *L'Oeuvre*, 24 April 1942, 3.
38. René Martel, "Les étrangers et le terrorisme," *Paris Soir*, 22 January 1944, 3. My emphasis.
39. Martel, "Les étrangers et le terrorisme," 3.
40. AN F7 15312, "Les sept terroristes avouent tous les crimes qui leur sont reprochés," *L'Oeuvre*, 6 March 1942.
41. Jean-Pierre Bertin-Maghit, *Les documenteurs des années noires. Les documentaires de propagande, France 1940–1944* (Paris: Nouveau Monde Editions, 2004), 263–64.
42. "L'action de la police contre le terrorimse communiste," *La Croix*, 3 March 1942.
43. AN BB30 1709, "'Répression impitoyable' a déclaré M. de Brinon en parlant des attentats récents," *La France au travail*, 25 August 1941.
44. Déat, "Politique des assassins," 1–2.
45. "Les auteurs de l'attentat contre M. Marcel Déat sont tous arrêtés," *Le Matin*, 28 April 1943, 1.
46. "En deux mois, la gendarmerie a saisi plus de 1,400 armes et de grandes quantité de munitions," *Le Matin*, 26 November 1943, 1.
47. P. H., "Attentats et machines infernales," *La Croix*, 22 June 1942, 3.
48. Georges Beaumont, "Paris, centre important de recrutement du banditisme," *Le Matin*, 17 December 1943, 1–2.
49. Francisque Laurent, "230 attentats ou sabotages ont eu lieu du 1er juillet 1941 au 18 février 1942," *L'Echo d'Alger*, 4 March 1942, 1.
50. On this topic, see Millington, *Fighting for France*.
51. Luc Capdevila, "The Quest for Masculinity in a Defeated France, 1940–1945," *Contemporary European History* 10, no. 3 (2001): 427. See also Joan Tumblety, "Revenge of the Fascist Knights: Masculine Identities in *Je suis partout*, 1940–1944," *Modern and Contemporary France* 7, no. 1 (1999): 11–20.
52. Capdevila, "The Quest for Masculinity," 433.
53. Philippe Henriot, "Crime et châtiment," *Combats*, 4 September 1943, 1. A similar protrayal may be found in Déat, "Politique des assassins," 1–2.
54. AN F7 15312, "Il y a les Français et il y a les autres," *L'Oeuvre*, 16 December 1941. See also Georges Claude, "Réprobation de tous les vrais Français," *Le Matin*, 29 December 1941; and "Terrorisme, Communisme, Banditisme," *L'Oeuvre* 4 June 1942, 1.
55. Philippe Henriot, "Aux portes de l'abattoir," *Combats*, 18 November 1943 (the date of this document is practically illegible), 1–2.
56. François Bout-de-l'An, "La Bataille ne nous fait pas peur!" *Combats*, 27 November 1943, 1.

57. See, for example, AN F7 15312, "Les auteurs des attentats ne sont pas des héros mais des lâches," *Le Petit Parisien*, 25 October 1941; "Montrons-nous dignes d'un destin indulgent," *Paris-Soir*, 10 December 1941; D'Orsay, "Une mesure bien accueillie,"; Laurent, "230 attentats," 1.

58. See, for example, "Pour la première fois Darnand parle à Paris," *Combats*, 19 June 1943, 1; "Face aux assassins," *Combats*, 4 September 1943, 1; "La Milice en deuil," *Combats*, 4 September 1943, 1.

59. Marcel Déat, "La tâche civique des Miliciens," *L'Oeuvre*, 16 July 1943, 1.

60. Marcel Déat, "Durcissement révolutionnaire," *L'Oeuvre*, 7 August 1943, 1–2.

61. "La Révolution Nationale: Notre déception," *La Trique. Organe de combat SOL des Alpes-Maritimes*, 1 April 1942, 1; "Si tu frappes, frappe dur," *La Trique. Organe de combat SOL des Alpes-Maritimes*, 1 April 1942, 2.

62. P.-A. Cousteau, "Une interview de Joseph Darnand: 'Aucun des crimes de nos ennemis ne restera impunis'," *Je suis partout*, 7 January 1944, 1.

63. Cousteau, "Une interview de Joseph Darnand," 1.

64. "Le mauvais calcul des assassins," *Combats*, 16 October 1943, 1.

65. AN F7 15312, "Vichy commencerait-il à comprendre?"

66. Paul Marion, "Un devoir patriotique s'impose à chaque Francais: Lutter contre le terrorisme," *L'Oeuvre*, 9 December 1941, 3; "Pour sauvegarder l'avenir de la France un devoir patriotique s'impose à chaque Français: Lutter contre le terrorisme," *Le Matin*, 9 December 1941, 1–3.

67. Maurice Levillain (RNP head for the Paris region), "Le RNP flétrit les auteurs des attentats," *Nouveaux Temps*, 10 December 1941, n.p.

68. AN F7 14888, "Note pour Monsieur le Sous-Directeur chargé des Services Administratifs de la Police Nationale dans les Territoires Occupés," 19 January 1944; "An das Französische Innenministerium—Direction Générale de la Police Nationale," 12 February 1944.

69. AN F7 14888, "A MM. les Maires du département du Doubs et et [sic] l'Ain Occupé. Objet: Attentats terroristes," 8 October 1942.

70. AN F7 14888, "Appel à la Population. Le Terrorisme est un Crime contre la Nation," signed by Prefect of the Yonne E.-A. Gardas and Courrier, "l'intendant de Police de la Région de Dijon."

71. AN F7 14905, "Le Délégué du Secrétaire Général au Maintien de l'Ordre à Madame Madeleine, Pontécoulant (Calvados)," n.d.

72. "Alerte au terrorisme qui va affamer nos villes si...," *Le Matin*, 12 October 1943, 1–2; "Dans le Cantal. Deux réfractaires au service du travail obligatoire exécutés par des meneurs communistes," *L'Oeuvre*, 21 June 1943, 1.

73. Simon Sabiani, "Pour venger nos morts," *Le Cri du Peuple*, 23 December 1943, 1 and 3.

74. Robert de Beauplan, "La France commence à respirer," *Le Matin*, 4 February 1944, 1.

75. François Marcot, "Sabotage et attentats," in *Dictionnaire historique de la*

Résistance. Résistance intérieure et France libre, ed. François Marcot, with Bruno Le Roux and Christine Levisse-Touze (Paris: Robert Laffont, 2006), 693.

76. "La campagne contre le 'terrorisme'," *Libération. Organe des Français libres (Nord)*, 23 November 1943, 3–4.

77. "La campagne contre le 'terrorisme'," 3–4.

78. "Pour le maquis…contre le terrorisme," *Courrier français du témoignage chrétien* 10 (1944): 1.

79. "Pour le maquis," 1.

80. See *L'aube de la Liberté, organe des prisonniers politiques, prison Chave, Marseille*, 1 March 1944, n.p.

81. *L'aube de la Liberté*, n.p.

82. *Coup d'oeil sur la presse libre….Petite revue des journaux français*, February 1944, 3; AN Z 4/79, dossier 532, document 2, "Les Terroristes: Ce sont les policiers…," n.d.

83. *L'aube de la Liberté*, n.p.

84. "Terrorisme milicien," *Le Patriote Berrichon. Organe de Lutte des Forces Unies de la Jeuneese Patriotique*, 15 August 1944, 2.

85. "Le fait de la resistance," *Défense de la France. Organe du Mouvement de la Libération Nationale. Edition de Paris*, July 1943, 2; "Nous, les terroristes…," *Libération: Organe des Français libres (Nord)*, 12 October 1943, 4; G. Le Mainois, "Terrorisme ou resistance," *Défense de la France. Organe du Mouvement de la Libération Nationale. Edition de Paris*, 15 December 1943, 1–2.

86. "Un bilan," *L'Humanité. Edition de la Zone Sud*, 1 May 1943, 1.

87. "Contre la terreur hitlérienne!" *La Bourgogne Combattante. Organe du Front National de la Côte-d'Or*, October 1943, 2.

88. "Contre la terreur hitlérienne!" 2.

89. "'Terrorisme' et insurrection nationale," *Libération. Organe du Mouvement uni de la résistance* 38 (30 October 1943), 1–2; Le Mainois, "Terrorisme or résistance," 1–2; "Grâce aux 'terroristes' nos cheminots ne sont plus bombardés," *Combat*, 1 February 1944, 2.

90. Le Mainois, "Terrorisme or résistance," 1–2.

91. Le Mainois, "Terrorisme or résistance," 1–2, emphasis in the original text.

92. "Pour le maquis," 1.

93. Indomitus (Philippe Viannay), "Le devoir de tuer," *Défense de la France. Organe du Mouvement de la Libération Nationale. Edition de Paris*, 25 February 1944, 1. See also "Le fait de la resistance," 2.

94. "'Terrorisme' et insurrection nationale," 1–2.

95. "'Terrorisme' et insurrection nationale," 1–2.

96. Indomitus (Philippe Viannay), "Résister," *Défense de la France. Organe du Mouvement de la Libération Nationale. Edition de Paris*, 15 March 1943, 1.

97. "Terroristes? Non: Justiciers!" *Combat. Edition de Paris*, 15 October 1943, 3.

98. "Contre la terreur hitlérienne!"2; "Crime terroristes??? Non…Justice de patriotes," *L'Aube libre. Organe du CDL. Numéro Spécial*, August 1944; ; Indomitus

(Philippe Viannay), "Le devoir de tuer," 1. See also Franck Liaigre, *Les FTP. Nouvelle histoire d'une résistance* (Paris: Perrin, 2015), 296.

99. "Parisiens, constituez dans chaque immeuble un comité de vigilance," *Combat*, 1 September 1944, 2.

100. See, for example, "Traqués par les FFI, les bandits seront bientôt mis hors d'état de nuire," *Ce soir*, 28 August 1944, 1–2; "Le CNR transmet au gouvernement le projet de statut de la Garde civique républicaine," *Ce soir*, 5 November 1944, 1.

101. "Les FFI seront le noyau de l'armée nationale nouvelle," *L'Humanité*, 29 August 1944, 2. See also Georges Cogniot, "Trente-quatre morts, quarante blessés au château de la Timone," *L'Humanité*, 28 November 1944, 1.

102. See https://www.legifrance.gouv.fr/affichTexte.do?cidTexte=LEGITEXT000006071212 (accessed August 18, 2020).

103. AN 19950398/25, "Circulaire. Le Garde des Sceaux, Ministre de la Justice, à Monsieur le Premier Président de la Cour d'Appel," 4 October 1944.

104. *Journal Officiel*, 1 July 1943, 14.

105. AN 19950398/25, "Circulaire."

106. AN 19950398/25, "Circulaire."

107. P. A., "Le nouveau statut des étrangers', *Le Petit Journal*, 17 September 1937, 4, mentioned in Schor, *L'opinion française et les étrangers en France, 1919–1939* (Paris: Publication e la Sorbonne, 1985), 649.

108. Haupt and Weinhauer, "Terrorism and the State," 208.

GLOSSARY OF THE FRENCH PRESS

1. This glossary draws on mainly two sources: Maurice Chavardès, *Une campagne de presse: La droite française et le 6 février 1934* (Paris: Flammarion, 1970), 109–13, and Pierre Milza, *L'Italie fasciste devant l'opinion française 1920–1940* (Paris: Armand Colin, 1967), 255–60. A valuable recent source on the press at the end of the 1930s is David Wingeate Pike, "La transition de la press parisienne entre juin et novembre 1940: Dissolution, fuite, exil, retour," *Guerres mondiales et conflits contemporains* 268, no. 4 (2017): 117–34.

2. Amélie Chabrier and Marie-Ève Thérenty, "Détective, histoire, imaginaire, médiapoétique d'un hebdomadaire de fait divers (1928–1940)," https://doi.org/10.4000/criminocorpus.5537 (accessed October 26, 2022).

3. Marina Bellot, "'Je suis partout,' hebdomadaire antisémite et collaborationniste," *Retronews*, https://www.retronews.fr/histoire-de-la-presse/echo-de-presse/2018/04/11/je-suis-partout-hebdomadaire-antisemite-et (accessed October 26, 2022).

SELECT BIBLIOGRAPHY

Archives Nationales, Pierrefitte-sur-Seine

3W Haute cour de justice
603 AP Fonds Henri Géraud
AJ 40 Archives allemandes de l'Occupation
BB18 Division criminelle du ministère de la Justice
BB30 Secrétariat général du ministère de la Justice
F7 Police générale
F60 Secrétariat général du Gouvernement et services du Premier minister

Archives de la Préfecture de Police, Le Pré-Saint Gervais

BA Cabinet du Préfet de Police
W Fonds contemporains

Dépôt Central des Archives de la Justice Militaire at Le Blanc Indre

Attentat du 19 février 1919 contre Georges Clemenceau, available at https://www.memoiredeshommes.sga.defense.gouv.fr/fr/arkotheque/navigation_facette/index.php?f=AffaireCottin

Newspapers and Magazines

L'Aube
L'Aurore
L'Avenir

Ce Soir
Le Cri du Peuple
La Croix
Détective
L'Echo d'Alger
L'Echo de Paris
Excelsior
Le Figaro
Gil Blas
L'Humanité
L'Intransigeant
Je suis partout
Le Journal
Journal des débats politiques et littéraires
Journal Officiel
La Lanterne
La Liberté
Le Matin
L'Oeuvre
L'Ouest-Éclair
Paris-Soir
La Patrie
Le Petit Journal
Le Petit Marseillais
Le Petit Parisien
Le Petit Provençal
Police-Magazine
Le Populaire
Le Temps

Printed Primary Sources

Bajanov, B., and N. Alexeiev. *L'enlèvement du Général Koutepov*. Paris: Editions Spes, 1930.

Barbusse, Henri. *J'accuse!...un réquisitoire implacable*. Paris: Bureau d'Editions, 1932.

Beaudéant, Jean. *L'attentat contre les chefs d'état*. Thèse pour le doctorat, Université de Toulouse, Faculté de Droit. Toulouse: Ch. Dirion Librairie-Editeur, 1911.

Belin, Jean. *My Work at the Sûrete*. London: George G. Harrap, 1950.

Boisson, Marius. *Les Attentats Anarchistes sous la Troisième République*. Paris: Editions de France, 1931.

Chandan, Krsta S. Chantitch. *Le Terrorisme devant la Société des Nations. Réquisitoire contre la Hongrie apostolique soutenue par le Vatican et Cie...* Paris: Publications Contemporaines "Frances-Les Balkans," 1935.

Darlix, Paul. *Terrorisme sur le monde*. Paris: Editions Baudinière, 1932.
Dmitriev, Valentine. *Le Terroriste*. Traduit du Russe par G. Savitch et E. Jaubert. Paris: Plon, 1912.
Franklin-Marquet, Henri. *La vérité sur l'affaire Gorgoulov. Ceux qui ont tué Doumer*. Paris: Bureau d'Editions, 1932.
Girard, André. *Anarchistes et bandits*. Paris: Les Temps Nouveaux, 1914.
Gorel, Michel. *Pourquoi Gorguloff a-t-il tué?* Paris: Editions Nilsson, 1932.
Julia, Edouard. *Papiers, 1895–1933*. Paris: Editions du Temps, 1936.
La fin tragique du Président Paul Doumer racontés par deux témoins oculaires. Paris: Librairie contemporaine, 1932.
Londres, Albert. *Les comitadjis ou le terrorisme dans les Balkans*. Paris: Albin Michel, 1932.
Longuet, Jean, and Georges Silber. *Terroristes et policiers. Azev, Harting et Cie. Les dessous de la police russe*. Paris: Librairie Félix Juven, 1909.
Lovitch, Joseph. *Tempête sur l'Europe. Roman. Préfacé de Henry Rollin*. Paris: Editions La Flèche d'Or, 1932.
Mondanel, Antoine. "Notes sur l'attentat de Marseille, 9 octobre 1934." Undated. https://www.interieur.gouv.fr/Le-ministere/Organisation/Mission-des-archives-nationales/Exposition-virtuelle/Attentat-du-9-octobre-1934 (accessed 19 February 2020).
Reber, Charles. *Terrorisme et diplomatie*. Paris: La Technique du Livre, 1935.
Rollin, Henri. *L'Apocalypse de notre temps. Les dessous de la propaganda allemande d'après des documents inédits*. Paris: Gallimard, 1939.
Seton-Watson, Robert William. "King Alexander's Assassination: Its Background and Effects." *International Affairs* 14, no. 1 (January-February 1935): 20–47.
Stepniak, Sergei. *La Russie souterraine*. Paris: J. Lévy, 1885.
———. *Underground Russia; Revolutionary Profiles and Sketches from Life*. Westport, CT.: Hyperion Press, 1973.
Vizetelly, Ernest Alfred. *The Anarchists: Their Faith and Their Record Including Sidelights on the Royal and Other Personages Who Have Been Assassinated*. London; New York: John Lane/The Bodley Head, 1911.
Waciórski, Jerzy. *Le terrorisme politique*. Paris: Edition A. Pedone, 1939.
West, Rebecca. *Black Lamb and Grey Falcon: The Record of a Journey Through Yugoslavia in 1937*, Vol. I. London: Macmillan, 1946.

Secondary Sources

Adriano, Pino, and Giorgio Cingolani. *Nationalism and Terror: Ante Pavelić and Ustasha Terrorism from Fascism to the Cold War*. Budapest: Central European University Press, 2018.
Amar, Marianne, and Pierre Milza. *L'immigration en France au XXe siècle*. Paris: Armand Colin, 1990.
Andress, David. "The Course of the Terror, 1793–94." In *A Companion to the French*

Revolution, edited by Peter McPhee, 293–309. Chichester, UK: Blackwell, 2013.

Avrich, Paul. *The Russia Anarchists*. Princeton, NJ: Princeton University Press, 1967.

Aydinli, Ersel. "Before Jihadists There Were Anarchists: A Failed Case of Transnational Violence." *Studies in Conflict & Terrorism* 31, no. 10 (2008): 903–23.

Baele, Stéphane J. "Are Terrorists 'Insane'? A Critical Analysis of Mental Health Categories in Lone Terrorists' Trials." *Critical Studies on Terrorism* 7, no. 2 (2014): 257–76.

Baker, Donald N. "The Surveillance of Subversion in Interwar France: The Carnet B in the Seine, 1922–1940." *French Historical Studies* 10, no. 3 (1978): 486–516.

Bantman, Constance. *The French Anarchists in London, 1880–1914: Exile and Transnationalism in the First Globalisation*. Liverpool, UK: Liverpool University Press, 2013.

Beauchamps, Marie. "Perverse Tactics: 'Terrorism' and National Identity in France." *Culture, Theory and Critique* 58, no. 1 (2017): 48–61.

Berezovich, Elena L., and Galina Kabakova. "Stéréotypes du 'Russe' et du 'Français' regards croisés." *Revue des études slaves* LXXXVI, no. 4 (2015): 389–412.

Bergman, Jay. "Vera Zasulich, the Shooting of Trepov and the Growth of Political Terrorism in Russia, 1878–1881." *Terrorism: An International Journal* 4, no. 1 (1980): 25–51.

Blatt, Joel. "The Cagoule Plot." In *Crisis and Renewal in France, 1918–1962*, edited by Kenneth Mouré and Martin S. Alexander, 84–104. New York: Berghahn Books, 2002.

Bloom, Mia. *Bombshell: Women and Terrorism*. Philadelphia: University of Pennsylvania Press, 2011.

Bogain, Ariane. "Terrorism and the Discursive Construction of National Identity in France." *National Identities* 21, no. 3 (2019): 241–65.

Bouhey, Vivien. *Les Anarchistes contre la République. Contribution à l'histoire des réseaux sous la Troisième République 1880–1914*. Rennes, FR: Presses Universitaires de Rennes, 2008.

Bourdrel, Philippe. *La Cagoule. Histoire d'une société secrète du Front Populaire à la Ve République*. Paris: Albin Michel, 1992.

Broche, François. *Assassinat de Alexandre Ier et Louis Barthou. Marseille, le 9 octobre 1934*. Paris: Editions Balland, 1977.

Brouard, Sylvain, Pavlos Vasilopoulos, and Martial Foucault. "How Terrorism Affects Political Attitudes: France in the Aftermath of the 2015–2016 Attacks." *West European Politics* 41, no. 5 (2018): 1073–99.

Brown, Keith. "The King Is Dead, Long Live the Balkans! Watching the Marseilles Murders of 1934." Unpublished paper delivered at the Sixth Annual World Convention of the Association for the Study of Nationalities, Columbia University, New York (5–7 April 2001).https://watson.brown.edu/files/watson/imce/research/projects/terrorist_transformations/The_King_is_Dead.pdf, (accessed 21 February 2020).

Brunelle Gayle K., and Annette Finley-Croswhite. *Assassination in Vichy: Marx Dormoy and the Struggle for the Soul of France*. Toronto: University of Toronto Press, 2020.

———. *Murder in the Metro: Laetitia Toureaux and the Cagoule in 1930s France*. Baton Rouge: Louisiana State University Press, 2012.
Bryan, Dominic, Liam Kelly, and Sara Templer. "The Failed Paradigm of 'Terrorism'." *Behavioral Sciences of Terrorism and Political Aggression* 3, no. 2 (2011): 80–96.
Callahan, Michael D. *The League of Nations, International Terrorism, and British Foreign Policy, 1934–1938*. Basingstoke, UK: Palgrave Macmillan, 2018.
Caron, Vicki. *Uneasy Asylum: France and the Jewish Refugee Crisis, 1933–1942*. Stanford, CA: Stanford University Press, 2002.
Ceci, Giovanni Mario. "A 'Historical Turn' in Terrorism Studies?" *Journal of Contemporary History* 51, no. 4 (2016): 888–96.
Clutterbuck, Lindsay. "The Progenitors of Terrorism: Russian Revolutionaries or Extreme Irish Republicans?" *Terrorism and Political Violence* 16, no. 1 (2004): 154–81.
Coeuré, Sophie, and Frédéric Monier. "Paul Gorgulov, assassin de Paul Doumer (1932)." *Vingtième Siècle, revue d'histoire* 65 (January-March 2000): 35–46.
Colombani, Roger, and Jean-René Laplayne. *La mort d'un roi. La vérité sur l'assassinat d'Alexandre de Yougoslavie*. Paris: Albin Michel, 1971.
Corne, Jonah. "Regicide on Repeat: The Pensive Spectator in Rebecca West's *Black Lamb and Grey Falcon*." *Criticism* 60, no. 1 (2018): 47–73.
Cox, Rory. "History, Terrorism and the State." In *The Cambridge History of Terrorism*, edited by Richard English, 571–93. Cambridge, UK: Cambridge University Press, 2021.
Dháibhéid, Caoimhe Nic. *Terrorist Histories: Individuals and Political Violence Since the 19th Century*. Abingdon, UK: Routledge, 2017.
Ditrych, Ondrej. "'International Terrorism' as Conspiracy: Debating Terrorism in the League of Nations." *Historical Social Research/Historische Sozialforschung* 38, no. 1 (2013): 200–210.
———. *Tracing the Discourses of Terrorism: Identity, Genealogy and State*. Basingstoke, UK: Palgrave Macmillan, 2014.
Drapac, Vesna. "A King Is Killed in Marseille: France and Yugoslavia in 1934." *French History and Civilization* 1 (2005): 224–33.
English, Richard. "History and the Study of Terrorism." In *The Cambridge History of Terrorism*, edited by Richard English, 3–27. Cambridge, UK: Cambridge University Press, 2021.
Feinberg, Myriam. "States of Emergency in France and Israel—Terrorism, 'Permanent Emergencies,' and Democracy." *Z Politikwiss* 28 (2018): 495–506.
Ferragu, Gilles. *Histoire du terrorisme*. Paris: Perrin, 2019.
Foley, Frank. "France." In *Routledge Handbook of Terrorism and Counterterrorism*, edited by Andrew Silke, 528–39. Abingdon, UK: Routledge, 2019.
Foshko, Katherine. "The Paul Doumer Assassination and the Russian Diaspora in Interwar Paris." *French History* 23, no. 3 (2009): 383–404.
Fragnon, Julien. "'We Are at War': Continuity and Rupture in French Anti-Terrorist Discourse." *Media, War & Conflict* 12, no. 2 (2019): 131–52.
Frampton, Martyn. "History and the Definition of Terrorism." In *The Cambridge History of Terrorism*, edited by Richard English, 31–57. Cambridge, UK: Cambridge

University Press, 2021.

Gage, Beverley. "Terrorism and the American Experience: A State of the Field." *The Journal of American History* 98, no. 1 (2011): 73–94.

Geifman, Anna. "Aspects of Early Twentieth-Century Russian Terrorism: The Socialist Revolutionary Combat Organization." *Terrorism and Political Violence* 4, no. 2 (1992): 23–46.

———. *Thou Shalt Kill: Revolutionary Terrorism in Russia, 1894–1917*. Princeton, NJ: Princeton University Press, 1993.

Gentry, Caron E., and Laura Sjoberg. *Beyond Mothers, Monsters, Whores: Thinking About Women's Violence in Global Politics*. London: Zed Books, 2015.

———. *Mothers, Monsters, Whores: Women's Violence in Global Context*. London: Zed Books, 2007.

Gerwarth, Robert, and Heinz-Gerhard Haupt. "Internationalising Historical Research on Terrorist Movements in Twentieth-Century Europe." *European Review of History—Revue européenne d'Histoire* 14, no. 3 (2007): 275–81.

Goldin, Vladislav I., and John W. Long. "Resistance and Retribution: The Life and Fate of General E. K. Miller." *Revolutionary Russia* 12, no. 2 (1999): 19–40.

Gooderham, Peter. "The Anarchist Movement in Russia, 1905–1917." PhD diss., University of Bristol, 1981.

Gourlay, Patrick. *Nuit franquiste sur Brest. L'attaque du sous-marin républicain C-2, 1937*. Kerangwenn, FR: Editions Coop Breizh, 2013.

Goussef, Catherine. *L'exil russe. La fabrique du réfugié apatride (1920–1939)*. Paris: CNRS Editions, 2008.

Graves, Matthew. "Memory and Forgetting on the National Periphery: Marseilles and the Regicide of 1934." *PORTAL. Journal of Multidisciplinary International Studies* 7, no. 1 (2010): 1–21. https://www.researchgate.net/publication/272731584_Memory_and_Forgetting_on_the_National_Periphery_Marseilles_and_the_Regicide_of_1934 (accessed 5 October 2022).

Gregory, Shaun. "France and the War on Terrorism." *Terrorism and Political Violence* 15, no. 1 (2003): 124–47.

Grey, Marina. *Le Général meurt à minuit. L'enlèvement de Koutiépov 1930 et de Miller 1937*. Paris: Plon, 1981.

Guillaume, Gilbert. "France and the Fight Against Terrorism." *Terrorism and Political Violence* 4, no. 4 (1992): 131–35.

Hagenloh, Paul M. "State Terrorism in Early Twentieth-Century Europe." In *The Routledge History of Terrorism*, edited by Randall D. Law, 159–77. Abingdon, UK: Routledge, 2015.

Haupt, Heinz-Gerhard, and Klaus Weinhauer. "Terrorism and the State." In *Political Violence in Twentieth-Century Europe*, edited by Donald Bloxham and Robert Gerwarth, 176–209. Cambridge, UK: Cambridge University Press, 2011.

Hellmuth, Dorle. "Countering Jihadi Terrorists and Radicals the French Way." *Studies in Conflict & Terrorism* 38, no. 12 (2015): 979–97.

Hillis, Faith. "The 'Franco-Russian Marseillaise': International Exchange and the

Making of Antiliberal Politics in Fin de Siècle France." *The Journal of Modern History* 89, no. 1 (2017): 39–78.

Hoffman, Bruce. "A First Draft of the History of America's Ongoing Wars on Terrorism." *Studies in Conflict & Terrorism* 38, no. 1 (2015): 75–83.

———. *Inside Terrorism*. New York: Columbia University Press, 2006.

Honig, Or, and Ido Yahel. "A Fifth Wave of Terrorism? The Emergence of Terrorist Semi-States." *Terrorism and Political Violence* 31, no. 6 (2019): 1210–28.

Hughes, Michael J. "British Opinion and Russian Terrorism in the 1880s." *European History Quarterly* 41, no. 2 (2011): 255–77.

Hülsse, Rainer, and Alexander Spencer. "The Metaphor of Terror: Terrorism Studies and the Constructivist Turn." *Security Dialogue* 39, no. 6 (2008): 571–92.

Jackson, Richard. "An Argument for Terrorism." *Perspectives on Terrorism* 2, no. 2 (2008): 25–32.

———. "In Defence of 'Terrorism': Finding a Way Through a Forest of Misconceptions." *Behavioral Sciences of Terrorism and Political Aggression* 3, no. 2 (2011): 116–130.

———. "The Literary Turn in Terrorism Studies." In *The Routledge History of Terrorism*, edited by Randall D. Law, 487–501. Abingdon, UK: Routledge, 2015.

Jareb, Mario. "Marseilles 1934: The Death of the King." In *A Transnational History of Right-Wing Terrorism: Political Violence and the Far Right in Eastern and Western Europe Since 1900*, edited by Johannes Dafinger and Moritz Florin, 115–28. Abingdon, UK; New York: Routledge, 2022.

Jarvis, Lee, and Michael Lister. "State Terrorism Research and Critical Terrorism Studies: An Assessment." *Critical Studies on Terrorism* 7, no. 1 (2014): 43–61.

Jensen, Richard Bach. *The Battle Against Anarchist Terrorism: An International History, 1878–1934*. Cambridge, UK: Cambridge University Press, 2014.

———. "The First Global Wave of Terrorism and International Counter-Terrorism, 1905–14." In *An International History of Terrorism: Western and Non-Western Experiences*, edited by Jussi M. Hanhimaki and Bernhard Blumenau, 16–33. Abingdon, UK: Routledge, 2013.

———. "The 1904 Assassination of Governor General Bobrikov: Tyrannicide, Anarchism, and the Expanding Scope of 'Terrorism'." *Terrorism and Political Violence* 30, no. 5 (2018): 828–43.

———. "Nineteenth Century Anarchist Terrorism: How Comparable to the Terrorism of Al-Qaeda?" *Terrorism and Political Violence* 20, no. 4 (2008): 589–96.

Kaplan, Jeffrey. "Terrorism's Fifth Wave: A Theory, a Conundrum and a Dilemma." *Perspectives on Terrorism* 2, no. 2 (2008): 12–24.

Keep, John. "Terror in 1905." In *Reinterpreting Revolutionary Russia: Essays in Honour of James D. White*, edited by Ian D. Thatcher, 20–35. Basingstoke, UK: Palgrave Macmillan, 2006.

Knight, Amy. "Female Terrorists in the Russian Socialist Revolutionary Party." *The Russian Review* 38, no. 2 (1979): 139–59.

Kovács, Péter. "Le grand précédent: la Société des Nations et son action après l'attentat contre Alexandre, roi de Yougoslavie." *Europe Integration Studies* 1, no. 1 (2002): 30–40.

Krauss, Charlotte. *La Russie et les Russes dans la fiction francaise du XIXe siècle 1812–1917. D'une image de l'autre à un univers imaginaire*. Amsterdam; New York: Rudopi, 2007.

Kunzi, Daniel, and Peter Huber. "Paris dans les années 30. Sur Serge Efron et quelques agents du NKVD." *Cahiers du monde russe et soviétique* 32, no. 2 (1991): 285–310.

Lambauer, Barbara. "D'une 'dûreté douce pour le futur': le terrorisme selon l'Allemagne nazie et sa repression." In *Terrorismes. Histoire et droit*, edited by Mireille Delmas-Marty and Henry Laurens, 89–162. Paris: CNRS Editions, 2010.

Laqueur, Walter. *The Age of Terrorism*. Boston: Little, Brown, 1987.

———. *A History of Terrorism*. Abingdon, UK: Routledge, 2017 (originally published 2007).

———. "The New Face of Terrorism." *Washington Quarterly* 21, no. 4 (1998): 167–78.

Larabee, Ann. "Why Historians Should Exercise Caution When Using the Term 'Terrorism'." *The Journal of American History* 98, no. 1 (2011): 106–10.

Lauchlan, Ian. "The Accidental Terrorist: Okhrana Connections to the Extreme Right and the Attempt to Assassinate Sergei Witte in 1907." *Revolutionary Russia* 14, no. 2 (2001): 1–32.

Lavenir, Catherine Bertho. "Bombes, protes & pistolets. Les âges médiologiques de l'attentat." *Les cahiers de médiologie* 1, no. 13 (2002): 17–35.

Law, Randall D. "Introduction." In *The Routledge History of Terrorism*, edited by Randall D. Law, 1–11. Abingdon, UK: Routledge, 2015.

———. *Terrorism: A History*, 2nd ed. Cambridge, UK: Polity Press, 2016.

Le Naour, Jean Yves. *L'Assassinat de Clemenceau* (Paris: Perrin, 2019).

Lewis, Mary Dewhurst. *The Boundaries of the Republic: Migrant Rights and the Limits of Universalism in France, 1918–1940*. Stanford, CA: Stanford University Press, 2007.

Lorin, Amaury. "Un 'régicide républicain': Paul Doumer, le président assassiné 6 mai 1932." *Criminocorpus: histoire de la justice, des crimes et des peines*. https://doi.org/10.4000/criminocorpus.435 (last accessed 26 October 2022).

———. *Une ascension en République. Paul Doumer 1857–1932, d'Aurillac à l'Elysée*. Paris: Dalloz, 2013.

Maga, Timothy. "Closing the Door: The French Government and Refugee Policy, 1933–1939." *French Historical Studies* 12, no. 33 (1982): 424–42.

Maitron, Jean. *Le Mouvement anarchiste en France. Tome 1. Des Origines à 1914*. Paris: François Maspero, 1975.

Marston, Geoffrey. "Early Attempts to Suppress Terrorism: The Terrorism and International Criminal Court Conventions of 1937." *British Yearbook of International Law* 73, no. 1 (2002): 293–313.

Matheson, Mary Carol. "Reframing Russia in France: 'Popular Diplomacy' and the Franco-Russia Military Alliance, 1871–1901." PhD diss., University of British Columbia, Vancouver, 2018.

McDermid, Jane. "Mariya Spiridonova: Russian Martyr and British Heroine? The Portrayal of a Russian Female Terrorist in the British Press." In *Reinterpreting*

Revolutionary Russia: Essays in Honour of James D. White, edited by Ian D. Thatcher, 36–54. Basingstoke, UK: Palgrave Macmillan, 2006.

Merriman, John. *Ballad of the Anarchist Bandits: The Crime Spree That Gripped Belle Époque Paris*. New York: Nation Books, 2017.

———. *The Dynamite Club: How a Bombing in Fin-de-Siècle Paris Ignited the Age of Modern Terror*. London: JR Books, 2009.

Miller, Martin A. *The Foundations of Modern Terrorism: State, Society and the Dynamics of Political Violence*. Cambridge, UK: Cambridge University Press, 2013.

Miller, Michael B. *Shanghai on the Metro: Spies, Intrigue, and the French Between the Wars*. Berkeley: University of California Press, 1994.

Millington, Chris. *Fighting for France: Violence in Interwar French Politics*. Oxford, UK: Oxford University Press, 2018.

———. *A History of Fascism in France: From the First World War to the National Front*. London: Bloomsbury, 2020.

Monier, Frédéric. "Défendre des 'terroristes' dans la France de 1935. L'avocat des 'oustachis croates'." *Le Mouvement social* 240 (July-September 2012): 105–20.

———. "L'attentat de Marseille 9 octobre 1934: Régicide et terrorisme dans les années trente." *La Révolution française. Cahiers de l'Institut d'histoire de la Révolution française* 1 (2012). https://lrf.revues.org/461 (accessed 1 March 2017).

Moore, Jean-Gaston. "Gorguloff, ou le procès de la démence." In *Les grands procès*, edited by Daniel Amson, Jean-Gaston Moore, and Charles Amson, 120–33. Paris: Presses Universitaires de France, 2007.

Morawski, Konrad Sebastian. "The Assassination of King Alexander I of Yugolsavia in the Light of Archival Press Articles." *Studia z Dziejów Rosji i Europy Środkowo-Wschodniej* 51, no. 1 (2016): 47–76.

Murray-Miller, Gavin. *Revolutionary Europe: Politics, Community and Culture in Transnational Context, 1775–1922*. London: Bloomsbury Academic, 2020.

Néaumet, Jean-Emile. *Les Grandes enquêtes du commissaire Chenevier. De la Cagoule à l'affaire Dominici*. Paris: Albin Michel, 1995.

Neboit-Mombet, Janine. *L'Image de la Russie dans le roman français 1859–1900*. Clermont-Ferrand, FR: Presses Universitaires Blaise Pascal, 2005.

Noiriel, Gérard. *Le Creuset français. Histoire de l'immigration XIXe–XXe siècle*. Paris: Editions du Seuil, 1989.

Norris, Pippa, Montague Kern, and Marion Just. "Framing Terrorism." In *Framing Terrorism: The News Media, the Government, and the Public*, edited by Pippa Norris, Montague Kern, and Marion Just, 3–27. New York; London: Routledge, 2003.

Parker, David, Julia M. Pearce, Lasse Lindekilde, and M. Brooke Rogers. "Press Coverage of Lone-Actor Terrorism in the UK and Denmark: Shaping the Reactions of the Public, Affected Communities and Copycat Attackers." *Critical Studies on Terrorism* 12, no. 1 (2019): 110–31.

Parry, D.L.L. "Counter Revolution by Conspiracy, 1935–1937." In *The Right in France: From Revolution to Le Pen*, edited by Nicholas Atkin and Frank Tallett, 161–81. London: IB Taurus, 2003.

Pavlović, Vojislav. "L'Attentat de Marseille 1934. La fin symbolique d'une alliance atypique." In *La Serbie et la France. Une alliance atypique. Relations politiques, économiques et culturelles, 1870–1940*, edited by Dušan T. Bataković, 575–97. Belgrade: Académie serbe des Sciences et des Arts, 2010.

Phillips, Hugh. "The War Against Terrorism in Late Imperial and Early Soviet Russia." In *Enemies of Humanity: The Nineteenth-Century War on Terrorism*, ed. Isaac Land. New York: Palgrave Macmillan, 2008.

Preston, William. *Aliens and Dissenters: Federal Suppression of Radicals, 1903–1933*. Urbana: University of Illinois Press, 1994.

Raflik, Jenny. "La France face au terrorisme d'hier à aujourd'hui." *Outre-Terre* 51, no. 2 (2017): 202–14.

Rapoport, David C. "Fear and Trembling: Terrorism in Three Religious Traditions." *The American Political Science Review* 78, no. 3 (1984): 658–77.

———. "The Four Waves of Modern Terrorism." In *Terrorism Studies: A Reader*, edited by John Horan and Kurt Braddock, 41–61. London; New York: Routledge, 2012.

———. *Waves of Global Terrorism: From 1879 to the Present*. New York: Columbia University Press, 2022.

Rapport, Mike. "The French Revolution and Early European Revolutionary Terrorism." In *The Routledge History of Terrorism*, edited by Randall D. Law, 63–76. Abingdon, UK: Routledge, 2015.

Raymond, Gino G. "After *Charlie*: The Unravelling of the French Republican Response." *Patterns of Prejudice* 52, no. 1 (2018): 24–38.

Richards, Anthony. "Conceptualizing Terrorism." *Studies in Conflict & Terrorism* 37, no. 3 (2014): 213–36.

———. "Defining Terrorism." In *Routledge Handbook of Terrorism and Counterterrorism*, edited by Andrew Silke, 13–21. Abingdon, UK: Routledge, 2018.

Roberts, Adam. "The 'War on Terror' in Historical Perspective." *Survival* 47, no. 2 (2005): 101–30.

Rosenberg, Clifford. *Policing Paris: The Origins of Modern Immigration Control Between the Wars*. Ithaca, NY: Cornell University Press, 2006.

Ross, Nicolas. *De Koutiépov à Miller. Le combat des russes blancs, 1930–1940*. Geneva: Editions des Syrtes, 2017.

Sadkovich, James J. "Terrorism in Croatia, 1929–1934." *East European Quarterly* 22, no. 1 (1988): 55–79.

Sageman, Marc. *Turning to Political Violence: The Emergence of Terrorism*. Philadelphia: University of Pennsylvania Press, 2017.

Sansico, Virginie. *La justice déshonorée, 1940–1944*. Paris: Tallandier, 2015.

———. "Le terrorisme, vie et mort d'une notion juridique 1930–1945." *Archives de la Politique Criminelle* 38, no. 1 (2016): 27–45.

Saul, Ben. "Attempts to Define 'Terrorism' in International Law." *Netherlands International Law Review* 52, no. 1 (2005): 57–83.

———. "The Legal Response of the League of Nations to Terrorism." *Journal of International Criminal Justice* 4, no. 1 (2006): 78–102.

Schmid, Alex. "The Revised Academic Consensus Definition of Terrorism." *Perspectives on Terrorism* 6, no. 2 (2012): 158–59.

———. "Terrorism: The Definitional Problem." *Case Western Reserve Journal of International Law* 36, no. 2 (2004): 375–419.

Schor, Ralph. *Histoire de l'immigration en France de la fin du XIXe siècle à nos jours.* Paris: Armand Colin, 1996.

Schraut, Sylvia. "Gender Politics and Terrorist Histories." In *The Cambridge History of Terrorism*, edited by Richard English, 623–44. Cambridge, UK: Cambridge University Press, 2021.

Shapiro, Jeremy, and Bénédicte Suzan. "The French Experience of Counterterrorism." *Survival* 45, no. 1 (2003): 67–98.

Shaya, Gregory. "How to Make an Anarchist Terrorist: An Essay on the Political Imaginary in Fin-de-Siècle France." *Journal of Social History* 44, no. 2 (2010): 521–43.

Silke, Andrew. "The Study of Terrorism and Counterterrorism." In *Routledge Handbook of Terrorism and Counterterrorism*, edited by Andrew Silke, 1–10. Abingdon, UK: Routledge, 2019.

———. *Terrorism*. London: Hodder & Stoughton, 2014.

Smith, Benjamin K., Scott Englund, Andrea Figueroa-Caballero, Elena Salcido, and Michael Stohl. "Framing Terrorism: The Communicative Constitution of the Terrorist Actor." In *Constructions of Terrorism: An Interdisciplinary Approach to Research and Policy*, edited by Michael Stohl, Richard Burchill, and Scott Englund, 91–107. Oakland: University of California Press, 2017.

Smith, M.L.R. "Review Article: William of Ockham, Where Are You When We Need You? Reviewing Modern Terrorism Studies." *Journal of Contemporary History* 44, no. 2 (2009): 319–44.

Smith, Stephen. *Russian in Revolution: An Empire in Crisis, 1890–1928*. Oxford, UK: Oxford University Press, 2017.

Sonn, Richard D. *Sex, Violence, and the Avant-Garde: Anarchism in Interwar France.* Philadelphia: Pennsylvania State University Press, 2010.

Stampnitzky, Lisa. "Can Terrorism Be Defined?" In *Constructions of Terrorism: An Interdisciplinary Approach to Research and Policy*, edited by Michael Stohl, Richard Burchill, and Scott Englund, 11–20. Oakland: University of California Press, 2017.

———. *Disciplining Terror: How Experts Invented "Terrorism."* Cambridge, UK: Cambridge University Press, 2013.

Thorup, Mikkel. *An Intellectual History of Terror: War, Violence and the State.* Abingdon, UK: Routledge, 2010.

Townshend, Charles. "'Methods Which All Civilized Opinion Must Condemn': The League of Nations and International Action Against Terrorism." In *An International History of Terrorism: Western and Non-Western Experiences*, edited by Jussi M. Hanhimäki and Bernhard Blumenau, 34–50. London: Routledge, 2013.

Tuman, Joseph S. *Communicating Terror: The Rhetorical Dimensions of Terrorism*, 2nd ed. Los Angeles; London: SAGE, 2010.

Vallé, Jean-Pierre. "L'assassinat politique du roi Alexandre Ier de Yougoslavie. Un tournant dans la censure des actualités cinématographiques sous la IIIe Répub lique?" *Hypothèses* 20, no. 1 (2017): 221–35.

Verhoeven, Claudia. "The Making of Russian Revolutionary Terrorism." In *Enemies of Humanity: The Nineteenth-Century War on Terrorism*, edited by Isaac Land, 99–119. New York: Palgrave Macmillan, 2008.

Viet, Vincent. *La France immigrée. Construction d'une politique, 1914–1997*. Paris: Fayard, 1998.

Vincent, Karelle. "Le régicide en République." *Crime, Histoire & Sociétés/Crime, History & Societies* 3, no. 2 (1999): 73–93.

Weil, Patrick. *La France et les étrangers. L'aventure d'une politique de l'immigration, 1938–1991*. Paris: Calman-Lévy, 1991.

Weinberg, Leonard. "A History of Terrorism." In *Routledge Handbook of Terrorism and Counterterrorism*, edited by Andrew Silke, 34–56. Abingdon, UK: Routledge, 2019.

Weinberg, Leonard, Ami Pedahzur, and Sivan Hirsch-Hoefler. "The Challenges of Conceptualizing Terrorism." *Terrorism and Political Violence* 16, no. 4 (2004): 777–94.

Wieviorka, Michel. "Espaces, niveaux et temporalités du terrorisme." *The Conversation* (French edition). Last modified 31 August 2017. https://theconversation.com/espaces-niveaux-et-temporalites-du-terrorisme-83263 (accessed 30 April 2020).

———. "France Faced with Terrorism." *Studies in Conflict & Terrorism* 14, no. 3 (1991): 157–70.

———. "From Classical Terrorism to 'Global' Terrorism." *International Journal of Conflict and Violence* 1, no. 2 (2007): 92–104.

———. "Une nouvelle ère du terorrisme?" Last modified May 29, 2013. https://wieviorka.hypotheses.org/171 (accessed 30 April 2020).

———. "Terrorism." In *Concise Encyclopedia of Comparative Sociology*, edited by Masamichi Sasaki, Jack Goldstone, Ekkart Zimmerman, and Stephen K. Sanderson, 418–26. Leiden; Boston: Brill, 2014.

Wight, Colin. "Theorising Terrorism: The State, Structure, and History." *International Relations* 23, no. 1 (2009): 99–106.

Zulaika, Joseba, and William Douglass. *Terror and Taboo: The Follies, Fables, and Faces of Terrorism*. Abingdon, UK: Routledge, 1996.

INDEX

Action Française, 55, 131, 156, 163
AIDP. *See* Association Internationale de Droit Pénal
Alexander I (King of Yugoslavia), 3, 17, 24, 151; assassination of, 108, 113, 114, 190; foreign policy of, 113–14; media reporting of assassination, 115–16; memorial to, 135–36; newsreel of assassination, 116–18, 119; police investigation into assassination, 118; response of the League of Nations to assassination of, 137–39; threats to life of, 121. *See also* Ustashe
Alexander II (Tsar of Russia), 7, 27, 30, 31
Anarchism, 3; anarchist community in Paris, 42; attacks of the 1890s, 34; historical work on, 14, 16–17; "propaganda by the deed," 29; repression of, 4, 34–35; representation of activists, 9, 27, 41–42; representations in fiction, 47–49; representations on film, 50–51; and Russia, 39–41, 43–44; and terrorism, 7, 26, 29, 30–31, 35, 37; under Vichy, 18; and women 42
Anarchist. *See* Anarchism

Assassination. *See* Alexander I (King of Yugoslavia); Doumer, Paul (President of France)
Association Internationale de Droit Pénal (AIDP), 111, 123

Bakunin, Mikhail, 29
Balkans, The, 113, 136; terrorism in, 124, 132, 133
Bantman, Constance, 148
Barthou, Louis (French Foreign Minister), 18, 106; death of, 108, 114–15; memorial to, 135–36; relationship with Yugoslavia, 113
Bidault, Georges, 143, 144
Blondet, Jacqueline, 158–60
Blum, Léon, 81, 131, 199
Bonnot, Jules, 16, 17, 38, 55
Bolsheviks. *See* Bolshevism
Bolshevism, 77, 176, 180; accusations of terrorism against, 57, 61, 62, 63, 77, 189, 192; and Emile Cottin, 74; and Paul Gorguloff, 81, 82, 86, 88
Bouchardon, Pierre, 63, 65, 69, 72–74
Bouvet, Gustave (alias Juvénis); attempted assassination of Alexandre Millerand, 55, 56, 77–79
Brinon, Fernand de, 175, 180, 181

285

Brousse, Paul, 29
Brunelle, Gayle K., 14, 18, 156, 159
Bulgaria, 117, 120, 132, 136
Burtsev, Vladimir, 43–44

C-2 affair, 143, 160; attempted theft of the C-2 submarine 163–64; planning of the raid in Brest, 160–63; trial of the perpetrators, 165–66;
Caferio, Carlo, 29
Cagoule (OSARN/CSAR), 191; attacks in, 1937 142–43; attempted coup, 157; Etoile bombing, 153–54; public exposure of, 143, 156, 157; and terrorism, 158, 173; and women, 158–60
Caron, Vicki, 129
Caserio, Santo Geronimo, 34, 35, 55, 66, 67, 79, 80, 81, 83, 95, 106
Cerbère; bombings in, 145, 146, 147, 148, 149, 150, 151, 161, 165, 166, 169
Chaix, Robert, 162, 163, 164, 166, 172
Chautemps, Camille, 156, 173–74
Chernozemski, Vlado, (assassin of Alexander I, alias Petrus Kelemen and Veličko Kerin) 120, 121, 122, 125, 126, 136, 151
Clemenceau, Georges (Prime Minister), 3, 36, 62, 63, 64; attempted assassination of, 54, 58–59, 72, 189. *See also* Cottin, Emile.
Collette, Paul, 175–76, 177
Combat Organization, 38, 41, 90; Azev affair, 41, 43. *See also* Party of Socialist Revolutionaries (Russia)
Comitadjis, 120, 132–34
Comité Secret d'Action Révolutionnaire/CSAR. *See* Cagoule
Communism, 2, 10, 20, 81, 82, 100, 176, 178; abduction of General Miller (1937), 144, 169; Communist Party (of France), 2, 20, 81, 82, 89, 100, 128, 131, 144, 156, 161, 169, 185, 187; communist resisters, 185; communists and terrorism, 3, 4–5, 57, 61, 78, 83, 89, 95–96, 179, 183–84, 187; response to assassination of Alexander I, 110, 111, 121, 128, 131; response to the C-2 affair, 161, 165; response to the Cagoule, 156
Communist Party (of France). *See* Communism
Conseil National de la Résistance (CNR), 178, 184
Convention for the Prevention and Punishment of Terrorism. *See* League of Nations
Convention for the Creation of an International Criminal Court. *See* League of Nations
Cottin, Emile, 3, 77, 78, 79, 188, 189; and anarchism ,55, 66, 68, 69, 70–71, 73; attempt on Clemenceau's life, 54, 58–59; background, 54–55, 65–66; "foreignness" of, 61; life after prison, 76; mental health of, 72, 74; motive, 55–56, 61–62, 63–64, 72; private life of, 67, 68–69; trial of, 63, 73–75
Coty, François, 83, 94, 98, 99, 195, 196
Croatia, 120–21; and the Ustashe, 18, 108, 109, 110, 111, 121, 151. *See also* Ustashe
Croix de Feu, 109, 128, 131, 161, 162, 172

Daladier, Edouard, 129, 173–74, 198
Darlix, Paul, 90, 95
Darnand, Joseph, 182
Darnar, Pierre-Laurent, 128, 169
Déat, Marcel, 175, 176, 178, 180, 181, 182
Deloncle, Eugène, 18, 142, 143, 157
Desbons, Georges, 124
Ditrych, Ondrej, 8
Doriot, Jacques, 143
Dormoy, Marx, 143, 157, 159
Doumer, Paul (President of France), 17, 24, 91, 94; assassination of, 80–81, 84–86, 88, 92, 105–6, 108, 139, 189–90. *See also* Gorguloff, Paul
Doumergue, Gaston, 131, 137

Eckhardt, Tibor, 137
Eden, Anthony, 112, 138
Etoile bombing (1937), 153–54. *See also* Cagoule (OSARN/CSAR)

Femme fatale. See Women
Ferrando (Talayero), José Luis, 162–63, 164, 166
Finley-Croswhite, Annette, 14, 18, 156, 159
Francs Tireurs et Partisans (FTP), 185
French Empire, 19–21
FTP. *See* Francs Tireurs et Partisans

Gabolde, Maurice, 177
Gallo, Charles, 34
Geneg, Anne-Marie, 87
Georges, Alphonse-Joseph, 114
Géraud, Henri, 99, 101, 103, 104
Germany, 5, 21, 57, 62, 63, 64, 82, 88, 90, 91, 106, 113, 129, 145, 167, 173, 175, 189, 190
Giobellina, Honorine, 68, 69, 70
Godina, Antun (or Ante), 127, 250n172
Godina, Stana. *See* Voudracek, Maria
Gorguloff, Paul (assassin of Paul Doumer); assassination of Paul Doumer, 80, 86, 106–7; descriptions of, 96–97; education, 86; execution of, 105; mental health, 83, 100–104, 106; motive, 88; presumed motive, 81–83, 87, 89, 97, 102–3; private life, 87, 92, 102; profession, 87, 102; trial of, 92, 99–104
GPU (Gosudarstvennoe politicheskoe upravlenie), 89, 143, 167, 169, 170, 179
Great Britain, 4, 41; and the League of Nations, 111, 137, 139
Guépéou. *See* GPU

Henriot, Philippe, 182
Henry, Emile, 16–17, 34, 35, 55, 69

Hitler, Adolf, 82, 113, 143, 152, 165, 169, 180, 196
Hoffman, Bruce, 10
Hungary; and the League of Nations, 111, 138; and the Ustashe, 110, 111, 121, 122, 134

Immigration, 2, 173, 188; "Foreigners' Statute," 156; to France from Russia, 93–94; and perceived links to terrorism, 4, 84, 98, 106, 130, 145, 169, 190; proposed legislation on, 128, 129, 191
IMRO. *See* Internal Macedonian Revolutionary Organization
Internal Macedonian Revolutionary Organization (IMRO), 108, 120, 125, 132, 134
Italy, 5, 29, 113, 130, 144, 145, 152; and the Union Générale Militaire Russe, 167; and the Ustashe, 111, 121, 127, 134, 137

Jackson, Richard, 8
Janka-Puszta, 110, 122, 133, 134, 135, 137, 151
Jeantet, Gabriel, 156, 179
Jensen, Richard Bach, 14, 17, 27
Jeunesses Patriotes, 109
Jevtitch, Bogoljub, 113, 133, 137

Kalifa, Dominique, 9
Kelemen, Petrus. *See* Chernozemski, Vlado
Kerin, Veličko. *See* Chernozemski, Vlado
Koenigstein, François Claudius. *See* Ravachol
Kralj, Mijo, 122–24, 151
Kramer, Eugon (alias of Eugen Dido Kvaternick), 122–24
Kropotkin, Peter, 30
Kutepov, Alexander Pavlovich, 95, 143, 167, 169, 172

La Rocque, François de, 128, 143, 198
Las Heras, Jesus de, 162, 163, 164
Lapidus. See Stryga, Vladimir
Laqueur, Walter, 7, 12, 13, 14
Laval, Pierre, 137, 175–76
League of Nations, 17, 137–38; Convention for the Creation of an International Criminal Court, 138, 139; Convention for the Prevention and Punishment of Terrorism, 11, 111–12, 138
Lebrun, Albert, 105, 135
Lewis, Mary Dewhurst, 129, 173
Liberation (of France); and terrorism, 187–88
Locuty, René, 142, 153, 154, 158
Lois scélérates. See Villainous laws
Londres, Albert, 132–33
Longuet, Jean, 43
Lorin, Amaury, 88, 105
Lovitch, Joseph, 92

Macon, Léon, 142, 153,
Macedonia, 117, 132, 136
Malatesta, Errico, 29
Marion, Paul, 183
Mata Hari, 6, 63, 171
Maurras, Charles, 131
Merriman, John, 14, 16–17
Méjat, Georges; newsreel of the assassination of Alexander I, 116–18
Méjat, Raymond. See Méjat, Georges
Menga, 162–63, 190
Méténier, François, 153, 154, 158, 160
Mihailov, Ivan, 120, 132
Milice Française, 3, 19, 182–83, 185
Milicević, Vladeta, 120
Miller, Martin A., 29
Miller, Michael B., 22, 170
Miller, Yevgeny (General), 18, 89, 143, 144, 172; kidnapping of, 166–68
Millerand, Alexandre, 55, 77, 78, 79, 80, 89
Mondanel, Antoine, 120, 123, 127

Montarron, Marcel, 92, 144, 151
Moreau de la Meuse, Jean, 153
Mornet, André, 73, 74
Mussolini, Benito, 82, 110, 113, 119, 144, 169, 196; and the Ustashe, 123

Narodnaia Rasprava (People's Vengeance), 29
Narodnaia Volya (People's Will), 7, 30, 32, 36, 49
Nechaiev, Sergei, 29, 30
Nihilism, 61, 95, 127, 189, 192; activists in France, 33, 42; in French fiction, 47, 50, 51; French understandings of, 28–29, 30, 31–33, 37 41; and terrorism, 16, 27, 28, 29, 40; and women, 33–34, 44, 46, 51, 127
Nihilist. See Nihilism
NKVD (Naródnyy Komissariát Vnútrennikh Del), 166, 167, 168

OSARN (Organisation Secrète d'Action Révolutionnaire Nationale). See Cagoule

Pardo, Léon, 163, 165
Parti Populaire Français (PPF), 143, 176, 178, 184, 197
Parti Social Français (PSF), 142, 143, 162, 163, 165, 198
Party of Socialist Revolutionaries (Russia), 27, 28, 53, 90
Pavelić, Ante (leader of the Ustashe), 121, 123, 124, 127
People's Vengeance. See Narodnaia Rasprava
People's Will. See Narodnaia Volya
Perčec, Gustav, 133–34
Perčević, Ivan, 123, 124
Plevitskaya, Nadezhda, 168, 169, 170, 171, 190
Pogorelec, Jelka, 133–34
Poincaré, Raymond, 80, 82, 119
Pospisil, Zvonimir, 122–24, 134, 151

PPF. *See* Parti Populaire Français
PSF. *See* Parti Social Français

Radical Party, 109, 198
Rajic, Ivan, 122–24, 134, 151
Rassemblement National Populaire (RNP), 175, 183
Ravachol (François Claudius Koenigstein), 16, 34, 35, 55, 79, 81
Resistance, 4; repression of, 180, 182, 183, 192; and terrorism, 10, 19, 178, 184, 185; use of violence, 3, 185, 186
Richards, Anthony, 10–11
Rips, Marcel, 43, 44, 45
RNP. *See* Rassemblement National Populaire
Rollin, Henri, 91, 106, 107
Rosario, Dominique Fusciardi. *See* Menga
ROVS (Rossijskij Obŝevoinskij Soûz/ Union Générale Militaire Russe), 143, 167, 168
Russia; characteristics of, 44–46, 58, 61, 97–98; in French entertainment, 47–52, 91; French perceptions of revolution in, 3, 4, 16, 17, 27, 31, 36, 52, 56–57; French perceptions of Russians as terrorists, 25–26, 27, 30–32, 33, 37–38, 39–42, 57, 66, 82–83, 96; Russian community in France, 32–33, 42–43, 93–94; Russian immigration to France, 94–96; terrorism in Russia, 3, 7, 29–30, 37–38, 38–39, 90; White Russians, 82, 89, 91, 92, 95, 100, 143, 166–8. *See also* Gorguloff, Paul; Nihilism; Soviet Union

Sampaix, Lucien, 165, 169, 176
Sarraut, Albert, 130, 131, 174
Savinkov, Boris, 90, 95
Schmid, Alex; Revised Academic Consensus Definition of Terrorism, 7

Schor, Ralph, 94
Schwartzbard, Sholom, 55, 94
SFIO. *See* Socialist Party
Shaya, Gregory, 9
Six février (1934) crisis, 109, 128
Skoblin, Nikolai, 167, 168, 169
Socialist Party (of France, Section Française de l'Internationale Ouvrière, SFIO), 10, 110, 128, 148, 152, 199
Sokoloff, Alexandre, 25–26, 42
Sokoloff, Viktor, 42
Solidarité Française, 129
Soviet Union (USSR), 3, 21, 81, 82, 88, 89, 90, 91, 92, 106, 113. *See also* Russia
Spain, 5, 26, 76, 145, 149, 188, 191; anarchists in, 37; and the C-2 affair, 161, 165, 166; civil war in, 141, 144, 172; and terrorism in France, 142, 147–48, 149, 150, 154
Special Sections, 18, 176, 177, 187; law of 14 August 1941, 176, 187–88; law of 5 June 1943, 18, 177
Spéranska, Sophie, 42
Stavisky Affair, 109, 128
Stepniak, Sergius, 32
Stryga, Vladimir (alias of "Lapidus"), 25–26, 27, 42, 43, 46

Tardieu, André, 81, 82, 87, 89, 91, 99, 100, 139
Terrorism; approaches to French terrorism, 15–16; bombings of 1937, 4, 18, 24, 141–42, 145–53; and collaborationists, 176, 179–84; and communism, 4, 10, 18–19, 33, 57, 61–62, 78, 81–82, 83, 89, 95, 110, 128, 131, 144, 156, 169; constructivism, 8–9, 17; cultures of terrorism, 1–2, 4, 9, 20, 57, 77, 83, 105–6, 112, 156, 173, 181, 183, 188, 192; definition of, 6–7, 9–12; and fascism, 5, 18, 82, 110, 128, 152–53, 158, 165, 169, 193;

in fiction, 46, 48–49, 51–52, 91, 170; and the French Empire, 19–22; in French entertainment, 48–52; and the French Revolution, 6; and "Frenchness," 4, 5, 35, 40, 53, 83, 145, 166, 172, 179, 180, 188, 191, 193, 202n6; and gender, 5–6, 51, 72, 110, 169–70, 181–82, 186, 192; and historians, 12–14; "imaginaries" of 9; international attempts to define, 111, 139; in interwar Europe, 3; and Islam, 5, 13, 15, 17; media framing of, 12, 22–24; in Occupied France, 176–77, 178, 179–80, 183; rejection of definitions, 7–8; and resisters, 184–88; Revised Academic Consensus Definition of Terrorism, 7; terrorism experts, 90, 111, 176; terrorism studies, 12, 15; twenty-first century attacks, 15; works on anarchism in France, 16–17; works on the interwar period in France, 17–18; works on the Vichy years, 18–19. *See also* Immigration

Troncoso, Julián, 143, 160–6

Turgenev, Ivan, 28–9

Union Générale Militaire Russe. *See* ROVS

United Nations, 139

Ustashe, 110, 124, 128, 151; alliance with the IMRO, 120; assassination of Alexander I, 109–10; founding of, 120–21; French understandings of, 125; links to foreign governments, 111, 137–38; political program, 121; training camps, 133–34; and women, 127

Vabres, Henri Donnedieu de, 111, 176, Vaillant, Auguste, 34, 79, 115
Vaillant-Couturier, Paul, 161, 169
Viannay, Philippe, 186
Vichy, 2–3, 183, 187; legislation on terrorism, 16, 18, 176–78
Villain, Raoul, 75–76
Villainous laws (lois scélérates), 4, 16, 34–35
Voudracek, Maria (alias of Stana Godina), 110, 122, 123, 126–27, 190

Wieviorka, Michel, 13, 15
West, Rebecca, 111, 118
Women: fictional representations, 46, 51–52, 170; and sexuality, 44, 46, 48, 110, 126–27, 159; as terrorists, 5–6, 30–31, 33–34, 42, 44, 91–92, 110, 127, 158–60, 171, 181, 190;

Yugoslavia, 3, 17, 22, 106, 108, 136, 190; appeal to the League of Nations (November 1934), 111, 137; founding of the dictatorship in 1929, 120–21; relations with France, 113–14; terrorism in, 121

Zasulich, Vera, 30, 51

The authorized representative in the EU for product safety and compliance is:
Mare Nostrum Group
B.V Doelen 72
4831 GR Breda
The Netherlands

www.ingramcontent.com/pod-product-compliance
Lightning Source LLC
Chambersburg PA
CBHW030609230426
43661CB00053B/1910